Growing Annuals

A.G.W. Simpson

Kangaroo Press

Contents

First published in 1988 by Kangaroo Press Pty Ltd
3 Whitehall Road (P.O. Box 75) Kenthurst 2156
Typeset by G.T. Setters Pty Limited
Printed in Hong Kong by Colorcraft Ltd

ISBN 0 86417 182 X

Introduction

Each word you read from here on shows *just how easy it is for you to grow annuals successfully.* You don't have to be a professional gardener to succeed. Many of today's great annuals were bred by talented amateur gardeners.

Openly and frankly, and without the use of fancy or technical jargon, I would like to share with you my experience, and secrets, gleaned from gardening worldwide, in a variety of climates, so that you can enjoy your gardening even more.

For you, I painstakingly took my photographs in close-up, to show just how a particular flower looks.

Why grow annuals from seeds?

It is possible that you may produce a world first, although the odds against producing a world-wide winner are great.

Another reason for growing flowers from seeds is to save money. You can get lots of plants from a packet of seeds. It may even be possible to get seeds from your own plants, or acquire them from a gardener friend.

And if you grow your own plants from seeds you can select those seedlings which are sturdiest, and discard the weaker. Those sturdy plants will be raised and grown on in the environment where they are to live out their lives.

But, surely, the most important of all the reasons to grow your flowers from seed, is that you take a small, or even minute seed, and sow it, water and nurture it, protect it, encourage it to flower, and comfort it all its life, so that it becomes as precious as if it were your own child.

But also visit annual seedling plant nurseries to keep abreast of cultivar trends. You can, if necessary, use nursery bought seedlings to supplement your garden design.

Annuals—Biennials—Perennials

A plant is either an annual, biennial or perennial. An annual, botanically, completes its life cycle in the space of twelve months. Horticulturally, an annual will germinate, grow, flower, produce seeds, and die within one season; although ephemeral annuals will produce more than one crop during the 'annual' season. But many plants which are biennials, or perennials are included in this book. Why? Either because they always look better in their first year; or it saves the bother of housing them during inclement weather; or they have been bred to be treated as annuals; or their distinctive foliage can be used as a foil; and so on. Three of the world's most famous 'annuals': petunia, blue lobelia, and scarlet salvia, are perennials. There are many beautiful annual plants used in garden displays.

A biennial germinates and grows vegetatively (leaves, roots and stems) for the first year, then in the second year it still grows, but also produces flowers and seeds, then dies.

A perennial is a plant that lives for three years or more, usually flowering and fruiting each year until it dies, although it may take a few years before it reaches the flowering and fruiting stage. Some perennials are deciduous, and some are evergreen.

Annuals are sub-divided into hardy annuals, half-hardy annuals, and tender annuals. Hardy annuals can be sown directly where they are to grow and flower, and will withstand a certain amount of frost. Half-hardy annuals can only be planted out when all danger of frost is past. Tender annuals can only be grown in a controlled indoor temperature such as a greenhouse.

But these plant categories do not have such a clear cut meaning in Australia as they do in cold climate countries. Plants that can be hardy annuals in far north Queensland are possibly half-hardy, or tender annuals in Tasmania or parts of Victoria and Canberra. Biennials and perennials can also be sub-divided into hardy, half-hardy and tender categories.

Therefore one has to be flexible and bear in mind local conditions when referring to hardy, half-hardy and tender annuals, biennials and perennials. Your local weather conditions will be peculiar to your area, so if in doubt seek local, sound, top-class, professional advice. On the back of seed packets you usually see seasonal planting times for Australia and New Zealand.

Before we go further we shall establish seasons, and the months of those seasons. We shall stick to the following definitions, throughout the book:

Australia	*England*
Summer	
December	June
January	July
February	August
Autumn	
March	September
April	October
May	November
Winter	
June	December
July	January
August	February
Spring	
September	March
October	April
November	May

Major Australian Climates

Australia can be divided roughly into seven major climates, and more specific information can be obtained from the excellent books available on climate, soils and vegetation. But it is important to bear in mind that Australia also has innumerable local-general and local-microclimates.

Most gardeners have heard of the tropical areas; the subtropical areas; the dry inland areas; the temperate areas; and the cool mountain-highland areas.

What you have to ascertain from sound, local professional advice is whether your local climate is: *tropical, subtropical, temperate* or *cold*. And what kind of tropical, subtropical, temperate or cold climate? For example is it dry temperate, cool temperate, warm temperate, Mediterranean temperate and so on? Planting can vary from State capital to State capital; for example, Melbourne's seed sowing times will be slightly different from Sydney's, or Adelaide's. Seek local, expert opinion on seedling propagation times for a particular plant at your locality. And remember that Australia's micro or local climates can be so variable that a seedling can be growing happily in one place, but after only a 20 minutes drive it can be correctly planted in a climate that could place it under stress.

Types of Border Design

The typical 'herbaceous' border, so beloved in 'old-fashioned' (late Victorian-Edwardian) English gardens is composed of only perennial, herbaceous plants, whose foliage, mostly, dies down after flowering.

But with today's smaller gardens, a mixed border of annuals, biennials and perennials has greater popularity. Mixed borders can provide colour all the year round, and any suitable type of plant can be used: annuals, biennials, bulbs, herbaceous perennial plants, roses, shrubs and trees. Trees can provide a succession of flowers; shrubs can provide a 'main' colour effect in autumn, winter and spring; annuals, biennials and/or perennials can provide spring and/or summer colour; and bulbs can supply colour in autumn, winter, spring and summer.

The points to consider before beginning a mixed border are:

1. Availability of the plants.
2. Colour of plant.
3. Height of plant, and the possible need to stake it, although breeders have endeavoured to breed sturdier plants. Staking, if begun when the plant's shoots are not too high, is not such a chore.
4. Growth span (width).
5. Season of flowering.
6. Longevity of flowering.
7. Any idiosyncrasies, such as invasive roots or seeds; prefers shade or full sun; and so on.
8. The labour needed to maintain it weed-free, and invasive-root free.
9. The desirability, or not, of top dressing the border each year with well-prepared and well-rotted compost or farmyard manure.

Spring-Summer (Annual) Bedding Schemes

In Australia we tend to call this type of display 'annual' bedding, although in colder northern hemisphere climates plants such as wallflowers, forget-me-nots and tulips are planted the previous year, that is, after the summer annuals have finished flowering.

Spring-summer bedding schemes can be split up into 3 convenient groups, although plants used in one group, can possibly be used in the others:

1. Traditional bedding flower scheme
2. Sub-tropical bedding scheme
3. Carpet-bedding.

Traditional flowering schemes contain the popular types of flowers such as: alyssum, ageratum, bedding dahlias, English daisies, French and African marigolds or their hybrids, lobelia, pansies, red salvias, wallflowers, and so forth.

Sub-tropical bedding schemes are comprised, usually, of 'so-called' sub-tropical foliage, such as *Begonia semperflorens* (cvs); *Celosia a. plumosa* (cvs); *Celosa a. cristata* (cvs); *Coleus* (cvs); *Cuphea ignea*; *Fuchsia* (cvs); *Iresine herbstii*, and so on.

Carpet bedding is a refined state of the gardening art, and was highly popular during Victorian and Edwardian times. The object is to create a painting using flowers or foliage. All of the plants are dwarf forms, slow and low growing, for the obvious reason that they could not otherwise be kept in check. Some annuals are used, but mostly perennials. Usually the bed is raised, like a wedge of cheese, or constructed on a bank so that it can be viewed easily.

Carpet bedding is still carried out today by various public parks departments, to commemorate special events, or as floral clocks, coats-of-arms or initials, and so forth.

Raised Beds

For various reasons it is often convenient to raise a flower garden above its surrounds; in this case the retaining walls may be built of brick, stone, railways sleepers, or specially treated wooden logs and planks. Drainage holes are usually made at the bottom of the wall to allow excess moisture in the bed to escape. The area between the retaining walls is filled with top quality, free draining soil, and the plants are then planted in the bed and grown on. I found this type of bed useful around public carparks to isolate the cars from the surrounds, and to provide a splash of colour for those entering the carpark. Gardeners who find difficulty in bending often have raised gardens constructed.

Rock Garden and Rockery

Rock gardens are made by placing rocks to simulate an outcrop of natural rock, and planting dwarf non-invasive true alpine plants within the rock area. Annuals that are not true alpines should not be used. A rockery is a series of scalloped beds, which look like those grand box-seats at the opera. Rocks are used to form the outside shape of the beds, and free draining soil is placed inside the rocks, and planted up. Gardeners use a wide range of annual plants in a rockery. Constructing rocks gardens and rockeries calls for expertise. Never lose sight of the fact that you are placing rocks above ground level. Also be aware that moving heavy rocks can be dangerous in many ways.

Container Planting (Tubs-Boxes-Baskets)

Tubs and boxes have come into their own in recent years because they can be used to great effect by providing dazzling displays in small areas such as balconies, patios, courtyards, and the like. Tubs and boxes can be made from clay, concrete or plastic, while boxes can also be made from wood. All forms are available in a multitude of designs and shapes. Remember that they may be very heavy, so take adequate precautions and care when moving them. Use the correct flowers, the best of compost, the correct balance of fertiliser, and supply adequate water. Check out any special irrigation watering systems for container plants. Hanging baskets are also highly desirable, providing excellent floral displays. They can dry out quickly so attention to their watering is of paramount importance. You can buy irrigation systems designed for watering hanging baskets.

Colour Combinations

There are three primary colours: red, yellow and blue. Mix red and yellow, and you get orange. Mix red and blue, and you get purple. Mix yellow and blue, and you get green. Orange, purple and green are secondary colours. Mix these secondary colours and you get intermediate or tertiary colours (see 'Colour Wheel' diagram).

Therefore, by mixing two or three primary colours you can achieve any colour. A colour that is intense and rich is known as a hue. Add black and the hue moves through shades of that colour. Add white and the hue moves through tints of that colour. A chromatic colour is one full of bright colour. You can reduce this chromatic saturation by adding black or white.

Warm colours are red, yellow-red, yellow, yellow-green, and green. Cold colours are red-purple, purple, purple-blue, blue, and blue-green.

Some colours advance to catch the eye: red (as in red traffic lights); orange (as in marigolds). Too much red or yellow can dominate a garden. Nevertheless, there have been many famous orange, red and yellow gardens. A colour such as red or yellow placed close to the house will contain the eye, mesmerised, in that one spot. But a drift of cool colours in that same area, followed by a small drift of warm colours, which in turn is followed by more cool colours, will allow the eye to travel over the cool colours, hit the warm colours, and then continue past these on to the cool colours, creating the illusion of distance.

Some colours are relaxing, and lead our vision ever outwards; blue skies for example; or a lake of bluebells in a green beechwood. There have been many famous all-blue gardens, and blue-silver grey gardens.

One of the greatest painters, J.M.W. Turner, and one of the greatest gardeners, Gertrude Jekyll, used colours to create atmosphere. People see solid objects in a garden such as trees, shrubs, rocks, a summer house, a pergola, but Turner would capture the atmosphere that existed between these solid objects using variations of red, yellow, blue and white, and Gertrude Jekyll did the same using various coloured flowers and foliage.

Colour Wheel

A 'colour wheel' has been devised to demonstrate colour combinations. Segments of red, yellow-red, yellow, yellow-green, green, blue-green, blue, purple-blue, purple, and red purple, are spaced evenly around the outside of the wheel. Inside the wheel is an equilateral triangle, which can be spun. The colours where the triangle corners touch will harmonise; for example: blue-green, yellow and red-purple. Colours that fall opposite will complement each other: for example yellow-red and blue. Colours that are next to each other will harmonise: for example red and yellow-red. You may be able to buy a colour wheel from your local art store.

Thus you can see that colour combinations are easy to achieve, but you have to bear in mind how much dominance of one colour you require. Can you plant favourite flowers that create disharmony next to each other? Yes! for two reasons: (1) They don't flower at the same time. (2) You don't agree with the suggestions on colour given above and are going to do your own thing anyway.

Light and Colour

There are other factors which will have a great effect on the flowers in your garden: 1. *Light:* A red rose on a wet morning will have more glow than on a sunny morning. Light early in the morning before the sun is high is golden. Then after a while you will notice blue in the shadows as the sun climbs higher. In the evening as the sun goes down the garden becomes golden again.

Some plants do not open fully on a dull day, Livingstone daisies for example. *Osteospermum fruticosum* is called the 'government flower' by unkind people, because they reckon it opens at ten in the morning, and closes at four in the afternoon. This means, of course, that you have much green leaf before the flowers show.

I lived in Europe for years, the Middle East for a year and a half, and Australia, and each of these countries seems to me to have its own light value. England has a soft, misty atmosphere. The atmosphere of mainland Europe is not as kind. The Middle East has harsh, vivid colours, and dense 'black and white' knife-edge shadows. Australia, on the other hand, is all over the place, with very varied light values. The light in Cairns seems to have a scrubbed-clean appearance, whereas the light in South Australia is harsher, particularly on the plains. Southern Victoria is different again, much softer. And when I left gardening in South Australia to garden in New South Wales it was like going to another country.

The point being that your local light value can influence your garden colour scheme. The soft, muted, misty flowered English herbaceous border will not have the same effect in the harsh South Australian light. Neither would powerful, tarty-coloured flowers go down well in an old English Tudor mansion. And our own Australian bush has a pastel mood all its own.

2. *Texture, form, shape of leaves and branches:* Some plants such as impatiens have shiny leaves, while others such as coleuses have felty leaves, and both types reflect light differently. There are plants with massed foliage which produces strong shadows, and plants with sparse foliage which lets more light through.

Many people like to have mixed colours in a bed while others like solid blocks of colour. Of the two, blocks of colour always seem to have more impact, as you will notice when viewing garden-bed designs in our public parks. But the occasional bed of mixed cinerarias, or tuberous begonias, and other like plants which, individually, have a studded, dramatic quality of their own, are very acceptable.

The blocks of colour in your garden need not be as vast, but the larger the area the more impact the design has. Single plants, or small, spotty groups do little

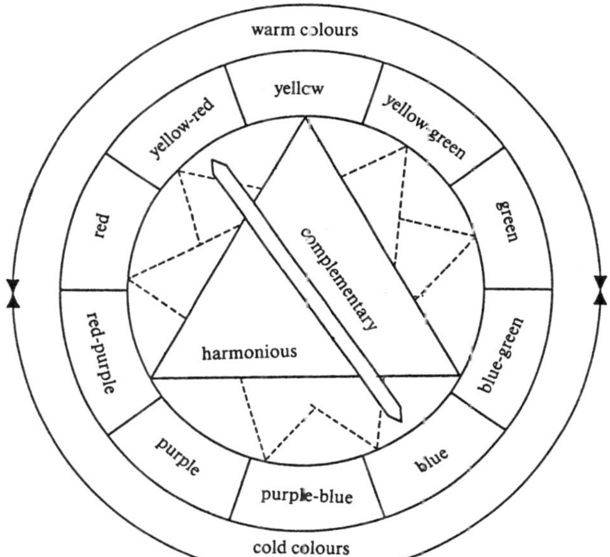

Colour Wheel

to enhance a garden, indeed they do the opposite. The powerful designs in our public parks have to create the necessary effect, because of the size of the area usually involved; and look the better for it.

For years I have been involved with public garden-bed designs; many in the London area. Fortunately for me, expense was not the prime consideration, but producing a public display of flowers that would be admired by tourists and locals was; and mostly I went for the dramatic display.

What factors affect the choice of colour schemes? Personal taste is most influential. An old-fashioned house or building could demand a different colour scheme to an ultra modern one. Many gardeners are patriotic, and subconsciously link national colours to beliefs they hold precious. Some gardeners use eye-stopping reds and yellows. Some prefer to use soothing colours. Some use mysterious colours. Some use cool colours. Some use bright pinks and white. Some use neon glowing colours. The list and the reasons are almost endless, but I feel it all comes down to the gardener's attitude, or what he or she feels like doing at the time.

Do not lose sight of the fact that there are many pastel shades of flowers available. And, in your garden, if a particular colour you liked becomes oppressive, then you can tone it down using flowers of a lighter shade, or by using suitable foliage. Silver or grey foliage always cools down hot colours, but too much golden foliage, because it is closely linked with the 'hot' colours red and yellow, can increase the feeling of heat. As can dramatic reds, purples or magentas.

There are great garden schemes that consist of only two colours such as blue and silver-grey, or white and green. There are also great gardens that are all golden, or all green. These gardens are often referred to as monocolour (one colour) gardens, and one might get the mistaken impression that such gardens were monotonous. But how many different shades of green can you picture? Many, of course! Green foliage should be considered more important than it is. All golden? Think of all the shades of yellow you can visualise: from ruddy apricot, to butter-yellow, to tangy lemon, to palest cream.

Other colours are copper, purple, grey, silver-grey, yellow variegated, white variegated and flushed yellow. In my opinion the secret of design is observation, and planning. You might use a flowering scheme because you saw it somewhere, but you find it does not fit in with your garden. Never despair. Eventually you will come up with a design that is essentially what you want.

Borders-Beds—Accent Plants

Annual flower beds and borders should be wide enough to create an effective splash of flower colour, and a 900 mm (3 ft) width would be the minimum, as anything less than that can look apologetic. (Except, of course, when it succeeds; for example, the way some gardeners plant low-growing flowers in the middle of a car driveway.) A 1.8 m (6 ft) wide garden bed would create a more powerful splash of flower colour. Try not to have flower beds too close to each other, separated only by a narrow path, as this can look jumbly.

Beds designed with fussy curves like a snake going beserk are irritating to look at. Curves should be as long and as gentle as possible, but they should look like pronounced curves, and not so gradual as to give the impression of a straight line that isn't 'quite' straight.

The overall flower height of your annual border can vary from small, low growing plants around the edge, graduating to larger plants in the centre; or you can have beds of plants that are all the same height, such as bedding geraniums, or bedding dahlias.

It is often advisable to have taller 'accent' plants placed judiciously throughout the bed. These can break up the flat plane an annual border can become. There could be two or three in the centre, or only one; but not too many, or the effect will be jungley and defeat the purpose. The purpose of accent plants is to focus your eyes to prevent them from travelling over the bed, and then wandering off to another flower bed or feature. You look at the low-growing plants, and your eyes travel up the accent plant(s), then back to the low-growing plants. I call them 'exclamation mark' plants. Why? If, in a novel, you read 'stop', it does not carry the same impact as if you read 'Stop!' And that is precisely what 'accent', 'dot' or 'exclamation mark' plants do; they 'Stop!' your eyes from wandering. I shall refer to them as accent plants from here on.

These accent plants can be traditional plants such as standard fuchsias, tall gladioluses, cannas, verbenas trained as standards, cordylines, or any suitable plant that gives say 900 mm (3 ft) height to the bed, and can be easily removed when the flowering has finished and a new bedding scheme is to be planted. Accent plants can be grown in large pots so that they can be easily removed after flowering, before they come a nuisance. Special attention would have to be paid to watering these 'pot-bound' plants during dry weather. Also, bear in mind that some plants can increase from root-suckers, and when you lift the pot root sections can snap off, continue to grow, and become a nuisance.

Planting Up Beds

If your bed is to be designed with small edging plants around the outside, taller plants in the centre, and accent plants in the middle, then begin by planting the small edging plants. But be aware that they are there when planting around them. Follow this by spacing and planting your accent plants. Then fill in with your main groundwork plants using the 'five-spot dice (die)' method.

What is the 'five-spot dice' method? You know how the five spots are arranged on a dice (die). You place one plant in the centre of the square, and the other four plants towards the corners, allowing the correct spacing between each plant. This distance will depend on the speed at which the plant will spread, and this is something you must find out.

You do not place them too closely together so that they quickly smother each other, or too far apart so that they take too long to join up to form the effect you are trying to create. They have to reach perfection together.

You don't have to use accent plants in a flower bed. A brilliant, eye-catching, flat-planed garden bed design I once saw contained only red salvias intermingled with dark-blue aquilegias.

If I intend to plant tulip bulbs to surmount a bed of wallflowers or other 'spring-bedding' plants, then I always plant the bulbs first. Why? Imagine the damage you might do to the foliage and roots of the wallflower plants if you planted the bulbs last. Just scatter the bulbs over the surface of the bed, making sure that they are not too close to each other, and plant them.

Those of you who own gardens where you can grow tulips with ease, or have a United Kingdom type climate, can underplant the tulips with various flowers to create a sea of colour below the exotic-looking tulip cups. One of the oldest, and still most popular of garden-bed designs is bright-red tulips over golden bedder wallflowers. Rich pink tulips above creamy wallflowers, which in turn are surrounded by dark-blue forget-me-nots, look mouth-watering. Or red-purple tulips over light-blue, foamy forget-me-nots. Or butter-yellow tulips over 'brown' polyanthus. Or white-pink English daisies intermingled with white pansies and 'Cambridge Blue' forget-me-nots, canopied by pink and white tulips. Pansies have been used as an under-plant with good effect.

There are many variations you can use. You can mix Siberian wallflowers with forget-me-nots; or pansies with daisies; or polyanthus and daisies; or daisies, aubretia and crocus; or red salvias, blue mealycup sage cultivars, and silver foliage; or massed beds of *Amaranthus tricolor* 'Joseph's Coat'; or massed beds of petunias; or tagetes, coleus, and silver foliage. Your imagination, your local climate and local planting times, and seeing what others do, is all you need to achieve great results. Just sit down with a pencil and some paper and work through a few flower colour combinations.

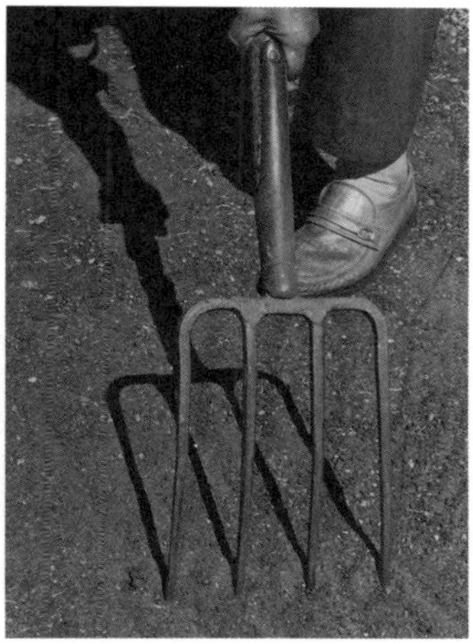

Breaking down soil using the back of the fork

Raking the seed bed into a fine tilth before use

Soil Preparation

Begin by digging the plot a spit deep (fork depth). You can incorporate well-rotted, well-made compost, or well-rotted, well-prepared farmyard manure. Do not use too much manure or compost as this could lead to rank growth in the plants, and possible scorching on some plants. If you bring up clay from the subsoil when you dig, then stop and ascertain the depth of the topsoil. You do not want to bring clay up to the surface, because it dries, becomes lumpy, and can play havoc when you try to prepare a fine seed bed. You just have to cultivate the humus topsoil.

You can double dig the plot. This means that you remove the humic, organic topsoil from the surface, and stack it to one side. You then dig the subsoil and thus you break through any hard pan, creating a deeper soil structure that will hold more moisture. This is of great value to the plant roots. Moisture that is held in the top spit can be rapidly evaporated, and because of this the soil may be too dry for the plant roots to take up nutrients. You can fork over the subsoil incorporating completely rotted manure or completely rotted compost. You can also use peat or clean sharp sand. Do not add fertiliser or green vegetable matter that can grow and produce weed problems, for example, grass clippings containing couch grass (*Cynodon* sp.), or kikuyu grass (*Pennisetum* sp.) roots. You then replace the topsoil on top of the forked-over, broken-down subsoil. Double-digging is hard work, but it may be rewarding. Once you have done all this, do not tramp backwards and forwards over the plot on wet days.

You should also appreciate the value of suitable mulches in hot weather to keep the moisture in the soil, which assists in plant nutrient uptake. However, the value of using organic mulches and well-rotted farmyard manures in the flower garden is being questioned by one authority.

Do not use compost made from grass clippings that have been treated with lawn-weedkiller, or weeds treated with total weedkiller, just in case the weedkilling ingredient of the poison is still active.

It may be that your soil is all clay. Then you cultivate the top spit incorporating well-rotted farmyard manure, or peat, or compost, and clean sharp sand.

Remove all weeds while digging, as they will soon establish themselves during the growing season, and become a nuisance. This is very important in a perennial border, which is to remain undisturbed for a considerable while. And couch grass (*Cynodon* species), although good as a lawn grass, is one of the worse weeds to contend with in a flower bed.

Compost, farmyard manure and peat moss, help to break up heavy clay soils and improve the moisture retention of light, sandy soils. Using a moderate dressing of farmyard manure or a well prepared compost, once a year, may mean that you don't need to use artificial (inorganic) fertilisers, but keep a check on the plants just in case they begin to fail. Also, farmyard manure that isn't properly collected to include urine will contain little potash, and potash is essential for flowering.

A quick word about peat. Peat is partly-decomposed plants, and can be formed in two distinct ways:

1. Water running down a hill may collect like a dam, with oxygen excluded, but with plants like sedges predominating. This water can contain various mineral salts, and the peat may not be acid. It is for this reason that you should ascertain the pH value of the peat you are using. (See section on soil pH testing.)
2. Peat can also be formed in raised bogs, where the water is mostly rain, and practically no nutrients are available to the moss plants. This peat is usually acid. But always make a habit of checking the pH of the peat you are using before you buy or use it.

A little peat does not go a long way! If you think that sprinkling a little peat over a sandy soil will solve all your moisture retention problems: or digging it in a clay soil will break down all your clay soil problems, then you will be sadly disillusioned. If you can only afford a little peat this year, then treat only a small part of the garden, and at least try to get that section right. Peat should be granulated to allow free drainage. But too much 'fine' peat dust will be lost in the soil.

If you have to firm the soil then do it on a dry day, and only on a dry day, by walking over it, making it just firm enough to receive the seeds and plants. Seeds planted in loose soil will disappear. Plants that are planted in loose soil are subject to root damage (wrench) through soil or wind movement.

An ideal garden soil should be well drained, but have the humic qualities that will retain moisture. Ideally, it should have a pH of 6.5 to 7.5, with pH 6.5 being preferred. Acid soils will only grow plants (such as camellias) that can tolerate acid soils. Alkaline soils can cause chlorosis in acid loving plants. But cruciferous plants, such as cabbage and stocks, grow well in a reasonably limy (alkaline) soil.

Humus is the 'black stuff' left when vegetable matter has been composted thoroughly and properly. The smell of a well-made, fully-rotted compost is one of the most beautiful on earth. And it even looks delicious.

Testing the Soil—The pH Test

Some gardeners feel that they have to apply a dressing of lime, because they are led to believe that it sweetens the soil. Never apply lime unless you are sure that the soil is in need of it, as you may be creating problems for the plants you are about to grow. Too much lime leads to trace element deficiencies. For example, it may inhibit the plant's uptake of the essential trace element iron. The plant, as a result, suffers and yellowing of the leaves (chlorosis) may occur.

Scientists have devised a system for testing the lime content in soil, which is called the 'pH Test'. ('pH' stands for 'potenz hydrogen', the power of hydrogen or: *'The negative decimal logarithm of the hydrogen ion concentration in the soil'.* I learned that definition parrot-fashion as a student and, strangely enough, *then* I knew what it meant.)

To simplify soil testing, a scale from pH 0 to pH 14 has been devised where pH 7 is deemed as neutral. From pH 7 down to pH 0 the soil is becoming progressively more acid (sour). From pH 7 up to pH 14 the soil is becoming progressively more alkaline (sweet or limy). I have included the words 'sour' and 'sweet' because some gardeners define soils as being either sour or sweet. Being a scion of an ancient horticultural family, who for generations grew cruciferous plants as a main crop for major British cities, I'm sure that two of the first words I ever learned were 'sour' and 'sweet'. But we should forget these words and settle for 'acid' or 'alkaline'.

You can buy soil-testing kits from your nurseryman to test your garden soil, to ascertain if it is acid, alkaline or neutral. If you find that the soil is extremely acid or extremely alkaline, then check, and double check, and check again, because excessively acid or alkaline soils are not normally found. Get the soil checked professionally if you are in any doubt. Take soil samples from all over the bed area where you are growing plants. Take samples from just below the soil surface, where the roots will grow, and reject any surface litter, which could give a false reading. Take your time doing this, as your garden will be there for a long time. Remember, if you have any doubts then seek professional advice on soils.

It is easy to make an acid soil neutral or alkaline, but is that what you really want? You can grow a wide range of acid-loving plants in an acid soil. It is difficult, perhaps impossible, to change an alkaline soil to an acid one. So think carefully before you change the pH value of your soil.

Acid Neutral Alkaline

0 1 2 3 4 5 6 6.5 - 7 - 7.5 8 9 10 11 12 13 14

pH Scale

Soil is treated with suitable pH soil testing fluid

Suitable pH testing powder is added

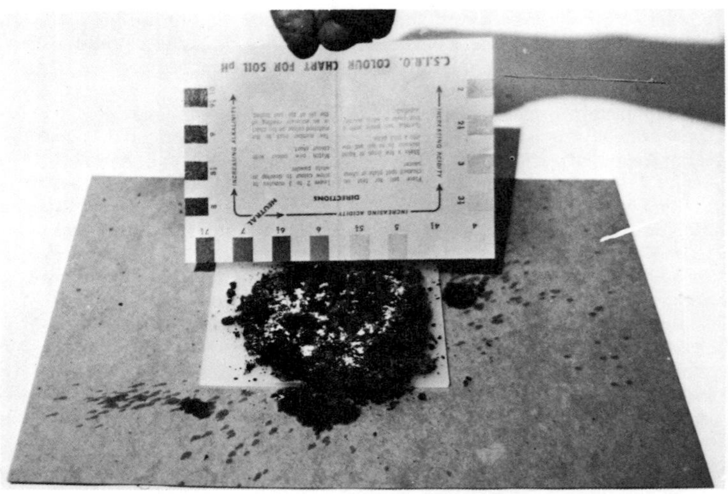

Colour of powder is matched against colour on the chart

Gypsum is the compound *calcium sulphate*, and is neutral in reaction. Many gardeners use gypsum to supply plants' calcium needs, calcium being the main ingredient of lime, (*calcium carbonate* or *calcium hydroxide* or *calcium oxide*).

Many plants thrive in a soil between pH 6.5 and pH 7.5, with pH 6.5 being deemed as most generally suitable. Some plants, known as calcicoles, prefer a reasonably alkaline soil. Some plants, known as calcifuges, prefer a reasonably acid soil.

If your soil has a reading of pH 6.5 then be very grateful. If it is between pH 7.0 and pH 7.5 or between pH 5.5 and pH 6.0 then also be grateful. The point being that you grow annual, biennial and perennial plants that prefer your particular soil pH.

But if you intend to use lime then use one that is suitable and prepared specifically for use on home garden soils. Read the information on the pack.

Plant Food

Plants have to eat, as indeed, we have to eat plants in one form or another, to survive. Plants take in carbon, oxygen and hydrogen either from the soil, water or from the atmosphere. The 'green' leaves, using chlorophyll and sunlight, transform carbon dioxide and water into soluble carbohydrates, such as glucose, and transport them to the growing tips of the plant. Glucose can be transformed into the more complex sugars and starches, and in combination with other plant foods can become complex proteins.

The three major plant foods, apart from those mentioned above, are nitrogen, phosphorus (phosphates) and potassium (potash), or N:P:K. 'N' stands for nitrogen; 'P' for phosphorus (phosphates); 'K' for kalium (potassium—potash: kalium being the scientific name for potassium). And these can be supplied by fertiliser application, or well-prepared manures.

Calcium, magnesium and sulphur are needed in smaller amounts, but mostly these are already available in the soil. Calcium is found in garden lime and gypsum (calcium sulphate). Sulphur is found in certain fertilisers such as sulphate of ammonia and sulphate of potash. Magnesium also is usually available to the plant. If you suspect a magnesium deficiency, do seek qualified, professional advice on soil and plant deficiencies. Remember, over-application of one element can depress the uptake of another, which could lead to plant failure.

'Trace' or 'minor' elements are also necessary, but usually these are available in the soil, and any attempt to supply them without knowing what you are about could lead to toxic soils, for a long, long time.

To put it very simply plants need nitrogen for leaf and green stem growth; phosphate for healthy root growth; and potash for flower colour-fruit-seed production.

There are two major groups of fertilisers: organic and inorganic. Organic fertilisers are obtained from the residues of plants and animals. The nutrients of these materials are slowly broken down by soil bacteria, and the food becomes available to the plant in that form. Examples are blood and bone, bone meal, dried blood, and hoof and horn meal. Blood and bone contains goodly amounts of nitrogen and phosphates. Bone meal contains small amounts of nitrogen and relatively high amounts of phosphate. Dried blood contains high amounts of nitrogen, and hoof and horn contains much nitrogen and a small amount of phosphates. The percentages they contain are usually written on the pack.

Farmyard manure from properly fed animals will contain dung, urine and straw, and supply the major plant foots and trace elements, but it is low in nitrogen. Pig and poultry manures are rich in concentrated plant foods, and should be treated with caution; a little goes a long way.

You can use artificial (inorganic) fertilisers, and possibly most of you gardeners who grow annuals, biennials, and perennials do this.

Chemical fertilisers are available in various 'balanced' or 'straight' forms. 'Balanced' fertilisers usually contain a balanced percentage of nitrogen, phosphates and potash, for a particular application (read the information on the pack). A 'straight' fertiliser is where only one nutrient is supplied, although there are 'straights' which may contain slight amounts of other nutrients.

There are the traditional bags of fertilisers, that have been around for years. There are the more recent ones, which are known as 'controlled-release' fertilisers, and these are becoming very popular. These 'controlled-release' fertilisers allow their nutrients to be released to the plant slowly over a period of time; a time specified on the pack. And some may be specially designed for annuals, biennials or perennials. Some are compounded for general use; or specially prepared for a particular group of plants. Read the instructions on the pack. This is of the utmost importance if you are using artificial fertilisers of any kind.

Then there are the balanced, liquid, soluble flower fertilisers and foliar feeds, the content and correct use of which are usually given on the pack. It is vitally important to read these instructions, particularly the method of application and suitability for given plants.

Nitro-chalk supplies nitrogen (ammonium nitrate) and calcium (lime), and is alkaline in reaction. Sulphate of ammonia (ammonium sulphate) is a quick acting fertiliser that supplies nitrogen. It can have a scorching effect on leaves and roots if not used correctly. Sulphate of potash (potassium sulphate) supplies potassium. Superphosphate supplies phosphate.

Remember, read the manufacturer's instructions on any pack of fertiliser before buying and using it. Also remember that over-application of fertiliser may lead to the death of young seedlings and mature plants.

Seed Sowing and Growing

There are good reasons why seeds fail:

1. Sowing them too deeply, or too shallowly, according to their needs.
2. Using an inferior compost, or sowing them in soil which stifles them, or cracks easily causing root damage.
3. Allowing the compost, or soil, to dry out, thus destroying the seeds or seedlings.
4. Not giving the seeds, or seedlings, the necessary protection during hot, or cold, weather.
5. The wrong sowing times.
6. Sowing the seeds when the soil temperature is below that required for the seeds to germinate; thus causing the seeds to rot.
7. Inferior seeds, but this is unlikely with reputable seed firms, who put a 'last-sowing' date stamp on the packet.
8. Heavy-handed watering by the grower. Or too little watering.
9. Heavy rain before the seeds and seedlings are established.
10. Too much fertiliser in the soil.

Spring and Summer Flowering Annuals

We tend to divide annuals up into either spring or summer flowering, the spring flowering plants being sown in autumn, and the summer flowering plants being sown in spring-mid summer. But this is too pat as many spring and summer annuals can be winter or autumn annuals depending on climate, or sown at times other than those mentioned. Nevertheless, the definitions 'spring' and 'summer' annuals help to pinpoint the groups.

Popular examples of 'spring-flowering' annuals are: *Bellis perennis* (daisy); *Brassica oleracea acephala* (ornamental kale); *Calendula officinalis* (pot marigold); *Cheiranthus cheiri* (wallflower); *Dianthus barbatus* (sweet william); *Linaria maroccana* (toadflax); *Myosotis sylvatica* (forget-me-not); *Nigella damascena* (love-in-a-mist); *Papaver nudicaule* (Iceland poppy); *Ranunculus asiaticus*; *Senecio cruentus* (cineraria).

Popular examples of 'summer-flowering' annuals are: *Amaranthus tricolor* (Joseph's coat); *Celosia argenta cristata* (cockscomb); *Limonium sinuatum* (statice); *Petunia × hybrida*; *Salvia splendens* (scarlet sage); *Phlox drummondii*; *Tagetes erecta* (African marigold); *Zinnia elegans*.

There are many, many more plants, and some of you will say, but they flower in winter, or in autumn, where I live. Possibly they do, but I think you see the point I am trying to make.

Seed Sowing Times

The correct seed sowing times are usually critical, but they vary considerably in Australia, even within local communities.

For this section I did much research on seed sowing times for the various states and territories within the Commonwealth, but the resulting information was complex and peculiar to each state, with wide variations for some areas within the same state or territory. An example is the Northern Territory, where the weather variations can be significantly different between the wet top end, and other parts of the Territory.

Such a complex of climates, and sowing times! And these climates are further complicated by a multitude of localised or microclimates, with only the gardener in residence knowing his own microclimate. The point being that it is the responsibility of Australian gardeners to seek local, professional advice for the correct and best sowing times for their locality. And, usually, such information is available. And never lose sight of the fact that your own commonsense is a great source of knowledge! But always read the sowing times and instructions given on the seedmen's seed packets.

I feel that, because of the quick growth-rate in certain areas, many annuals can be treated as ephemeral annuals; that is two, or more, plantings of a particular annual during the year.

In cold, frost-prone climates half-hardy annuals or plants that are grown as half-hardy annuals, cannot be sown outside in the open when there is a risk of frost, as frost would kill them. They are, therefore, sown after all risk from frost is past and the ground has warmed up. Alternatively, the seeds of half-hardy annuals are sown in a greenhouse, or similar warm place, at a temperature of between 15–25°C (59–77°F), according to the seed's germination requirements, but usually between 18–21°C (64–70°F), in late winter to spring (August-September), or approximately 6 to 8 weeks before the last frost, or 6 to 8 weeks before the usual planting out time in those areas. It all depends on how long it takes the plant to germinate and be ready for planting outside after any danger from frost is past and the ground has warmed up. The seedlings are gradually hardened off in cold fame or similar, and then planted out mid-late spring-early summer (late September-October-November-December), but only if all danger from frost is past and the ground has warmed up.

Hardy Annuals

You should follow a few basic rules when sowing seeds directly where they are to grow and flower, or in prepared seedbeds.

Dig over the soil when it is easy to work, on a dry day, directly where the plants are to grow and flower, breaking it down into a fine tilth. Rake out any debris, and firm the soil gently but thoroughly to take the seeds. A soil that is loose is no good for sowing seeds, as the seeds drop into the soil crevices, and are lost. Loose soil is no good for planting young seedlings as the seedling's roots will suffer from excessive wrenching (movement). Walking over the soil backwards and forwards, when it is dry, on your heels, is one way to consolidate a loose soil. But this can be very tiring, and taxing on your leg muscles, as I found out all those times when consolidating cricket square, bowling green, and lawn foundation soils. But walking ordinarily, normally, over the soil will also be effective. You can also flood the soil with water to settle it.

Water the soil a few hours before sowing the seeds, and let the top surface dry out, so that you can walk over it without damaging the soil structure. Many gardeners work from a plank to minimise soil damage. If possible choose a cool, calm day, but the soil surface must be dry.

Seeds should be sown thinly to avoid unnecessary thinning out later on. The seeds can be sown either broadcast fashion, or in shallow drills (rows). Sowing seeds broadcast fashion creates a very informal effect, but I can assure you from personal experience that if young weeds grow up with young, desirable seedlings, then it is hard to distinguish between them. If, however, you sow the seeds in drills then the seedlings will come up in straight rows, and are easier to detect. But, you may ask, won't that look regimented?

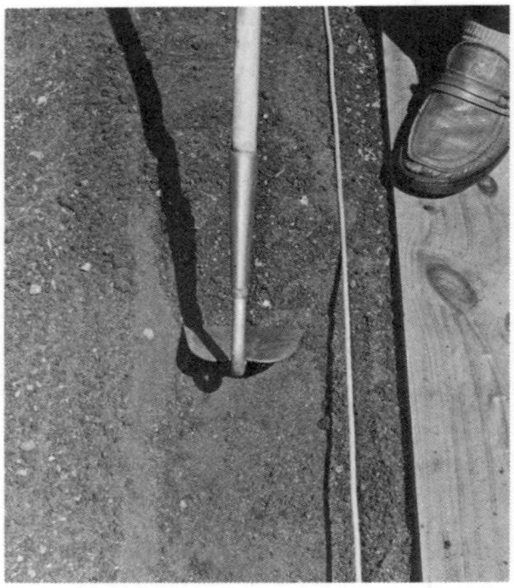

Using a swan-necked hoe to draw out wide drills (rows)

Using a swan-necked hoe on edge to draw out a shallow drill

Using the head of the rake to make a shallow drill

Not if you vary the angle of the rows, making them run sideways, or at angles from where you are viewing.

Most seeds need light to germinate (check the packet), and some seeds are best sown on the soil surface, and then pressed lightly and gently on to the soil surface to anchor them, so that they come into contact with the moisture held by the soil particles. Others are sown at the required depth, and a rough approximation is twice the diameter of the seeds; some say the length of the seed deep, but these

Using a broom handle to create a shallow drill

Using a small trowel to draw out a shallow drill (row)

Adding sand or peat to the bottom of a seed drill

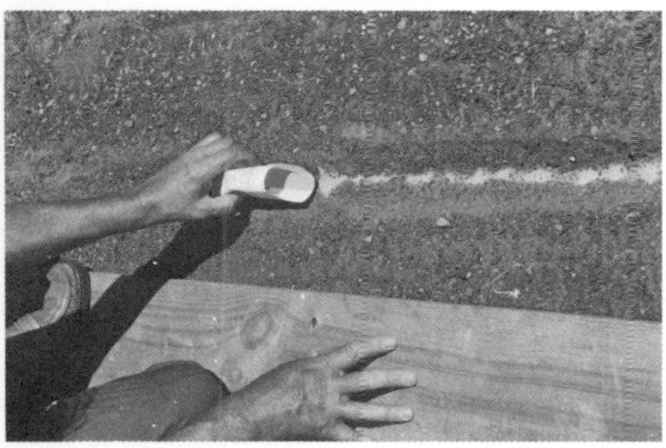

Sowing seeds mixed with clean fine sand out of doors

Raking soil over seeds from both sides

Gently firming seed rows with the head of a rake

Gently firming seeds with a wooden trowel

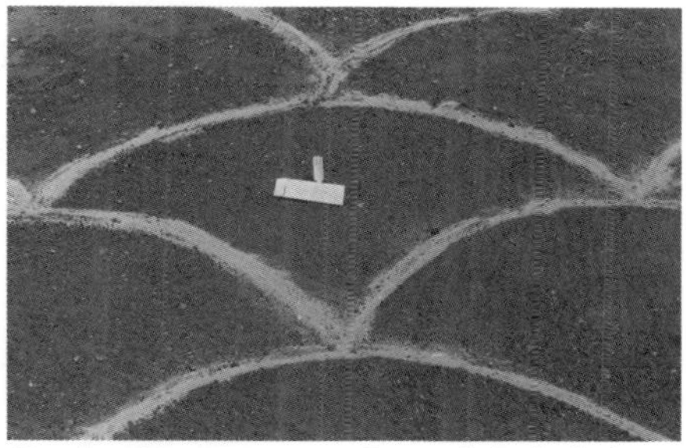

Showing the arrangement of annuals in the bed

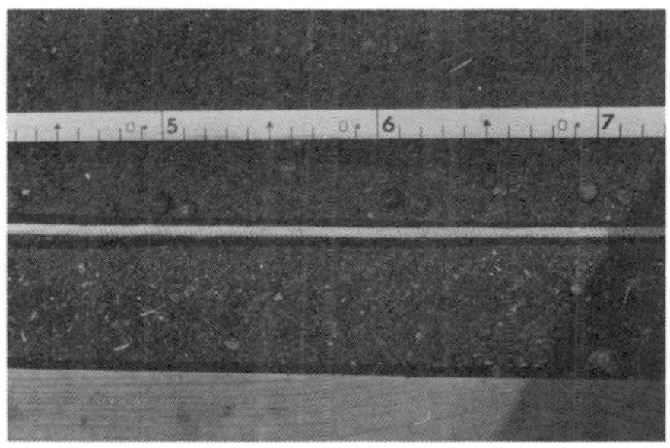

'Station-Planting' seeds

Shows spacing of large seeds in a drill (row)

depths are not infallible, and more correct information is given on the seed packet. Lightly-gently firm the soil to anchor the seeds; I have used the head of the rake, or a wooden float, and sometimes a flat-board punner (a light block of wood attached to the end of a broom handle). Gently, but thoroughly, water the seeds using a fine spray, and do not allow the seedbed soil or seedlings to dry out. Keep the soil pleasantly moist until the seedlings are well established (unless the directions on the seed packet state differently), and then water the plants as, and when, they need it. Some seeds can also be sown in nursery seedbeds, using the same methods as above, and then transplanted into their permanent quarters.

Thinning Out

The seeds, usually, will come up thicker than required for the display you want, and will have to be thinned out. You carefully, and thoughtfully, remove the surplus seedlings before the plants crowd each other. Try to choose a cloudy day, when the soil is dry enough to walk over without damaging the surface, or instead of walking over the soil, work from a plank. Wait until germination is well established. Thin out the seedlings over a period of days, or say 3 or 4 weeks; commonsense is needed here.

In the first sweep, thin out the weakest. Gently mist-water around the roots of those seedlings left, to settle the roots, and then let these seedlings grow on. Carry out another sweep at a later date, using the same procedure. Then another, if necessary, until you have achieved the required distance apart, and have strong, sturdy seedlings left.

Or in the first sweep leave double the seedlings you need. For example if you need 25 plants, then leave 50 seedlings. Two to three weeks later carry out the second, and usually final, thinning; but the time of thinning, and how many sweeps are needed, depends on the growth of the seedlings.

A rough guide to the 'thinned-out' distance between seedlings is half the final height of the plant, but the seed packet gives a more comprehensive account, as some plants are wide spreading, but at the same time low growing. Don't just grab at a seedling, and pull at it, as you will invariably end up with a handful of those seedlings you wanted to leave. Take your time when thinning seedlings.

Moving Seedlings

To move a seedling from an outdoor seedbed to where it is to grow and flower,

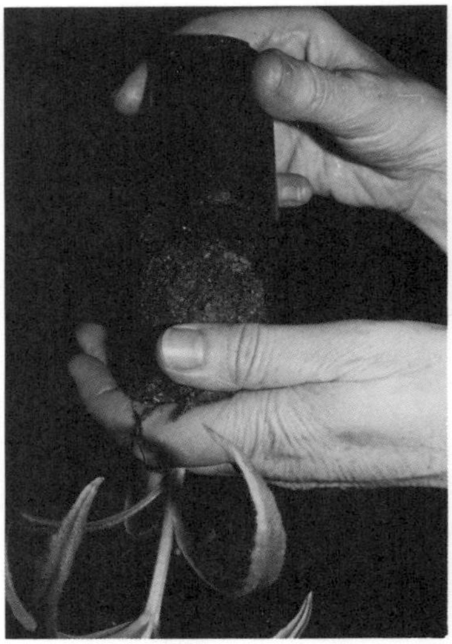

Removing a seedling from a pot (n.b. stem is between fingers)

Using 'notched' label to prick out small seedlings

Pricking-out, holding young seedling gently by the leaf

Gently settling seedlings using the fingers; gloves can be used

Using fork to ease up seedlings from seedling container

you begin by gently watering the plant roots only, but not the surrounding soil, as you have to walk over it. Preferably on a cloudy day or at evening, when the soil is dry enough to walk over without damaging its structure, lift the seedling with a garden-trowel taking as much root ball soil as is feasible. Transfer the plant into a scooped out hole where it is to grow, gently firm the soil around it, and water it in. By using this method of transplantion shock should be reduced. Should a hot sun suddenly appear, then you may have to shade the seedlings temporarily, until the roots have settled and struck into the new soil. Commonsense is needed here.

Sowing Seeds in Seed Compost Containers

There are many seed raising and potting composts on the market. But do choose a reputable one.

The University of California and University of Cornell composts (U.C. composts), are mixed to a strict set of rules laid down by these august bodies. What about John Innes composts? There are no better composts than properly prepared John Innes composts, and the emphasis is on proper preparation, according to the inventor's instructions. In John Innes composts a suitable fibrous loam is the main ingredient, and it is the quality of this loam that makes the compost good or bad.

Also be aware that when soil is 'sterilised' all the injurious organisms are killed off, but the nitrogen-fixing bacteria survive. Without competition these bacteria thrive exceedingly well, producing an excess of ammonia salts which is injurious to the young seedlings' roots. Flush out ammonia salts from the 'sterilised' soil with water before the soil is used as compost material.

Other reputable composts are made from a mixture of acid, granulated peat, and clean, sharp sand, with the necessary fertiliser ingredients added. If unsure, seek local, professional advice on composts.

Throughout this book, for convenience, I will not refer to 'named' composts, but use the phrase 'recommended seed raising compost', or 'recommended potting compost'; but you will know what I mean. I will, mostly, refer to flats, boxes, punnets, seed pans and half pots as seed compost containers, or potting compost containers, and again you will know what I mean. The seed compost containers are approximately 63 mm (2.5 in) in depth, although if you use ordinary pots the depth can be greater. Wooden seed boxes should be soaked in water before use to prevent them absorbing moisture from the compost.

You will come up against various expressions such as 'pricking out'; 'pricking on'; and 'pricking off'. As far as I am concerned, all mean to move crowded seedlings from the seed compost container, and space them apart into seedling-boxes, punnets or pots of potting compost. To make life easier space out the seedlings 50 mm or 75 mm (2 in or 3 in) apart; 75 mm (3 in) apart being for pot plant seedlings. Other expressions are 'potted up' and 'potted on', referring to plants being moved from one pot to a wider pot. Again these expressions, as far as I am concerned, mean the same, although to be honest I prefer 'potted on'. And, generally, when moving a plant on into a larger pot, I prefer to go on two sizes each time; from a 75 mm (3 in) pot to a 125 mm (5 in) pot; from the 125 mm (5 in) pot to a 175 mm (7 in) pot; to a 225 mm (9 in) pot. Or from a 50 mm (2 in) pot to a 100 mm (4 in) pot; to a 150 mm (6 in) pot; and so on. I don't think there is anything to be gained by potting plants on one size at a time. But many gardeners disagree with this, and prefer to pot plants on one size at a time, to prevent the plant from being surrounded by too much cold wet compost. Also there are certain plants that need 'tight potting' all their lives.

Fluorescent Light Propagating Systems

To maintain a large greenhouse at high temperatures is an expensive business, but reasonably priced 'propagating cases', 'fluorescent-lighted seed stands', 'seed starter lamps', 'propagating table top plant lights' and other propagation systems are available. (Read the manufacturer's instructions carefully.) It is vitally important to remember that you are dealing with electricity in the presence of water, therefore make sure the system is perfectly safe to handle and use and, if necessary, installed by a qualified electrician. Don't take chances with electricity and water. Your local electricity authority may have information on seed propagating systems.

Sowing Seed in Compost

The compost is placed in the seed compost container and firmed moderately by pressing down with the fingers. You can wear gloves to prevent your hands from coming into direct contact with the compost. Thoroughly firm the corners and sides of the container, although with some plastic seed punnets the sides tend to bow out under pressure. Make sure the compost is perfectly level, and then flatten the top by pressing it with a smooth, clean block of wood. The compost should be approximately 12 mm (½ in) below the top of the container, to allow for watering.

Thinly sow the seeds on to damp seed raising compost, at the correct time, under glass in a greenhouse, or indoors under plant growing fluorescent lights, at the required temperature. In frost-free climates where seeds can be grown in seed compost containers without the need for a greenhouse or a cold frame, then it is possible to use a shade frame covered with 'white' shadecloth (check with your local supplier/manufacturer) suitable for seed raising.

Germinating temperatures are variable, and range from 15–25°C (59–77°F), but usually 18–21°C (64–70°F). Some seeds may demand a temperature lower than 15°C (59°F), and will fail in high temperatures; while others may require a temperature higher than 25°C (77°F). The sowing times and sowing temperatures are usually given on the seed packet or in the seedmen's catalogues.

One method of ensuring that the seeds are sown thinly enough, is to empty sufficient seeds into the palm of your right hand. Hold the hand say 125 mm (5 in) above the compost. Move the hand over the compost, while at the same time tapping gently with your left hand, slowly releasing the seeds. Do dummy runs with clean, dry sand to get the hang of it. Avoid sowing seeds in thick patches, as this can lead to overcrowding, and possible damping-off disease. Sow half of the seeds in one direction, and the other half in the opposite direction.

How do you estimate just how many seeds you need for a particular container? Place a sheet of snow-white paper on to a flat surface. Turn the thoroughly dry, empty container upside down on the sheet of paper, and draw its outline. Remove it, and carefully scatter the seeds over the white paper, and within the boundaries of the container outline, until you have sufficient coverage. Now carefully tip the seeds back into an empty packet or small envelope, and begin from there. Many professional nurserymen use a seed sowing gadget, which makes most seed sowing easy, and these gadgets may be available at your local nursery.

The above form of sowing can only be done with dry, easy-running seeds, as sticky, fluffy, or very fine seeds will not scatter. The sowing of very fine seeds is discussed below. Sticky seeds can be mixed with very fine, sharp, silver sand, and then sown straight out of the packet. Fluffy seeds can be fluffed out, and placed near enough individually. Larger seeds can be placed individually. Many gardeners sow certain seeds in the compost, but along lightly marked rows, a sort of 'furrow' effect.

You'll soon become proficient at seed sowing. Cover the seeds with the required depth of sieved compost, or fine, clean sharp sand. Hold a fine sieve above the seed container and sift the required layer of sand or compost over the seeds. Do not bury them too deeply.

Gently firm the compost to anchor the seeds. Stand the container in a shallow dish of tepid water, with the water level below the rim of the container, but at the compost level, allowing moisture to soak up through the compost until it just glistens on the surface. Then remove the container. Don't let the water pool on the surface or the seeds may be washed to the sides of the container. The compost must be kept pleasantly moist.

Grow the seedlings at the required temperature in a frost-free greenhouse, cold frame or seed propagating case, in good light, but not with direct sunlight scorching through the glass.

In warm, frost-free areas, the seeds can be sown in containers, which are placed in a propagating case. Or the container can be covered with a small sheet of suitable strong glass to conserve moisture, keep out the rain and aid germination. Some gardeners place the container in a suitable, clear plastic bag, but it would need propping up above the seeds as rain can flatten a plastic bag. In hot weather place the container in a suitable shade-house for the seeds to germinate. But as stated previously, 'white' shadecloth is being used for growing seeds and seedlings in temperate and warmer areas. There are Australian gardeners who protect their seeds and seedlings from hot sun and heavy rain by making a frame or tent over the seed compost container using fibreglass insect gauze.

The glass or plastic bag is removed immediately the seedlings show. Or you can raise one end of the glass temporarily to allow air circulation, but it must be removed soon afterwards to prevent the seedlings from becoming drawn and spindly. However, those seedlings not growing in a frame, case, or greenhouse will still need protection from inclement weather, as heavy rain coming through the shadecloth may spoil the compost and seedlings.

Having got the seeds to germinate at a reasonably high temperature, you remove the container from the propagating case, but still keep it in a greenhouse environment, in good light but not hot sunlight. Shade if necessary. The temperature is usually gradually reduced, depending on the nature of the plant.

The plants are grown on until ready to be transplanted. Then the seedlings are pricked out into containers. They are grown on in a compatible, warm, atmosphere, free from frost. The seedlings are gradually temperature-adjusted, until they are ready to be moved out into the cold frame, where they will be hardened off.

It is imperative to watch for signs of seedling 'damping off' disease, which if noticed must be treated with a suitable fungicide. Prick out (transplant) the seedlings from the seed compost container when they are large enough to handle easily, and before they stifle each other, into containers or pots of well-firmed, damp, potting compost, and grow them on.

There are seedlings that resent any transplantation, and here a few seeds are planted in individual pots, and then thinned out in the pot leaving only the sturdiest. You can also use the same treatment for those seedlings that do not mind transplantation, to achieve unchecked seedlings.

It is important, that the temperature of the potting compost is the same as the seedling compost, to help prevent transplantation shock.

Back to the seedlings: ease them up with a label, blunt pencil or similar, and carefully ease them apart. Hold each seedling gently by the leaf rather than by the vulnerable stem. Make a hole in the potting compost with a dibber (a pointed stick like a blunt pencil), deep and wide enough to take the seedling's roots straight down without bending them upwards. Gently place the seedling into the hole, so that it is snug, upright, and not flopping. Very, very gently firm the soil around the seedling with your fingers or the dibber; don't be heavy-handed around seedling roots as subsequent watering will settle the compost around them.

When you have finished pricking out the seedlings, mist-water the root area very carefully with a fine spray to settle the compost around the roots. Or place the container in a shallow dish of tepid water until the compost just glistens with moisture, then remove it. Keep the seedling compost pleasantly moist at all times. Place the seedlings in a good light, but not strong, baking sunlight, to grow on. Shade them if necessary.

In frost-prone areas gradually harden these seedlings off in a cold frame, or a shade frame in warmer areas, and plant them out, once they are thoroughly hardened off, directly where they are to grow and flower, assuming any danger from frost is past and the ground has warmed up; or in warmer areas once the seedlings have adjusted to the warm sunlight. You will gain nothing from planting seedlings into cold soil or, as is more likely, you will lose them. You will also lose by planting seedlings into hot soil. How would you feel were you a delicate seedling?

Starting Seeds Indoors on a Windowsill, or Similar

For the purpose of this book I grew approximately 50 separate genera of annuals, not species (*Lobelia, Salvia, Petunia*, are all separate genera), using a spare bedroom window. It is unlikely that you would grow as many for your garden. But I have to be honest and state that I was available during the day, all through the seeds' germination and seedlings' growth process.

I had no option but to use a north facing window, which in the southern hemisphere faces the equator, but I installed a suitable curtain shade for the seeds to protect them during hot sunlight. I also safely installed suitable lighting to provide any lighting necessary for the seeds' propagation.

1. Choose a window that receives a goodly amount of daylight, but don't subject the seeds to hot sunlight baking through the glass. Also many Australian houses have a wide roof-overhang which cuts out much sunlight, and could cause light availability problems.
2. Choose small, convenient, seed raising containers, and use top quality seed raising compost. Make sure the compost is pleasantly moist, not wet. Sow the seeds. Some seeds demand to be sown in pots, with the seedlings being thinned out leaving only the strongest in each pot. The compost must be kept pleasantly moist and warm to ensure germination, but not waterlogged.
3. You can cover the seeds with glass, which could prove to be awkward, difficult, and possibly dangerous with young children around; or put the container in a clear plastic bag and seal it; or cover the top of the container with top quality, transparent, plastic cling wrap, such as is used in the kitchen for wrapping food.

Selection of seed and seedling containers

Showing author's window-sill propagation set up

This helps to seal in the moisture and to keep the seeds warm. Those seeds that demand darkness to germinate can be covered with black plastic or kitchen aluminium foil. Those seeds completely enclosed in a clear plastic bag should not need any extra watering, but keep a check on them just in case. Otherwise, any watering can be done by standing the 'top-closed' containers in a shallow dish of water until the compost surface just glistens with moisture. Then the container is removed. Large seeds in open containers can be mist-sprayed with water; fine seeds in open containers are watered from below. Constantly check to ensure that the seeds and compost do not dry out.
4. Condensation will form under the cling wrap, which can be removed by gently tapping the wrap. Condensation will form inside the plastic bag, therefore make sure the plastic is not in direct contact with the compost.
5. Seeds need the correct temperature, as suggested in the ABC of Plants, to germinate.
6. Stand the containers in a waterproof tray, or make a tray of plastic, so that water will not drop on the floor or walls. And definitely ensure that water does not drip on to electrical devices, plugs etc.
7. Safety is vitally important, therefore make sure that no electrical device, or cable, comes into contact with the water you are using for the plants. And remember that inquisitive young children will have to be protected from any likely danger.
8. Constantly check the container for signs of germination. Remove the glass, plastic bag, cling wrap, black plastic or

Pot for seeds can be divided into two, or even four sections

Sowing seeds by hand

Firming compost with fingers (but use gloves)

Firming compost using a simple, clean block of wood

aluminium foil immediately the seeds germinate.

9. The seedlings will lean towards the strongest light source. Therefore, turn them regularly so that all parts receive equal amounts of sunlight.

10. Remember that seedlings can stew next to a hot window; or they can freeze at night next to a cold one. Therefore protect them where necessary from excessive heat or cold.

11. The seedlings will tolerate a slightly lower temperature after germination. But not too suddenly; or too cold. Eventually, of course, they will have to be hardened off sufficiently to cope with outside temperatures.

12. Prick out the seedlings, when they are large enough to handle, into containers of potting compost; say 50 mm (2 in) apart each way. Or prick them off singly into small pots of potting compost.

13. The plants must be hardened off before they can be planted outside, and this is where a cold frame is of great value. But the transition from the warm growing area to the cold frame has to be gradual, as sensitive seedlings object to sudden fluctuations of temperature. Just think how you would feel, going from a warm room into a cold greenhouse.

14. Gradually harden off those seedlings that are destined to be planted outside, and plant them out when all danger from frost is past and the ground has warmed up. Conversely, the problem in some areas could be that the outside temperature is too hot for the soft-grown seedlings, and they will have to be hardened off in a suitable shade house or shade frame. Australian gardeners have to realise that seedlings can be decimated by frost and/or hot sun.

Covering seeds with glass and paper

Hardening Off Seedlings in Cold Climates

Seedlings grown inside or in a hothouse are 'soft', and before they can be planted outside, directly where they are to grow and flower, they have to be 'hardened off' in a cold frame, or similar, to gradually acclimatise them to outside temperatures. Bear in mind that some winter temperatures average just above freezing point, and in frost-prone areas it is vital to harden seedlings off. This is usually done 2–4 weeks (depending on the natural hardiness of the plant, and how late it is in the season) before the accepted planting-out time, when all danger from frost should be past, and the ground should have warmed up.

The frame is kept closed for the first few days to let the plants become accustomed to their new environment. Then start by giving the seedlings a crack of air during the warmest part of the day, then close down the frame and protect them during the night, with matting or similar, against any damaging frost; and, if necessary, also protect them from frost, or too cold a weather during the day. Also bear in mind that the seedlings may need shading from unexpected, hot sunlight, but not heavy shade, as this can lead to 'drawn' seedlings.

Gradually, over a period of weeks, expose the seedlings little by little, more and more, to the outside temperature, until they are fully hardened off and ready to be planted out; but only when all danger from frost is past and the ground has warmed up. Do not leave the cold frame lights (window) off until you are absolutely positive that all danger from frost is past.

As I have pointed out, time and time again, to gardeners, to my gardening students, to my gardening apprentices, commonsense is the most important qualification needed in gardening, and never more so than when hardening off seedlings.

Sowing fine seeds mixed with clean, sharp, fine sand

Ongoing Care of Seedlings

Water the seedlings gently, but thoroughly, before planting them out, and then water them gently with a fine-rose watering-can, once they are planted, to settle the soil around the roots. This tends to keep the plants turgid (full of water). Try to water the young planted seedlings, and mature plants if possible, without washing soil over the leaves and flowers, as this leads to spoiling and possible fungus attack.

Screeding seeds with fine compost and sharp sand

Sowing and Raising Fine Seeds

The energy contained in fine seeds such as begonias, calceolarias, petunias, and such like is not great, and if buried too deeply they will not survive.

Firstly, make sure the compost is fine and not lumpy, otherwise the seeds could disappear among the crevices. Secondly, thoroughly saturate the compost with tepid water and allow the surplus to drain away, leaving a dark, damp compost. Don't ever sow seeds in dry compost, as dry peat in a seed or potting compost takes a long time to absorb moisture and could float to the top.

Fill the seed compost container with the compost, and firm it thoroughly, particularly into the corners. If the compost is loose, then the seeds could be lost in the crevices. Place the container in a shallow dish of tepid water so that the level of the water is below the rim of the container, but at the level of the compost inside. Do not allow water to flow over the top of the container. Remove the container when the surface of the compost glistens with moisture, but has not pooled.

Plunging pots of seeds in water

Thinly sprinkle the seeds over the

compost surface, and lightly press them with a clean, dry, flat board to anchor them to the compost. To aid distribution, you can mix the seeds, in the packet, with several times their own volume of very fine, clean, sharp, silver sand. Cover the container with a piece of top quality glass and the seeds should germinate without further watering, but keep a constant check on this. Some gardeners use a suitable, clear plastic bag.

As soon as the seedlings appear remove the container from the plastic bag or lift up one side of the glass to allow air circulation; but don't keep the glass over the seedlings too long, or they will become drawn; better that you remove the glass altogether, as soon as the seedlings appear.

When the seedlings need water, place the container in a dish of tepid water, again with the level of the water below the container rim, but at the level of the compost inside. Do not allow water to flow over the top of the container, as this could wash out the seedlings. Control this operation carefully, and remove the container once the surface compost just glistens with moisture, but has not pooled.

If, for some reason, you wish to water the seeds, or seedlings, without placing them in a container of water, then use a very, very, fine mist-spray, similar to a scent atomiser. I would suspect that more seedlings are lost through careless watering, than from any other operation; but I may be wrong. Always, when growing seeds and seedlings, use lukewarm water as cold water could have a very sobering effect on them.

Hardy Annuals in English (UK) Gardens

Ideally, the hardy annual area should be dug over roughly in the autumn, incorporating compost, well-rotted manure, or clean sharp sand on heavy soils. It is left to be broken down by winter frosts. Hardy annuals are sown early to late spring (but do seek competent, local, professional advice on correct seed sowing times for your locality), directly the ground is dry enough to be worked and broken down easily, and is warmed up sufficiently after the winter frost period to allow germination.

Half-hardy Annuals in English (UK) Gardens

Half-hardy annuals are usually sown, under glass, mid winter—mid spring—late spring (January—early April), depending on how long it takes the plant to grow from seed to planting-out size (but do seek competent, local, professional advice on correct seed sowing times at your locality). Planting out is usually done late spring—early summer (late May—early June), but only after any danger from frost is past and the ground has warmed up. The temperature needed to germinate the seeds depends on the seed's genetic temperature requirements. The seeds are sown in a recommended seed raising compost (U.C., John Innes, or similar) in shallow trays of either wood, clay, or as is more likely, plastic, these containers being approximately 50–63 mm (2–2.5 in) deep.

Germinating temperatures are variable, and range from 15–25°C (59–77°F), but usually 18–21°C (64–70°F). Some seeds may demand a temperature lower than 15°C (59°F) and will fail in high temperatures; while others may require a temperature higher than 25°C (77°F). The sowing times, and sowing temperatures are usually given on the seed packet or in the seedmen's catalogues. For more information please refer to previous section on half-hardy annuals.

Weed Competition

It is a good idea to keep the soil around the seedlings free from weeds, which are very aggressive and will grab most of the soil's goodness. But be careful when cultivating around seedlings and plants as the roots are usually near the surface and can easily be damaged by the hoe. Careful hand weeding can be the answer to many weed problems.

Feeding

To keep certain annuals growing strongly they are given occasional feedings with a suitable, balanced, liquid, soluble, flower fertiliser, which is applied as the manufacturer recommends. Not all annuals need this form of feeding.

Dead-heading

Dead-heading (removing spent flowers), unless you are keeping the seeds for your own seed bank, will pay dividends in as much as all the plant's goodness will be directed to producing new flowers or foliage.

Light and Shade

Generally speaking most annuals like sunlight. There are a few that will tolerate partial or filtered shade, but none that I can think of will prosper well in heavy shade. A sun-loving annual in shade will not thrive. A shade tolerant annual in hot sunlight will scorch and, no doubt, die.

Pinching Out

You may be under the impression that certain leggy plants may be improved by 'pinching out'; this is cutting or nipping off the growing tip with clean scissors, or between the thumbnail and forefinger, to produce sturdier plants. But this is only partly true. It is only successful with those plants that produce flowers from sideshoots. Be aware that certain plants will remain blind, and produce no flowers, if the growing tip is pinched out. So be selective before attempting to pinch out the growing tips of seedlings.

Pots

Pots, usually, are either clay, plastic, or peat. They can round, or square. In my opinion clay pots look better, but I prefer to work with plastic pots. Square pots take up less space than round. Peat-pots, made from peat, are similar in shape to conventional round or square pots, and are used extensively to avoid root disturbance, as the plant plus the peat-pot are planted out. These pots need supporting, for example in boxes, in case the pot walls break down under movement; particularly when they are saturated with water.

Plant Measurements

I shall use only millimetres, or metres, or inches, or feet in my measurements. I shall refer to a flower as being . . . mm (. . . in) 'wide', and not 'across', even though grammatically 'across' may be correct.

Botanical Names

Plants are split up into families, genera, species, varieties, and cultivars. Asteraceae (Compositae) is the daisy family. Let us assume that the common daisy, (genus) *Bellis*, (species) *perennis*, known botanically as *Bellis perennis*, has a naturally occurring variety called *rosea*. Thus botanically we have *Bellis* (genus) *perennis* (species) *rosea* (variety); or *Bellis perennis* var. *rosea* (variety may be abbreviated as 'var.' or as plural 'vars'). Let us now assume that a person has created a garden hybrid 'cultivated-variety' (known as a 'cultivar'). 'Rob Roy' is a famous daisy cultivar. Now we have *Bellis perennis* 'Rob Roy'. Genus, species, and naturally occurring variety names are written in italics. The cultivar is written in roman type beginning with a capital, and is put between single inverted commas: 'Rob Roy'. Thus you can see that natural varieties and man-made cultivars are different, and in this book they will not generally be lumped together under 'varieties'. You will come across the word 'cultivar' throughout the book, but it may be abbreviated as 'cv.' or plural 'cvs'.

F_1 Hybrids

To produce F_1 hybrids, a few plants with desirable characteristics are selected from 'field' garden plants. They are grown on in isolation, allowed to set seed naturally, and again plants with desirable characteristics are selected. These seeds are sown in isolation, away from plants of their own kind, so that they become inbred lines. They are allowed to set seed which is used to produce the next generation of plants. The plants are selected again, in isolation, always selecting better and better plants. This is known as mass selection. Eventually, two isolated, pure-breeding lines are crossed, producing F_1 hybrids with their renowned hybrid vigour. Or simplified:

1. Select plants from 'field' garden plants
2. Establish pure breeding lines
3. Cross two pure breeding lines to get F_1 hybrids.

Pluralising 'Latin'

I prefer the 'es' plural, and not 'i'. For example, I do not write the plural of amaranthus as 'amaranthi', but as 'amaranthuses'.

Lists of Plant Uses

Cut Flowers

Many annuals can be used as cut flowers, and a comprehensive book on floral art should give details on the best type of flowers to grow, and their subsequent treatment after picking. Also be aware of any family flower-allergy problems, and poisonous plants.

Acroclinium roseum
Ageratum houstonianum (floss flower)
Agrostemma githago 'Milas' (corncockle)
Anemone (various)
Antirrhinum majus (snapdragon)
Arctotis × *hybrida* (arctotis)
Bellis perennis (English daisy)
Brachycome iberidifolia (Swan River daisy)
Briza maxima (large quaking grass, pearl grass)
Calendula officinalis (pot marigold)
Callistephus chinensis (China aster)
Campanula medium (Canterbury bell)
Celosia argenta plumosa (Prince of Wales feathers; tall cvs)
Centaurea cyanus (cornflower)
Centaurea moschata (sweet sultan)
Cheiranthus × *allionii* (Siberian wallflower)
Cheiranthus cheiri (wallflower)
Chrysanthemum carinatum (annual chrysanthemum)
Clarkia elegans
Consolida ajacis (annual larkspur)
Coreopsis (various)
Cosmos (various)
Cosmos sulphureus
Dahlia (various)
Delphinium × *hybrida*
Dianthus (carnation, pink, sweet william)
Digitalis purpurea (foxglove)
Emilia javanica
Felicia (various) (blue marguerite, kingfisher daisy)
Gaillardia aristata cvs
Gaillardia pulchella
Gerbera jamesonii
Godetia amoena
Gomphrena globosa (globe amaranth)
Gypsophila elegans
Gypsophila paniculata
Helianthus annuus (small-flowered hybrid sunflowers)
Helichrysum bracteatum
Hunnemannia fumariifolia (Mexican tulip poppy)
Iberis amara (giant hyacinth-flowered candytuft)
Ipomopsis rubra (sky rocket)
Lathyrus odoratus (sweet pea)
Lavatera trimestris
Limonium sinuatum (statice)
Limonium suworowii (Russian statice)
Linaria maroccana
Lupinus (hybrids) (lupins)
Malope trifida (malope)
Matricaria eximia (feverfew)
Matthiola incana (stocks)
Moluccella laevis (bell of Ireland)
Myosotis sylvatica (forget-me-not)
Nemesia strumosa
Nigella damascena (love-in-the-mist)
Papaver nudicaule (Iceland poppy)
Penstemon × *gloxinioides*
Phlox drummondii
Primula malacoides
Primula polyantha
Reseda odorata (mignonette)
Rudbeckia hirta 'Tetra' (gloriosa daisy)
Salpiglossis sinuata
Salvia (various)
Scabiosa atropurpurea (pincushion scabious)
Scabiosa stellata (star scabious)
Scizanthus × *wisetonensis*
Silene coeli-rosea (rose of heaven)
Tagetes erecta (African marigold)
Tagetes patula (French marigold)
Tagetes × *hybrida*
Tagetes tenuifolia pumila (*signata*) (dwarf marigold)
Thymophylla tenuiloba (Dahlberg daisy)
Tithonia rotundifolia (Mexican sunflower)
Trachelium caeruleum (throatwort)
Trachymene coerulea (*Didiscus*) (blue lace flower)
Tropaeolum majus (nasturtium)
Venedium fastuosum (monarch of the veldt)
Verbena × *hybrida*
Viola (various) (violas and pansies)
Xeranthemum annuum (immortelle)
Zinnia elegans

Long-lasting Cut Flowers

Acroclinium roseum
Celosia argenta plumosa
Gomphrena globosa
Gourds (fruits)
Gypsophila elegans
Helichrysum bracteatum
Helipterum (various)
Limonium sinuatum (statice)
Lonas inodora
Lunaria annua (honesty)

Moluccella laevis
Nigella damascena
Ornamental grasses
Scabiosa stellata
Trachymene coerulea (*Didiscus caeruleus*)
Xeranthemum annuum

Hanging Basket and Pot Plants

Ageratum houstonianum (floss flower, dwarf cvs)
Browallia speciosa
Begonia (various)
Brassica (ornamental kale)
Calendula officinalis (pot marigold)
Coleus blumei (× *hybridus*)
Dianthus (carnation, pink, sweet william)
Exacum affine
Gazania × *hybrida*
Gerbera jamesonii
Helichrysum bracteatum (strawflower)
Heliotropium × *hybridum* (cherry pie)
Impatiens (various)
Lavatera trimestris (rose mallow)
Lobelia erinus
Mimulus × *hybridus* (monkey flower, various cvs)
Petunia × *hybrida* (particularly trailing cvs)
Primula (various; but be aware of skin allergy species and cvs)
Ranunculus asiaticus
Salpiglossis sinuata (velvet flower)
Schizanthus pinnatus (poor man's orchid)
Senecio cruentus (cineraria)
Tagetes patula (French marigold)
Tagetes × *triploid* (triploid marigolds)
Thunbergia alata (black-eyed Susan)
Tropaeolum majus (nasturtium cvs)
Zinnia (various species; cvs)

There are many more plants that can be used.

Edging Plants

Many small plants can be used as edging plants.

Ageratum houstonianum (floss flower; dwarf cvs)
Antirrhinum (snapdragon; dwarf cvs)
Arctotis × *hybrida*
Bellis perennis (English daisy)
Begonia semperflorens (wax begonia)
Brachycome iberidifolia (Swan River daisy)
Brassica (ornamental kale)
Calendula officinalis (pot marigold)
Celosia argenta cristata (cockscomb)
Callistephus chinensis (China aster; dwarf cvs)
Catharanthus rosea (vinca, periwinkle; dwarf cvs)
Cheiranthus cheiri (wallflower; dwarf cvs)
Cuphea ignea (cigar plant)
Dahlia (dwarf bedding cvs)
Dianthus (carnation, pink, sweet william; dwarf cvs)
Dorotheanthus (mesembryanthemum, Livingstone daisy)
Eschscholtzia (California(n) poppy; dwarf cvs)
Gazania × *hybrida*
Gilia tricolor
Godetia (dwarf cvs)
Gomphrema globosa (globe amaranth; dwarf cvs)
Iberis amara (hyacinch-flowered candytuft)
Iberis umbellata (candytuft)
Impatiens balsamina (balsam)
Linaria (various cvs)
Lobelia erinus
Lobularia maritima (white alyssum; also various colours)
Malcomia maritima (Virginia(n) stock)
Mimulus moschatus (various cvs)
Myosotis sylvatica (forget-me-not)
Nemesia strumosa (cvs)
Nierembergia hippomanica
Nolana (various)
Petunia × *hybrida*
Phlox drummondii (cvs)
Portulaca grandiflora (cvs)
Reseda odorata (mignonette)
Sanvitalia procumbens (creeping zinnia)
Tagetes patula (French marigold)
Tagetes tenuifolia (*signata*)
Tagetes × triploid (dwarf cvs)
Torenia fournieri (wishbone plant)
Tropaeolum majus (nasturtium; dwarf cvs)
Verbena (various cvs)
Viola (violas and pansies; various cvs)
Zinnia (dwarf species and cvs)

Plants with Colourful Foliage

Amaranthus (various species and cvs)
Aptenia cordifolia variegata
Atriplex hortensis var. *rubra*
Brassica (ornamental kale, cabbage)
Coleus blumei cultivars
Euphorbia heterophylla
Euphorbia marginata
Hunnemannia fumariifolia
Impatiens (New Guinea variegated cultivars)
Kochia scoparia var. *triphylla*
Lunaria annua
Matricaria eximia 'Aureum' (syn. *Chrysanthemum parthenium* 'Aureum')
Ocimum basilicum (purple form)
Onopordium bracteatum
Perilla frutescens (purple form)
Pyrethrum ptarmicaeflorum
Ricinus communis
Senecio bicolor
Zea mays (variegated leaf cvs)

Climbing and Vine Plants

Calonyction aculeatum
Cobaea scandens
Ipomoea (species and cvs)
Gourds (climbing cvs)
Luffa aegyptica
Luffa cylindrica
Maurandya barclaiana
Momordica balsamina
Momordica charantia
Thunbergia alata
Tropaeolum (various climbing species and cvs)

Pests and Diseases

How much do you really know about insecticides, fungicides and other garden chemicals? Note well! The information contained in this book on garden chemicals and their uses is, to the best of my knowledge and experience, complete and true. But all suggestions and recommendations are given without any guarantees. It is the responsibility of the reader to check the details of these chemicals and their effects on people, animals and plants.

This brings me to the point I will now make. In my opinion, I feel that all home gardeners should possess an authoritative book, written by a professional, on garden pests and diseases and the correct treatment of these pests and diseases. These books are available in bookshops and are not unduly expensive. An authoritative book on the use and abuse of weedkillers would also be a useful addition to your library.

In my opinion, there are 3 golden rules when considering the use of garden chemicals:

1. Do not use any pesticide, insecticide, herbicide-weedkiller, fungicide or nematicide unless you have to.
2. Use the least toxic substance that will do the job.
3. Read the instructions on the manufacturer's label *before* you buy the product and *before* you use it.

Certain plants may be allergic to a particular product. Malthion (maldison) dust may damage carnations, dahlias, gerberas, primulas, petunias, snapdragons and stocks. Malathion (maldison) may damage crassulas, ferns, and gerberas. Dimethoate (Rogor) may damage begonias, chrysanthemums, and gloxinias; Omethoate is a similar related insecticide. Metasystox (dimeton-S-methyl) may damage chrysanthemums, gerberas, and zinnias. Azobenzene may damage gerberas, schizanthus and many types of seedlings. Diazinon may damage asters. Kelthane (dicofol) may damage chrysanthemums. Thiram may cause skin irritation. Zineb may cause skin and other irritations. White oil may stunt ferns, and salvias. Copper oxychloride may injure young chrysanthemums. Oxycarboxin may damage some chrysanthemums and carnations. Copper hydroxide may damage chrysanthemums. And so on.

By reading the label on the pack, and by studying a professionally-written, authoritative book on pests and diseases and seeking advice from people professionally qualified to advise on pests and diseases, you should be able to ascertain which product can cause injury to a particular plant. Television, radio (particularly the talk-back shows), gardening magazines and gardening columns or sections in newspapers and 'glossy' magazines are sources of information.

Cleanliness (dare I say it?) comes before godliness in the garden. Plants that are grown in a clean, healthy environment are remarkably free from pests and diseases. Stale air and overcrowding of the seedlings leads rapidly to deterioration. It is so important to work cleanly around seeds and plants. Use top quality composts, clean pots or compost containers, clean plant labels, clean dibber or fork-prong (for pricking out seedlings), and so on. Grow the plants in a healthy, buoyant atmosphere to reduce the incidence of pest and disease infection.

Damping-off disease is the most obvious of plant diseases in young seedlings, and red spider, aphids, and slugs are the most obvious of pests.

There are offices in most States where gardeners can get information concerning gardening problems. Many garden chemicals are poisonous, therefore don't take chances with fungicides, pesticides, insecticides, herbicides, weedkillers, nematicides or any garden chemical. Always check the pack before buying it. And always check the pack before using it.

1. Read the label on the container to ensure that the fungicide, pesticide, insecticide, nematicide, herbicide or garden chemical you intend to use is suitable for the job you have in mind. Also check the legal requirements specified by various State governments.
2. Certain plants are allergic to certain insecticides, pesticides, fungicides, and so on. Certain insecticides, fungicides or others, may be flammable. *Read the label.*
3. *Read the label* and follow the manufacturer's instructions.
4. Use the least toxic substance that will do the job you have in mind. Protect yourself with suitable clothing.
5. Some herbicides are volatile, as are some fungicides, pesticides, insecticides, and others. Off-target damage can be considerable. Use the least volatile material to reduce spray drift. If feasible, use a coarse nozzle to help reduce spray drift.
6. Choose a cool, calm, windless day, when no rain is expected, to use the spray.
7. Keep children, pets, and onlookers well out of the way.
8. Certain insecticides, fungicides and others will kill fish or may poison bees. Some insecticides are toxic to animals and birds. Some garden chemicals can cause irritation to the nose and mouth. *Read the label.*
9. Certain fungicides, insecticides and others should not be used anywhere near edible crops, especially at harvest time. *Read the label.*
10. Do not smoke while using garden chemicals. Do not spray chemicals in confined spaces.
11. Lock up the chemicals, after use, in a sensible spot that is well out of the reach

Caterpillar damage on ornamental cabbage

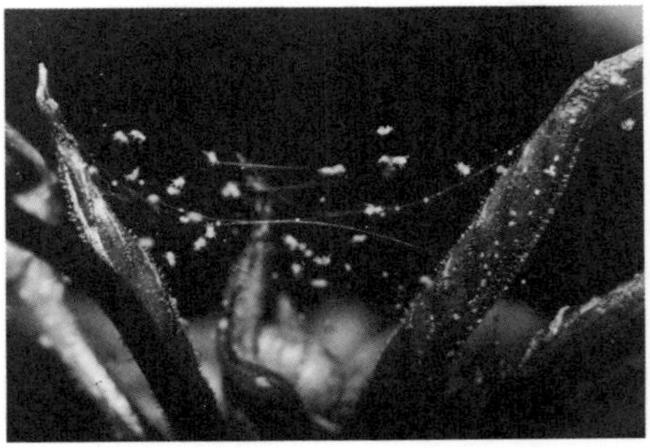

Spider mite on young shoots

Downy mildew fungus attack on leaves

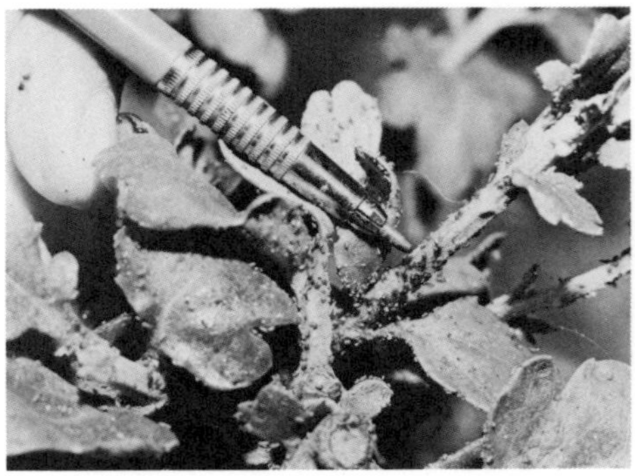

Aphids attacking young shoots

of children, but not so high that the chemicals will fall into your eyes, face and mouth when you reach for them. Keep the key so only responsible individuals know where it is.

12. Wash your hands and other exposed parts of the body after using chemicals.

13. Do not use any garden chemicals unless you have to. Remember! the pest's natural predators will substantially control the pest.

Crop rotation will help reduce the incidence of soil-borne diseases. The removal and destruction of infected leaves may prevent a more serious outbreak.

Bearing in mind what has been written above about some plants being allergic to particular insecticides or fungicides, read below for the suggested treatment of some of the more common problems:

Pests

Aphids dimethoate, malathion (maldison), omethoate, pyrethrum spray
Caterpillars carbaryl, derris, Dipel HG
Cutworms endosulfan, diazinon
Leafminers dimethoate, diazinon
Mealy bugs dimethoate, omethoate
Red spider dicofol, dimethoate, omethoate
Scales dimethoate, malathion (maldison) and white oil, white oil
Snails-slugs metaldehyde (some brands contain dog repellant, check the pack), methiocarb
Thrips malathion, omethoate
White fly dimethoate, omethoate, pyrethrum

Diseases

Damping-off disease furalaxyl, Cheshunt compound
Downy mildew furalaxyl, zineb, mancozeb
Leaf spot benomyl, copper oxychloride, mancozeb
Powdery mildew benomyl, dinocap
Root rots benomyl, mancozeb
Rusts Choose rust-resistant cultivars, thiram, zineb
Stem rots benomyl

Garden chemicals can be known by brand names, or by *active constituent* (ingredient) names. A few of these brand names are listed below, but *always* I repeat *always* check the *active constituent* (ingredient) the pack contains and its effects on the plants you have in mind:

Benlate (benomyl); Manzate (mancozeb); Fongarid (furalaxyl); Karathane (dinocap); Terraclor (quintozene); Thiram (T.M.T.D.); Zineb (zineb); Carbaryl (carbaryl); Derris (rotenone dust); Gesapon (diazinon); Endosulfan, Thiodan (endosulfan); Kelthane (dicofol); Lebaycid (fenthion); Malathion, Maldison (maldison); Metasystox (demeton-S-methyl); Nemacur (fenamiphos); Folimat (omethoate); Rogor (dimethoate); Slug and Snail Killer (metaldehyde); Baysol Methiocarb (methiocarb).

Be alert when physically picking up a product from the nurseryman's shelf. Check the pack for details of what it contains; its action on pest and diseases; its effects on certain flowers and plants; safety precautions and so on.

Poisonous Plants

Some people are allergic to particular plants. Some plants, or parts of a plant, are poisonous if ingested, for example *Agrostemma githago, Ricinus communis* (castor oil plant) and delphiniums. Some seeds are specially treated with chemicals; *read the seed packet label.* For information on poisonous plants contact your local library and Poisons Information Centre, address in the front of the phone book. You can also check with your local Department of Agriculture. Read the information on the seed pack. Seeds produced by the plant *Abelmoschus moschatus* must be kept away from children. Think carefully about the types of plants to use in areas frequented by young children.

Pest Plants

Many beautiful annuals have become pest plants in certain agricultural areas. *Echium platagineum*, Salvation Jane or Patterson's curse, is probably the most famous. But cultivars of this plant are widely grown in colder climates. *Mimosa pudica*, the sensitive plant, is spreading across many warm parts of the world, particularly where it is not controlled by its natural predators. Ageratum, Mexican poppy, and many other plants, are causing concern in certain areas. It may be that a particular plant is not available to Australian gardeners, and no doubt there are good reasons for this. We are an agricultural nation, and plants that could cause agricultural problems are certainly not wanted. Therefore, if a plant is not available or disappears from the seedmen's shelves, just accept the fact. Each State has an authority for pest plants. Check your phone book under the State offices.

Quarantine

Each State Department of Agriculture has a section that deals with plant and seed quarantine. For more information contact the relevant section. There are strict quarantine laws concerning the importation of seeds and plants into Australia.

Irrigation

I have designed and installed irrigation schemes, both automatic and manually controlled, and some of them very large. I have worked in the irrigation section of a very large nursery complex designing schemes for home gardens. And I now tell you that by using modern piping, modern sprinklers, modern drippers and jet sprays, irrigation for the home gardener can be a simple service to instal.

Visit your local nursery or irrigation store that specialises in home garden irrigation to find out just how many convenient and varied irrigation systems there are available. What you also need to know is the pressure of the water (metric = kPa: kiloPascals; or imperial = psi: pounds per square inch) and flow rate (metric = Lpm: litres per minute; or imperial = gpm: gallons per minute) at your house. Give this information to the irrigation firm, plus your proposed irrigation plan, and they, using the manufacturer's charts, will rapidly work out your requirements. You may be charged for this service, so check to make sure. Ring up your State water supply, ask for their advice, explain what you wish to know about their water supply to your house, and tell them what you intend doing. Find out all the facts on when to use high-pressure piping or low pressure piping. Are your water pipes old and corroded? If so this has to be considered.

But first visit the store or nursery, talk to the qualified irrigation staff, and pick up a pamphlet guide(s) issued by the irrigation equipment manufacturers on do-it-yourself garden watering systems. Read it thoroughly.

You can buy drippers that deliver, usually, 4 or 8 or 0–100 (adjustable) litres an hour, that can be placed by individual plants. You can buy full-circle, or part-circle jet sprays, or micro jets, hanging basket sprays, mist sprays, narrow border sprays, sprays that can be attached to a fixed-riser pipe to spray above the plants, and so on. Or flexible tubes can be taken along pergola roofs, and the like, with the sprays or drippers being attached to the tubes.

You can also buy lawn sprinklers or lawn sprinkler jets in full-circle, three-quarter circle, two-thirds circle, one-half circle or one-third circle; or watering squares, centre strips, end strips or side strips. These lawn sprinklers and their jets can be adapted for use in the flower garden. Talk it over with the qualified irrigation staff.

You can buy automatic timers that switch the water on and off at the intervals you programme. Or manual timers that do the same thing. The versatility of these timers varies proportionally with their cost.

Some irrigation systems can be attached directly to the garden tap. Other more complicated systems demand the use of a qualified plumber and/or a qualified electrician. Discuss this problem with your local irrigation installation expert.

Where to obtain the seeds?

The obvious start would be the seed packet stands at your local nurseries or seed shop; I even see them for sale in book shops. Seeds are advertised for sale in garden and other magazines; check out your local newsagents, bookstores and libraries. Your local parks department, botanical garden and like organisations, and local horticultural experts could all prove valuable sources of information. The yellow pages may contain the names of seed firms.

Always thoroughly read the information given on the seed merchant's seed packet for colour, height and so on. And seek out any 'Caution' or 'Special Note' or similar information given. Also reread information on plants and seeds given in seed catalogues as it is easy to accidentally skip a couple of lines.

Also thoroughly read the manufacturer's instructions and information given on fertiliser packs.

Note well! The information contained in this book on plant descriptions, seed sowing dates, plant uses and so on are to the best of my knowledge and experience complete and true. But all the descriptions, suggestions and recommendations contained herein are given without any guarantees. It is the liability and responsibility of the reader to check his local correct seed sowing times, plant uses, suitability of fertilisers for a given plant and so on.

Also be aware that sowing times can be extended for certain flowers. You will now notice that growers offer various seedlings for sale over a reasonably lengthy period of time.

The seed germination times and flowering times which are given are only approximate, as there are many factors which influence both operations. Always, after having sown the seeds, be prepared for germination.

Gardeners living in tropical areas can use the sowing guidelines given for subtropical areas. But as in a single year tropical areas can receive 1600 mm (63 in) to 2400 mm (94 in), or in certain areas even more rain, much of it between November and February, there are periods when seed sowing times will have to be adjusted. And there are occasions when growers in tropical areas have an edge on seed sowing, when others are more restricted. This is where local, expert knowledge on seed sowing times comes to the fore.

The expression 'under glass' which appears throughout the book usually means: 'indoors in a greenhouse, or similar'.

The expressions: 'Use (or) using a damp, recommended, seed raising compost' (or 'damp, recommended potting compost'), which appear frequently throughout the following pages, mean 'a compost that has been thoroughly moistened, drained of surplus water, but is still well moistened'. It is assumed that seed raising compost and potting compost will always be used damp; read section on seed composts, earlier in this book.

Throughout the book you will see the following: (sow seeds) 'at . . . – . . . °C (. . . – . . . °F): that is the 'temperature area' immediately where the seeds and/or seedlings are actually growing.

The expression tepid warm when referring to watering plants means lukewarm water. Water temperature extremes can put the seeds or seedlings under unnecessary stress.

Paying regular visits to retail plant seedling nurseries means that you are keeping abreast of the latest cultivar trends. Use nursery bought seedlings, if necessary, to supplement your garden design.

Drip irrigation is being used more and more for watering annuals. Not only does this save water by reducing evaporation, it avoids damaging the flowers and foliage, which can happen with heavy, overhead watering.

It may be that the plant you are seeking is not listed under the name you know it by. In these cases please refer to the index, to see if it is listed under an alternative name.

Removing Seedlings from Pots

You realise, of course, that seedlings in clay or plastic pots will have to be removed from the pots for a normal garden bedding scheme, otherwise they would soon become root-bound. But take great care when removing the pot from the seedling, as all the good work that has gone before can be destroyed in seconds. Water the pot seedling prior to removing it as this may ease its passage from the pot. Hold the pot in one hand, and carefully slide your other hand over the mouth of the pot with the seedling stem supported gently between the index and second fingers. This will prevent the seedling from falling on to the ground once the pot is inverted. Don't squeeze the delicate seedling shoot. Turn the pot upside down and with luck the pot will lift off easily from the seedling. Don't use force to remove the pot as this could injure the roots. If the seedling is reluctant to come out then, still holding the stem between your fingers, gently tap the rim of the pot on to a solid object, such as the edge of a bench top, taking great care not to damage the seedling's shoots or leaves. The pot should lift off. Experiment with any spare potted seedlings, if available. Take your time.

By using peat pots you can plant the seedling pot and all, as the roots will grow through the sides of the pot. Read the instructions on the manufacturer's label.

English (UK) Gardens Seed Sowing Times

At the end of all plant descriptions, there is a small section, written especially for English (United Kingdom) gardeners, giving seed sowing times.

ABC of Plants

***Abelmoschus* (muskmallow)** The East Asian *Abelmoschus manihot* (syn. *Hibiscus manihot*), the sunset hibiscus: height 1.5–2.4 m (5–8 ft); will bloom in the first year from seeds, and although perennial can be grown as an annual. The large, 150–225 mm (6–9 in) wide, radardish, light-yellow flowers, with their maroon centres are fleeting, but soon replaced by other flowers up the stem.

It is used as a border plant, although sprawly, or as a border backing plant, as the long, narrow, pointed-toothed foliage and reddish stems form an effective backdrop. It is early-mid summer flowering in temperate areas.

A. manihot prefers a rich, moist soil, and a sunny location.

The newish *Abelmoschus* species; height: 450 mm (18 in); listed in a recent seed catalogue as *Abelmoschus* sp. or on a seed pack as *Abelmoschus moschatus* (syn. *Hibiscus abelmoschus; H. moschatus*), silk-flower, has been recently discovered in Central Asia.

It is a frost-tender plant which requires a sunny, warm position in the garden. The five 'aeroplane-propellor' petalled, bright-red, white-centred, fleeting blooms can be from 63–100 mm (2.5–4 ins) wide; mine were 100 mm (4 in). From out of the centre of each bloom protrudes a golden-yellow, longish seed stem similar to a limp, but skinny, finger.

The deeply-lobed foliage varies from rosy-green, to bright green.

A. moschatus can be grown as a pot plant, container plant or summer bedding plant.

It likes ample water when growing well and a well-balanced soluble, liquid, flower fertiliser, suitable for this hibiscus and applied as the manufacturer instructs.

Propagation: (Abelmoschus manihot) Sow the seeds in 75 mm (3 in) peat pots, using a damp, recommended, seeding raising compost; late winter in sub-tropical areas; spring in temperate areas; and 6 to 8 weeks before the last frost is expected in frost prone areas, under glass, at 16–18°C (61–64°F). Thin out the seedlings, keeping the strongest in each pot.

Harden off the seedlings if necessary in a cold frame. Plant them out, peat pot and all, when all danger from frost is past and the ground has warmed up, directly where they are to grow and flower, 600 mm (24 in) apart.

Propagation: (Abelmoshus moschatus) Sow the seeds in seed compost containers, late winter, or 6 to 8 weeks before the last frost in your locality, under glass, at 18–24°C (64–75°F). Use a damp, recommended, free-draining seed compost. Cover the seeds with a sheet of glass, but check regularly to make sure that the compost does not dry out. Remove the glass as soon as germination occurs to prevent 'drawing up' of the seedlings.

Germination should occur in approximately 10–21 days at 24°C (75°F).

Prick out the seedlings when they are large enough to handle into 75 mm (3 in) pots of a damp, recommended potting compost and grow them on. They can be hardened off in a cold frame and planted out into the garden 250–300 mm (10–12 ins) apart, when all danger from frost is past and the ground has warmed up. Or they can be potted on into 150 mm (6 in) pots and grown as pot plants.

Flowers should appear 3½–5 months from sowing, depending on location.

If kept as pot plants they need shading from hot sunlight.

In English gardens sow the seeds of *A. manihot* in 75 mm (3 in) peat pots, late winter-early spring (Feb–March), under glass, at 14–16°C (57–61°F), and treat as half hardy plants. Sow seeds of *Abelmoschus moschatus* at 18–24°C (64–75°F). Treat seedlings as tender plants. Summer flowering.

Pests and diseases: Reasonably free.

Cultivars/varieties: Abelmoschus manihot. A. moschatus 'Mischief', red outer, white centre. (Carefully read the instructions on the seed pack.)

Family: Malvaceae.

***Abutilon* (flowering maple, Chinese lantern)** The Central and South American evergreen perennial *A.* × *hybridum*; height 450–900 mm –2 m (18–36 in–6 ft); is not a true maple, but has maple-leaf shaped leaves.

The 37 mm (1.5 in) long by 37–56 mm (1.5–2.2 in) wide, yellow or orange, pendant, funnel-shaped flowers hang down from the branches like colourful lamp-shades. Flowers appear late-spring or summer, or later, depending on how and where they are grown.

Abutilons can be grown in the warm parts of Australia as shrubs, but will succumb to frost elsewhere.

They are usually grown as pot plants, patio, or window-box container plants in cooler areas, and protected from frost. But they make fascinating pot plants and container plants in any climate.

Abutilons thrive in a warm, moist soil, preferably fibrous loam, in partial shade with sun part of the day. They need ample water when growing well, but otherwise should be kept just pleasantly moist. They also need feeding with a well-balanced, soluble, liquid, flower fertiliser, suitable for abutilons, and applied as the manufacturer instructs.

Propagation: Sow the seeds in seed compost containers, using a damp, recommended seed raising compost, in autumn in warm areas, or spring in frost-prone areas, or 8–9 weeks before the last frost is expected, at 18–21°C (64–70°F).

Germination takes approximately 20 days. Prick out the seedlings into pots of damp, recommended, potting compost, and grow them on either as pot plants or future garden shrubs.

Plants to be used outside in the garden must be hardened off thoroughly, and planted out only when all danger from frost is well past and the ground has warmed up. Abutilons will not survive outside in frost-prone areas during winter.

In English gardens, sow the seeds of the *Abutilon* species in seed compost, late winter-early spring (Feb–April) at 16–21°C (61–70°F). Treat them as half-hardy plants, and grow on as greenhouse pot plants requiring a minimum winter temperature of 10–13°C (50–55°F). Flowers appear late spring-mid autumn (May–Oct).

Pests and diseases: Scale, white fly, mealy bugs.

Varieties/cultivars: Abutilon, large-flowered mixed (yellow, orange, pink, red); *Abutilon* Giant Mixed.

Family: Malvaceae.

***Acanthus* (bear's breeches, oyster plant, biblical lily)** The Italian-Southern European *Acanthus mollis*; height 750–900 mm–1.8 m (30–36–71 in); is the most popular of the acanthuses. It is included in this book for its effectiveness as an architectural foliage specimen, although strictly speaking it is a perennial border plant.

The leaves are 650–750 mm (or even 1 m) long by 250–300 mm wide (26–30 in by 10–12 in). They are distinctive, glossy, mid-to-dark green, scalloped, but deeply-cut, deeply divided and sharply pointed. Acanthus leaves are depicted on certain ancient Greek architectural columns.

From the mass of green leaves appears in late spring-summer a 450–750 mm–1.8 m (18–30–72 in), spike of green-pink, hooded bracts over tubular, white and purple 'snapdragon' flowers. Dangling from the inside top of the flower is a minute, golden ball of pollen organs and under each flower is a small, spiny bract.

Acanthuses prefer a fertile, moisture holding, but well-drained soil in a partially shaded site, or sunny in cold areas. Water acanthuses adequately when they are growing well. Cut down the spent, flowering stems and remove any dead leaves after they have flowered. *A. spinosus* and *A. balcanicus* are also grown.

Propagation: Sow the seeds in seed compost containers using a damp, recommended seed raising compost, in spring. Place the containers in a greenhouse or cold frame for the seeds to germinate. Prick out the seedlings, when they are large enough to handle easily, into 75 mm (3 in) pots of damp, recommended potting compost. Don't let them stew under the glass during any hot sun.

Grow the seedlings on until they are well established, harden them off, and either transplant them into a nursery holding bed 150 mm (6 in) apart, and from there into their permanent quarters in late winter; or plant them out, directly where they are to grow and flower 600–900 mm (24–36 in) apart, in dramatic groups to show off the leaves.

Acanthus resent root disturbance once established, although they can outstay their welcome and have to be divided eventually. Divide the roots in winter.

In English gardens sow the seeds in seed compost, early spring (March-April), and place in a greenhouse or cold frame. Prick out the seedlings singly into pots. Flowers appear mid summer-early autumn (July-Sept).

Pests and diseases: Snails and slugs.
Cultivars/varieties: Species as above.
Family: Acanthaceae.

***Acroclinium* (paper everlasting daisy)** The Western Australian spring-summer flowering annual *Acroclinium roseum* (syn. *Helipterum roseum*); height 375–600 mm (15–24 in); is a prolific, decorative flower.

The paper-texture, 25–50 mm (1–2 in) wide, yellow-centred, semi-double, saucer-shaped, daisy flowers can be red, pink or white, or shades and tints of those colours. They are used as cut flowers and everlasting dried flowers, and some gardeners grow acrocliniums as pot plants.

The narrow, pointed, greyish-green leaves are insignificant.

Acrocliniums grow in a well-drained, sunny, even poorish soil, although during the flowering season, they seem to benefit from regular, but weak, dressings of a well-balanced, liquid, soluble fertiliser, suitable for acrocliniums, and applied as the manufacturer instructs.

Propagation: Acrocliniums are usually sown directly where they are to flower and grow. Dig over the soil where the plants are to grow and flower when it is easy to work, breaking it down into a fine tilth. Rake out any debris, and firm the soil gently, but thoroughly, to take the seeds.

Draw out (mark out) drills (rows), 12 mm (0.5 in) deep, 250 mm (10 in) apart; or 'station-sow' a few seeds 250 mm (10 in) apart. You can also broadcast the seeds.

Sow the seeds evenly and thinly, autumn to spring sub-tropical-tropical areas; autumn or early spring temperate areas; or early spring in cool areas. Cover them with a thin layer of clean, sharp sand, and water in the seed, gently but thoroughly, using a fine spray. Keep the seeds pleasantly moist until they germinate and become well established, and then water the plants when they need it.

Seedlings should appear in 8–28 days depending on temperature. Carefully thin out the seedlings to 150–300 mm (6–12 in) apart.

In English gardens sow the seeds evenly and thinly mid-spring (April) over the area where the seeds are to grow and flower. They should flower mid-late summer. For earlier flowers sow the seeds indoors in pots of damp, recommended seed raising compost in a cool 15°C (59°F), frost-free place, 6 to 8 weeks before the last expected frost. Keep only the strongest seedling in each pot to avoid transplantation shock.

Pests and diseases: Aphids.
Cultivars/varieties: Double mixtures.
Family: Asteraceae.

***Ageratum* (floss flower)** The Mexican *A. houstonianum* (syn. *A. mexicanum*); height 75–200–600 mm (3–8–24 in) depending on cultivar ('Tall Blue' being to 900 mm–36 in); is an easily grown, frost-sensitive annual which produces masses of minute powder-puff flowers.

It has many delightful cultivars, including tetraploids and F_1 hybrids, in white, pale-blue, mid-blue, deep-blue, rose-pink and reddish-mauve flower colours. Flowers can appear all year round depending on location.

Ageratum is grown extensively as an edging plant for spring and summer bedding decoration, in window boxes, as pot plants, or the tall cultivars as cut flowers.

It thrives in most well-drained soils, in a sunny site, although in hot summers it will tolerate some filtered shade, but it must be kept in bounds in warm, moist areas to prevent it becoming a pest plant. It will even tolerate poor soils, but it must never be allowed to dry out, so keep the soil just pleasantly moist.

To prolong the flowering period, feed the plants during the growing season with a well-balanced liquid, soluble, flower fertiliser, but suitable for ageratum (i.e. low in nitrogen, as you want flowers and not too much foliage), and applied as the manufacturer instructs. Remove spent flowers to keep the plants bushy, neat and floriferous.

Propagation: Ageratums are warm-season annuals. Sow the seeds, under glass where necessary, at 16–21°C (61–70°F), in seed compost containers using a damp, recommended, seed raising compost; most seasons in frost-free, sub-tropical areas, but mostly late summer-mid autumn; late winter-spring-summer-autumn in temperate areas; early spring-late summer in cooler areas. Just press the seeds on to the top of the damp compost, as they need light to germinate. The seeds germinate in 5–21 days at 18–21°C (64–70°F).

Prick out the seedlings, when they are large enough to handle, into containers or 75 mm (3 in) pots of damp, recommended potting compost. Grow the seedlings on.

Harden off the plants (those grown under glass harden off in a cold frame) and plant them out when all danger from frost is past and the ground has warmed up.

The seeds can also be sown in a properly prepared seed-bed after any frost risk, and transplanted out to their permanent quarters later.

Or they can be sown directly where they are to grow and flower, and thinned out 100–150–225–300 mm (4–6–9–12 in) apart, depending on the spread of the cultivar.

In English gardens sow the seeds in seed compost, under glass, in late winter-early-mid spring (Feb-March-April), at 16–21°C (61–70°F). Treat seedlings as half-hardy plants. Flowers early summer on.

Pests and diseases: Slugs, snails, mildew, foot and root rot.
Cultivars/varieties: 'Blue Blazer' F_1, height 200 mm (8 in), blue mauve. 'Blue Mink', height 150–200 mm (6–8 in) soft blue. 'Giant Tetra Blue', height 250 mm (10 in), light blue. 'Mosaic of Mauves', height 200 mm (8 in), mauve shades. 'Spindrift', height 200–250 mm (8–10 in) white. 'Southern Cross' F_1, height 250–300 mm (10–12 in) blue and white. 'Think Pink', height 200 mm (8 in), rosy pink. Many more.
Family: Asteraceae.

***Agrostemma* (corn cockle)** The southern European-Turkish hardy annual *Agrostemma githago* is an insignificant cornfield weed, but it has a cultivar known as *Agrostemma githago* 'Milas'; height 600–900 mm (24–36 in); and it is the cultivar that is grown.

A. g. 'Milas' is a plant for hot, dry summers and is used by some gardeners as a 'cottage-garden' style or annual border plant, or as an unusual cut-flower.

The 5 reflexed-petalled, deep-rose shading inwards to light-pink, 50–75 mm (2–3 in) wide, flat trumpet-like flowers have black sighting-dashes, which form lines leading from the petal edge to the nectar-sac. The petal texture reminds me of elegant, pin-stripe, fine flanellette.

These flowers are borne on long, slender stems, usually in summer, but this depends on location and method of growing as I have seen them in late spring.

The leaves are narrow-pointed, grass-like and approximately 150 mm (6 in) long.

Corn cockles grow in a wide variety of soils, but prefer a well-drained, neutral soil in full sunlight. They resent root disturbance.

Caution: Be aware that the seeds of this plant are poisonous if eaten.

Propagation: Dig over the soil when it is easy to work, directly where the plants are to grow and flower, breaking it down into a fine tilth. Rake out any debris and firm the soil gently but thoroughly to take the seeds.

Broadcast the seeds thinly and evenly over the prepared surface in early spring although they can be sown in autumn in mild winter areas. Rake them lightly into the surface tilth, or lightly cover them with sieved soil, or similar.

Gently water the seeds to anchor them to the soil. Keep the soil, seeds and seedlings pleasantly moist. If sown sparsely enough thinning out is unnecessary.

Germination is reasonably swift in warm soils, approximately 5 to 14 days. But if the seedlings appear too close for the effect you are trying to create, then you can thin them out up to 300 mm (12 in) apart.

Flowers should appear in approximately 3 months from sowing, maybe longer or shorter, depending on sowing time and local growing conditions.

In English gardens, sow the seeds in spring (March-April) directly where the plants are to grow and flower, just raking them into the top tilth. Some gardeners also make an autumn sowing. Agrostemmas are summer-flowering (June-Aug).

Pests and diseases: Generally free.
Cultivars/varieties: 'Milas'.
Family: Caryophyllaceae.

***Alcea* (hollyhock)** Originally from China and southwestern-central Asia, the perennial *Alcea rosea* (syn. *Althaea chinensis*) is now thought to be a hybrid of *A. setosa* (Turkey) and *A. pallida* (eastern Europe); height: 'tall' cultivars, 2–2.7 m (7–9 ft) high; 'dwarf' cultivars, 600–750 mm (24–30 in). It has both 'annual' or 'biennial' forms.

In late spring-summer hollyhock spikes bear approximately 100 mm (4 in) wide, radar-dish, or funnel-shaped, or the more popular, crinkly-petalled, double flowers, in shades and tints of white, yellow, pink or red. In temperate areas hollyhocks flower occasionally during the winter.

Plant hollyhocks in bold groups of say 4 to 6 plants. The taller cultivars are used as accent plants to draw the eye, or as screening plants. The really dwarf cultivars can be used as bedding plants.

Certain named cultivars can be used as annuals in mild-winter locations, or as half-hardy annuals in cold climates. Other cultivars can be sown in autumn, and will flower the first season.

Hollyhocks that are grown as perennials can suffer badly from rust.

They prefer a deep, fertile soil, not too rich, preferably sheltered, but they will grow in a range of soils provided these are neither too acid nor too alkaline and receive adequate water during dry spells.

The taller flowering spikes are vulnerable to wind damage and usually need suitable support.

Although reasonably hardy, hollyhocks are susceptible to heavy-hard frost and need glass cloche protection.

When growing well, they appreciate applications of a well-balanced, liquid, soluble flower fertiliser suitable for hollyhocks and applied as the manufacturer instructs.

Propagation: Prepare a fine, friable seedbed, and thinly sow (space) the seeds, autumn sub-tropical areas, late-summer-autumn temperate and cool areas, in shallow rows 6 mm (¼ in) deep. Seeds germinate in approximate 5–21 days depending on temperature.

Transplant the seedlings as soon as they are ready, directly where they are to grow and flower 375 mm (15 in) apart for dwarf cultivars and 600 mm (24 in) apart for the taller ones.

Don't put off transplanting for too long, otherwise the plant's tap root would be well formed, and root damage may occur.

Alternatively, the seeds can be sown directly where they are to grow and flower, in a well lit sheltered area.

Or thinly space (sow) the seeds in seed compost containers, using a damp, recommended seed raising compost, 6 to 8 weeks before late-spring planting, under glass, if necessary, at 13–18°C (55–65°F). Cover the seeds with a light dressing of compost, or vermiculite.

Mist-water the seeds using a fine spray, and don't let them or the seedlings dry out, but don't overwater them either, as hollyhock seedlings are prone to damping-off disease. Just keep the compost pleasantly moist.

Seeds should germinate in approximately 5–21 days, depending on temperature. Prick out the seedlings in 75 mm (3 in) pots of damp, recommended potting compost, and harden the plants off in a cold frame. Plant them out directly where they are to grow and flower, when all danger from frost is past and the ground has warmed up.

In English gardens sow 'annual' hollyhock seeds in seed compost containers, late winter-early spring (Feb-March), under glass at 13–18°C (55–65°F) and treat them as half-hardy plants. In mild-winter areas sow (space) biennial seeds, late spring-early summer (late May-June-July), in shallow drills (rows) directly where the plants are to grow and flower or in a nursery seed-bed. In hard-frost winter areas, sow 'biennial' seeds, early-summer, in seed compost containers. Overwinter in cool greenhouse or cold frame and plant them out mid-spring (April). Flowers mid summer on.

Pests and diseases: Chewing insects, snails, slugs, red spider mites, anthracnose, hollyhock-rust, leaf spot.

Cultivars/varieties: Powder Puffs Mixed, height 1.5–2 m (5–6 ft), pink, reds, yellow, apricot. Marjorette Mixed, height 600 mm (2 ft), white, light pink, rose, salmon, crimson red, yellow. Pinafore, height 900 mm–1 m (36–39 in), up to 5 flower spikes on a plant, semi double or single, full colour range. Summer Carnival, height 2–3 m (6–10 ft), mixed colours. Tall Cottage Mixed, height 2 m (6–7 ft).

Family: Malvaceae.

***Alonsoa* (mask flower)** The Andean-Peruvian *Alonsoa warscewiczii* (syn. *A. grandiflora*); height 250–600 mm (10–24 in); is a half hardy, bushy perennial that is usually grown as a half-hardy annual in cold climates, but in temperate areas is grown as a perennial, flowering late-spring and on.

The lightly-spurred, 25 mm (1 in) wide, rich-scarlet flowers, fading to orange-red as they age, are deep-dish, 5-scalloped petalled, with a texture reminiscent of red marzipan.

The flower spike stems are ribbed, slightly hairy to the touch, green or reddish, and bear dark, bright-green, toothed-edged, oval-pointed leaves.

Alonsoas are used as pot plants, bedding plants, and grouped in small clumps in the flower border.

Mask flowers are not really suited to hot climates. They prefer a fertile, well-drained soil, in a sunny position in cool to temperate locations, but deteriorate in prolonged wet conditions.

A. acutifolia (syn. *myrtifolia*), the narrow-leaved mask flower, is also grown, but is not as popular. The upside-down, twisted flowered *A. incisifolia*; height 600 mm (24 in); a frost-sensitive plant, is used in Australian gardens.

Propagation: Mask flowers take approximately 4 months from seed to flower.

In frost-prone areas sow the seeds in seed compost containers, using a damp, recommended, seed raising compost, under glass, late winter-spring, at 13–18°C (55–64°F). Press the seeds gently on to the compost surface.

Mist spray the seedlings with water, and don't let them dry out, but just keep the compost pleasantly moist. Prick out the seedlings into small pots of damp, recommended, potting compost, and grow them on.

Harden off the seedlings, if necessary in a cold frame, and plant them out, late spring, but only when all danger from frost is past and the ground has warmed up, directly where they are to grow and flower, 225–300 mm (9–12 in) apart.

Or the seeds can be sown, early autumn in frost free areas, or spring in other areas, directly where they are to grow and flower, when any danger from frost is past. Thin out the seedlings to 225–300 mm (9–12 in) apart.

In English gardens sow the seeds in seed compost containers, early spring (March), under glass at 13–18°C (55–64°F). Treat mask flowers as half-hardy plants. Flowers appear in summer, and on.

Pests and diseases: Aphids.

Cultivars/varieties: *A. warscewczii* 'dwarf form'.

Family: Scrophulariaceae.

***Amaranthus* (love-lies-bleeding, tassel flower, Joseph's coat, flaming fountain, amaranth, prince's feathers)** These long-lasting, warm-season, summer annuals are renowned for their brilliantly-coloured, crested foliage or tassel flowers.

The tropical American *Amaranthus caudatus*; height 900 mm–1.5 m (36 in–5 ft); is the popular love-lies-bleeding or tassel flower. It has long, droopy, egg-shaped, pointed, pale-green leaves. The flower racemes, reminiscent of twisted ropes of pink millet, can be from 150–450 mm (6–18 in) in length. The cultivar *A. c.* 'Viridis' has green flowers.

The American *A.* × *hybridus* looks like a thin relation of *A. caudatus*.

The tropical American *A. hypocondriacus*, prince's feathers, has a dense, deep-red brush of flowers.

The Asian-Indian *A. tricolor*; height 600–900 mm (24–36 in); has ovalish lance-like leaves, with banded mixtures of red, yellow and green, and shades and tints of these colours where the bands meets. *A t. perfecta* 'Joseph's Coat' is an outstanding fusion of colour. *A. tricolor* var. *splendens* is also worth growing.

A. salicifolius 'Flaming Fountain' with 'fountains' of brilliant foliage is also grown.

Amaranthuses are used as background plants, in small groups as spectacular accent plants, or as bedding or container plants.

They require sunshine, sufficient water, but not in excess and a well-drained, neutral, friable garden soil to which a well-balanced flower fertiliser has been added according to the manufacturer's instructions. But to me, however, the colours seem to be more intense in poorer soils, although the foliage is not as luxurious.

Amaranthuses resent root disturbance.

Propagation: To minimise root disturbance, thinly sow a few seeds in 75 mm (3 in) peat-pots, using a damp recommended seed raising compost, winter-mid spring (late summer leaves are best) sub-tropical areas, winter-early spring-early summer temperate areas, spring-early summer in cold areas, at 21–24°C (70–75°F).

Or thinly sow the seeds in seed compost containers, using a damp, recommended, seed raising compost. Lightly cover the seeds with sieved compost or vermiculite.

Stand the container in a shallow dish of tepid water until the compost just glistens, then remove it. Or you can mist-water the compost using a fine spray. Keep the compost just pleasantly moist. The seeds germinate in approximately 8–21 days, depending on temperature.

Prick out the 'best coloured' seedlings, when they are large enough to handle, into 75 mm (3 in) pots of a damp, recommended potting compost, and grow them on until they are approximately 75 mm (3 in) tall.

Gradually harden the seedlings off in a shade frame, or if necessary in a cold frame, and plant them out directly where they are to grow and flower, when any danger from frost is past and the ground has warmed up. They can also be grown as 125 mm (5 in) or wider pot-plants, using a damp, recommended potting compost.

Amaranthus species and cultivars can be sown directly where they are to grow and flower, but only when any danger from frost is past in cold areas. 'Station sow' a sprinkling of seeds in clumps, 400–450 mm (16–18 in) apart, depending on cultivar. Carefully thin out the seedlings, keeping the strongest at each station.

In English gardens thinly sow a few seeds into 75 mm (3 in) peat-pots, earliest-mid spring (March-April), under glass, at 21–24°C (70–75°F). Or thinly sow the seeds in seed compost containers. Treat seedlings as half-hardy plants. Summer bedding foliage; flowers late summer.

Pests and diseases: Snails, caterpillars, fungus when young.

Cultivars/varieties: 'Flying Colours', height 1.2–1.5 m (4–5 ft), gold, pink, or scarlet. 'Flaming Fountain', height 900 mm (3 ft), red. 'Illumination', height 1.2 m (4 ft), crimson topped gold. 'Early Splendour', height 900 mm (3 ft), red, purple. 'Joseph's Coat', height

600 mm (2 ft), yellow, green, crimson. 'Starburst', height 900 mm (3 ft), rich red, yellow, and fresh green.
Family: Amaranthaceae.

Ammi majus **(bishop's flower, white lace flower)** The Mediterranean cool season annual *Ammi majus*; height 900 mm (3 ft); is a mid-late spring-summer (depending on when, and how, the seed is germinated) flowering plant that produces 125–150 mm (5–6 in) wide, flower heads, made up of explosions of minute, white 'star-snowflake' flowers that can be used in floral arrangements. *A. majus* is principally a cool or temperate locality bedding plant.

You may see *A. majus* referred to as 'Queen Anne's lace'. However, this name is also attributed to a plant known as *Daucus carota* var. *carota*; height 1 m (39 in) or more; which is a biennial, or treated as an annual, with finely dissected foliage, like a carrot. *Daucus carota* var. *carota* has small, white flowers, with occasional pink ones, borne in wide sprays. Both forms are beautiful and can be obtained from seedsmen, but make sure you get the one you want.
Propagation: Dig over the soil when it is easy to work, directly where the plants are to grow and flower, breaking it down into a fine tilth. Rake out any debris, and firm the soil gently, but thoroughly, to take the seeds.

'Station sow' the *A. majus* seeds, late winter temperate areas, late spring cool areas, but only if no medium to heavy frosts are expected in your locality. Plant in clumps 350–400 mm (14–16 in) apart. Lightly rake the seeds into the top surface tilth.

Gently but thoroughly water the seeds using a fine spray, and don't allow the seeds or seedlings to dry out. Keep the soil pleasantly moist. Germination takes approximately 15 days, but depends on soil temperature. Thin out the seedlings to 400 mm (16 in) apart.

In English gardens, sow a few seeds in individual 75 mm (3 in) pots, late winter, indoors in a cool place, say 6–8 weeks before outdoor planting time in your area. Or 'station sow' the seeds, in mid-late-spring (March-April), but not if medium to heavy frosts are likely.
Pests and diseases: Reasonably free.
Cultivars/varieties: Species as above.
Family: Apiaceae.

Anagallis **(pimpernel)** The frost-sensitive, North African-western Mediterranean *A. linifolia* (syn. *A. monelli* ssp. *linifolia*), the flax-leaved pimpernel; height 300 mm (12 in); has 18–31 mm (0.7–1.2 in) wide, saucer-shaped, summer flowers of a most intense-blue; but there are red and purple forms.

The small leaves are dark-green, narrow and lance-like. Although a tender perennial it is usually grown as a tender annual.

The European scarlet pimpernel, *Anagallis arvensis*, a hardy annual, has small, orange-red flowers, and accompanied by its close relative the blue pimpernel, *Anagallis femina* (syn. *A. arvensis* var. *foemina; A. coerulea*), is found growing wild in many parts of the world, including temperate Australia.

But it is the cultivated form of the blue pimpernel, *Anagallis arvensis* 'Caerulea'; height: clambering, or some shoots to 300 mm (12 in); that we shall discuss. The 18 mm (0.7 in) wide, 5 round-pointed, petalled, saucer-shaped flowers are of a most intense blue, each with a pink-purple, fluffy ovary, that 'glows' in the centre of the flower. The flowers are borne on single, fine, fuse-wire stems, with up to three stems arising from a single source.

The oval-pointed, dull-green, stemless leaves, 18–25 mm (0.7–1 in) long, by 8–12 mm (0.3–0.5 in) wide, are borne in opposite pairs up the squareish ribbed stems.

Possibly, the major difference between the two principal blue periwinkles discussed above, apart from their original localities, is their respective leaf formation, although the flowers of *A. linifolia* may be wider.

A. a. 'Caerulea' blue periwinkles can be used as hanging-basket plants, edging plants or pot-plants. But clump them in small, bold groups, to get the best effect from the blue flowers. Pimpernels like sunlight, but not hard-hot sunlight, a well-drained, light, sandy-loam, and ample water during dry spells. *A. a.* 'Caerulea' pimpernels are principally cool soil, temperate climate plants.

Blue pimpernels bloom late spring-early summer, and on, in temperate areas; later in cooler areas. Although in temperate areas you may see the wild forms of the blue pimpernel flowering early spring, and on.
Propagation: Sow the seeds of *Anagallis arvensis* 'Caerulea' in seed compost containers, under glass, late-winter in temperate areas, early-mid spring cool areas, or say a month or two before the normal outdoor planting time in your locality at 15–18°C (60–65°F).

Use a damp, recommended seed raising compost. Mist water the seeds using a fine spray and keep the seeds, seedlings and compost pleasantly moist. Prick out the seedlings into 50 mm (2 in) pots of damp, recommended, potting compost and grow them on.

Harden off the seedlings in a cold frame, and plant them out directly where they are to flower and grow, 150 mm (6 in) apart, when any danger from frost is past and the ground has warmed up, for flowering late spring or summer.

I have sown the seeds in late winter, and had them flowering outside earliest summer, and on.

In temperate areas, and cooler areas, sow the seeds thinly, after any danger from frost is past, directly where the plants are to grow and flower. Firm the soil gently, but thoroughly, to take the seeds, as they have to stay close to the surface for germination. You can sprinkle the merest breath of sieved compost or fine sand over them, but usually they trickle down in between the soil crumbs anyway.

Gently but thoroughly water the seedlings using a fine spray, and don't allow the seeds or seedlings to dry out, but keep the soil pleasantly moist. Thin out the seedlings to 150 mm (6 in) apart.

In English gardens thinly sow the seeds in seed compost, early-mid spring (March-April), under glass at 15–18°C (60–65°F), and treat them as half-hardy plants. They should flower early summer-early autumn (June-Sept).

Or sow the seeds of *A. arvensis* 'Caerulea' in mid spring (April), directly where they are to grow and flower.
Pests and diseases: Aphids.
Cultivars/varieties: Species, cultivars, as above.
Family: Primulaceae.

Anchusa **(Cape forget-me-not, summer forget-me-not)** The South African biennial-annual *Anchusa capensis*; height 250–450 mm (10–18 in); is a mild-frost resistant plant. It is similar to, but more showy than the *Myosotis* sp. forget-me-not.

The 6–12 mm (0.2–0.5 in) wide, 5-petalled, star, saucer-shaped flowers are vibrantly blue with creamy-white centres. Other colours are also available, shades of clear-blue to ultramarine.

Masses of summery flowers borne on branched, hairy, leafy stems arise from out of the dwarf, 150 mm (6 in) tall, dull-green, hairy, lance-shaped foliage.

Anchusas grow well in poor soils. Do not overfeed them as they are used to semi-starved conditions.

They are used as border plants in most gardens in a semi-shaded position, or in a sunny location in the cooler areas. They are also used as pot plants. Anchusas prefer good sunlight, and a soil that retains moisture, but in hot areas they prefer semi-shade. They can fail in hot, humid conditions. They tolerate a poor soil, flowering in abundance, and excessive nitrogen fertiliser will encourage leaf growth at the expense of flowers.

Cut down the flowering stems after the first flush of flowers. Feed the plant with a well-balanced, soluble, liquid, flower fertiliser, suitable for anchusas and applied as the manufacturer instructs, to build up the plant's depleted food reserves and encourage further blooms.
Propagation: Thinly sow the seeds in a small properly prepared seed-bed, late summer-autumn in sub-tropical areas, autumn or spring temperate areas, or spring in colder areas, after frost risk.

Rake the seeds lightly into the fine tilth, 6 mm (0.2 in) deep. Cover the seed with sieved soil, or clean, sharp-sand, or vermiculite. Keep the seeds and seed-bed pleasantly moist at all times. Transplant the seedlings, as soon as they are large enough to handle, from the nursery-bed into their permanent quarters.

Or the seeds can be sown directly where they are to grow and flower, and then thinned out to 225–300 mm (9–12 in) apart.

The seeds can also be sown in seed compost containers, using a damp, recommended seed raising compost, and placed in a cold frame or shade frame. Water gently but thoroughly keeping the ground or compost pleasantly moist until the seeds germinate. This usually takes 14–30 days at 20°C (68°F), but mine came through in only 7 days.

Transplant the seedlings, properly hardened off and when they are large enough to handle easily, into their permanent quarters 225–300 mm (9–12 in) apart.

In English gardens, provided the ground is easy to work, sow the seeds mid-spring (March-April), directly where they are to grow and flower. Or for pot plants sow the seeds mid-winter (January) in seed compost, under glass, at 16–18°C (61–64°F). Flowers appear mid-summer on.
Pests and diseases: Snails, slugs, cucumber mosaic virus.
Cultivars/varieties: 'Blue Angel', height 200–250 mm (8–10 in), ultramarine blue.
Family: Boraginaceae.

Anemone **(windflower)** The Mediterranean,

spring-flowering *Anemone coronaria* and its hybrids; height 150–300 mm (6–12 in); are magnificently exotic both in colour and form.

The 'De Caen' singles; height 150–300 mm (6–12 in); and 'St Brigid' semi doubles; height 150–300 mm (6–12 in); are justly famous for their 50–100 mm (2–4 in) poppy-like blooms in red, lavender, purple and blue.

Anemones prefer a rich, sheltered, well-drained soil in sun or partial shade.

Propagation: Sow anemone seeds, mid-summer-early autumn, in seed compost containers, using a damp, recommended seed raising compost, but barely cover the seed, i.e. just to their own depth.

Prick out the seedlings into beds once they are large enough to handle easily, 200 mm (8 in) apart, and 250 mm (10 in) between rows, and let them grow on and eventually flower.

Or sow seeds outside, directly where they are to flower and grow. Fluff out and separate the seeds and scatter them over the seedbed or place them in rows. Lightly cover the seeds with sieved, sandy soil, or compost, to a seed's depth.

Water the seed gently with a fine rose on the hosepipe. Continue to water if dry conditions persist. Thin out the seedlings to the required distance.

In English gardens sow ripe seeds late summer-mid autumn (Aug-Oct) in seed compost. Place the container in a cold frame or greenhouse to germinate. Prick out the seedlings into containers. Grow them on. Transplant them to a nursery holding bed. Grow them on and plant them out in due season. Flowers spring.

Pests and diseases: Aphids, caterpillars, slugs, snails, virus.

Cultivars/varieties: 'St Brigid' Mixed, height 375 mm (15 in). Creagh Castle Strain, double and semi-double mixed. 'Mona Lisa' Mixed F_1 Hybrid, height 600 mm (24 in).

Family: Ranunculaceae.

***Antirrhinum* (snapdragon)** The southwestern European Mediterranean, spring-summer flowering *Antirrhinum majus*; height 100 mm–1.2 m (4–48 in); although a hardy perennial in warmer districts, is usually treated as an annual.

Antirrhinums, with their stately flowering spires, are used principally as bedding plants, border plants, and cut flowers some having a very spicy fragrance. They seem to bloom and bloom until cut down by severe frost. Frost will also kill young antirrhinum plants.

A. majus can be conveniently split up into 3 height groups: 'Tall Giant Snaps' 750 mm–1.2 m (30–48 in); 'Intermediate Snaps' 300–600 mm (12–24 in); and 'Dwarf Snaps' 150–250 mm (6–10 in). The 'Giant Snaps' are used as cut flowers (but check the packet to make sure as some cultivar flowers shatter); the others mainly as bedding plants. 'Giant Snaps' have to be supported with stakes, or similar, in exposed sites.

These bag-faced, dragon-mouthed, plants are justly famous, particularly now with the improved rust-resistant cultivars, F_1 hybrids, and tetraploids, but even the open-pollinate lines are highly acceptable. Snaps are available in a multitude of shades and tints of white, yellow, pink, and red, but unfortunately no blue. They can be single or double flowered.

Traditionally, snapdragons have closed mouths, but some of the tetraploids are open-mouthed (open-faced). Some have description names, such as azalea-flowered, butterfly-flowered, or hyacinth-flowered.

Some gardeners pinch out the tips once the young plants have made a reasonable height, say 75–100 mm (3–4 in) tall, to produce stocky, side-branched, floriferous plants. Others prefer to let the plants grow on naturally.

Antirrhinums thrive in a sheltered, well-drained, approximately neutral soil, not too fertile, as this could lead to soft, vulnerable plants. They like the sun, except in hot, dry areas, when they will tolerate some shade. Faded and spent blooms are removed to prolong the flowering period.

Antirrhinums can be grown much of the year in sub-tropical locations, but early-spring flowering snapdragons are grown extensively in these areas. They can also be grown for much of the year in mild-winter, temperate climates.

Propagation: Seed can be sown in seed compost containers, using a damp, recommended peat-sand seed raising compost, late summer-autumn-winter in sub-tropical areas, late summer-autumn or early-spring temperate areas, spring-late summer-early autumn in cool areas, under glass where necessary, at 13–21°C (55–70°F).

The fine seeds should not be covered as they need light to germinate. Lightly press the seeds with a flat board on to the top of the compost to anchor them to the compost surface. Place the container in a shallow dish of water and remove it when compost surface just glistens. Or gently mist water the seeds with a fine spray, keeping the compost pleasantly moist.

The seeds germinate in approximately 5–14 days. Prick out the seedlings, when they are large enough to handle, into containers or pots of damp, recommended potting compost.

Harden them off, if necessary in a cold frame, before planting them directly where they are to grow and flower, 200 mm (8 in), or 300–400 mm (12–16 in) apart, depending on whether they are dwarf, intermediate, or tall cultivars, when all danger from frost is past and the ground has warmed up.

Seeds can take approximately 4 to 5 months to flower.

Or the seeds can be sown in prepared seedbeds outside, after any risk from frost is past, but don't necessarily expect the same uniformity as from those grown under controlled conditions.

In English gardens, sow the seeds on top of the compost in seed compost containers, late winter-early spring (Feb-March), under glass, at 13–21°C (55–70°F), and treat as half-hardy plants. Flowers midsummer, and on.

Pests and diseases: Aphids, caterpillars, nematodes, damping-off, botrytis, downy mildew, foot and root rot, leaf spot, powdery mildew, stem rot, rust, verticillium wilt.

Cultivars/varieties: There are so many! Bright Butterflies Hybrids, height 750 mm (30 in), pink, red, orange. Love Letters Mixed, height 250 mm (10 in), many contrasting bicolours. Little Darling Mixed, height 300 mm (12 in), butterfly type. Madame Butterfly F_1 Hybrid, height 600 mm (2 ft), double, azalea-flowered, open faced. Sweet Heart F_1 Hybrid, height 300 mm (12 in), mixed colours, double azalea-shaped flowers. Tetra Mixed, height 750 mm (30 in), frilled fluted petals. Tom Thumb Mixed, height 250 mm (10 in). There are many, many more.

Family: Scrophulariaceae.

***Aptenia* (dew plant, heart-leaved moonflower)** The South African frost-sensitive, evergeen, perennial creeper, *Aptenia cordifolia* (syn. *Mesembryanthemum cordifolium*); height 150 mm (6 in); is a fleshy, succulent, small-leaved plant, that is seen frequently in the milder parts of Australia as a ground-cover.

It can also be grown on banks, or as a specialist bedding plant, or window-box and planter-box feature.

It requires similar treatment to the Livingstone daisy, the difference being that in mild climates it is grown as a perennial. It is grown as an annual in the cooler, frost-prone areas as it is cut down by frost.

The 12–19 mm (0.5–0.7 in) wide, intense pink daisy flowers are borne in reasonable quantities from late spring-early summer and on, depending on location. There is a variegated leaf form *A. c.* 'Variegata', and a white form *A. c.* 'Alba'.

Aptenia prefers a well-drained, open soil, in full sun. It thrives well in mild, temperate climates. It is not a greedy plant, so do not over-feed or overwater it. Obtaining a suitable supply of *A. cordifolia* seeds could be difficult.

Propagation: Thinly sow the seeds in containers, using a damp, recommended seed raising compost, late summer-early autumn in sub-tropical areas, and autumn in mild winter areas.

In colder areas, sow the seeds, under glass, say 2–3 months before the last frost is expected in your locality, at 15–18°C (59–65°F). If you are prepared to maintain such a temperature from autumn to spring, then sow the seeds in autumn.

Prick out the seedlings into 75 mm (3 in) pots of damp, recommended potting compost and grow them on.

Or sow a few seeds in individual pots and thin out the seedlings, keeping only the strongest in each pot.

Grow the aptenia seedlings on and harden them off, if necessary in a cold frame, before planting them out directly where they are to grow and flower, when all danger from frost is past and the ground has warmed up.

Or the fine seeds can be sown in autumn or spring, directly where they are to grow and flower, but only if there is no risk from frost and the ground has warmed up. Mix the seeds with several times their own volume of fine, sharp sand and broadcast them over the prepared area. Do not bury the seeds, but gently press them with a board, or similar, to anchor them to the soil.

Gently but thoroughly water the seeds using a fine spray, and do not allow the seeds, or seedlings, to dry out, keeping the soil just pleasantly moist until the seeds germinate. Thin out the seedlings to required distance apart say 150 mm (6 in) for a quicker cover, or 450 mm (18 in) apart where they are to become perennial.

In English gardens sow the seeds on to seed compost, under glass, late winter-early spring (Feb-March), at 15–18°C (59–65°F). Treat as half-hardy plants. Or seeds can be sown outside, in mid-late spring, but only when all danger from frost is past and the ground has warmed up, directly where they are to grow and flower. Summer flowering.

Pests and diseases: Reasonably free, although mealy bugs.

Cultivars/varieties: Species, cultivars as above.
Family: Aizoaceae.

***Aquilegia* (columbine, granny's bonnet)** The European, spring-summer flowering, perennial *Aquilegia vulgaris*; height 450–600 mm (18–24 in); produces reasonable white, pink or blue, short-spurred flowers.

But it is the long-spurred hybrids from *A. vulgaris* and American species, available in cream, yellow, pink, red, crimson and blue, and shades and tints of these colours, and bicolours, that are in such demand.

These 'border garden' aquilegia hybrids are used massed as bedding plants, or as rockery plants or cut flowers. They produce a mass of funnel-horned blooms, five horns forming one 75 mm (3 in) flower, surmounting blue-green, 'maidenhair fern' type foliage.

Aquilegias are cool-climate plants, and like a rich, moisture retaining, but free-draining soil, in a partially shaded spot that receives sun for part of the day. But they will need semi-shade in hot, hard-sun areas.

The southern United States-Mexican *A. longissima*; height 600–900 mm (24–36 in); grows well in temperate Australia and has a pale lemon centre with bright red spurs. The Colorado Rocky Mountain *A. caerulea*; height 300–600 mm (12–24 in); has sky-blue and white flowers. There are also dwarf border cultivars of aquilegia.

Aquilegias can be planted in dramatic clumps with say 300–375–650 mm (12–15–26 in) between plants, depending upon how long they are kept as perennials. Or they can be scattered among bedding plants to create an interesting effect. Water them regularly, particularly during dry spells. Plants can be kept for from 2 to 5 years, but in sub-tropical areas new seedlings produce the best results. Late summer-mid autumn sown seeds should take approximately 6–8 months to flower.

Dead-head (remove) spent flowers to prevent them from going to seed, and thus extend the flowering period. Feed the plants, when the buds are forming, with a well-balanced, liquid, soluble flower fertiliser, suitable for aquilegias, applied as the manufacturer instructs.

Propagation: Thinly surface-sow the seeds in seed compost containers, using a damp, recommended, seed raising compost; late summer-autumn in sub-tropical and temperate areas; autumn or early-spring in cool areas. Gently press the seeds to anchor them to the compost.

Stand the container in a shallow dish of lukewarm water until the compost surface just glistens with moisture, then remove the container. Or mist spray the seeds using a fine spray. Don't let the compost dry out, but keep it just pleasantly moist.

Seedlings germinate in approximately 21–30 days at 21–25°C (70–77°F). Prick out the seedlings once they are large enough to handle into containers or pots of damp, recommended potting compost.

Transplant the seedlings, once properly hardened off, and when they are large enough to handle easily, say 50–75 mm (2–3 in) tall, to directly where they are to grow and flower, spacing them 300–375–650 mm (12–15–26 in) apart.

Or you can transfer the plants into 75 mm (3 in) pots of damp, recommended potting compost, grow them on, and then plant them out directly where they are to grow and flower.

Or in cold areas seeds can be sown, early spring, in seed compost containers indoors, 8 to 10 weeks before transplanting them outdoors, hardened off properly, directly to where they are to grow and flower.

Aquilegias can be used as pot or container plants.

In English gardens sow the seeds outdoors mid spring-early summer (April-May-June). Or sow the seeds in compost containers, early spring, indoors, 8 to 10 weeks before planting them out directly where they will grow and flower. Harden off the seedlings before planting them outside. Aquilegias are spring or summer flowering.

Pests and diseases: Aphids, leaf miner, cluster-cup rust, crown rot-wilt, cucumber mosaic virus.

Cultivars/varieties: Dragonfly Hybrids Mixed, height 450 mm (18 in), pink, rose, crimson, yellow, copper. McKana's Giant Mixed, height 750 mm (30 in). Music F_1 Hybrid Harmony Mix, height 500 mm (20 in), blue and white, pink and white, red and white, yellow, red and gold, and white.

Family: Ranunculaceae.

***Arctotis* (African daisy, blue-eyed African daisy, aurora daisy)** The perennial, spring-summer-autumn flowering, South African daisy, *Arctotis × hybrida*; height 300–600 mm (12–24 in) is popular as a ground cover because of its arrogant, long-stemmed, eye-catching, glowing, 75–100 mm (3–4 in) wide blooms.

Flowers are available in white, ivory, yellow, orange, apricot, carmine, wine, ruby-crimson, or brownish, and shades and tints of these colours; some have a contrasting-colour centre disc which can be surrounded by a small, golden ring.

The leaves are lobed, notched, semi-narrow, woolly-grey or grey-green.

Arctotis are grown as bedding plants, cut flowers and pot plants.

The plants can look scruffy as they age, and that is why some gardeners treat them as annuals, planting up with fresh stock regularly. Arctotis are adaptable to most well-drained soils. They like plenty of sun, although not in excess, and they close up in dull weather.

A. stoechadifolia 'Grandis' (syn. *A. venusta* 'Grandis') is popular, although its flower colour range is limited.

Water the plants during dry weather, but not excessively as they are semi-drought resistant, and excess watering may cause stem rot. Feed them, once the plants have budded up, with a well-balanced, liquid, soluble, flower fertiliser, suitable for arctotis and applied as the manufacturer instructs.

Some gardeners pinch out the growing tips of the young plants, when they are approximately 125 mm (5 in) tall, to encourage side-branching. The taller plants may need some form of support. Dead-heading (removing spent flowers) helps to prolong the flowering season. Arctotis are susceptible to severe frost.

Propagation: Thinly sow the seeds in seed compost containers, using a recommended, damp, seed raising compost, in autumn-winter sub-tropical areas, late summer-early autumn temperate areas, early-spring in cool areas, under glass if necessary, at 16–21°C (61–70°F).

Mist water the seedlings using a fine spray. Keep the compost just pleasantly moist. Seedlings germinate in approximately 10–30 days, depending on soil temperatures.

Prick out the seedlings into, preferably, small pots, harden them off, if necessary in a cold frame, and plant them out 300–400 mm (12–16 in) apart, but only when any danger from frost is past and the ground has warmed up.

Or you can sow the seeds in early spring directly where they are to grow and flower, once any damaging frost risk is past and the temperature does not drop below 10°C (50°F). Thin out to the required distance. Flowers should appear in approximately 16 weeks from sowing.

In English gardens thinly sow the seeds in seed compost, under glass, early-mid spring (March-April), at 16–21°C (61–70°F). Flowers appear mid summer-autumn.

Pests and diseases: Aphids, grey mould, stem rot.

Cultivars/varieties: Giant Hybrids Mixed, height 350 mm (14 in), wide colour range. Large-flowered Mixed.

Family: Asteraceae.

***Argemone* (Mexican poppy, devil's fig, prickly poppy, crested poppy, Mexican prickly poppy)** The summer flowering annual *Argemone mexicana*; height 600 mm (24 in); is more or less rapidly becoming a serious pest plant in Australia and in warm, temperate areas throughout the world.

Although popular in cooler, northern hemisphere gardens, it is, even in such climates, a strong growing plant with the ability to self-seed.

It has 60 mm (2–4 in), wide, yellow-white, sometimes orange, flowers. The leaves are silver-veined, glaucous, scalloped, prickly and 60–125 mm (2.4–5 in) long. Its seeds have spines which stick to clothing and animal hides, and are transported; and the plants thrive in hot, well-drained soil, hence the problem in Australia.

The North, Central and South American *A. platycerus* (crested poppy); height 300 mm–1.2 m (1–4 ft); is a better looking plant, with its white, 6-petalled, 50–100 mm (2–4 in) wide, tissue-paper flowers and glaucous, blue-green, prickly foliage.

Propagation: I feel that *Argemone mexicana* should not be grown in Australia.

In English gardens *Argemone* species seeds are sown in peat-pots, indoors at 18°C (64°F), approximately 6 to 8 weeks before the last frost, or early spring (March), and grown on. The roots resent disturbance. The seedlings are thinned out leaving only the strongest in each pot. They are then hardened off in a cold frame and planted out, peat pot and all, when all danger from frost is past and the ground has warmed up.

Or the seeds can be sown, when any danger from frost is past and the ground has warmed up, directly where they are to grow and flower. Thin out the seedlings to 250–300 mm (10–12 in) apart. Argemones need a hot, sunny sheltered location. They are summer-flowering.

Pests and diseases: Reasonably free.

Cultivars/varieties: Species as above.

Family: Papaveraceae.

***Asclepias* (bloodflower)** The tropical American *Asclepias curassavica*; height 1 m (39 in); is an attractive, perennial evergreen with a loose cluster of 18 mm (0.7 in) wide, scarlet-orange, blood-red, 5-lobed 'flowers', with a centre column of stamens which are partially enclosed by golden-yellow hoods.

The bloodflowers are swept back, like arrow feathers, from the golden centre petals. The seed pods are approximately 200 mm (4 in) long.

The leaves, arranged in opposite pairs up the stem, are narrow, lance-like and shiny green.

Bloodflowers are reasonably hardy in many warm parts of Australia, but they still must be protected from inclement weather and are treated as tender perennials, grown in pots in a cool greenhouse, or as frost-sensitive annuals in cooler areas. They are used as warm border plants and, taking their height into consideration, are grown towards the back of the border.

They require a reasonably fertile, well-drained, reasonably moist soil in a sunny location. Flowers appear in summer-autumn.

The eastern North American and Canadian butterfly weed, *A. tuberosa*; height 600 mm (24 in); is a half-hardy, sun-loving, border perennial that bears masses of bright-orange or bright-yellow flowers, depending on species or cultivar, on 125 mm (5 in) wide clusters, giving a 'flame' appearance to the summer garden.

Butterfly weed resents root disturbance. It prefers a well-drained, slightly acid soil.

Plant out bloodflowers 300–600 mm (12–24 in) apart, in sunny, reasonably moist, slightly acid soil. Fertilise the plants with dressings of acid compost.

Propagation: Sow only ripe seeds of *A. curassavica* in 75 mm (3 in) pots using a damp, recommended seed raising compost, autumn in sub-tropical areas, late winter-early-spring in temperate areas, and early spring in cooler areas at 16–21°C (61–70°F), under glass where necessary. Thin the seedlings out, keeping only the strongest in each pot. Grow them on, harden them off, and plant them out directly where they are to grow and flower, 400 mm (16 in) apart, when all danger from frost is well past and the ground has warmed up.

Or pot the seedlings on into progressively larger pots, going up 2 sizes each time; from 75 mm (3 in) to 125 mm (5 in) to 175 mm (7 in), using a damp, recommended potting compost, and grow them on as frost sensitive greenhouse perennial pot plants.

Propagation of A. tuberosa: Sow only ripe seeds of butterfly weed, in early spring, indoors, into 75 mm (3 in) pots of slightly acid, damp, recommended seed raising compost.

Seedlings germinate in approximately 30 days. Thin out the seedlings leaving the strongest in each pot. Grow the seedlings on, harden them off, and plant them out directly where they are to grow and flower, 300–600 mm (12–24 in) apart.

Or sow the seeds in winter, under glass, at 16°C (61°F), for setting out in early spring, but hardened off, and after any danger from frost is past in cold areas.

The seeds can also be sown under glass in a cool place 8–10 weeks before planting them out directly where they are to flower and grow.

Alternatively, in warm areas sow the seeds in summer for planting out into their permanent quarters in early autumn.

In English gardens, *A. curassavica* is usually treated as a greenhouse pot plant requiring a minimum winter temperature of 10°C (50°F). But in mild parts of the country, in a sheltered spot, it can be grown outside as an annual, but planted out only when all danger from frost is well past, and the ground has warmed up. Sow the seeds in 75 mm (3 in) pots, late winter-early spring (Feb-March), under glass at 16–21°C (61–70°F). Treat seedlings as half-hardy plants. Bloodflowers are summer-autumn flowering.

Pests and diseases: Reasonably free.
Cultivars/varieties: Species as above.
Family: Asclepiadaceae.

***Atriplex* (orach)** The European-Siberian summer flowering *Atriplex hortensis*; height 900 mm–1.2–1.8 m (3–4–6 ft) and taller, depending on cultivar; is an annual grown in the flower garden for its foliage, particularly for the contrast provided by the soft-green, arrowhead, 75–175 mm (3–7 in) long leaves.

There are popular purple forms, *A. h.* var. *atrosanguinea* and *A. h.* var. *rubra*, which are also grown. The only problem being that their unusual colour is hard to fit into bedding schemes. But it can be, and indeed is, done.

The flowers are insignificant but the seed pods are reasonably attractive.

Atriplex prefers a neutral, or slightly limy (alkaline) soil. It is reasonably drought resistant, but water the plants well during hot weather to keep the foliage growing, and feed with a well-balanced, soluble, liquid, flower fertiliser, suitable for atriplex and applied as the manufacturer instructs.

Keep down any weeds, but be careful when weeding around the plants as the roots object to disturbance.

Atriplex is a member of the goosefoot family of plants, and has been in cultivation since ancient times.

Propagation: Thinly sow the seeds in small rows, as soon as the ground can be worked, late-winter, subtropical areas, spring in other areas, after danger from frost is past, directly where they are to grow and flower. Thin out the seedlings to 200–300 mm (8–12 in) apart.

Or sow a few seeds in 75 mm (3 in) peat pots, thinning out the seedlings to leave the strongest in each pot. Let them grow on and plant them out directly where they are to grow and flower.

In English gardens sow the seeds, early-mid spring (March-April), directly where they are to grow and flower. Thin out the seedlings to the required distance.

Pests and diseases: Reasonably free.
Cultivars/varieties: Species, cvs as above.
Family: Chenopodiaceae.

***Begonia* (wax begonia)** The popular Brazilian fibrous-rooted, wax begonia, *A. semperflorens-cultorum*; height 150–300 mm (6–12 in); although a perennial, is used as a warm season annual in public parks and home gardens.

Wax begonias can be split up into two convenient groups:

1. Dwarf 250–300 mm (10–12 in).
2. Extra dwarf 150–200 mm (6–8 in).

Wax begonias are mounded, floriferous plants studded with 25–50 mm (1–2 in) wide, single, double or mass-double flowers, in shades and tints of white, pink or red, or picotee-bicolours.

Their oval, waxy leaves can be yellowish, green, reddish, bronze-green, or chocolate-brown.

Wax begonias can be used as bedding or edging plants, in window boxes, or as pot plants and house plants.

But they cannot survive frost, or hot, hard sunlight. They thrive in a sheltered, rich, organic, free-draining soil in filtered, dappled light, such as that which comes through a leafy tree, or in bright shade; but bear in mind that wax begonias planted close to a tree will have to cope with competition from the roots and pollution from the leaves.

Some of the new F_1 hybrids will cope with full sun where temperatures do not exceed 32°C (90°F); but be sure to check these details on the seed packet. Wax begonias like adequate water when they are growing well, but don't like to be waterlogged.

Feeding with a well-balanced, liquid, soluble, flower fertiliser, suitable for wax begonias and applied during the growing season as the manufacturer instructs, helps to ensure continuous blooming.

Propagation: The seeds, which are as fine as a trace of snuff, can be mixed with several times their own volume of clean, dry, fine, silver sand, to aid distribution.

Thinly sow the seeds, indoors, on to the top of damp, recommended seed-raising compost, winter-spring in tropical areas, late winter-spring in temperate areas, spring in cold areas, under glass where necessary at 16–24°C (61–75°F), say 21°C (70°F).

Finely screed the top 3 mm (0.1 in) of compost to provide a suitable bed for the fine seeds which are pressed gently on to the compost to anchor them, but not buried, as they need light to germinate.

Stand the container in a shallow dish of water, allowing moisture to soak up through the compost. Remove the container once the water glistens on the surface. Cover the container with a sheet of glass, but remove the glass immediately the seedlings show to prevent them from being 'drawn' or unnecessarily exposed to damping-off fungus.

If you opt to mist water, then use a very, very fine spray and apply the moisture gently, without disturbing the compost. Keep it just pleasantly moist, but not waterlogged.

Germination should occur in approximately 14 to 21 days. Prick out the seedlings once they have made their first 'true' leaf. You may find out that the seedlings are not easy to handle when transplanting. But you could use a V-notched plant label, the 'V' being free from jagged edges, or similar, to transfer the seedlings.

Prick them out into containers or 75 mm (3 in) pots of damp recommended, potting compost and grow them on. Harden them off, if necessary in a cold frame, and plant them directly where they are to grow and flower, 200–300 mm (8–12 in) apart, depending on whether they are extra-dwarf or dwarf, when all danger from frost is past and the soil has warmed up.

Wax begonias will bloom until cut down by frost. They can be taken inside before frost risk and grown on as pot plants.

In English gardens, sow the seeds under glass, in seed compost, late winter-early spring (Jan-Feb-March), at 16–24°C (61–75°F). Treat as half-hardy plants. They will bloom in summer, and on, until cut down by frost.

Pests and diseases: Aphids, eelworms, mealy bugs, mites, bacterial leaf-spot-wilt, botrytis blight, cucumber mosaic, crown and stem rot, damping-off, grey mould, powdery mildew, stem rot.

Cultivars/varieties: Organdy Mixed F_1 Hybrid, height: 200 mm (8 in), white, rose, carmine, scarlet. Thousand Wonders, various and varied flowers and leaves. There are many more cultivars.
Family: Begoniaceae.

***Bellis* (daisy, English daisy)** It is the spring-flowering cultivars of the perennial lawn-weed daisy, *Bellis perennis*; height 25–100–175 mm (1–4–7 in); that we grow in our gardens, where they are treated as cool season annuals.

Cultivars are available with 12–25 mm (0.5–1 in) wide, double flowers of white, pink or red, or bicolours, all with bright-golden centres, although some miniatures are pompon shaped. There are also the huge-headed 'Monstrosa' cultivars, 50 mm (2 in) wide and more; height 125–150 mm (5–6 in).

Daisies are used as edging plants, bedding plants or pot plants. They prefer a well-drained, not too fertile, organic soil, a cool location, in sun or in partial shade with sun for part of the day, in warmer areas.

Feed them, once the buds are formed, with a well-balanced, soluble liquid fertiliser, suitable for daisies, and apply it as the manufacturer instructs.

Remove spent leaves, and spent flowers to prolong the flowering period and prevent inferior self-seeding. Daisies are sometimes treated as biennials in cold locations.

'Daisy' comes from the Old English *daegeseage*: 'day's eye'.
Propagation: Easy by seed, provided that the cultivar is fertile, as some cultivars, such as 'Dresden China' and 'Rob Roy', are not.

Thinly sow the seeds in seed compost containers, 3 mm (0.1 in) deep, using a damp, recommended, seed raising compost, autumn in sub-tropical areas, late summer-autumn in temperate areas, and late summer-autumn or early spring in cold areas, just covering the seed with vermiculite or sand.

Mist water the compost using a fine spray, and keep the compost pleasantly moist. Germination usually takes 10–25 days.

Prick out the seedlings, when they are large enough to handle, into containers, and grow them on, then plant them out into their permanent quarters, 100–150–225 mm (4–6–9 in) apart, depending on cultivar.

Or the seeds can be sown thinly in a prepared seed-bed and from there, when they are large enough to handle easily, planted out directly where they are to grow and flower.

Or they can be sown indoors in a light, frost-free place, 6 to 8 weeks before normal spring planting time. They are pricked out into boxes of damp recommended potting compost, grown on, and then planted out in spring.

In English gardens thinly sow the seeds directly into nursery seed-beds, late spring-early summer (May-June), in shallow drills (rows) 3 mm (0.1 in) deep. Transplant the seedlings when they are large enough to handle easily, in early-autumn (Sept), directly to where they are to grow and flower. Or the seeds can be sown in seed compost containers. Flowers appear spring-mid summer (March-July).
Pests and diseases: Reasonably free.
Cultivars/varieties: Giant Mixed, large flowered strain. Double Mixed, 25 mm (1 in) wide flowers. Pomponette, height 150 mm (6 in), button type, red, rose, white, 13 mm (0.5 in) flowers. Monstrosa Mixed, height 150 mm (6 in), flowers 60 mm (2.4 in) wide.
Family: Asteraceae.

***Brachycome* (Swan River daisy)** The Western Australian *Brachycome iberidifolia*; height 200–300–450 mm (8–12–18 in); is a delicately-fragrant, easily grown annual, with 18–50 mm (0.7–2 in) wide, summer flowers in violet-blue, pale-blue, white, pink, or shades and tints of these colours; all with blackish or yellow centres.

The flowers appear on 250 mm (10 in), or taller, stems; a tufted, mound of colour.

The foliage is delicately-lacy, deeply cut, even fern-like.

They make attractive edging, pot or bedding plants.

Brachycomes prefer a light, free-draining, loamy soil in a site that receives good sunlight as they are hot weather plants. But they do not like excess water. Provide a twiggy support for the plants if necessary. Dead-heading these plants is a fiddly, but useful, job, as the brownish seed heads can look scruffy.
Propagation: Sow the seeds, 3 mm (0.1 in) deep in damp, recommended seed raising mix; late autumn-winter in sub-tropical areas; late winter-midsummer in temperate areas; spring in cold areas, under glass where necessary, at 16–21°C (60–70°F). Gently firm the seeds and compost.

Seeds germinate in approximately 10–21 days. Prick out the seedlings into containers or pots of damp, recommended, potting compost and grow them on. Harden them off, if necessary in a cold frame, and plant them outside directly where they are to grow and flower, 200–375 mm (8–15 in) apart.

Carefully nip the young growing tips cleanly out of the plants when seedlings are approximately 50–60 mm (2–2.4 in) high, to encourage branching, although they will branch naturally.

Flowers appear approximately 14–16 weeks from germination. I have had them flowering in 8 weeks.

Seeds can also be sown directly in the garden in a sunny position. Break down the ground into a fine tilth and firm the seedbed to prevent the seeds from being lost. Sprinkle the seeds thinly over the ground or sow in drills. Rake the seeds lightly into the top 3 mm (0.1 in) tilth surface. Water the seed gently using a fine spray.

In English gardens sow the seeds in seed compost, under glass, early spring (March), at 16–21°C (60–70°F), and treat them as half-hardy plants. Or sow the seeds, in late spring (April-May), directly where they are to grow and flower, but only when any danger from frost is past. Summer flowering.
Pests and diseases: Reasonably free.
Cultivars/varieties: Species as above. 'Purple Splendour', height 230 mm (9 in), violet blue flowers.
Family: Asteraceae.

***Brassica* (ornamental kale or cabbage)** *Brassica oleracea acephala*, the ornamental kale; height 150 mm (6 in); is a technicolor variation of the common kale, with its crinkled, or shredded, or frosted-looking leaves in various shades of cream, green or pink.

The cabbage-flowers are a drab yellow.

Ornamental kale can be treated as a hardy or half-hardy annual. Ornamental cabbage is also grown.

It is used as a bedding-out feature clustered in small groups to give effect, or grown as a winter pot-plant feature in a greenhouse.
Propagation: Sow seeds late summer-early autumn (February-March) for winter display, directly into the ground, or in seed compost containers of a damp, recommended, seed-raising compost, and grow them on. In cold areas seeds can be sown late winter-early spring under glass. Or sow outside when all danger from frost is past.

Cold weather helps to establish ornamental kale colour.

Prick out the seedlings into 75 mm (3 in) peat-pots, or into their permanent quarters; 300–375 mm (12–15 in) apart in good sunlight.

Or sow them under glass in early summer. Prick out seedlings into 75 mm (3 in) pots or peat-pots, and grow them on in shade until the hottest part of summer is past, then plant them out into their permanent quarters. The problem with kale/cabbage is that they can 'bolt' (go to seed) in hot weather.

In English gardens sow the seeds late winter-early spring (Feb-March), under glass. Or sow them directly where they are to grow once the danger from frost risk is past.
Pests and diseases: Cabbage root, fly-flea beetle, clubroot.
Cultivars/varieties: Fringed Mixed, height 300 mm (12 in), red, or pink on green. Red and White Peacock F_1, height 300 mm (12 in), ornamental, feathery foliage. Ornamental Cabbage Mixed, height 450 mm (18 in), white on green, green on red.
Family: Brassicaceae.

***Briza* (large quaking grass)** The Mediterranean annual *Briza maxima*; height 375–600 mm (15–24 in); is the best known of the *B.* species.

It is a broad-leaved grass, and from the clump erect stems bearing drooping, loose panicles of egg-shaped seed spikelets appear in spring-summer.

But it's the hissing and quaking of the *Briza* species, which occurs in the slightest breeze, that evokes the feeling of summer and buzzing insects.

Plant quaking grass in bold clumps. Its neutral, golden colour makes a good foil for colourful or subdued bedding plants.

It prefers a rich, free-draining soil, and a sunny site.

The panicles are used by floral arrangers.
Propagation: Thinly sow seeds in spring or autumn in temperate areas directly where they are to grow and flower. Thin out the seedlings, 150–225 mm (6–9 in) apart, allowing the strongest to form accent plants.

In English gardens sow the seeds early-mid spring (March-April), or early autumn (Sept) in mild winter areas, directly where they are to grow and flower.
Pests and diseases: Reasonably free.
Cultivars/varieties: Species as above.
Family: Poaceae.

***Browallia* (amethyst flower, bush violet)** The South American-Colombian *Browallia speciosa*; height 300–350 mm or to 750 mm (12–14–30 in); is a frost-tender perennial of the nightshade family, but it can be treated as an annual.

It makes a superb pot or hanging-basket plant, particularly its newer cultivars. These cultivars are available in navy-blue, violet, mauve-blue, light blue or white. The flowers are 37–50 mm (1.5–2 in) wide or more, with bell, fused, star-shaped petals and white centres.

The leaves are delicately soft, glossy, bright green, egg shaped and pointed.

Browallias can also be planted in the frost-free garden, in a semi-rich, moist soil in a semi-shaded spot or a sunny position that does not get too hot.

Feed browallias when they are growing well with a weak-strength, well-balanced, soluble, liquid flower fertiliser, applied as the manufacturer instructs for browallias.

Keep the plants watered, using a fine spray.

Propagation: Thinly sow the seeds in early-spring, under glass, on top of a firmed, damp, recommended, seed raising compost, at 18–24°C (64–75°F), and gently firm down the seed to anchor it on to the compost.

Water the seeds by immersing the pot in water until the compost surface just glistens with moisture, then remove the pot from the water. Cover seed with a sheet of glass and place in good light, not direct sunlight. Make sure that the compost does not dry out.

Or very carefully mist water the compost, using a very fine spray.

Germination takes place in approximately 14–21 days. Prick out the seedlings, once large enough to handle, into containers of damp, recommended, potting compost, and from there into 75 mm (3 in) pots, and subsequently into 125 mm (5 in) pots for indoor work. Harden off browallias intended for outdoor use, if necessary in a cold frame. These can be planted outside in the garden when danger of frost risk is over and the ground has warmed up; 200–250 mm (8–10 in) apart.

Seed can also be sown in summer-early autumn, in a shady spot, for indoor, winter flowers.

In English gardens sow the seeds under glass, late winter-early spring (March), at 18–24°C (64–75°F), and treat them as half-hardy plants. Summer flowering.

Pests and diseases: Reasonably free.

Cultivars/varieties: Browallia 'Vanja', height 350 mm (14 in), navy blue. Jingle Bells Mixed, height 250 mm (10 in).

Family: Solanaceae.

***Calceolaria* (slipper flower)** The Chilean-South American *C.* × *herbeohybrida*; height 200–375 mm (8–15 in); is a tender, winter-spring flowering 'annual' (biennial) plant, although some of the newer F_1 hybrids will flower most of the year, except during very hot weather.

The 25–37 mm (1–2.5 in) baggy, inflated, but eye-catching blooms resemble slippers, hence their common name. Colours include yellow, orange, red; as well as specked, spotted and blotched. Water calceolarias regularly when in flower.

Propagation: Calceolarias are grown principally as pot plants under glass, in a cool, humid, minimum winter temperature of 8–10°C (46–50°F).

Thinly sow the seeds on top of the compost, in seed compost containers using a damp, recommended seed raising compost; summer-early autumn in temperate areas; spring-summer in cold areas, for winter-spring flowers; at 18°C (64°F). Make sure that the compost is firmed.

The seeds are minute and must be handled carefully. Press them on to the compost surface just sufficiently to make contact.

Germination occurs in 8–21 days. Prick out the seedlings when large enough to handle, into containers of damp, recommended, potting compost. Grow the seedlings on in a cool, not cold or hot, humid temperature. Pot them on into 75 mm (3 in) pots, filled with damp, recommended, potting compost.

Grow the plants on, and later transfer them into 125–175 mm (5–7 in) pots of compost for flowering. They flower approximately 15–28 weeks from sowing; some of the newer hybrids will flower 4–4½ months from germination.

Feed the plants with a well-balanced, liquid, soluble, flower fertiliser, suitable for calceolarias during the final stage. Calceolarias like good light, but shaded from hot sunlight, or partial shade. The day or night minimum winter temperature for mature plants is 8–10°C (46–50°F).

In English gardens sow the seeds in seed compost, under glass, early summer (June), at 18°C (64°F), and grow the plants on in a cool and humid greenhouse where the winter temperature does not drop below 8–10°C (46–50°F). Flowers late spring-summer.

Pests and diseases: Aphids, whitefly.

Cultivars/varieties: Anytime Series F_1, height 225 mm (9 in), flowers in red, rose, yellow spotted-brown, red and yellow, and rose and white flowers. Bright Bikinis F_1 Hybrid, mixed colours, height 250 mm (10 in). Dwarf Hybrids mixed colours, height 250 mm (10 in). F_1 Hybrid Multiflora (Japan).

Family: Schropulariaceae.

***Calendula* (pot marigold)** The cultivars of the Mediterranean hardy annual pot marigold, *Calendula officinalis*; height 300–600 mm (12–24 in); are to be seen in most public garden displays.

They are easy to grow from seeds, are not fussy, and their 50–75–100 mm (2–3–4 in) wide, 'chrysanthemum-like' blooms are available in eyecatching colours of apricot, orange or yellow.

They grow on tall, thickish, but floppy stems, and bloom continuously.

You can use pot marigolds in the garden, or as pot plants or cut flowers.

The drawbacks of pot marigolds, possibly, are: (1) they are too eyecatching, and (2) their powerful scent may be objectionable to some.

They are used for displays at any time of the year.

Dead-head spent blooms to keep the plant compact and tidy, and to prevent weedy seedlings.

Propagation: Thinly sow the seeds, 12 mm (0.5 in) deep, in seed compost containers, using a damp, seed raising compost, late summer-autumn-early winter in warm areas for flowers in winter-spring.

Sowings can be made most of the year in cooler areas, except winter, but usually early spring.

Germination can take 6–14 days in warm conditions. Seedlings grow rapidly, and can be planted out 250–400 mm (10–16 in) apart, depending on hybrid.

Calendulas take 6–10 weeks to flower in warm climates, and correspondingly longer in colder areas.

They like a medium, moderately fertile, moist soil and full sun, but they will grow in a well-drained, poor soil. Too rich a soil could lead to much leaf growth, but poorer flower production. Calendulas do not transplant readily.

Seeds can be sown directly in the garden, the seedlings being thinned out to 250–300 mm (10–12 in) apart. Water the plants regularly in dry spells.

In English gardens sow the seeds, early-mid spring (March-April), directly where they are to grow and flower, or sow 4 weeks earlier under glass in seed compost. Seeds can also be sown in early autumn in the garden for spring flowering.

Pests and diseases: Caterpillars, damping off, foot rot, fusarium, leaf blight, rust, yellows.

Cultivars/varieties: Campfire, height 450–500 mm (18–20 in), orange. Fiesta Gitana Mixed, height 300 mm (12 in), creamy-yellow, tangerine, orange. Kablouna Gold, height 500 mm (20 in), shades of yellow, strikingly crested. New Crested Mixed, height 450 mm (18 in), yellow, orange. Pacific Beauty Mixed, height 400 mm (16 in), cream, yellow, apricot, orange.

Family: Asteraceae.

***Callistephus* (China aster)** The Chinese-Japanese *C. chinensis*; height 200–750 mm (8–30 in); is popular as a cut flower, particularly the 125 mm (5 in) wide, 'ostrich-feathered' hybrids.

Asters are also popular garden plants, with their purple, blue, pink or white flowers.

Previously, asters have been notorious for their susceptibility to 'wilt disease', and to help avoid this, you can plant the seedlings in a fresh soil site each year, using wilt-resistant cultivars. Asters like a sandy-loam, fertile, neutral soil, in a sheltered, sunny position.

Propagation: Thinly sow the seeds 2 mm (0.1 in) deep in seed compost containers, using a damp, recommended seed raising compost; much of the year, but usually winter-spring, in subtropical areas; spring-summer in temperate areas; spring-summer in cold areas.

Or sow a few seeds in small, peat-sand compost blocks, removing surplus seedlings leaving only one to grow as a single plant, thus minimising root disturbance.

Grow the seeds at 13–18°C (55–64°F).

Germination takes place in 11–20 days. Prick out the seedlings into containers of damp, recommended, potting compost and grow them on.

Harden off the seedlings, if necessary in a cold frame. Plant them out directly where they are to grow and flower, when all danger from frost is past and the ground has warmed up, 150–350 mm (6–14 in) apart, depending on spread of hybrid. Flowers appear in approximately 3–4 months.

Seeds can be sown in spring, directly outside once any danger from frost is past. Keep plants watered in dry weather.

Feed the plants, when the flowers are budding and flowering, with a well-balanced, suitable, liquid, soluble, flower fertiliser, applied as the manufacturer instructs.

In English gardens sow the seeds under glass, early-mid spring (March-April) at 13–18°C (55–64°F), in seed compost, and treat them as half-hardy plants. Or sow the seeds outside in the garden directly where they are to grow and flower, when any danger from frost is past. Flowers midsummer, and on.

Pests and diseases: Aphids, caterpillars, nematodes, powdery mildew, wilt, rust, foot and root rot.
Cultivars/varieties: Colour Carpet Dwarf (Seven Dwarfs Mixed). Disco Dancer Mixed, height 500 mm (20 in), many colours, some with white centres. Dwarf Divinity Mixed, height 200 mm (8 in), mixed colours. Early Sparkle, mixed colours. Giant Crego Mixed, height 750 mm (30 in) curled, twisted petals. Perfection Mixed Colours, height 900 mm (3 ft). Powderpuffs Mixed, height 600 mm (2 ft). There are many more cultivars.
Family: Asteraceae.

***Calonyction* (moonflower)** The frost-sensitive, tender-perennial, tropical-South American *Calonyction aculeatum* (syn. *Ipomoea alba, I. bona-nox*); height 3–6 mm (10–20 ft); is a greenhouse plant for most areas, excepting warm, moist, northern regions where the evening-night temperature does not drop below 12–13°C (54–55°F). Indeed, given the right growing conditions moonflowers may naturalise. But this may not be what you want. It would also be environmentaly undesirable.

Moonflower is a rapid, twining-climbing plant, but because of its vigorous nature and frost sensitivity it is usually grown as an annual.

It is very similar to a morning glory plant, but its spectacular, 150 mm (6 in) wide, flat-trumpet, white flowers, with their delicious evening fragrance sets it apart. The trumpet face is divided by a 5-pointed, narrow, creamy-green star.

It is called moonflower because it opens suddenly in the late afternoon-evening, and stays open to mid morning, depending on how dark is its location. You can imagine the 'Victorian' ghostliness of these white flowers caught by moonbeams! Plants under glass produce flowers early summer, and on. Flowers outside, summer-autumn.

The dense leaves are large, delicately textured, heart-shaped, and when broken or damaged exude a milky sap.

Don't overfertilise moonflowers, or you end up with leaves at the expense of flowers. Moonflowers like a light, well-drained soil in a sunny location, but not hot, direct sunlight through greenhouse glass. The plant roots resent disturbance, so be extra-careful when working close to them. Flowers appear approximately 4 months after germination.
Propagation: Begin by soaking the hard-coated seeds overnight in warm water to speed up germination.

Sow the seeds, in spring, under glass, 18–25 mm (0.7–1 in) deep, individually into 75 mm (3 in) peat pots to avoid transplantation shock as the roots resent any disturbance. Use a damp, recommended, seed raising mix. Grow them on at 21°C (70°F).

Carefully water the seeds and seedlings and do not let them dry out, keeping the compost pleasantly moist. They can be potted on, peat pots and all, into 225-300 mm (9–12 in) sturdy containers of damp, recommended potting compost, bearing in mind that the roots are powerful, thriving exceedingly well in the right climate, and could crack susceptible containers.

I have seen moonflowers planted directly into the greenhouse border but they do tend to take up considerable space, as they grow on as perennials.

In warm areas, where the night temperature does not drop below 12–13°C (54–55°F), they can be sown directly, or planted in their peat pots, outside, 300 mm (12 in) apart, in front of already erected sturdy, approximately 2.4–3 m (8–10 ft) tall supports, such as a trellis or pyramid.

Sow 2 or 3 seeds to a 'station', keeping only the strongest seedling at each point.

In cooler areas, in late spring, sow the seeds in individual 75 mm (3 in) peat pots, under glass, 4–8 weeks before the last frost, at 21°C (70°F), and grow them on. Harden off the seedlings in a cold frame and plant them out, but only when the night temperature from then on is not expected to go below 12–13°C (54–55°F). In such climates the plants are treated as tender annuals.

In English gardens treat the plants as tender annuals or perennials and sow the seeds in spring under glass.
Pests and diseases: Slugs.
Cultivars/varieties: Species as above.
Family: Convolvulaceae.

***Campanula* (bellflower)** The southern European Canterbury bell, *Campanula medium*; height 375–900 mm (15–36 in); is probably the best known of the vast *Campanula* family.

Canterbury bells can be single, semi-double or double flowered. The taller plants usually need staking.

If grown as a biennial, then in the first year of growth the plant produces a rosette of lance-shaped leaves, and in the second year the flowering stems arise bearing the bellflowers.

There are cultivars which can be treated as annuals.

The 'Calycanthema' 'cup and saucer' form can be had in pink, blue or white. The outer calyx-petals of *C. m.* 'Calycanthema' act as a saucer for the 50–75 mm (2–3 in) centre bellflower-cup.

Canterbury bells prefer a well prepared, neutral, rich, organic, well-drained soil, open or partially shaded, but not heavy shade.
Propagation: Thinly sow seeds of *C. medium* biennial forms on seed compost containers of damp, recommended, seed raising compost, autumn-early winter in temperate areas, but late summer-autumn in cold areas, barely covering the seeds with sand or compost, as they need light to germinate.

Seeds should germinate within 21 days. Prick out seedlings, when large enough to handle, into containers of damp, recommended potting compost, and from there into 75 mm (3 in) pots. The next move can be to the site where they are to grow and flower, 300 mm (12 in) apart.

In severe frost areas these young plants need protection over winter.

In English gardens sow the seeds in seed compost, in a cold frame, late spring-early summer, or in a nursery seed bed, late spring-early summer. *C. m.* 'Calycanthema' may be grown as a half-hardy annual if sown indoors in a well lighted place at 18–21°C (64–70°F), 8–10 weeks before the usual frost-free, spring planting-out time in your location. Flowers late spring-early summer.
Pests and diseases: Slugs, snails, leaf spot.
Cultivars/varieties: Cup and Saucer Mixed, height 750 mm (38 in). Bells of Holland Mixed (dwarf), height 450 mm (18 in); colours: canary yellow, pink, mauve and white.
Family: Campanulaceae.

***Capsicum* (ornamental peppers)** The cultivars of the tropical, South American, frost tender 'annual' *C. annuum*; height 200–375 mm (8–15 in), depending on cultivar; are grown for their bright, glossy, green-ivory, cream-yellow-red, tweaked, sharply-pointed, cone-shaped fruits, 25–50 mm (1–2 in) long, borne in spring-midsummer-autumn. Some cultivars bear round fruits.

The flowers are small, white and insignificant, but interesting.

The soft leaves, which are fair game to hole-making insects, are glossy, mid-green, egg-shaped and bluntly pointed; some cultivars can have variegated leaves.

Capsicums prefer a sheltered, well-drained organic soil, to which a well-balanced fertiliser, suitable for capsicums, has been added in accordance with the manufacturer's instructions.

Feed the plants, once the flowers appear, with a well-balanced, liquid, soluble, flower fertiliser, suitable for capsicums, and applied as the manufacturer instructs.

Water the plants regularly during dry spells. Capsicum cultivars are used extensively as pot plants, although they can be planted outside, hardened off, once frost risk is past and the ground has warmed up.

But be aware that some cultivar fruits are extremely hot, and keep children away from such fruits.
Propagation: Thinly sow the seeds 6 mm (0.2 in) deep, in seed compost containers using a damp, recommended seed raising compost; late winter to mid spring in subtropical areas; late winter to early summer in temperate areas; spring in cold areas, under glass where necessary; at 18–24°C (64–75°F).

Germination can take 10 to 21 days. Prick out the seedlings, when large enough to handle, into 75 mm (3 in) pots of damp, recommended, potting compost, and grow them on. Harden them off, if necessary in a cold frame, and plant them out directly where they are to grow and flower, when any danger from frost is past and the ground has warmed up.

Or pot them on into 125 mm (5 in) pots of potting compost for small cultivars, and 175 mm (7 in) for the larger, and grow them on as pot plants.

Fruits appear in approximately 14 weeks from sowing.

In English gardens sow the seeds late winter-late spring (Feb-May), under glass, at 18–24°C (61–70°F), and treat them as half-hardy pot plants.
Pests and diseases: Leaf eating insects, red spider, fungus, leaf spots, and more.
Cultivars/varieties: 'Candlelight', cone tapered. 'Festival', cone tapered. 'Fireball', round fruits. Inferno Mixed, height 250 mm (10 in), cone, tapered, and round fruits.
Family: Solanaceae.

***Catananche* (cupid's dart)** The western Mediterranean *Catananche caerulea*; height 450–750 mm (18–30 in); is an easy perennial to grow from seed.

Its sparkling sky-blue cornflower-like, 37 mm (1.5 in) wide flowers (bracts) with deeper-blue centres, borne on wiry stems, dart above its grey-green, grass-like foliage. These tissue-like flower petals are unusual in that the ends look as though they have been notched with paper scissors. They are long-lasting blooms that will light up any garden border during summer.

1. *Abelmoschus manihot* (sunset hibiscus)

2. *Abelmoschus moschatus* (silk flower)

3. *Abutilon* × *hybridum* (flowering maple)

4. *Acanthus mollis* (bear's breeches)

5. *Acroclinium roseum* (paper everlasting daisy)

6. *Ageratum houstonianum* (floss flower)

7. *Ageratum houstonianum* white cv.

8. *Agrostemma githago* 'Milas' (corn cockle)

9. *Alcea rosea* double-form cv. (hollyhock)

10. *Alonsoa warscewiczii* (mask flower)

11. *Amaranthus caudatus* (tassel flower)

12. *Amaranthus salicifolius* cv. (flaming amaranth)

13. *Ammi majus* (bishop's flower)

14. *Anagallis arvensis* 'Caerulea' (blue pimpernel)

15. *Anchusa capensis* (Cape forget-me-not)

16. *Anemone* 'St Brigid' (windflower)

17. *Antirrhinum* open-faced cv. (snapdragon)

18. *Antirrhinum* double-flowered cv.

19. *Aptenia cordifolia* (dew plant)

20. *Aquilegia hybrid* cv. (columbine)

21. *Arctotis* × *hybrida* cv. (aurora daisy)

22. *Argemone platycerus* (crested poppy)

23. *Asclepias curassavica* (bloodflower)

24. *Atriplex hortensis* (orach)

25. *Begonia semperflorens* cv. (wax begonia)

26. *Bellis perennis* cv. (English daisy)

27. *Brachycome iberidifolia* (Swan River daisy)

28. *Brassica* (ornamental kale)

29. *Briza maxima* (large quaking grass)

30. *Browallia speciosa* cv. (amethyst flower)

31. *Calceolaria* × *herbeo hybrida* cv. (slipper flower)

32. *Calendula officinalis* cv. (pot marigold)

33. *Callistephus chinensis* cv. (China aster)

34. *Callistephus chinensis* pompon cv. (China aster)

35. *Calonyction aculeatum* (moonflower)

36. *Campanula medium* cv. (Canterbury bell)

37. *Capsicum annuum* cv. (ornamental pepper)

38. *Catananche caerulea* (Cupid's dart)

39. *Catharanthus rosea* cv. (Madagascar periwinkle)

40. *Celosia argenta cristata* coxcomb cv.

41. *Celosia argenta plumosa* cv. (Prince of Wales feathers)

42. *Centaurea cyanus* cv. (cornflower)

43. *Centranthus ruber* (red valerian)

44. *Cherianthus cheiri* double-flowered cv. (wallflower)

45. *Chrysanthemum carinatum* cv. (painted daisy)

46. *Clarkia concinna* cv.

47. *Cleome hasslerana* (spider flower)

48. *Clianthus formosus* (Sturt's desert pea)

49. *Cobaea scandens* (cup and saucer vine)

50. *Coix lachryma-jobi* (Job's tears)

51. *Coleus × hybridus* cv. (painted nettle)

52. *Consolida ajacis* (annual larkspur)

53. *Convolvulus tricolor* cv. (dwarf convolvulus)

54. *Coreopsis tinctoria* cv. (tickseed)

55. *Cosmos bipinnatus* cv. (cosmea)

56 *Cosmos sulphureus* cv. (yellow cosmos)

57. *Cucurbita pepo ovifera* (male and female) (gourd)

58. *Cuphea ignea* (cigar plant)

59. *Cyclamen persicum* cv.

60. *Dahlia* cv. (bedding form)

61. *Datura metel* (angel's trumpet) (plus fruits)

62. *Delphinium elatum* × *grandiflorum* cv.

63. *Dianthus barbatus* (sweet william) cv.

64. *Dianthus chinensis* cv. (Indian-China pink)

65. *Dianthus caryophyllus* cv. (Chabaud carnation)

66. *Diascia barberae* (twinspur)

67. *Digitalis purpurea* cv. (foxglove)

68. *Dimorphotheca aurantiaca* cv. (star-of-the-veldt)

69. *Dorotheanthus bellidiformis* (Livingstone daisy)

70. *Echinacea purpurea* (purple cone-flower)

71. *Emilia javanica* (Cupid's paintbrush)

72. *Eschscholtzia californica* cv. (Californian poppy)

73. *Euphorbia marginata* (snow-on-the-mountain)

74. *Exacum affine* cv. (Persian violet)

75. *Felicia amelloides* (blue marguerite)

76. *Freesia* × *hybrida* cvs

77. *Gaillardia* × *hybrida* (perennial) cv. (blanket flower)

78. *Gazania* × *hybrida* cv. (treasure flower)

79. *Gerbera jamesonii* (Transvaal daisy)

80. *Gilia tricolor* (bird's eye)

81. *Godetia amoena* cv. (satin flower)

82. *Gomphrena globosa* cv. (globe amaranth)

83. *Gypsophila elegans* cv. (chalk plant)

84. *Helianthus annuus* double-flowered cv. (sunflower)

85. *Helichrysum bracteatum* (strawflower)

86. *Heliotropium × hybrida* cv. (heliotrope-cherry pie)

87. *Helipterum floribundum* (paper daisy)

88. *Hibiscus moscheutos* cv. (rose mallow)

89. *Hunnemannia fumariifolia* (Mexican tulip poppy)

90. *Iberis amara* cv. (hyacinth candytuft)

91. *Iberis umbellata* cv. (candytuft)

92. *Impatiens balsamina* cv.

93. *Impatiens* New Guinea cv.

94. *Impatiens wallerana* cv.

95. *Impomoea violacea* (morning glory)

96. *Ipomopsis rubra* (skyrocket)

97. *Isatis tinctoria* (dyer's woad)

98. *Kochia scoparia* var. *triphylla* (burning bush)

99. *Lagurus ovatus* (hare's tail grass)

100. *Lathyrus odoratus* cv. (sweet pea)

101. *Lavatera trimestris* cv. (annual mallow)

102. *Leptosiphon hybridus* (stardust flower)

103. *Limnanthes douglasii* (poached egg flower)

104. *Limonium sinuatum* cvs (statice)

105. *Linanthus grandiflora* (mountain phlox)

106. *Linaria* × *hybrida* cv. (toad flax)

107. *Linum grandiflorum* (scarlet flax)

108. *Lisianthus russellianus* (prairie gentian)

109. *Lobelia erinus* cv.

110. *Lobularia maritima* cv. (sweet alyssum)

111. *Lobularia maritima* white cv. (sweet alyssum)

112. *Lonas inodora* (golden ageratum)

113. *Luffa cylindrica (aegyptiaca)* (loofah)

114. *Lunaria annua* (honesty)

115. *Lupinus* × *hybridus* (annual) cv. (lupin)

116. *Lychnis chalcedonica* (Maltese cross)

117. *Lythrum salicaria* (purple loosestrife)

118. *Machaeranthera tanacetifolia* (Tahoka daisy)

119. *Malcolmia maritima* (Virginia stock)

120. *Malope trifida* (mallow-wort)

121. *Matricaria eximia* (feverfew)

122. *Matthiola bicornis* cv. (night-scented stock)

123. *Matthiola incana* double-flowered cv. (stock)

124. *Maurandya barclaiana* (climbing penstemon)

125. *Mentzelia lindleyi* (blazing star)

126. *Mimosa pudica* (sensitive plant)

127. *Mimulus* × *hybridus* cv. (monkey flower)

128. *Mirabilis jalapa* (marvel of Peru)

129. *Moluccella laevis* (Irish bells)

130. *Momordica charantia* (balsam pear)

131. *Myosotis sylvatica* cv. (forget-me-not)

132. *Nemesia strumosa* cv.

133. *Nemophila menziesii* (baby blue eyes)

134. *Nicandra physalodes violacea* (shoo-fly plant)

135. *Nicotiana* × *hybrida* cv. (flowering tobacco)

136. *Nierembergia hippomanica* cv. (blue cup flower)

137. *Nigella damascena* cv. (love-in-the-mist)

138. *Nolana paradoxa* (Chilean bell-flower)

139. *Ocimum basilicum* purple-form cv. (ornamental basil)

140. *Oenothera missouriensis* (evening primrose)

141. *Onopordum bracteatum* (scotch thistle)

142. *Osteospermum fruticosum* cv. (veldt daisy)

143. *Papaver nudicaule* cv. (Iceland poppy)

144. *Pelargonium* × *hortorum* cv. (geranium)

145. *Penstemon* × *gloxinoides* cv. (bearded tongue)

146. *Perilla frutescens crispa lacinata*

147. *Petunia* × *hybrida* double-form cv

148. *Petunia* × *hybrida* single-flowered cv.

149. *Phacelia tanacetifolia* (wild heliotrope)

150. *Phlox drummondii* cv.

151. *Phlox drummondii* stellaris cv

152. *Physalis alkekengi* (Chinese lantern)

153. *Platycodon grandiflorum* (balloon flower)

154. *Portulaca grandiflora* cvs (sun plant)

155. *Primula malacoides* cv. (fairy primrose)

156. *Primula* × *polyantha* cv. (polyanthus)

157. *Pyrethrum ptarmicaeflorum*

158. *Pyrethrum roseum* cv.

159. *Ranunculus asiaticus* cv. (turban buttercup)

160. *Ratabida columnaris* (red Mexican hat)

161. *Reseda odorata* cv. (mignonette)

162. *Ricinus communis* (castor oil plant)

163. *Rudbeckia hirta* cv. (black-eyed Susan)

164. *Salpiglossus sinuata* cv. (painted tongue)

165. *Salvia splendens* cv. (scarlet sage)

166. *Salvia spendens* purple cv.

167. *Sanvitalia procumbens* (creeping zinnia)

168. *Scabiosa atropurpurea* cvs (pincushion flower)

169. *Schizanthus pinnatus* cv. (poor man's orchid)

170. *Senecio bicolor* cv. (dusty miller)

171. *Senecio* × *hybridus* cv. (florists' cineraria)

172. *Silene coeli-rosa* cv. (rose of heaven)

173. *Stylomecon heterophylla* (wind poppy)

174. *Tagetes erecta* (African marigold) cv.

175. *Tagetes erecta* (African marigold) white cv.

176. *Tagetes patula* (French marigold cv.)

177. *Tagetes tenuifolia* cv. (signet-fine leaved marigold)

178. *Thunbergia alata* (black-eyed Susan)

179. *Thymophylla tenuiloba* (Dahlberg daisy)

180. *Tithonia rotundifolia* cv. (Mexican sunflower)

181. *Torenia fournieri* (wishbone flower)

182. *Trachelium coeruleum* (throatwort)

183. *Trachymene coeruleus* (blue-lace flower)

184. *Tropaeolum majus* cv. (nasturtium)

185. *Ursinia anethoides* (jewel-of-the-veldt)

186. *Venedium fastuosum* (monarch-of-the-veldt)

187. *Verbascum longifolia* (mullein)

188. *Verbena* × *hybrida* cv. (vervain)

189. *Viola* × *wittrockiana* cv. (pansy)

190. *Xeranthemum annuum* (immortelle)

191. *Zea mays* (showing silks) (corn)

192. *Zinnia* × *hybrida* cv.

Even the silvery-green buds are attractive. The flowers can be used for dried flower arrangements.

Catananches will succeed in a dry sandy soil and sunny location. The plants will need supporting as wind can knock them around. Cut back the flowering stems once flowering has finished.

Propagation: Sow the seeds thinly in seed compost containers, using a damp, recommended seed raising compost, under glass from late winter to early summer, at 14–18°C (57–64°F).

Cover the seeds with clean sharp sand, compost or vermiculite, 6 mm (0.2 in) deep. Gently firm the seeds and compost. Gently water the compost, keeping it pleasantly moist. Seeds can take 7–28 days to germinate.

Prick out seedlings, when large enough to handle, into small pots of damp, recommended, potting compost. Grow them on, harden them off if necessary in a cold frame and plant them out where they are to grow and flower.

Or you can sow seeds directly into a prepared seedbed, choosing a sunny or partially shaded site.

Dig over and break down the soil into a fine tilth. Firm the soil gently to take the seeds. Plant the seeds in drills and cover them with a 6 mm (0.2 in) depth of compost or vermiculite. Gently firm the soil using the head of the rake or a board.

Water the soil gently but thoroughly, and keep it pleasantly moist until the seeds germinate. Then water the seedlings when they need it. Transplant the seedlings, 250–300 mm (10–12 in) apart, into a sunny location.

In English gardens sow the seeds in seed compost, under glass, late winter-early spring (Feb-March), at 13–18°C (55–64°F). Prick out seedlings into small pots of potting compost and treat as half-hardy plants. They flower outside early summer on.

Pests and diseases: Slugs and snails.

Cultivars/varieties: Species as above.

Family: Asteraceae.

Catharanthus **(Madagascar periwinkle)** The tropical *Catharanthus rosea* (syn. *Vinca rosea*); height 150–600 mm (6–24 in); is a spring-summer blooming perennial.

It has 25–50 mm (1–2 in) wide, 5 aeroplane-propellor petalled flowers in pink or white, some having a deeper colour centre-eye.

Its oblong egg-shaped, blunt pointed leaves are dark and glossy green.

Catharanthus prefers a free draining soil and sunny site. Keep the plants well watered when they are growing well.

Feed with a well-balanced, liquid, soluble, flower fertiliser, suitable for these plants, and applied as the manufacturer instructs.

C. rosea is treated as a bedding annual now that better cultivars, with their mass of flowers, are available.

Propagation: Sow the seeds thinly at compost level, in seed compost containers, using a damp, recommended, seed raising compost; autumn, subtropical areas; spring elsewhere; under glass if necessary, at 19–21°C (65–70°F).

Keep the seeds close to compost surface level as sowing too deeply can hinder germination. Seeds usually germinate within 7–21 days. Mist water the seeds gently using a fine spray, keeping the compost and future seedlings pleasantly moist.

Prick out seedlings into containers, and from there into pots, of damp, recommended, potting compost. Harden off the seedlings, if necessary in a cold frame, and plant them out directly where they are to grow and flower, 200–250 mm (8–10 in) apart, when all danger from frost is past and the ground has warmed up.

In English gardens sow the seeds in containers of seed compost, under glass late winter (Feb) at 19–21°C (65–70°F), and treat as half-hardy plants. They flower in summer.

Pests and diseases: Reasonably free.

Cultivars/varieties: Species as above. Little Mixed (five colour mix). Magic Carpet Mixed, prostrate, brilliant colour mix. Mixed Colours, height 300 mm (12 in), white, rose, white with crimson. 'Polka Dot', 200 mm (8 in), white, cherry red 'eye'.

Family: Apocynaceae.

Celosia **(cockscomb, Prince of Wales' feathers)** Cultivars of the summer flowering, warm-season, tropical Asian, annual *Celosia argentea*; height 300–600 mm (12–24 in) depending on cultivar; have been developed to produce brilliant flowers in red or yellow, shades and tints.

C. a. cristata has 75–150 mm (3–6 in) long, rippled, velvety, cockerel-combs, above light green, narrow egg-shaped, sharply-pointed leaves.

C. a. plumosa (syn. *C. a. pyramidalis*), has 75–125 mm (3–5 in) tall flower plumes, like miniature pampas grass plumes, borne above mid-green, egg-shaped, sharply-pointed leaves.

Celosias grow in most good garden soils, but prefer a well-drained sandy loam, rich in organic material, in a sunny, sheltered position.

Be careful when watering celosias, as indiscriminate flooding spoils the flower combs and plumes, and excess moisture around the roots causes rot.

Propagation: Sow the seeds thinly, 6 mm (0.2 in) deep, in seed compost containers, using a damp, recommended, seed raising compost; winter-spring subtropical areas; in late winter-spring-early summer, temperate areas; spring, cool areas; under glass, where necessary, at 18–24°C (64–75°F).

Germination can occur in 10–21 days. Prick out the seedlings into small pots of damp, recommended potting compost, and grow them on at 16°C (61°F). Pot them on into 125 mm (5 in) pots of damp, recommended, potting compost. Keep them in a warm, buoyant ventilation, with adequate shade during hot weather.

Harden off those seedlings destined for planting outside, if necessary in a cold frame, and space them out directly where they are to grow and flower, 225–300 mm (9–12 in) apart according to cultivar, when all danger from frost is past and the weather has warmed up. Remember that celosias are tropical plants.

Or seeds can be sown directly where they are to grow and flower, when all danger from frost risk is past. Thin out as required.

In English gardens sow the seeds in seed compost containers of seed raising compost in late winter-mid spring (Feb-April), under glass, at 18–24°C (64–75°F), and treat them as half-hardy plants. They flower mid summer on.

Pests and diseases: Foot and root rot.

Cultivars/varieties: Apricot Brandy, height 450 mm (18 in), apricot-orange plumes. Cockscomb Coral Garden Mixed, height 250 mm (10 in), rose, red, yellow, orange. Cristata Prize Strain (cockscomb), brilliant, varied selection. Fairy Fountains Mixed, 300 mm (12 in), light pink, salmon, scarlet, yellow golden plumes. Kewpie Red, Extra-Dwarf. Kewpie Yellow. Pampas Plume Mixed, height 600 mm (2 ft), red, yellow. Tall Golden Triumph, 900 mm (36 in). There are more.

Family: Amaranthaceae.

Centaurea **(cornflower, sweet sultan)** The southeastern European summer-flowering, annual cornflower of British cornfields, *Centaurea cyanus*; height 225–900 mm (9–36 in); has been developed to produce many sparkling hybrids.

The 25–50 mm (1–2 in) wide flowers are available in shades and tints of white, pink, red, blue and blue-purple. There is also a cultivar that has the same colours, but its petals are tipped with white. Examine each petal of a cornflower and you will find that it opens up into its own little flower.

The florists' cornflowers are, usually, the taller blue hybrids; 600–900 mm (24–36 in). The compact dwarf cornflowers, 225–300 mm (9–12 in) tall, are used for bedding and pot work. But both can be used for either cut flowers or bedding.

Cornflowers, although they do well in temperate areas such as Adelaide, seem to thrive better in cooler areas.

The oriental, sweetly scented annual sweet sultan, *C. moschata*, is also grown, and is available in white, yellow, pink or purple.

Perennial cornflowers are also grown, and none is more spectacular than the Caucasian cornflower, *C. dealbata*, with its tight, brilliant, pink flowers, 50–75 mm (2–3 in) wide.

Cornflowers grow well in a well-drained, ordinary, fertile, garden soil.

Propagation: Dig over the soil, when it is easy to work, breaking it down into a fine tilth. Gently but thoroughly firm the soil ready to take the seeds. Cornflowers do not take transplantation well and are therefore best sown directly where they are to grow and flower.

Thinly sow the seeds of *C. cyanus* either broadcast or in drills, 3 mm (0.1 in) deep; autumn-early winter subtropical areas; late summer-autumn temperate areas; late summer-mid autumn or early spring in cold areas.

Gently press the seeds to anchor them to the soil. Gently water the seeds using a fine spray. Germination should take place within 14 days.

Thin out the seedlings as soon as feasible, 225–300 mm (9–12 in) apart, taking great care not to disturb the roots of those left behind. Gently water those seedlings left in the ground to settle the roots.

Or a few seeds can be sown in patches throughout the border, keeping only the strongest seedlings.

Seeds can also be sown indoors in good light in small pots, using damp, recommended, seed raising compost, say 6 weeks before your normal planting out time. Thin out the seedlings keeping only the strongest in each pot. Harden them off, and plant them outside when all danger from frost is past.

Water the plants during dry weather. Feed them once the buds have formed with a weak solution of a well-balanced, liquid, soluble, flower fertiliser, suitable for cornflowers.

Keep down weeds, but remember the roots

of the cornflower are susceptible to damage and they will quickly wilt and die if disturbed unnecessarily. The plants may have to be supported in windy areas.

In English gardens sow the seeds of annual cornflowers in early autumn or early mid-spring, (Sept or March-April), directly where they are to grow and flower. Flowers early summer, and on.

Pests and diseases: Snails.

Cultivars/varieties: 'Blue Boy', double, bright cornflower blue. 'Blue Diadem', height 600 mm (2 ft), intense, deep blue. Double Mixed, pink, red, dark red, blue. 'Florists' Blue', height 900 mm (3 ft), double, cornflower blue. 'Frosty', height 600–750 mm (2–2.5 ft), pink, crimson, purple, blue, tipped with silver-white. Polka Dot Mixed, height 400 mm (16 in), double blooms.

Family: Asteraceae.

***Centranthus* (red valerian)** The Mediterranean, summer-flowering (although it can be late-spring to autumn) *Centranthus ruber* (syn. *Kentranthus ruber*); height 450–900 mm (18–36 in); is the best known of the valerians.

The long-lasting, small explosion of bright-pink, or red, 'twinkly', long-tubed, 6 mm (0.2 in) flowers, borne on 600 mm (24 in) stems, are attractive.

The blue-grey-green, narrow, egg-shaped, sharply-pointed leaves are borne opposite each other on the stem. But some find the smell of bruised or damaged leaves unattractive. To me the smell is bland.

The name 'centranthus' means 'spur-flower' and on examination you will see that the 'spur' is longer than the flower ovary.

Red valerian will thrive in most soils, indeed it is so adaptable that many dismiss it as a weed, particularly when they see it growing out of wall cracks. But it seems to do better in a neutral or limy (alkaline), well drained garden soil.

Propagation: Thinly sow the seeds, in spring, in seed compost containers, using a damp, recommended seed raising compost.

Prick out the seedlings, when large enough to handle, into 75 mm (3 in) pots of damp, recommended potting compost, and transplant them, once established, directly where they are to grow and flower.

Or the seeds can be sown directly where they are to grow and flower. Thin out the seedlings, or transplant them when they are very small, as red valerians dislike being transplanted when older.

Plant, or thin out, 300 mm (12 in) apart.

In English gardens sow the seeds in seed compost containers, mid-spring (April-June), and place the containers in a cold frame. Prick out the seedlings into 75 mm (3 in) pots of potting compost, harden them off, and plunge them outside. Or sow the seeds directly where they are to grow and flower; or in a nursery seedbed, and then transplant later. Young potted seedlings may need protecting over-winter. Flowers appear early summer and on.

Pests and diseases: Reasonably free.

Cultivars/varieties: Various red and white vars and cvs.

Family: Valerianaceae.

***Cheiranthus* (wallflower)** The southern European *Chieranthus cheiri*; height 200–450 mm (8–18 in); although often treated as a biennial, is a short-lived perennial. In warm areas of Australia it is treated as an annual.

The sweet, penetratingly-scented, winter or spring wallflowers, with blooms 25 mm (1 in) wide, can be single-petalled or double-petalled, the double-petalled flowers looking like upright spikes of double stocks.

Blooms are yellow, gold, orange, pink, blood-red, mauve or chocolate, or shades and tints of these colours. And of these the 'golden bedder' forms are most popular, although the blood-reds seem to be more fragrant.

Wallflowers are used for bedding, border, cut flowers and rockeries.

They flower late winter-spring, although the flowering period can be extended to summer and autumn in clement climates. They are 'cabbage family' plants, preferring a well-drained, slightly acid to slightly alkaline, but not too acid soil, and a sunny location.

Seedlings growing in severe frost areas can suffer from 'winter kill' and need protection during winter. But sensibly ventilate the frame when the outside temperature goes above freezing point, 0°C (32°F).

Feed them, once the flower buds have formed, with a weak solution of a well-balanced, soluble, liquid, flower fertiliser, suitable for wallflowers and follow the instructions.

C. allionii (syn. *Erismum*), the Siberian wallflower, is also grown for its later, orange or golden flowers.

Propagation: Sow seeds, 6–9 mm (0.2–0.4 in) deep, in a nursery seedbed; late summer-autumn subtropical areas; summer-autumn temperate areas; and late summer cool areas.

Germination occurs in approximately 7 days. Thin out the seedlings 50 mm (2 in) apart when large enough to handle, and gently firm soil around their roots.

Transplant them into their final quarters when they are 37–50 mm (1.5–2 in) tall, and the site has been prepared to receive wallflowers. But lift them using a garden trowel as this removes a root-ball around the sensitive roots, and transfer the whole into a scooped-out hole.

Gently water in the seedlings, and pay particular attention to their watering to get them established.

Or sow seeds, 10 mm (0.5 in) deep, in containers of seed raising compost. The seeds will germinate within 5–10 days. Prick out the seedlings into deep boxes of damp, recommended, potting compost, and grow them on. Transfer them to their permanent quarters 200–300 mm (8–12 in) apart. Flowers appear approximately 24 weeks from sowing.

In English gardens sow seeds in late spring-summer (May-June), into nursery-bed drills 6–9 mm (0.2–0.4 in) deep, the drills being 300 mm (12 in) apart. Thin out seedlings to 50 mm (2 in) apart. Gently firm the soil around the roots to settle them. Plant them out in autumn, directly where they are to grow and flower. Flowers mid spring, and on.

Pests and diseases: Root fly maggots, club root, various cabbage plant problems.

Cultivars/varieties: Early Flowered Gilded Giants. Early Flowering Russet Shades. Early Wonder Double Mixed. My Fair Lady, height 400 mm (16 in), burgundy, orange, purple. Paris Market, height 300–450 mm (12–18 in), mixed colours. Bedding Mixture, height 300 mm (12 in), primrose, gold, orange, scarlet.

Family: Brassicaceae.

Chrysanthemum There are many chrysanthemums that can be grown from seed.

The Mediterranean *Chrysanthemum carinatum* (syn. *C. tricolor*), painted daisy; height 600 mm (24 in); is an erect plant bearing summer blooms 60–75 mm (2.4–3 in) wide, with blackish-purplish-mauve centre discs, surrounded by 'outer-space' zoned bands of differing colours: white, yellow, pink, red, and so on.

Space the plants 300 mm (12 in) apart. Painted daisies prefer a sunny, sheltered spot or light shade, and a rich organic, fertile soil.

The Mediterranean *C. coronarium*, crown daisy; 300 mm–1.2 m (12–47 in) tall; a strongly-scented plant, has summer-flowering 37–50 mm (1.5–2 in) wide, single, semi or double white or yellow flowers surmounting light-green foliage. Space 375 mm (15 in) apart.

C. paludosum, a European chrysanthemum; height 300 mm (12 in); is a grey-leaved plant with single, summer-flowering, 25 mm (1 in) wide, white flowers. Space 225 mm (9 in) apart.

C. × *spectabile* is a 1–1.2 m (39–47 in) tall hybrid between *C. carinatum* and *C. coronarium*. Mostly single flowers with yellow centre disc, then a band of yellow, then a band of white. Space 450 mm (18 in) apart.

A small, yellow-flowered chrysanthemum cultivar known as *C.* 'Goblin' is becoming a popular spring pot or bedding plant.

C. parthenium (see *Matricaria eximia*).

Propagation of annuals: Thinly sow the seeds, 5 mm (0.2 in) deep, in seed compost containers, using a damp, recommended, seed raising compost; winter-spring subtropical areas; late winter-early spring temperate areas; spring-early summer cold areas; under glass if necessary, at 13–20°C (55–68°F).

Plants germinate in 5–18 days at 20°C (68°F). Prick out the seedlings, when large enough to handle, into containers of damp, recommended, potting compost. Harden them off, if necessary in a cold frame, ready to be planted out when all danger from frost is past and the ground has warmed up.

Or sow the seeds; early-late spring temperate areas; early summer cold areas, once the soil is warm and frost-free; directly where they are to grow and flower. Barely cover the seeds with sand, compost or vermiculite, 5 mm (0.2 in) deep. Thin out the seedlings 300 mm (12 in) apart.

Water the plants in dry spells, and feed them with a well-balanced, liquid, soluble, flower fertiliser suitable for these plants and applied as the manufacturer instructs.

In English gardens sow *C. carinatum* seeds in spring, once the soil has warmed up, directly where they are to flower, and thin out to correct spacing. Or sow seeds in seed compost, under glass, late winter (Feb), at 13–20°C (55–68°F), and treat seedlings as half-hardy plants. Flowers summer.

Pests and diseases: Many insects and diseases attack chrysanthemums.

Cultivars/varieties: 'Goblin', height: prostrate to 300 mm (12 in), yellow. *C. paludosum*, height 375 mm (15 in), white. Tricolor Daisy Mixed, height 600–900 mm (2–3 ft).

Family: Asteraceae.

***Clarkia* (clarkia; syn. *Godetia*, satin flower)** These colourful, slender-stemmed, leafy, hardy annuals, which can flower anytime between late spring and winter, are native to the U.S.A.

Although clarkias and godetias look different, both have been classified in certain countries, such as the U.S.A., as clarkias.

Because clarkias and godetias are United States native plants, I have decided to include them under the one section, although you may find *Clarkia* and *Godetia* listed separately in catalogues and on seed packets.

Several *Clarkia* species are grown in our gardens:

C. amoena (syn. *Godetia amoena*), satin flower; height 600–1 m (24–39 in); cup-like flowers.

C. amoena whitneyi (syn. *C. grandiflora; Godetia amoena whitneyi; G. grandiflora*); height 225–375 mm (9–15 in). Flower width 50–100 mm (2–4 in).

C. concinna (syn. *Eucharidium concinna*); height 600 mm (24 in); feathery flowers.

C. unguiculata (syn. *C. elegans*); height 600 mm (24 in); 'double stock' flower clusters.

C. pulchella; height 450 mm (18 in); frilly flowers; white, pink, red, lavender or purplish blooms.

The flower spikes vary in height from 225 mm–1 m (9–39 in). Flower width also varies between species, mostly 25–50 mm (1–2 in); some godetias, 50–100 mm (2–4 in).

Clarkias succeed well in sunny, ordinary, even poor, light, well-drained, but not dry soils. They dislike very hot summers.

Some gardeners grow clarkias under glass earlier in the year to get them into flower before the very hot weather. But be wary of the hot snaps and its effect on plants under glass. The glass may have to be shaded. We can experience very high temperatures in early spring, even in temperate areas.

Quick-acting nitrogenous, leaf-promoting fertiliser, in excess, could be detrimental to clarkias-godetias. They also suffer from wind damage, and may have to be supported.

Keep the plants free of weeds, but remember that they are surface-rooting, and any heavy-handed hoeing, or strenuous hand-tugging, can cause the plants to wilt and die.

Propagation (Clarkia and Godetia): Thinly sow the seeds, 5–8 mm (0.2–0.3 in) deep; late summer-autumn-winter in warm areas for winter-spring flowers; late summer-autumn or early spring in temperate areas; spring in cold areas when all danger from frost is past; directly where the plants are to grow and flower.

Thin out the seedlings very carefully as they resent root disturbance. They don't particularly like transplantation either.

Having said that, for the purpose of this book, I sowed *Clarkia* and *Godetia* seeds in punnets, and transplanted them into thumb pots of potting compost, when tiny, but easy enough to handle, and every seedling survived and grew exceedingly well. But I do not recommend this practice as the norm.

Clarkia/Godetia seeds germinate between 5–21 days at 20°C (68°F). Mine took 8 days *(Clarkia)* and 7 days *(Godetia)*.

Clarkias prefer a sunny site, but not direct, hot sunlight. Fork over the garden soil, breaking it up, and then rake it into a fine tilth, removing debris and weeds. Gently, but firmly, press the soil to take the seeds.

Thinly sow the seeds over the prepared soil in drills (rows) or broadcast fashion. Rake over the seeded area gently, just burying the seeds. Gently press the soil to anchor them.

Water the seeds gently, but copiously, using a fine spray. Keep the surface and seeds pleasantly moist until germination, and then water the seedlings as needed.

Thin out the seedlings 100–150–300 mm (4–6–12 in) apart, according to species or cultivar.

Clarkias can be grown as pot plants. Sow a few seeds into pots of damp, recommended, seed raising compost, and thin out the seedlings, eventually keeping only the best one in each pot.

In English gardens sow the seeds, early-mid spring (March-April), directly where they are to grow and flower, and thin out to the required distance. Flowers mid summer, and on.

Pests and diseases: Aphids, grey mould, foot and root rot, verticillium wilt.

Cultivars/varieties: Clarkia Double Mixed, height 900 mm (3 ft), pink, red, white. Clarkia Mixed Colours, height 600 mm (24 in), white, salmon, carmine, mauve, purple. *Clarkia* 'Pink Ribbons', height 600 mm (2 ft), deep rose feathery. Godetia Azalea Flowered Mixed, 400 mm (16 in), white, rose, lilac, rose, crimson, orange, some blotched. Godetia Dwarf Double Compact Mixed, height 300 mm (12 in). *Godetia* 'Grace F_1 Hybrid' Formula mixed colours, height 750 mm (30 in). *Godetia* 'Sybil Sherwood', height 450 mm (18 in), double, salmon pink, edged white. Godetia Squatters Mixed, height 300 mm (12 in), many blotched colours.

Family: Onagraceae.

Cleome (spider flower) The summer-autumn flowering, tropical American *Cleome hasslerana* (syn. *C. spinosa; C. pungens*); height 1–1.8 mm (39–71 in); has a 100–200 mm (4–8 in) wide cluster of white, white with a breath of pink, deeper pink or purplish spider flowers. Each of these flowers has a long, greenish-purplish tube, which protrudes well out from the petals. The flowers are short-lived, but are quickly replaced by others.

Cleomes have prickles on the stem and spiny thorns at the base of each mid-rich green, compound maple-like leaf; each leaf comprising 5–7 oblong pointed leaflets.

Not only is the flower unusual, but so is the habit of growth once the plants have reached maturity. They can produce spider-like branches, dripping with decorative seed-pods, and give the impression of weird creatures preparing to move menacingly across the garden.

Cleomes like a sheltered, well-drained, fertile soil in a sunny spot. They are fairly drought resistant.

Propagation: Thinly sow the seeds, barely covering them as they need light to germinate, in seed compost containers, using a damp, recommended seed raising compost, under glass, late winter-early spring, at 18–24°C (64–75°F).

Germination can take up to 18 days. Prick out the seedlings into 75 mm (3 in) pots of recommended potting compost, and then harden off the seedlings, if necessary in a cold frame, and plant them out into their permanent positions, 450–600 mm (18–24 in) apart, when all danger from frost is past and the ground has warmed up.

Or dig over the ground; late summer-autumn-late winter-early spring, subtropical areas; early spring, temperate areas; spring-summer, cold areas; and sow the seeds directly where the plants are to grow and flower, when all danger from frost is well past, at 20–24°C (68–75°F).

Break down the soil into a fine tilth, take out all the debris and weeds, and gently press the soil to firm it well enough to take the seeds.

'Station sow' a few seeds in clumps, or in drills (rows), or broadcast them. Barely rake in the seeds, hardly covering them. Press the soil to anchor them. Water gently but copiously using a fine spray. Thin out the seedlings 600 mm (24 in) apart. Or you can transplant them into other flowering quarters.

In English gardens sow the seeds under glass in early-mid spring (March-April), at 18–24°C (64–75°F), and treat them as half-hardy pot plants. Flowers mid summer, and on.

Pests and diseases: Aphids.

Cultivars/varieties: Formula Mixed. Various Mixed, height 900 mm (3 ft), white, pink, rose, purple.

Family: Capparidaceae/Capparaceae.

Clianthus (Sturt's pea, desert pea, glory pea) South Australia's State flower, *Clianthus formosus* (syn. *C. speciosus; C. dampieri*); height: clambering.

When gardeners see this frost-tender, glorious pea-flower thriving so effortlessly during winter-spring in the harsh areas of Australia they could be forgiven for thinking that the plant grows like a weed.

It is a silky plant with 9–15, or more, small grey, 10–30 mm (0.4–1.2 in) leaves, opposite each other on a prostrate or semi-erect stem. Although a perennial it is usually treated as an annual.

The 50–75 mm (2–3 in) tall scarlet flowers, pointed at the top (standard), and forked at the base (keels), with glossy black or brown protruding sightless, ball-like centre bosses, are held on short, hairy, erect stems like a snake rearing.

Sturt peas thrive in full sun. As they resent root disturbance remove any weeds near their roots very gently.

Propagation: Sturt peas can be sown in the garden where they are to flower, as they bitterly resent root disturbance, or grown as single plants in pots.

But first soak the seeds by pouring hot water over them, and then allowing the water to cool. Sow the seeds in spring-summer 3 mm (0.1 in) deep in the soil where they are to flower. Keep the seeds moist until they germinate, then water the plants when they need it.

Or sow the seeds singly in 75 mm (3 in) peat pots, using damp, neutral, sandy compost. Australian native plant gardeners go to great lengths to grow these plants successfully.

In English gardens sow the seeds singly in 75 mm (3 in) peat pots, of damp, neutral, seed raising compost, late-winter-early spring (Feb-March) at 16–20°C (61–68°F), potting on if necessary. Flowers spring-early summer.

Pests and diseases: Reasonably free.

Cultivars/varieties: Species as above.

Family: Fabaceae/Papilionaceae.

Cobaea (cup-and-saucer vine, cathedral bells) The Mexican *Cobaea scandens* is a vigorous, climbing plant; height 6–7.5 m (20–25 ft and more); but it is usually trained at a much lower height. It is an evergreen (or semi-evergreen), tendrilled, perennial plant, although many grow it as an annual.

Cobaea produces numerous 37–50 mm

(1.5-2 in) wide-mouth, 'cup-and-saucer', bell-shaped flowers. These are greeny-white tinged pink, to purple-green or mauvish, with stamens that seem to pour out of the flower.

The 62-100 mm (2.4-4 in) long leaves are deep-green, roughish-textured, and spring on opposite sides of the clambering stems. The hooked tendrils are extremely touch sensitive.

Cobaeas are suitable only for temperate or warmer areas as they can look scruffy during winter; even in Adelaide they can, sometimes, look a bit the worse for wear, but they do grow there.

Grow in a sunny, or partially shaded, sheltered, fairly poor soil as excessive, nitrogenous fertiliser produces very vigorous growth at the expense of flowers.

Cup-and-saucer vines can also be grown as pot plants, growing in 200-250-300 mm (8-10-12 in) pots, and trained up suitable trellis or wire frames.

Propagation: Sow ripe seeds in spring with the long edge downwards, leaving the top edge flush with soil, in containers of damp, recommended seed raising compost, and then grow under glass at 18-20°C (64-68°F).

Prick out the seedlings, when they are large enough to handle, into pots of damp, recommended, potting compost. Harden them off, if necessary in a cold frame, and plant them out directly where they are to flower and grow, 600 mm (24 in) apart, when any danger from frost is past and the ground has warmed up.

Or place two seeds, on edge, in individual 75 mm (3 in) pots of damp, recommended, seed raising compost, and once germinated, carefully remove the weakest seedling. Pot on the strong seedling as required.

In English gardens sow the seeds under glass in seed raising compost, at 18-20°C (64-68°F), in late winter-early mid spring (Feb-March-April), singly or two seeds, on edge, to a 75 mm (3 in) pot. Keep the strongest in each pot. Harden off the seedlings, and plant them out when all danger from frost is past and the ground has warmed up. Or grow them on as pot plants using large pots. Summer flowering.

Pests and diseases: Aphids, or a number of greenhouse pests.

Cultivars/varieties: Species as above.

Family: Polemoniaceae.

***Coix* (Job's tears)** The Chinese-East Indian *Coix lacryma-jobi*; height 600 mm-2.1 m (2-7 ft); is a strongly-rooted, coarsely broad-leaved (like sweet corn) grassy clump.

Gardeners grow it for the sprays of white, green, black-striped green, seed pods, that look like pointed peas, and which hang down along the stem in tear-like clusters; hence its common name. Job's tears likes a sunny site, and fertile soil.

Propagation: Soak the seeds the day prior to sowing them, so as to soften the hard seed testa.

Place seeds individually in pots of seed raising compost in late winter-spring, at 16-18°C (60-64°F), and grow them on. Transplant the seedlings into their permanent quarters, hardened off if necessary, when all danger from frost is past.

Seeds can also be sown outside in their growing quarters, when the danger of frost is passed and the soil has warmed up.

In English gardens sow the seeds late winter-early spring (Feb-March), under glass, individually in pots, at 16-18°C (60-64°F). Harden off the seedlings, and plant out when the danger from frost risk is past and the soil has warmed up. Seed heads appear midsummer on.

Pests and diseases: Reasonably free.

Cultivars/varieties: Species as above.

Family: Poaceae.

***Coleus* (flame nettle, painted nettle)** The Javanese *C.* × *hybridus (Coleus blumei)*; height 150-900 mm (6-36 in), but mostly 200-600 mm (8-24 in); is grown for its multi-coloured leaves. Its blueish flowers are insignificant, and not particularly wanted.

Coleus leaves can be had in various colour combinations: white, cream, yellow, orange, pink-maroon, red, purple, bronze or brown. A leaf can display 3 or 4 of the above colours, but most gardeners are satisfied with 2 distinct colours on a leaf.

The leaves can be egg-shaped pointed, or heart-shaped pointed, broad, squat-oval and pointed, medium width and pointed, or narrow, lancelike and pointed, with either deeply toothed, notched, scalloped or blunt-lobed edges.

Coleuses are perennial plants, but are usually treated as tender annuals.

They can also be trained as standards by 'legging' (removing) the side branches and leaves, leaving the main growing tip, and pinching out the flower buds, to produce a bare stem with a 'coma' of leaves at the top, like a palm tree.

You would use coleus cultivars that lend themselves to this type of treatment. The stem will need support.

Coleuses are frost sensitive and need to be grown under glass in cold areas, but can be planted outside provided all danger from frost is past and the ground has warmed up.

Their delicate foliage, however, is easily spoiled by rain, wind and hot sun, and the succulent shoots are damaged by heavy hands.

They make particularly useful shadehouse plants.

Pinch out any flower buds to prolong leaf formation.

Coleuses prefer a semi-shady site with good light, not hot sunlight, a rich soil, and ample moisture (not waterlogged) when they are growing well. Feed regularly, to keep the brilliance in the leaves, with a well-balanced, liquid, soluble, flower fertiliser, suitable for coleuses and applied as the manufacturer instructs.

Many cultivars are grown from cuttings, but excellent mixtures, strains, and separate colours are available from the seedsmen, some being 'self' lower-branching, ('extra-dwarf base branching'), thus, possibly, negating the need to pinch out the growing tips.

Propagation: Sow the fine seeds thinly, barely covering them with sieved compost or sand, in seed compost containers using a damp, recommended seed raising compost, under glass; winter-early spring in subtropical areas; spring to early summer elsewhere; at 20-24°C (68-75°F).

Place the container in a shallow dish of lukewarm water, and remove the container once the water barely glistens on the compost surface. Cover the container with a sheet of glass to retain the moisture, and place it in good light, but not direct sunlight.

Remove the glass once the seeds have germinated. Again place the container in a dish of water to water the minute seedlings. Alternatively, use a very, very fine mist spray, but take great care not to wash the seedlings out, which is easily done. Pay particular attention to watering coleuses as they soon dry out.

Germination should take place within 10-21 days. Keep the seedlings out of strong sunlight. Prick them out, when large enough to handle, into 75 mm (3 in) pots of damp, recommended potting compost, choosing the leaf colours you think are best.

Let them grow on, and then carefully pinch out the centre growing tip(s) (unless they are self-branching forms), when the plants have made a few inches growth, to encourage side-branching and bushier plants.

Pot them on into larger pots when they have outgrown their present ones. Keep the atmosphere warm and buoyant. They can be planted outside in the garden in a sheltered site when all danger from frost is past and the ground has warmed up, spacing them 250-300 mm (10-12 in) apart.

In English gardens sow the seeds mid winter-early spring (Jan-March), under glass at 20-24°C (68-75°F), and treat them as tender pot plants.

Pests and diseases: Caterpillars and other leaf eating insects, mosaic.

Cultivars/varieties: Blakehurst Mixed, formula of best sellers, especially for pot work. Fairway Mixed, height 200 mm (8 in). Fashion Parade Mixed, height 250 mm (10 in), brilliant colours. Rainbow Blend, 300 mm (12 in). Superfine Rainbow Mixed, height 300 mm (12 in). There are many more, including separate colours.

Family: Lamiaceae.

***Consolida* (larkspur)** The cultivars of the Mediterranean *Consolida ambigua* (syn. *Delphinium ajacis*), *Consolida regalis* (syn. *D. consolida*) and *Consolida orientalis*; height 300 mm-1.2 m (12-47 in); are neater, annual versions of the larger perennial delphinium.

Indeed, until recently they were known as delphiniums, and may still be called that in some catalogues.

Compact, upright spikes of star-shaped, tightly-knit single or double, 30 mm (1.2 in) flowers are produced in spring or summer, covering much of the slender stem in white, pink, rose, salmon, lilac-blue or violet. They are either branching or single column.

The lacy-feathery foliage droops down like pale-green hair from the stem nodes (knuckles). Larkspurs are useful plants for garden display and for cutting.

They do well in the temperate and cooler areas, but in the warm, moist north they suffer badly from fungus attacks, so be careful not to spray water indiscriminately over their vulnerable foliage.

Choose a sunny, sheltered site, and a well-drained, moderately fertile, neutral or slightly limy soil.

Feed larkspurs, when the buds appear, with a well-balanced, liquid, soluble, flower fertiliser, suitable for larkspurs and applied as the manufacturer instructs.

Be careful when weeding around larkspurs as they object to any root disturbance. The tall cultivars could need staking.

Remove dead blooms, and keep the seeds away from young children.

Propagation: Seeds can be sown; autumn-early winter in subtropical areas; late summer-autumn-early winter in temperate areas; or early spring in cold areas; directly where they are to grow and flower.

Fork over the ground breaking it down into a fine tilth, raking out weeds or debris, and firming it gently but thoroughly, ready to take the seeds.

Sow the seeds thinly in drills (rows), 3 mm (0.1 in) deep, directly where the plants are to grow and flower.

Or 'station sow' the seeds in clumps dotted over the garden area to produce small flower pools. Lightly rake the soil over the seeds and press down lightly, but firmly, to anchor them.

Water the seeds gently, but well, using a fine spray. Keep the seedbed and seedlings pleasantly moist, until the seedlings are well established, and then water the plants during dry spells.

The seeds germinate in 14–21 days, at 15–18°C (59–64°F), although I've had them germinate in 11 days at the higher temperature.

Thin out the seedlings 300–450 mm (12–18 in) apart; or as little as 200 mm (8 in) apart for the dwarf cultivars.

You could try transplanting any spare seedlings into another garden site, should you feel inclined. But only if they are very small and you are very careful. If you are prepared to take the chance, get the roots covered with the soil and gently watered in immediately. I have transplanted them with mixed-to-bad results.

Or you could try sowing a few seeds indoors in a cool spot, in individual 75 mm (3 in) peat-pots of damp, recommended, potting compost, say 6 to 8 weeks before the usual planting out time in your location. Thin out the seedlings keeping only the strongest in each pot.

In English gardens sow the seeds; early autumn (Sept) in mild winter areas; or early spring elsewhere (March); directly where they are to grow and flower, once the soil can be worked easily. Flowers appear early-mid summer.

Pests and diseases: Slugs, snails, aster yellows, bacterial bud rot, crown rot, stem rot, powdery mildew.

Cultivars/varieties: Double Dwarf Mixed, height 350 mm (14 in). Dwarf Hyacinth Flowered, height 300–380 mm (12–15 in), white, pink, salmon, lilac, violet, denim blue. Giant Regal Mixed, height 1 m (3 ft), white, rose lilac, carmine, scarlet, light blue, blue. Regal Strain Harlequin Mixed. Supreme, height 1–1.5 m (3–5 ft), good colour range.

Family: Ranunculaceae.

***Convolvulus* (dwarf-convolvulus)** The southern European *Convolvulus tricolor* (syn. *C. minor*); height 225–450 mm (9–18 in); is a late spring, and on, flowering annual.

It is a beautiful little plant, producing masses of fleeting, 37–50 mm (1.5–2 in) wide, trumpet-like blooms, each on its own little stem. Mostly, each trumpet has 3 colours (hence *tricolor*), in shades or tints of pink or blue, separated by a white band from the yellow throat; but there are white-flowered, yellow-throated flowers.

They make splendid pot plants, tub plants and hanging-basket specimens. Remove the spent flowers and seed pods regularly to keep the neat appearance of the plant. Do not confuse *C. tricolor* with the morning glory plant, *Ipomea* species.

Dwarf-convolvuluses prefer a sunny site and a fertile soil, but will manage in a poorer one. Water the plants well during dry spells and keep down any weeds, taking care not to disturb the dwarf-convolvulus's roots.

Feed them, once the flowering buds appear, with a well-balanced, liquid, soluble flower fertiliser, suitable for convolvuluses and applied as the manufacturer instructs.

Propagation: Soak the seeds overnight in warm water, and sow them late winter-spring in subtropical areas; spring in temperate areas; spring-early summer in cold areas. Sow them directly where they are to grow and flower, 8 mm (0.3 in) deep, and 300 mm (12 in) apart in drills (rows).

My last batch of convolvulus seeds germinated in 5 days in a warm temperature.

The seeds are more or less large enough to be handled singly, so you can place them accurately. Thin out the seedlings if they are crowding each other.

Or sow 2 or 3 seeds in individual 75 mm (3 in) peat pots of damp, recommended seed raising compost, keeping the strongest seedling in each pot and growing it on. Plant out seedlings pot and all.

Or the seeds can be sown in seed compost containers, under glass, early spring, at 18°C (64°F). Prick out the seedlings, when large enough to handle, into pots or containers of damp, recommended potting compost.

Harden off the plants, if necessary in a cold frame, and plant them out, 300 mm (12 in) apart, when all danger from frost is past and the soil has warmed up. Or use them as pot or hanging basket plants.

In English gardens sow the seeds under glass at 18°C (64°F), early spring, and treat them as half-hardy annuals. Or they can be sown early-mid spring (March-April), directly where they are to grow and flower. Flowers appear early summer, and on.

Pests and diseases: Reasonably free.

Cultivars/varieties: Species as above.

Family: Convolvulaceae.

***Coreopsis* (syn. *Calliopsis*) (tickseed)** *Coreopsis* species are late winter-mid spring, or spring-summer-autumn flowering North American annuals or perennials. Many species and cultivars can be grown from seed.

Coreopsis tinctoria (syn. *C. bicolor*); height 600–900 mm (24–36 in); has dark-green leaves and bears masses of 50 mm (2 in) wide flowers on stiffish stems, in yellow or 'blotch banded' variations of yellow to chestnut to mahogany-brown. There are dwarf (225 mm–9 in) cultivars of *C. tinctoria*, also with spectacular banding.

C. drummondii (syn. *C. basalis*); height 600 mm (24 in); has dark green leaves and bears masses of 50 mm (2 in) wide, bright-yellow flowers with a reddish-brown stain at the base of each petal, each flower having purplish-black centre discs.

C. grandiflora 'Sunray'; height 12–18 in; has 50–62 mm (2–2.4 in) wide, bright-yellow flowers.

Tickseeds like a neutral, light, well-drained, friable soil in a sunny location. Cut down the dead canes after flowering, for both annuals and perennials, to encourage future flowering.

Annual tickseeds will seed freely if the seed-cases are left on the plant, but is this desirable? The taller tickseeds have to be staked or supported in early growth, to prevent them flopping.

The spring-flowering, Californian-Mexican perennial *Coreopsis maritima* (syn. *Leptosyne maritima*) the sea dahlia; height 300–900 mm (12–36 in); is grown as an annual.

It has 100–125 mm (4–5 in) wide, yellow daisy-like flowers borne on 300–350 mm (12–14 in) stems above finely-divided, ferny foliage. Sea dahlias prefer a light, well-drained soil in a sunny location.

Propagation: Sow the seeds of annuals, or perennials treated as annuals; late summer-autumn-mid spring in subtropical areas; or autumn and early winter or spring in temperate areas; or spring in cold areas; when all danger of frost is past, 6 mm (0.2 in) deep, directly where they are to grow and flower. Firm the seeds with a board, or similar, to anchor them to the soil.

Keep the seedbed pleasantly moist. Pay particular attention to the plant's need for water.

Seeds will germinate in 8–21 days, depending on soil temperature. Thin out the seedlings 200–300 mm (8–12 in) apart, when large enough to handle easily.

Or for earlier flower, in cold areas, sow the seeds in seed compost containers, using a damp, recommended, seed raising compost, under glass, say 5 or 6 weeks before the last expected frost in your location.

The dwarf cultivars can also be grown as pot plants by sowing seeds in a damp, recommended, seed raising compost at 18°C (64°F) in autumn under glass. Plant 3 well-rooted seedlings into a 225 mm (9 in) pot and grow them on under cool-glass conditions.

Sow *C. maritima* seeds; autumn in subtropical and temperate areas; spring in cold areas; directly where the plants are to grow and flower, 6 mm (0.2 in) deep. Thin out the seedlings to 250–300 mm (10–12 in) apart. Seedlings should emerge in approximately 15 days, and flower in approximately 3 months.

In English gardens sow seeds of annuals in their permanent flowering quarters, early-late spring (April-May), once the weather begins to warm up. Sow perennial seeds in a prepared seedbed, mid spring (April). Transplant seedlings to a nursery holding-bed. Plant them out, mid-autumn (Oct), to directly where they are to grow and flower. Summer flowering.

Pests and diseases: Slugs, snails, leaf spot, rust, yellows.

Cultivars/varieties: Sunburst, height 750 mm (30 in), golden yellow; species as above.

Family: Asteraceae.

***Cosmos* (cosmos, cosmea)** The cultivars of the Mexican annual *Cosmos bipinnatus*; height 750 mm–1.20 m (30–47 in) or taller; usually flower summer and autumn. But mine sown under glass are in flower in mid-spring; temperate area with mild winters.

The 50–100 mm (2–4 in) wide, flattened, single or double dahlia-like flowers with ragged petal edges, can be had in white, pink, red, purple, or bicolor-edged with a deeper colour.

The flowers are borne at the top of the light-green, feathery foliage, which springs in opposite branchlets up the stem.

Cosmos sulphureus cultivars have petals with yellow or orange shades and tints. It is a coarser, darker-foliaged cosmea.

Cosmos prefers a sheltered, free-draining soil in a sunny spot. The taller cultivars may need staking.

Keep the plants well watered, but not flooded, as they are native to dry areas where they get occasional deep watering.

Weeding should be done with care. Cosmos makes a good cut flower. Dead-head (remove) the spent flowers to encourage further large blooms.

Feed the plants when the buds are forming with a well-balanced, liquid, soluble, flower fertiliser, suitable for cosmos and applied as the manufacturer instructs.

Propagation: Sow the seeds in nursery-beds, or directly where they are to grow and flower, and cover them with 6 mm (0.2 in) of sifted soil or sand.

Sow seeds mid winter-mid spring in subtropical areas; late winter early summer in temperate, mild winter areas; or mid-spring-early summer in colder areas, but only if the danger from frost is past and the ground has warmed up, as cosmos is frost-sensitive.

Seeds can be sown 2 to 3 weeks before normal spring sowing time, in seed compost containers using a damp, recommended, seed raising compost, under glass in a warm place, say 16°C (60°F), for earlier flowers.

Prick out the seedlings when large enough to handle into containers or small pots of damp, recommended potting compost. Harden them off, if necessary in a cold frame, and plant them out directly where they are to grow and flower, when any danger from frost is past and the ground has warmed up.

Thin out those seedlings sown in the flowering site, or transplant the seedlings from the nursery-bed, when large enough to handle, into their flowering site, to approx 250–600 mm (10–24 in) apart, depending on cultivar, but close enough to give each other physical support.

You can sow the seeds in drills (rows), or 'station sow' in clumps. 'Station sowing' means planting a few seeds in one spot, and then a few more at the next planting spot. Thin out the weakest and keep only the strongest plant at each station.

Seedlings should appear in approximately 21 days depending on soil temperature.

In English gardens sow the seeds under glass at 16–20°C (61–68°F), early-mid spring (March-April), and treat them as half-hardy annuals. In mild winters you can sow the seeds directly where they are to flower and grow, when all danger from frost is past and the ground has warmed up. Thin out to required distance apart. Flowers appear mid-summer on.

Pests and diseases: Aphids, bacterial wilt, leaf spot, powdery mildew.

Cultivars/varieties: Bright Lights, height 900 mm (3 ft), yellow, golden orange, scarlet orange. Candystripe, height 750 mm (30 in), flowers approximately 75 mm (3 in) wide; ice white or rose, petals bordered, splashed, stippled, with crimson. Polidor Mixed, height 750 mm (30 in), semi double flower, yellow, gold, orange, red. Sensation Mixed, height 1.2 m (4 ft), mostly pink, mauve, some white, red. Sunny Gold, height 500–900 mm (20–36 in), golden yellow double flowers.

Family: Asteraceae.

***Cucurbita* (gourds)** The half-hardy, tropical American annuals, *Cucurbita pepo* var. *ovifera*, small ornamental gourds, and *Lagenaria vulgaris* (syn. *L. leucantha*), large gourds, are grown for their decorative, dried fruits.

But gourds can be odd-looking fruits, some being 50 mm (2 in) in size, others being ridiculously large, 1.5 m (5 ft). They are a talking point among flower arrangers and, indeed, they are an art form, with books being devoted to them.

But you know, the large, golden-yellow, trumpet-funnel flowers are extremely lovely, and are often overlooked as a gourd-plant feature.

The leaves and habit are similar to a marrow or cucumber, and the plant can clamber to a height of 3–4 m (10–13 ft). It can also clamber over the ground, but the fruits can become deformed, and not so well coloured.

You can obtain large-fruited gourds, or small-fruited gourds, in apple shape, bottle shape, kidney shape, pear shape, warted, and so on.

Ornamental gourds prefer a warm, moist, well-drained, fertile soil in a sunny spot; not too hot a sun.

They need supporting with trellis, meshed column-supports, cone-frames, tripods or similar, as they are vigorous, tendrilled, clambering plants.

They can be grown as accent plants, if trained up garden-cone frames, garden-tripods or similar.

Propagation: Sow the seeds under glass (e.g. cold frame) in spring; late spring in cold areas; singly, 12 mm (0.5 in) deep, in pots of seed raising compost, as they are large seeds.

Seeds germinate in approximately 14–21 days at 21°C (70°F) soil temperature. Gourds grow rapidly so don't let them become pot-bound.

Harden off the seedlings and plant them out, 600 mm–1 m (24–39 in) apart, directly where they are to grow, flower and fruit, when all danger from frost is past, and the ground has warmed up.

Or sow seeds, late spring-early summer, when all danger from frost is past, outside directly where they are to grow and flower, in a sunny position. Cover the seeds shallowly only, with sieved soil or sand.

Keep the compost or soil just pleasantly moist.

Or sow 2 or 3 seeds directly where they are to grow and flower, when all danger from frost is past, and thin them out leaving the strongest seedling at each station. Gourds resent root disturbance.

Deep yellow flowers will be produced, either male or female. The female flowers have the little, bulbous bumps behind the flowers.

Cut off the fruits only when they have matured fully, and are hard-coated. Carefully clean them up, and let them dry.

In English gardens sow the seeds under glass in a greenhouse; early spring (March); or in a cold frame mid-late spring (April-May); individually in 75 mm (3 in) pots of seed raising compost, and grow them on. Pot on into larger pots, but only if the roots have outgrown their present pots. Do this carefully as the roots resent disturbance. Plant out in the garden, properly hardened off, when all danger from frost is past and the ground has warmed up. Pick fruits when matured.

Or sow the seeds in their flowering site outdoors, late spring-early summer (May-June), if all danger from frost is past.

Pests and diseases: Caterpillars, mildew.

Cultivars/varieties: Species as above; Bottle or Pre-History Gourd; Carving and Container Collection; Small or Large Mixed.

Family: Cucurbitaceae.

***Cuphea* (small cigar plant, cigar flower)** The spring-summer-autumn flowering, evergreen, Mexican *Cuphea ignea*; height 300–600 mm (12–24 in); is called the cigar plant because the 19–25 mm (0.7–1 in) long, by 4 mm (0.2 in) wide, flaming-red, tubular, flowers, borne singly on their own little stem, are tipped with 'cigar ash', or otherwise purplish-black and white, papery tissue that looks like cigar ash.

C. ignea is an attractive shrub, with satin-smooth, mid-green, 37 mm (1.5 in) long, oval, pointed leaves.

Although cigar plants succeed in temperate, mild winter conditions, they are severely cut back by frosts. Therefore, they could be grown under glass as 'annual' pot plants in severe frost areas. They are also grown as pot plants in other areas.

Cigar plants prefer an open, well-drained, fertile soil in full sun, or a little shade.

Give cigar plants ample moisture, and feed them when the buds form with a well-balanced, liquid, soluble fertiliser, suitable for cigar plants and applied as the manufacturer instructs.

Propagation: Sow the seeds in seed compost containers, under glass, using damp, recommended, seed raising compost, in mid-winter, temperate and cool areas, at 21°C (70°F).

Gently press the seeds on to the compost to anchor them. Gently mist water using a fine spray, keeping the compost just pleasantly moist. The seeds germinate in approximately 15 days.

Prick out the seedlings into containers of damp, recommended, potting compost, and from there into 75 mm (3 in) pots, and then harden them off in a cold frame.

Plant them out directly where they are to grow and flower, when all danger from frost is past and the soil has warmed up. Space the seedlings 200–300 mm (8–12 in) apart.

If they are to be grown as pot plants, then pot the seedlings on into 125 mm (5 in) pots of damp, recommended, potting compost; and wider pots, if necessary.

Eventually, the bushes become littered with hundreds of small, scarlet, tubular flowers smoking away like mad.

In English gardens sow the seeds in seed raising compost, mid-late winter (Jan-Feb), at 21°C (70°F), and treat them as tender pot plants. Pot first into 75 mm (3 in) pots, then 125 mm (5 in) pots, and then 175 mm (7 in) pots. Flowers mid spring, and on.

Pests and diseases: Reasonably free.

Cultivars/varieties: Species as above.

Family: Lythraceae.

Cyclamen The florists' cyclamen, *Cyclamen persicum*, has fascinating, 'swept-back', pink-nosed flowers with either smooth-edged, or fimbriated (fringed) edged petals, each flower on its own stem, with some cultivars having filagreed, marbled, silver leaves.

The colours range in shades and tints, from white through to pink and purple; some are bicoloured. Some flowers are fragrant.

Half-hardy cyclamen can be grown in bush-houses in warm temperate and subtropical areas, provided the plants are kept cool and moist.

Cyclamen thrive in an open, slightly acid, well-drained soil, rich in organic matter, shaded from hot sun and sheltered from strong winds, hot or cold.

It may surprise gardeners to know that

cyclamen are members of the primrose family.
Propagation: Place the seeds of *C. persicum* in rows, each seed 25 mm (1 in) apart, in seed compost containers, using a damp, recommended, seed raising compost, under glass, late summer-autumn, at 16–18°C (50–65°F). Or you can use pots.

Make sure the compost has been thoroughly dampened and drained, but is still moist, before you plant the seeds. The trays or pots must be deep enough to take the compost, plus a 25 mm (1 in) depth of granulated peat.

Press the seeds individually into the damp compost, as they are large enough to handle easily, to a depth of 3 mm (0.1 in). The seeds, in turn, are covered by a 25 mm (1 in) layer of damp, granulated peat to help prevent them drying out.

The compost is watered and the box covered with a sheet of glass and a sheet of newspaper, or cover seeds and container with aluminium foil. Constantly check on the seeds to make sure that the compost is not drying out, and to discover if they are germinating.

The seeds can be watered from below by standing the container in water until the compost surface is damp, and then letting the surplus moisture drain off. They must not be allowed to dry out. Patience is required when growing cyclamen.

Remove the glass, newspaper, peat or aluminium foil once germination occurs. Prick out the seedlings, when they have made one leaf, into seed trays filled with damp, recommended, potting compost, increasing the spacing to 75 mm (3 in) apart, making sure that the roots are below ground in the compost, but the tuber is just above ground.

Once a plant has made 4 leaves, transplant it singly into a 100 mm (4 in) pot of suitable damp, potting compost (John Innes No. 2 or equivalent), and grow it on at a temperature of 18°C (65°F), to encourage vegetative growth.

Take care when watering as any moisture on the leaves causes 'white-ring' staining.

Place the cyclamen in their flowering stations, say 200 mm (8 in) apart, and drop the temperature to 15.5°C (60°F) to encourage flowering.

In English gardens sow the seeds of *C. persicum* late summer-autumn, in seed compost containers using a damp recommended seed raising compost, spacing each seed 25 mm (1 in) apart. Check above for growing details.
Pests and diseases: Aphids, tarsonemid (cyclamen) mites, thrips, botrytis blight-grey mould; fusarium wilt, leaf spot, soft rot.
Cultivars/varieties: Amsterdam Giants, various single colours, or mixed. Giants of Aalsmeer Mixed, many colours. Miniature Fragrant Kaori Shades Mixed, marble marked leaves, various colours. New Wave F_1 Hybrid Mixture, soft waved flower edges. Silver Leaved Mixed, various colours. 'Victoria', height 250 mm (10 in), ruffled, pure white petals, with cherry red border and eyes. Fringed Mixed, fringed flowers.
Family: Primulaceae.

Dahlia There are many cultivars of the Central American dahlias seen in gardens, from the massive-headed decoratives to the exquisite, miniature pompons, all usually grown from cuttings.

But here we are more concerned with growing the 'annual', half-hardy, bedding forms of dahlia, 300–450 mm (12–18 in) tall, from seed. Although many seed forms can be used for pot work and cut flowers.

Bedding dahlias are relatively easy to grow, and make a bold, bright, splash in all colours, except true blue, in beds of their own. They can be either single or double flowered 50–75 mm (2–3 in) wide.

They like a sheltered, sunny site, and a neutral, well-drained, rich, organic soil, which has been dug deeply (spade-depth) to allow the subsoil to absorb moisture for the tuberous roots. A suitable fertiliser is added as the manufacturer instructs for dahlias, and dug in.

But if the ground has been heavily manured for a previous crop, then adding fertiliser may not be necessary, otherwise the plant will produce too much foliage and not enough flowers.

Dahlias, when budding and flowering, appreciate applications of a well-balanced, liquid, soluble fertiliser, suitable for dahlias, and applied as the manufacturer instructs. They also like ample water during hot weather.

Remember that young dahlia plants, and old for that matter, are susceptible to frost damage. It is a sobering sight to see dahlia plants as green as green one day, then black as charcoal the next.

You can take ripe seeds, before they have split and shed, from any dahlia. Dry off the seeds, store them in a cool, dry place, and grow them on the following 'dahlia year', anticipating with excitement the fantastic dahlias you will breed.

Indeed, some fine 'named' dahlias have been produced in this fashion. But don't bank on it, as the dahlia-world is littered with corpses of 'fantastic' dahlias.

But if you do breed a winner, then take great care of it, and propagate vegetatively in the correct manner, to ensure 'true to original cultivar' dahlias.

Your dahlia seed will produce tubers, which you can keep for future flowers.

Tubers are usually lifted and stored in a cool dry place after flowering to avoid frost damage, although they will over-winter in mild, warm areas. Seek local professional advice on leaving or storing dahlias.

Remove any spent flowers to prolong flowering period.
Propagation: Bedding dahlia seeds are sown in seed compost containers, using a damp, recommended, seed raising compost, and placed in a shade frame, or cold frame, or under glass, at 16–18°C (61–64°F). The type of protection needed depends on your local climate.

Space the seeds, 12 mm (0.5 in) deep, 50 mm (2 in) apart: winter-mid spring in subtropical areas; late winter-spring temperate areas; and spring-early summer in cold areas.

The seeds will germinate reasonably quickly, in 1 to 4 weeks. Prick out the seedlings when they are large enough to handle, and transplant them into pots, or 50 mm (2 in) apart into containers of damp, recommended, potting compost, and grow them on.

Harden the seedlings off, if necessary in a cold frame, and plant them out directly where they are to grow and flower, 300–375–600 mm (12–15–24 in) apart, depending on the height and spread of the plant, when all danger from frost is past and the ground has warmed up.

Or the seeds can be sown directly in a sheltered nursery bed in the open, after any frost risk. These nursery bed seedlings can be transplanted out directly where they are to grow and flower.

In English gardens sow the seeds in seed raising compost, under glass, mid winter-early spring (Feb-March), at 16–18°C (61–64°F). Treat them as half-hardy plants. Lift the tubers after flowering, and store them in a warm, airy, frost-free place for planting out in the next 'dahlia year'. Flowers midsummer, and on.
Pests and diseases: Aphids, earwigs, snails, slugs, caterpillars, botrytis blight, grey mould, leaf spot, petal blight, powdery mildew, stem rot, wilt, and more.
Cultivars/varieties: Dandy Mixed, height 500–600 mm (20–24 in), unusual 'collarette' flower form. Figaro Mixed Colours, height 300 mm (12 in), mostly double. Redskin Mixed, height 350 mm (14 in), bronze-red leaves, unusual colour range. Unwin's Dwarf Double Hybrids, height 600 mm (2 ft), semi double.
Family: Asteraceae.

Datura **(angel's trumpets, trumpet flower)** What angel, one wonders, are these plants named after, bearing in mind that these fragrant, summer flowering plants, including the seeds, are poisonous? Yet, you see them growing in many places; even as pot plants. Keep small children away from all daturas.

If you intend growing daturas then there is one which can be treated as annual, *D. metel*, which has attractive, dangling, fragrant, 150–200 mm (6–8 in) trumpets, with 100 mm (4 in) wide mouths, that are white inside and lavender-violet outside.

It grows to a height of 900 mm–1.5 m (3–5 ft). It is a vigorous, shrubby-bushy, grey-green, strongly-scented, oval-leaved plant that can be used for tall bedding, spaced 750 mm (30 in) apart, or as an accent plant. It likes a rich, open soil and sunny site.
Propagation: Sow the seeds in seed compost containers, using a damp, recommended, seed raising compost, late winter-mid spring, subtropical areas; early spring temperate areas; spring in cold areas; under glass if necessary, at 16–18°C (61–64°F).

Prick out the seedlings when large enough to handle into 75 mm (3 in) pots of potting compost, and grow them on.

Those plants destined to be planted directly where they are to grow are hardened off, if necessary in a cold frame, and planted out when any danger from frost is past and the ground has warmed up.

In English gardens sow the seeds in seed compost containers, under glass, early spring (March), at 16–18°C (61–64°F), and grow them as half-hardy pot plants before planting them out, properly hardened off, late spring (May), but only when all danger from frost is past and the ground has warmed up. Flowers early-mid summer.
Pests and diseases: Reasonably free.
Cultivars/varieties: Species as above.
Family: Solanaceae.

Delphinium **(larkspur)** The spring-autumn flowering Pacific Hybrid cultivars of the perennial, European Siberian *D. elatum* × other *D.* species; height 1.5 m (5 ft), or higher; are arguably the most stately plants in the garden.

The 38–64 mm (1.5–2.5 in) wide flowers are star-like, single, semi-double or double, mostly blue, purple or white, clustered on erect, rigid spikes.

Delphinium are fairly easy to grow from fresh seeds.

Although they are perennials and will last a few years in cooler areas, they will eventually deteriorate through various causes. Therefore, they are treated as annuals, particularly in subtropical areas.

Pacific Hybrids like a sheltered, reasonably sunny site, and a well-drained, rich, organic, neutral soil.

Other *D. elatum* groups, apart from the Pacific Hybrids are: *D. elatum*, a traditionally shaped delphinium, ranging in height from 1 m (39 in) to 2.4 m (8 ft); the flowering appearing to be more loosely arranged up the stem.

D. elatum × *D. grandiflorum* Belladonna Hybrids; height approximately 1 m (39 in); with a looser arrangements of flowers on the stem than those of the Pacific Hybrids.

The taller delphiniums need staking to keep their stately appearance, as there is nothing more distressing than drunken Pacific Giants. Create a tripod of three 1.2 m (4 ft) tall canes around each plant, when it is a few inches tall, joining the canes with rings of tying twine so that the plant's stems are not restricted, and can move gently within the canes.

Or failing this, insert sturdy garden stakes, at the same time as you plant the delphinium seedlings to avoid damaging the roots later on, upright into the ground behind each plant taking care not to drive splinters or pointed cane slivers into your hands and face. I speak from painful experience. Carefully and discreetly, tie the plant stems loosely, but securely, to the stakes, as the plant grows. Also, remember that you only want to see the foliage and flowers when in full bloom, and not the stake.

If the ground has been well prepared, using a well balanced delphinium fertiliser applied as the manufacturer intructs for delphiniums, then the plant should cope. Failing this, feed the plants, when they are growing well, with a well-balanced, liquid, soluble, flower fertiliser, suitable for delphiniums, and applied as the manufacturer instructs. Avoid the excessive use of nitrogenous fertiliser.

Give delphiniums copious water during dry spells, never letting the plants dry out. Remove spent flowers and seeds as soon as possible, and dispose of them safely, away from young children.

Propagation: Sow ripe, fresh seeds, as they quickly lose viability, in seed compost containers using a damp, recommended, seed raising compost; autumn in subtropical areas; autumn-winter in temperate areas; late summer-mid autumn or early spring in cold areas.

Young seedlings from a summer-autumn sowing will need winter protection in very cold areas. A spring sowing will produce later flowers. Germination can be slow: 14 days to one month.

Or in cold climates sow the seeds singly in 75 mm (3 in) pots of seed raising compost in a greenhouse or cold frame in late summer-early autumn, with the compost barely covering the seed.

Grow them on under glass until spring, but be aware of outside temperature fluctuations and do not let the young plants become heat-stressed.

The young plants can be hardened off and planted out directly where they are to grow, when all danger from frost is past and the soil has warmed up.

If you cannot give the seeds and seedlings under-glass protection from cold and frost, then sow the seeds in spring.

Space delphiniums 500–750 mm (20–30 in) apart, depending on height and spread of the plant.

Or you can sow the seeds in late winter under glass, in seed raising compost, at 14–16°C (57–61°F). Prick out the seedlings when large enough to handle into 75 mm (3 in) pots and grow them on, gradually reducing the temperature to say 11°C (52°F). Harden off the seedlings, and plant them out in late-spring, directly where they are to flower, once all danger from frost is past and the ground has warmed up.

In English gardens sow fresh seeds of delphinium in early autumn (Sept); or early spring (March); directly where they are to grow and flower, thinning out the seedlings to their required distance apart. Or sow seeds in seed compost containers using a recommended seed raising compost, and place the container in a cold frame for the seeds to germinate. Flowers early to mid summer.

Pests and diseases: Slugs, snails, thrips, aster yellows, bacterial leaf spot, crown, root and stem rot, powdery mildew and more.

Cultivars/varieties: Astolat Series, pink shades. Blue Fountains Dwarf Mixed, height 900 mm (3 ft), white, blue mauve, purple, Pacific Giant-like blooms. Connecticut Mixed, height 750 mm (30 in), pure white. Pacific Giants, height 1.5 m (5 ft), various blues and whites, some with contrasting 'bees'.

Family: Ranunculaceae.

Dianthus The genus *Dianthus* contains over 300 species, but we are only concerned with the following, which can be grown from seeds:

(1) The sweet william, *D. barbatus*.

(2) The Indian-China pink, *D. chinensis*.

(3) The annual carnation, *D. caryophyllus*. Chaubaud strain; and other like forms.

Dianthuses are late winter, or spring, or summer flowering plants, depending on climate, species or cultivar.

All dianthuses like a sunny site and free-draining, neutral soil, but object to excessive doses of nitrogenous fertiliser. You can buy fertilisers compounded for carnations.

The perennial, east European sweet william, *D. barbatus*, has colourful 'annual' or 'biennial' hybrids with frilly flowers of white, pink, red, or shades and tints of these colours; some are picotee edged. However, today modern 'annuals' are mostly grown.

Sweet williams have flat-faced, 25 mm (1 in) wide, single or double flowers, borne in 75-150 mm (3–6 in) flat, upfacing clusters. They can, according to species-cultivar, range in height from between 150–600 mm (6–24 in). They are used as cut flowers or edging or bedding plants.

I prefer them massed on their own, like a smouldering carpet.

Sweet william are easily grown from seeds. Prune off spent flowering stems to encourage further flowering.

The bushy, compact, late winter-spring-summer flowering (depending on climate), East Asian, Indian-China pink, *D. chinensis*, is a perennial that is usually grown as an annual or biennial.

It looks like an 'up-market' version of the sweet william.

Indian-China pinks are used as edging or bedding plants.

They are sweetly-scented, and grow approximately 150-300 mm (6–12 in) in height, producing masses of 25–56 mm (1–2.2 in) wide flowers in a brilliant colour range of white, pink, and red. The flowers can be crimped-edged, single, semi-double or double; some with contrasting deeper centre bands.

The foliage is fine-leaved, blue-grey-green and grassy-looking.

The best known of the summer flowering perennial 'annual' carnations, the Mediterranean-French *D. c.* Chabaud Strain; height up to 600 mm (24 in); is frost-sensitive in cold climates and is treated as an annual.

Although not as glamorous as the florist's carnation, it is very useful as a bedding plant and cut flower. It is available in white, pink, red, yellow, and shades and tints of these colours. The flowers have a clove-scent fragrance, although I find this hard to detect on some flowers. The double flowers are 37–50 mm (1.5–2 in) wide; possibly wider.

The foliage is blue-grey-green and grass-like.

Propagation: Thinly sow the seeds of sweet william, *D. barbatus*; autumn-winter-spring in subtropical areas; late summer-autumn or spring in temperate, mild-winter areas; late summer-autumn or early-spring in cold areas; 3 mm (0.1 in) deep, directly where they are to grow and flower. Thin out the seedlings to 300 mm (12 in) apart.

Or sow the seeds thinly distributed in containers of seed raising compost; early autumn and winter in subtropical areas; spring and autumn in temperate mild winter areas; spring and autumn in cool areas. Autumn sowings will provide spring and early summer blooms.

Prick out the seedlings when large enough to handle into containers of damp, recommended, potting compost 50–75 mm (2–3 in) apart. Or transplant them singly into 75 mm (3 in) pots, and grow them on.

Plant them out in the open, in spring, directly where they are to flower. In cold, severe frost areas the seedlings will need protection over the winter; if this is not available then make spring sowings.

Sow seeds of *D. chinensis* 3 mm (0.1 in) deep, thinly distributed in containers of seed raising compost; early autumn-winter in subtropical areas; late summer-autumn-winter-spring in temperate mild winter areas; autumn or spring in cold areas.

Prick out the seedlings when large enough to handle into containers of damp, recommended, potting compost 50–75 mm (2–3 in) apart, or into 75 mm (3 in) pots, and grow them on. Harden off the seedlings, and plant them out in the open, directly where they are to flower.

In cold, severe frost areas the seedlings will need protection over the winter; if this is not available make spring sowings.

Thinly sow seeds of *D. c.* Chaubaud 'annual' carnations, 6 mm (0.2 in) deep, thinly distributed in containers of seed raising compost, under glass if necessary; early autumn-winter-early spring in subtropical areas; autumn-late winter-early spring in mild winter temperate areas; late summer-autumn or late winter-spring in cold areas.

Prick out the seedlings when large enough to handle into containers of damp recommended, potting compost 50–75 mm (2–3 in) apart.

or into 75 mm (3 in) pots, and grow them on.

Harden off the seedlings, and plant them out in the open, directly where they are to flower. In cold, severe frost areas, the seedlings will need protection over the winter; if this is not available then make spring sowings.

Sweet william usually flower late spring-summer. Indian pinks flower mid winter-mid spring. Chabaud carnations flower spring to autumn.

In English gardens sow the seeds of 'biennial' sweet william in a garden nursery bed, early summer (June–July), and transplant the seedlings in mid-autumn (Oct). Or sow the 'annual' seeds under glass in seed raising compost, early spring (March) for early summer flowers at 13–15°C (55–59°F).

In English gardens sow seeds of *D. chinensis* carefully and thinly, mid-spring (mid-April), directly where the plants are to grow and flower, thinning them out to 150–225 mm (6–9 in) apart. Or sow the seeds under glass in seed raising compost in early spring (March) at 13–15°C (55–59°F). Flowers midsummer on.

In English gardens sow the seeds of Chaubaud carnations in containers of seed raising compost early winter (Jan-Feb) at 15–16°C (59–61°F), and treat them as half-hardy plants. Flowers midsummer on.

Pests and diseases: Aphis, thrips, red spider, alternaria blight, botrytis blight, fusarium stem rot, fusarium wilt, rust, septora leaf spot, viruses, and more.

Cultivars/varieties: Carnations: Chabauds Giants, height 500 mm (20 in), up to twelve different colours. The Knight Series F_1 Mixed, height 300 mm (12 in), various colours. Sweet William: Dwarf Wee Willi, extra dwarf, many colours. Early Brilliance, height 375 mm (15 in), bright colours. Indian Carpet, height 125–150 mm (5–6 in), white, pink, scarlet, crimson, solid or zoned. Pinocchio Mixed, height 150 mm (6 in), bright colours. Red Express, height 600 mm (2 ft), scarlet red. Roundabout, height 150 mm (6 in), white, pink, rose, carmine, red, zoned, 'eyed', bicolours. Dianthus: Baby Doll Dwarf Single Mixed, height 200 mm (8 in), large flowers. F_1 Hybrid Magic Charms, height 150 mm (6 in), white, pink, salmon, scarlet, crimson, and unusual bicolour-speckled; fringed petals. F_1 Telstar, height 200 mm (8 in), white, pink, rose, salmon, crimson, scarlet; plus variegated patterns.

Family: Caryophyllaceae.

***Diascia* (twinspur, dutchman's breeches)** The mid-late spring-summer flowering, South African annual *Diascia barberae*; height 300–450 mm (12–18 in); has bright-pink, small, 19 mm (0.7 in) wide, goblet-cup flowers, borne on tremulous, wavy stems.

The name 'twinspur' refers to the twin, curled, 'baggy-pants' spurs found at the back of the flower.

The leaves are small, oval-pointed, dark-green and glossy.

The plant's floppy habit may be considered unsightly, but that is its nature, and should be considered thus.

If you wish to prevent twinspurs following their natural, loose gangling habit, then you can very carefully pinch out the shoot's centre tip when it is 50 mm (2 in) tall, or when the plants have produced enough stem joints to provide sufficient sideshoots, to get the plant to branch. Once the side shoots have reached 4 leaves, approximately 50 mm (2 in) long, then they too can have their centre tips pinched out.

When the first flush of flowers is past cut back the spent flowers, and the plant will shoot and hopefully flower again.

Propagation: Diascia succeeds in temperate climates, such as Adelaide's, in a well-drained soil and sunny site.

Sow the seeds in seed compost containers using a damp, recommended seed raising compost, in early spring, under glass, at 16–18°C (61–64°F).

Barely cover the seeds. Keep the compost pleasantly moist. Prick out the seedlings into 75 mm (3 in) pots of damp, recommended potting compost, when they are large enough to handle.

Grow the seedlings on under glass, then harden them off in a cold frame and plant them out 150 mm (6 in) apart, directly where they are to flower, but only if danger from frost is past and the ground has warmed up.

In English gardens sow the seeds in seed raising compost, late winter-early spring (Feb-March), under glass at 16–18°C (61–64°F), and treat them as half-hardy bedding or pot plants. Flowers appear latest spring-summer.

Pests and diseases: Reasonably free.

Cultivars/varieties: Species as above.

Family: Scrophulariaceae.

***Digitalis* (foxglove)** The West European foxglove *Digitalis purpurea* is a biennial which in certain climates can be a short-lived perennial. But it has now been superseded with the introduction of the new hybrids, some of which can be treated as annuals.

From the broad, 450 mm (18 in) wide rosette of deep-green oblong-pointed, 200 mm (8 in) long, or longer, leaves arises the 750 mm–1.5 m (2.5–5 ft) spike of hanging, tubular, bell-shaped flowers.

These flowers are available in cream, pink, red or yellow, usually with white or yellow, dark-spotted throats, with the lower tip of the flower looking petulant.

The new dwarf hybrid plants can produce blooms on both sides of the flowering spike. They are not as tall as the species, or as the Excelsior hybrids, and therefore are not as wind-vulnerable, but they can still get damaged.

Foxgloves thrive in the moist, humid, cooler States. They grow well in a semi-shady spot, in a well-drained, but moisture retentive soil, not waterlogged, and best arranged in clumps as accent plants, so that their tall, stately spikes of flowers form eye-catching groups.

They can be grown to bloom in spring and summer. They self-seed readily, but generally this is not desired, although the resulting mass of flower-spikes can look casually attractive.

Cut down the flowers when the flowering has finished and usually smaller spikes of flowers will be produced.

Caution: Parts of the plant should be considered poisonous.

Propagation: Thinly sow the very fine seeds in seed compost containers on top of damp, recommended seed raising compost, late summer or autumn, in a reasonably cool, sheltered spot. Press the seeds carefully to anchor them to the compost.

Very carefully mist spray the seeds with water, or water them from below by standing the container in a dish of water, allowing the compost surface to just glisten with moisture and then removing the container. Keep the compost just pleasantly moist from then on.

Seed should germinate in up to 21 days. Prick out the seedlings, when large enough to handle, into 100 mm (4 in) pots. Plant them out in early spring.

Or the seeds can be sown, late spring-summer, outside in a sheltered, semi-shaded, nursery seed-bed, which has been dug, cleaned of debris and firmed ready to take the fine seeds. Barely rake the seeds into the surface tilth.

Water the seeds using a fine spray. Keep the soil just pleasantly moist. Thin out the seedlings to 150 mm (6 in) apart, and grow them on. Plant them out in autumn, directly where they are to grow and flower, spacing them 300–450 mm (12–18 in) apart.

Or the seeds of the 'annual' foxgloves can be sown under glass in mid-winter, in containers of damp, recommended, seed raising compost at 18–21°C (64–70°F).

Prick out the seedlings into containers of damp, recommended, potting compost, and from there into 100 mm (4 in) pots of recommended potting compost. Harden off the seedlings, if necessary in a cold frame, and plant them out directly where they are to grow and flower, 300 mm (12 in) apart.

In English gardens sow the seeds of biennials in the garden in a nursery seed-bed, late spring-early summer (May-June). Transplant autumn. (But check winter hardiness of resulting young plants in cold climates.) Or sow seeds of the 'annual' hybrids under glass, in late winter (Feb-March), at 18–21°C (64–70°F), and treat them as half-hardy plants. Flowers appear in summer.

Pests and diseases: Reasonably free, although chewing insects, wilt, and others may eventuate.

Cultivars/varieties: Foxy, height 1 m (39 in), white, cream, pink, carmine, throats attractively spotted with maroon. Excesior Hybrids, height 1.5 m (5 ft), wide colour range with spotted throats.

Family: Scrophulariaceae.

***Dimorphotheca* (Cape daisy, Cape marigold, star-of-the-veldt)** The South African perennial *D. aurantiaca* (syn. *D. sinuata*); height 300–450 mm (12–18 in); has been hybridised to produce an exciting range of 'annual' plants.

The single, daisy-like flowers are brightly-coloured, up to 50 mm (2 in) wide, in white, yellow, orange, salmon-pink or pink, and shades and tints of those colours, with contrasting yellow-brown centre discs. The backs of the petals, as with most daisies, are usually a deeper colour.

Star-of-the-veldt daisies flower summer, and on. They close at night and on dull days, like so many of the daisy family, but this fault is compensated for by their proliferation of flowers during sunny days.

The pale-green leaves are lobed, 100 mm (4 in) long, by 12 mm (0.5 in) wide. Star-of-the-veldt daisies make excellent bed and border plants, but are no good as cut flowers.

Dimorphothecas are frost sensitive and prefer a sheltered, sunny site, or may tolerate a slightly shaded one, and a free-draining, sandy-loam. They withstand semi-drought conditions reasonably well. They object to over-watering and over fertilising, although regular sensible watering is necessary to encourage leaf and flower growth.

Remove spent (dead) flowers to prolong the flowering period.

D. annua (syn. *D. pluvialis*) is an attractive plant which is grown in Australia, but is not as popular as those above. *D. chrysanthemifolia* is a fine looking yellow flowered species. *D. ecklonii* and *D. barberae* look so much like the Osteospermums, that I have included them under that heading.

Propagation: Thinly sow star-of-the-veldt seeds, 3 mm (0.1 in) deep, in seed compost containers, using a damp recommended seed raising compost; all year in subtropical areas, but usually winter-mid spring; late winter-early spring under glass; and also summer in the temperate mild winter areas; and spring under glass in the colder areas. Mist spray the seeds with water, keeping the compost pleasantly moist.

The seedlings should germinate within 15 days (mine germinated in 5 days) at 16–20°C (61–68°F). Prick them out when large enough to handle into 75 mm (3 in) pots of damp, recommended, potting compost, and grow them on. Harden them off, if necessary in a cold frame. They grow rapidly.

Plant them out directly where they are to grow and flower, 150–300 mm (6–12 in) apart, but only when all danger from frost is past and the ground has warmed up.

They should flower within approximately 3 months given fine, warm, pleasantly-moist growing conditions, and continue flowering.

The seeds can be sown directly where they are to grow and flower, but only when the danger of frost is past in the cooler areas.

Dig over the garden-bed breaking it down into a fine tilth, and removing any debris. Firm the soil ready to take the seeds.

Sow the seeds, late-spring (cooler areas), and lightly rake them into the tilth. Spray gently using a fine rose. Keep the seeds pleasantly moist. Carefully remove any weeds without disturbing the young seedlings. Thin out the seedlings to the required distance.

In English gardens sow the seeds, late-spring (May), directly where they are to grow and flower, and thin out the seedlings to the required distance. Or sow the seeds in seed raising compost, early spring (March), under glass at 16–18°C (61–64°F). Treat them as half-hardy plants. They flower in summer.

Pests and diseases: Leaf chewing insects, aster yellows, grey mould.

Cultivars/varieties: Mixed Colours.

Family: Asteraceae.

***Dorotheanthus* (Livingstone daisy)** The late winter-spring, or summer-flowering, South African *Dorotheanthus bellidiformis* (syn. *Mesembryanthemum criniflorus*); height 100–150 mm (4–6 in); can look either an incredibly spectacular carpet of colour or an incredibly drab one, depending on whether the sun is shining as they open only during hot sunlight.

The glowing, exotically-rayed daisy flowers are 25–30 mm (1–1.2 in) wide. They can be white, pink, red, crimson, purple, lemon, orange or apricot, or shades or tints of these colours.

The petals of some Livingstone daisies are zone-banded like an archery target; for example: a deep carmine-pink around the outside, gradually fusing to golden-yellow, to white, and then to a dark-pink centre-disc.

Their leaves and prostrate stems are fleshy and succulent, and appear to be speckled with minute ice crystals.

Livingstone daisies are reasonably hardy, but are treated as half-hardy plants. I used them principally as bedding plants for public display, massed on their own, although they can be used for hanging baskets, window boxes, and the like.

They prefer a well drained, average soil, which must be in full sun. Water them moderately but don't over-water them. Don't over-fertilise them either, as they are not greedy plants.

Livingstone daisies are easily raised from seeds.

Propagation: Thinly sow the seeds 3 mm (0.1 in) deep in seed compost containers using a recommended seed raising compost; autumn-early winter in subtropical areas; or autumn in temperate areas; spring in cooler areas, or say 10 weeks before the last frost in your location; under glass where necessary, at 15–18°C (60–65°F).

Gently press the seeds to anchor them to the surface of the compost. Mist spray them, and keep the compost pleasantly moist. Place them in a dark place to germinate, which should take 1 to 3 weeks.

But keep a constant watch for the seedlings to emerge, otherwise the darkness will cause them to become drawn and spindly.

Prick out the seedlings, once they are large enough to handle, 50 mm (2 in) apart, into containers of damp, recommended, potting compost. Grow the seedlings on, and, if necessary, harden them off in a cold frame.

Pot them on into 75 mm or 100 mm (3–4 in) pots of damp, recommended, potting compost, if they threaten to become root-bound in the containers.

Plant out the seedlings directly where they are to grow and flower, 150–300 mm (6–12 in) apart, but only if any danger from frost is past and the ground has warmed up. Livingstone daisies take approximately 5 months to flower.

Or the seeds can be sown; autumn in warm areas; spring in cooler areas, but only if danger from frost is past; directly where they are to flower and grow.

Dig over and break down the soil into a fine tilth, and firm it to take the seeds. Sow the seeds thinly, and rake them gently and lightly into the tilth surface. Gently firm the seeds to anchor them to the soil. Water carefully, using a fine spray. Keep the soil just pleasantly moist, to get the seedlings under way.

In English gardens sow the seeds under glass in early spring (March) at 15–18°C (60–65°F), and treat them as half-hardy annuals. They can also be sown outside in the garden, in mid-late spring (April-May), but only when any danger from frost is past. Flowers midsummer, and on.

Pests and diseases: Reasonably free.

Cultivars/varieties: Livingstone Daisy Mixed; *Mesembryanthemum criniflorus.*

Family: Aizoaceae.

***Echinacea* (purple cone-flower)** The mid summer-autumn flowering, North American perennial *Echinacea purpurea* (syn. *Rudbeckia purpurea*); height 1–1.2 m (39–47 in); has 75–100 mm (3–4 in) wide, radiating, daisy-like, swept-back flowers.

The petals, depending on cultivar (there is a white form), can be pale pink at their tips, deepening to crushed raspberry-carmine where they join the centre-disc. This centre-disc is a minutely-studded, yellow-brown, prominent, rounded cone, hence the plant's name. This cone, in time, produces rings of tiny, yellow stamens.

Purple cone-flowers tend to flop if not supported. The bright-green, lance-shaped leaves are lightly toothed and rough when touched.

Purple cone-flowers like a fertile, free-draining, deep, loamy soil. They make good cut flowers. Cut back the stems when the flowers are spent to prolong the flowering period. Tidy up the dead stems after the flowering period is finished.

Propagation: Sow the seeds in seed compost containers, using a damp, recommended, seed raising compost, 8 to 10 weeks before the normal planting out time in your location; or during spring, but under glass, at 13–15°C (55–59°F), if frost is still a threat.

The seeds need darkness to germinate. Germination takes approximately 20 days, or longer, but watch this carefully to prevent seedlings being 'drawn' in a dark location. Expose the seedlings to good light as soon as they germinate, but not hot sunlight.

Prick out the seedlings into containers of damp, recommended, potting compost, and grow them on. Harden them off, if necessary in a cold frame. Transplant the seedlings into nursery-beds, before planting them out directly where they are to flower and grow.

Or move them out into 100 mm (4 in) pots of potting compost, and grow them on, plunged up to the pot's rim in peat or clean sharp sand to keep the roots cool. Then plant them out directly where they are to grow and flower.

In English gardens sow seeds in seed raising compost, early spring (March) under glass, at 13–15°C (55–59°F). Prick out the seedlings into pots, and harden off. Plunge them in sand outside, or transplant them to a nursery holding-bed, prior to planting out in mid autumn (Oct). Or sow seeds in a seedbed late spring-early summer (May-June). Purple cone-flowers bloom midsummer on.

Pests and diseases: Reasonably free.

Cultivars/varieties: Species as above.

Family: Asteraceae.

***Emilia* (tassel flower, cupid's paintbrush)** The annual *Emilia javanica*; height 450–600 mm (18–24 in); is thought to have originated in tropical and central Africa, and spread to tropical Central America and tropical India.

The small, scarlet, pompon tufts of flowers, 13 mm (0.5 in) wide, grow out from tall, wiry stems. They make useful cut flowers.

The leaves are rough to the touch, arrow-shaped and enclose the stem.

Emilias prefer a sunny, sheltered location, and will thrive in a free-draining soil.

Water the plants regularly, and give them occasional feeds of a well-balanced, liquid, soluble, flower fertiliser, suitable for emilias and applied as the manufacturer instructs.

Remove spent flowers, and dispose of them carefully to prevent weed seeding.

Propagation: Dig over the site where emilias are to grow and flower, removing any debris. Rake the soil, breaking it down into a fine tilth, and firm gently ready to take the seeds.

Thinly sow the seeds early-spring in warm winter areas, or after the last frost, when the soil has warmed up, in other areas. Gently rake the seed into the top tilth, not too deeply, and gently firm the soil and seed.

Water the seeds gently, but copiously, using a fine rose so as not to wash them out. Keep the soil pleasantly moist.

Germination can take 7–15 days. Emilias seem to tolerate crowding, so only thin them out to 100–150 mm (4–6 in) apart.

Or sow the seeds under glass at 16–20°C (60–68°F), say 3 weeks before the last frost.

Prick out the seedlings when they are large enough to handle, into small pots, and grow them on. Emilias can grow 300 mm (12 in) under glass in 21 days. Harden them off, and plant them out directly where they are to grow and flower, but only when all danger from frost is past and the ground has warmed up.

In English gardens sow the seeds directly where the plants are to grow and flower, but only if any danger from frost is past. Or sow the seeds under glass at 16–20°C (60–68°F), say 3 weeks before the last frost is expected. Grow them on as half-hardy plants.

Pests and diseases: Reasonably free.
Cultivars/varieties: Species as above; plus a yellow form.
Family: Asteraceae.

Eschscholtzia **(syn.** ***Eschscholzia*****) (California(n) poppy)** The spring-summer flowering Californian *Eschscholtzia californica*; height 300–450 mm (12–18 in); is a widely grown bedding plant.

The colour of the 50–75 mm (2–3 in) wide, satiny, four-petalled, cupped, single, sometimes crinkly, poppy-like flowers is one of the most intense in the flower kingdom. And on hot, sunny days the flowers seem to glow and smoulder like orange embers.

The Californian poppy is grown as an annual. Flower cultivars are available in white, cream, rose, yellow, orange, scarlet or mauve; single or semi-double flowers.

They are easy to grow and in spring-summer they burst forth in their blaze of colour, but only when the sun shines.

They prefer a well-drained, preferably sandy, neutral loam; it doesn't have to be a rich soil, but it must receive full sun.

Propagation: Dig up and break down the soil into a fine tilth, directly where the Californian poppies are to grow and flower. Rake out and remove any debris.

Broadcast the seeds, or sow them in rows, or 'station-sow' them in patches, at the required distance apart, late winter-spring subtropical areas; late winter-spring-early summer in temperate areas; spring in cold areas. Rake in the seeds barely covering them.

You can mix the seeds with a little dry sand or compost to make their sowing easier. Carefully water the seeds using a fine spray. They will germinate in 5–15 days depending on soil temperature. Thin out the seedlings, when large enough to do so, 150–200–300 mm (6–8–12 in), usually 150 mm (6 in), apart.

The carrot or fern-like, blue-grey-green, tufty foliage is vulnerable to insect damage at this stage.

Californian Poppies resent root disturbance so take care when weeding around the plant.

Flowering will commence approximately 8–10 weeks after the seeds have germinated. The mature plants will produce seeds, and the resulting seedlings will naturalise and produce seedlings.

In English gardens sow the seeds in early autumn (Sept), or spring (March), preferably in a light, free-draining soil. Flowers appear early summer, and on.

Pests and diseases: Reasonably free.
Cultivars/varieties: Lemon Drops, height 250 mm (10 in), lemon yellow, 13 mm (0.5 in) wide flowers. Mission Bells Mixed, height 300–600 mm (12–24 in), mixed pastel and vibrant double, and semi-double blooms.
Family: Papaveraceae.

Euphorbia **(spurge)** The southern United States-Mexican annual poinsettia *E. heterophylla* (Mexican fire plant, fire-on-the-mountain, painted leaf); height 600–900 mm (24–36 in); has dark-green, variable, wavy or jagged edged, oval-shaped leaves. The top leaves, during summer, turn into layers of scarlet bracts, which surround smallish orangey-red flowers. It is treated as a half-hardy annual in cold areas.

The United States (Texas, Colorado, Minnesota) *E. marginata* (snow-on-the-mountain); height 600–900 mm (24–36 in); is treated as a hardy annual. It is one of the most beautiful spurges, with its light-green, white-edged leaves and ghostly-white bracts. But, unfortunately, it is a 'primary' declared pest plant in some States; check with your local Dept of Agriculture.

Euphorbias are not necessarily grown for their flowers as sometimes these can be insignificant. They are, however, grown for their false flowers (bracts) which, in the Christmas poinsettias, are shown to perfection.

Most spurges exude a milky, acrid sap, if cut or broken, and human or animal contact with this sap should be avoided.

Euphorbias grow in a poor or fertile, well-drained soil, in a sunny site.

Euphorbias are a remarkable group of plants, ranging from humble weeds such as the petty spurge *E. peplus*; to the spiny crown-of-thorns *E. milli* (syn. *E. splendens*); to the unusual, shrubby wulfen-spurge, *E. characias wulfenii* (syn. *E. wulfeni, E. veneta*), with its 'snobbish' ovary which sticks out sideways on its own little arm, away from the flowers; to the extremely popular dwarf forms of the Christmas scarlet poinsettia, *E. pulcherrima*.

Propagation: In those places where the spurges are not considered as pest plants, sow the seeds of snow-on-the-mountain, *E. marginata*, in mid-spring, directly where they are to grow and flower.

Dig over the soil, breaking it down into a fine tilth, ready to take the seed. Or patch sow the seed at the correct distance apart, 300–600 mm (12–24 in), keeping only the best seedling in the one patch.

Sow the seeds of the annual poinsettia under glass in early spring at 18–21°C (64–70°F), in containers of recommended seed raising compost. Prick out the seedlings into boxes and from there into small pots. Harden them off and plant them outside if all danger from frost is past and the ground has warmed up.

In English gardens sow the seeds of annual poinsettias, *E. heterophylla*, outside directly where they are to grow and flower, but only if the danger from frost is past. Or sow the seeds indoors under glass in mid spring (April) in containers of seed raising compost, at 18–21°C (64–70°F), and treat them as half-hardy plants. Flowers in mid summer.

In English gardens sow the seeds of snow-on-the-mountain, *E. marginata*, in early-mid spring (March-April), directly where they are to grow and flower. Or sow the seeds under glass in early spring in containers of seed raising compost, at 16°C (61°F), and treat them as a half-hardy plant. Flowers early autumn.

Pests and diseases: Grey mould.
Cultivars/varieties: Species as above.
Family: Euphorbiaceae

Exacum **(persian violet)** The popular, fragrant, partial-shade, warm season annual *Exacum affine*; height 225 mm (9 in); makes a sweet and useful house plant, greenhouse pot plant and container patio plant. In cooler areas they are warm-greenhouse plants.

The 5-petalled, fragrant, star-shaped flowers, 13–19 mm (0.5–0.7 in) across, are lavender-blue with a darker-blue centre and eye-catching yellow stamens.

The leaves are small, shiny, a little waxy-looking, and squatly oval-pointed.

Propagation: Thinly sow the 'trace of snuff' fine seeds, under glass, in seed compost containers, on top of dampened, recommended, seed raising compost, as they need light to germinate. Gently press the seeds on to the compost to anchor them.

The seeds can be sown for much of the year, but are usually sown in spring in cooler climates, at 18–24°C (54–75°F).

Mist spray the seedlings very carefully, otherwise the seed will float or be washed out. Or preferably, water the seeds by standing the container in a shallow dish of water, and allowing the water to percolate up through the compost, so that it just dampens the surface of the compost; then remove the container. Keep the compost pleasantly moist.

Seeds should germinate in approximately 15 days. Prick out the seedlings, when large enough to handle, into containers of damp, recommended potting compost, and grow them on.

Pot them on into 75 mm (3 in) pots. Grow them on, and pot them on two sizes into 125 mm (5 in) pots. Lightly shade the greenhouse during hot weather and ventilate if necessary, keeping the greenhouse warm, but buoyant.

In English gardens thinly sow the seeds on to the surface of dampened seed compost, under glass, during early spring at 18–24°C (64–75°F). Treat the plants as tender, warm-greenhouse pot plants. Flowers appear mid summer and on.

Pests and diseases: Usual greenhouse pests and diseases.
Cultivars/varieties: E. affine; 'Midget', height 150 mm (6 in), lavender blue with contrasting yellow-stamens centre.
Family: Gentianaceae.

Felicia: The South African, spring-summer flowering, *Felicia bergerana* (kingfisher daisy); height 100–200 mm (4–8 in); is a prolific, but frost-sensitive, annual daisy.

The 13–18 mm (0.5–0.7 in) wide, bright-blue, yellow-centred daisies appear in a mass over the cushion-mat of lance-like grey-green leaves.

But the kingfisher daisy is not as dramatic as its perennial relative *Felicia amelloides*.

F. amelloides (blue daisy, blue marguerite); height 300–450 mm (12–18 in); seen growing in most temperate areas, has pale mauve-blue flowers 25–31 mm (1–1.2 in) wide, which are borne on stiff stems, 200–225 mm (4–5 in) above the foliage.

Its mid-green leaves, 31 mm (1.2 in) long and ovalish, are hairy and rough to the touch.

Both species can be grown from seeds. In warmer climates *F. amelloides* is a perennial sub-shrub; it is, however, often grown as an annual in cold climates unless it is protected from frost. Overwinter under glass, minimum temperature 10°C (50°F).

Both these plants can be used as border or rockery plants, or pot, balcony or container plants.

They demand a sunny spot to keep the flowers open, in a well-drained, fertile soil, plus adequate watering during dry spells. Remove spent flowers to increase flower production, and to keep the plant looking tidy.

Propagation: Thinly sow seeds of *F. bergerana* in seed compost containers, autumn; or early spring cool areas; under glass where necessary, at 16–18°C (61–64°F), using a damp, recommended seed raising compost.

Prick out the seedlings, when they are large enough to handle, into containers of damp, recommended, potting compost, and grow them on. Harden them off, if necessary in a cold frame, and plant them out directly where they are to grow and flower, 150 mm (6 in) apart, but only if any danger from frost is past, and the ground has warmed up.

It is probably better, in the warmer and temperate areas where *F. amelloides* grows outside as a perennial, to increase the plant supply by taking 50–75 mm (2–3 in) vegetative, softwood cuttings in summer, after the first flowering flush. Plant the rooted, hardened off cuttings outside in the garden, 750 mm (30 in) apart.

In English gardens sow the seeds in seed compost containers, late winter-early spring (Feb-March), under glass, at 16–18°C (61–64°F), using a dampened, recommended seed raising compost, and treat felicias as half-hardy plants. Bear in mind that *F. amelloides* is grown here as an annual, not as a perennial, and therefore they are planted closer than suggested above. Kingfisher daisy flowers should appear mid-summer-early autumn (late June-September); blue marguerite flowers in summer (June-Aug).

Pests and diseases: Reasonably free.
Cultivars/varieties: Species as above.
Family: Asteraceae.

Freesia The winter-spring flowering South African freesia, *Freesia* × *hybrida*; height 150–600 mm (6–24 in); is grown extensively for its heavenly fragrance, although some cultivars are more fragrant than others.

Freesias are also grown for their exquisite bright or pastel colours in yellow, red, blue, and also white. The split-edged, 37–50 mm (1.5–2 in) long, fairy trumpets are borne on one side of the long, wiry stems. Double-flowered strains have been available for many years, but they are not much seen.

Blue freesias seem to be most popular, followed by yellow, red, then white, although mostly mixtures are available from the seedsmen.

Freesias prefer a well-drained, reasonably fertile, light soil, in a sunny position; but they will grow in lightly dappled shade, as is obvious from the way they have colonised some of our native woodlands.

Propagation: Seeds can flower in 8 to 12 months from sowing. Thinly sow the seeds in seed compost containers, using a damp, recommended seed raising mix, from mid to late summer. In hard frost areas grow them in a cool greenhouse at 5–6°C (41–43°F) winter temperature.

Soak the hard-coated seeds in tepid water for 24 hours, prior to sowing, to speed up germination.

Many years ago I was taught to grow freesias by soaking the seeds, contained in a hessian bag, for 24 hours, and then for 20 minutes a day until the seed chitted (germinated). The seeds were then planted immediately into damp, recommended, seed raising compost.

However, as stated, you can soak the seeds for 24 hours in tepid water. Sow a few seeds in individual 50 mm (2 in) pots of damp, recommended, seed raising compost, keeping only the strongest seedling in each pot. Or sow them in seed compost containers, thinning out to 50 mm (2 in) apart. Or sow a few seeds into a 125 mm (5 in) pot, leaving 5 seedlings in each pot. You can make a succession of sowings to lengthen the flowering period.

The seedlings can be planted out directly where they are to grow and flower, or grown as pot plants. Or the seeds can be sown in partially shaded garden rows.

Freesia seeds will develop into corms, which can be used for future plantings.

In English gardens sow the seeds from early spring to early summer (March-June); or mid-late spring (mid April-mid May); or up to mid summer (mid-July), for later flowers, in a cool greenhouse. Grow them on in a frost free greenhouse. The plants should be kept moist and properly shaded in summer.

Pests and diseases: Aphids, red spider mite, wilt and corm rot.
Cultivars/varieties: Emerald Rainbow Strain Mixed, height 750 mm (30 in), white, pink, dark red, violet, orange, dark blue. Super Giants Mixed, height 300–375 mm (12–15 in), very large perfumed strain, in choice colours.
Family: Iridaceae.

***Gaillardia* (annual gaillardia, blanket flower)** Mostly summer flowering, the United States gaillardias are either perennial species and cultivars, or annual species and cultivars. Both can bloom in the first year from seed.

The annual *G. pulchella* var. *picta*; height 300–600 mm (12–24 in); can have single, or semi-double, or ball-shaped flowers.

The Picta Lorenziana cultivars form fascinating, mostly 50–75 mm (2–3 in) wide, pompon flowers, in richly coloured shades and tints of cream, yellow, red, orange, or bronze. The 'Lollipops' cultivar has various colours and bicolours.

The cultivars of the perennial *Gaillardia aristata* × *G. grandiflora* × *G. pulchella*; height 600–750 mm (24–30 in), have satin-smooth, rayed-daisy, 60–100 mm (2.4–4 in) wide flowers with striking 'gypsy' coloured, fused, banded-zones in yellow, orange, scarlet or bronze, with dark brown or reddish centre-discs.

Gaillardia leaves are grey-green, lance-like, pointed with serrated edges.

Perennial gaillardias are relatively easy to grow from seed, and will flower, depending on sowing times and climate, from spring, through summer, and on into autumn. The annuals germinate and bloom quickly from seed, approximately 4 months.

Although the cultivars of the annual gaillardia are not as impressive as the perennial's, they withstand dry conditions. However, they are frost tender. They are used as bedding or border plants, providing a flow of blooms from seed sown in spring.

The perennial gaillardia is used as a border plant and has cultivars which flower in the first year from seed.

Gaillardias prefer a well-drained, fertile soil, in a sunny site. Both types may need supporting with twiggy sticks, or similar. Cutting back the spent flowers will prolong the flowering life of the plant. Gaillardias can be used for cut flowers.

Propagation: Thinly sow the seeds of annual gaillardias in seed compost containers, using a damp, recommended seed raising compost, autumn to spring subtropical areas; autumn or spring in temperate and cool areas.

They are frost sensitive. In hard frost-prone areas sow the seeds under glass at 13–16°C (55–61°F) a month or two before the last frost is expected. Gently press the seeds on to the surface of the compost.

Prick out the seedlings into containers of damp, recommended potting compost, and grow them on. Harden them off before planting them outside, directly where they are to grow, but only when all danger from frost is past and the ground has warmed up.

Or thinly sow the seeds directly where they are to grow and flower, when all danger from frost is over. Sow them broadcast-fashion or in drills (rows); or you can 'station-plant' the seeds: i.e. sowing a few seeds in clumps at the required spacing.

Begin by digging over the site when it is easy to work, breaking it down into a fine tilth to take the seed. Gently, but thoroughly firm the seed bed.

Rake in the seeds carefully keeping them close to the surface, and gently press them using the head of the rake, or a board, to anchor them to the soil. Thin out the seedlings, 300 mm (12 in) apart, keeping only the strongest.

Sow the seeds of perennial gaillardias in autumn to spring subtropical areas; autumn and spring temperate and cool areas, under glass where necessary, in containers of seed raising compost; or sow them broadcast, or in rows, or in 'station plantings' in a prepared seed bed, as described above.

In English gardens sow seeds of the perennial gaillardias indoors under glass at 13–16°C (55–61°F), in late winter-early spring (Feb-March). Also sow the seeds of annual gaillardias late winter-early spring in seed raising compost at 13–16°C (55–61°F). Treat both as half-hardy annuals.

Or sow the seeds of annual gaillardias, mid spring (April), directly where they are to grow and flower. Or sow seeds of perennial gaillardias outside in a propagating bed, late spring-early summer (May-June). Prick out the seedlings, into a nursery-holding bed. Transplant them mid-spring (April) the following year.

Pests and diseases: Mildew.
Cultivars/varieties: Grandiflora Perennial Mixed, height 600 mm (2 ft), various colours. *G. a.* Reselected Hybrids, height 600–750 mm

(2–2.5 ft), crimson to yellow, many zoned, bicoloured. Lollipops, height 300 mm (12 in). Lorenziana Double Mixed.
Family: Asteraceae.

***Gazania* (treasure flower)** Hybrids of the South African *G. linenaris, G. nivea* and *G. rigens* (syn. *G. splendens*), known as *Gazania × hybrida*; height 150–300 mm (6–12 in); are seen in numerous gardens throughout Australia.

Gazanias produce slightly hairy, single-stemmed 50–100 mm (2–4 in) wide, dahlia-daisy flowers, in white, yellow, pink, red, crimson, orange, brown-mahogany, bicolours, and shades and tints of those colours, with 'sighting splashes' of a deeper colour at the base of each petal. These flowers have contrasting, approximately 12.5 mm (0.5 in) wide, brownish, yellow, deep yellow or greenish-yellow centre zone discs.

The leaves are leathery-stiffish, lance-like, deeply-lobed or smooth-edged, sometimes on the same plant, mostly dark green on top (sometimes greyish), and grey-whitish hairy underneath.

Gazanias prefer a well-drained, sandy loam and revel in hot sun, closing up in dull or dark weather.

They are used as border plants or as massed-bedding plants, where their brilliant colours can be seen to perfection.

Seeds are available in mixed colours, and should you discover a desirable cultivar, then propagate it vegetatively.

Perennial gazanias flower spring-summer-autumn, and on until cut down by frost. They can be grown as pot plants, particulary the dwarf varieties.

They will deteriorate if over-fertilised, or excessively watered, particularly on moisture-retaining soils. They suffer badly in wet winters and humid, moist conditions. Gazanias are frost sensitive.

Propagation: Sow the seeds in seed compost containers using a damp, recommended seed raising compost, winter-spring, subtropical areas; late winter-early spring temperate areas; spring in cool areas; under glass if necessary, at 16°C (61°F) soil temperature. Cover the seeds with 6 mm (0.2 in) of compost. Keep the compost pleasantly moist.

Prick out the seedlings into 75 mm (3 in) pots. Harden them off, if necessary in a cold frame, and plant them outside when all danger from frost risk is past and the ground has warmed up, 200–300 mm (8–12 in) apart.

In English gardens sow the seeds in compost, under glass at 16°C (61°F), in mid-late winter (Jan-Feb), and treat as half-hardy annuals. Summer flowering.

Pests and diseases: Mildew, grey mould.
Cultivars/varieties: Sunshine Mixed, height 200 mm (8 in), pink, crimson, gold, orange, with contrasting zones. Chansonette, large flowered, dwarf plants. Mini Star Mixed, height 300 mm (12 in) white, pink, red, yellow, tangerine, mahogany, and intermediate shades and tints.
Family: Asteraceae.

***Gerbera* (gerbera, African-Transvaal daisy)** The South African *Gerbera jamesonii*; height 375–600 mm (15–24 in); is a spring-summer flowering, frost-sensitive perennial, which loves long, warm summers.

From a lobed, hairy, rosette of leaves, on long stems, gerberas produce single or double, daisy-like, rayed flowers, 75–125 mm (3–5 in) wide (although some of the newer hybrids are much larger), in white, yellow, orange, pink or red, and shades and tints of these colours.

Named cultivars are propagated vegetatively but, nevertheless, you can grow beautiful gerberas from quality seed and, who knows, you may produce a winner which you can propagate vegetatively to keep true to form.

Gerberas can be used as cut flowers, pot plants, bedding plants or specialist plants.

They will adapt to most Australian climates, except cold areas where they are grown in a greenhouse as pot plants. They prefer a sunny position, sheltered, in a well-drained, fertile, neutral-slightly acid soil.

Gerberas can be planted in raised beds 200 mm (8 in) above the surrounding soil to facilitate drainage around their roots. Take care when weeding around them as the roots are easily damaged. You can also mulch the soil during summer. Cut off spent flowers and stems to ground level.

Never cover the crowns with compost or soil, as this rots the plants.

Gerberas are becoming more and more popular as a show flower. There are societies dedicated to furthering the cause of this delightful plant and, if you are interested, then your local gardening authorities may have the address.

Propagation: Gerberas seeds are approximately 6 mm (0.2 in) long, often more, with a point at one end of the seed and a minute crown where the pappus 'parachute' was attached at the other. This may not be easy to detect, but do try to.

Or, possibly, the seeds may still have the fluffy 'parachutes' attached. (In nature these parachutes help the seeds to float through the air to find a new flowering site.)

Use fresh seeds as they soon lose their vitality and viability.

Sow the seeds in seed compost containers, using a damp, recommended, neutral-slightly acid, gerbera seed raising compost, under glass if necessary. Place the seeds individually, 25 mm (1 in) apart, with the parachutes still visible; that is pressing the seeds, points down, 5 mm (0.2 in) deep.

Do this winter-spring in subtropical areas; spring-early summer in temperate areas; and spring in cool areas; under glass where necessary. Don't cover the seeds with compost as they need light to assist in germination.

Water the seeds using a fine spray. Cover the container with a sheet of glass, and place it in a sheltered spot, in good light, but not direct sunlight. Don't allow the compost and the seeds to dry out, but keep the compost pleasantly moist.

Germination should occur within 5–21 days at 18–24°C (64–75°F); mine took 6 days. Remove the glass when germination has taken place or the seedlings will become drawn.

Gradually introduce the seedlings to sunlight, little by little, over a period of time (but not scorched under glass), to produce sturdy plants. The night temperature should not drop below 10–13°C (50–55°F).

When the seedlings reach the 4-leaf stage, pot them up into 100 mm (4 in) pots of recommended, neutral-slightly acid, gerbera, damp, potting compost, and grow them on. They can be planted out in the garden at the 100 mm (4 in) pot stage, properly hardened off, directly where they are to grow and flower, 300–500 mm (12–20 in) apart, but only when all danger from frost is past and the ground has warmed up.

Or let them grow on, and then transfer them into 175 mm (7 in) pots.

Never cover the crowns with compost or soil, as this will rot the plants.

Gerberas can take up to a year or more to flower from germination. But if the new cultivars are sown early enough, indoors, say 6 to 8 weeks before normal planting out time, and planted out, hardened off, after any frost risk, then they should flower in the first summer.

Feed with a reputable, well-balanced, liquid, soluble, gerbera fertiliser applied as the manufacturer instructs for gerberas.

Or you can pot the plants on into 200–250 mm (8–10 in) pots of recommended, neutral-slightly acid, gerbera, damp, potting compost, and treat them as pot plants.

Gerberas grown in pots in the greenhouse could 'stew' in hot weather, and need light shading during sunny weather, depending on your local climate. If in doubt seek local, professional advice on gerberas. Over-winter gerberas, if necessary, in a glasshouse ensuring that the temperature does not drop below 7°C (45°F).

In English gardens, gerberas are mostly greenhouse plants. Sow the seeds in a recommended, gerbera seed raising compost, under glass at 18–24°C (64–75°F), in late winter-early spring (Feb-March). Treat them as half-hardy, greenhouse pot plants, giving special attention to their feeding, watering and summer ventilation, and giving them light shading late spring-summer, when necessary. Make sure that the greenhouse winter temperature does not drop below 7°C (45°F). Keep these pot plants just moist during winter. Alternatively, grow as half-hardy bedding plants.

Pests and diseases: Slugs, snails, mite, red spider, foot rot, leaf spot, crown rot.
Cultivars/varieties: Black Heart Mixed, height 600 mm (2 ft), usual colour range, but with black centres. Californian Strain, height 600 mm (2 ft), wide range of colours. Farnell Double Mixed, height 600 mm (2 ft). Gigi, height 450–600 mm (18–24 in), large flowered duplex (double single flowered), some crested, 10 or more distinctive shades and tints. Dwarf Happipot Mixed, height 300 mm (12 in), cream, rose, pink, salmon, orange, yellow, good for pot work. Sunburst Mixed, 450 mm (18 in) mostly red, yellow, with twice as many petals as on single flowers.
Family: Asteraceae.

***Gilia* (bird's eye)** The Californian West Coast to British Columbian *Gilia tricolor*; height up to 600 mm (2 ft); is an easy-to-grow annual, which produces clusters of 18–25 mm (0.7–1 in) wide, 5-petalled blooms.

These flowers are pale pink, violet-tipped flushed white, bell-shaped, and star-mouthed, with contrasting violet throat blotches and pale yellow throat. From out of the throat issues a sweet (some say like milk chocolate, but to me like vanilla ice-cream) fragrance.

The foliage is feathery and fine, 75–10 mm (3–4 in) long, with 18–25 mm (0.7–1 in) branchlets.

Gilias prefer a free-draining, sandy loam soil, but will tolerate a range of soils. They are particularly sensitive to drought and heat and wilt rapidly. They are grown as bedding annuals.
Propagation: Seed can be sown; mid-summer to autumn in subtropical areas; autumn or early spring temperate areas; spring in the cooler areas, but once the soil has warmed up; directly where they are to grow and flower, in a sunny or slightly shady spot.

Dig over the soil, when it is easy to work, breaking it down into a fine tilth, to take the seeds. Remove any debris. Gently but thoroughly firm the soil.

Thinly sprinkle the seeds over the prepared area, or sow them in rows. Lightly rake the seeds into the top tilth, not too deeply, and firm gently to anchor them to the soil. Gently water them using a fine spray, and keep the seedbed pleasantly moist.

The seedlings should germinate in up to 21 days, or less depending on the soil temperature. Do not allow the seedlings to dry out. Thin them out, keeping only the strongest, 225 mm (9 in) apart.

I grew gilias under glass, sowing the seeds in punnets of damp, recommended, seed raising compost, in early-spring at 14–16°C (57–61°F). The seeds germinated in 4 days, like mustard and cress. I pricked out the seedlings into small pots of damp, recommended, potting compost, and grew them on as pot plants.

These pot plants began flowering in approximately 58 days from sowing. Some I hardened off and grew on outside when all danger from frost was past, in the spot where they flowered.

In English gardens sow the seeds in spring, but only when the soil has warmed up, directly where they are to grow and flower. They are summer flowering.
Pests and diseases: Reasonably free.
Cultivars/varieties: Species as above.
Family: Polemoniaceae.

***Godetia* (see *Clarkia*)** Certain authorities classify godetias and clarkias as being of the same genus, *Clarkia*. I have also listed godetias under *Clarkia*. But in some seed catalogues, godetias and clarkias are listed under separate headings, so be aware of this.

***Gomphrena* (globe amaranth)** The Indian *Gomphrena globosa*; height 200–750 mm (8–30 in); is a summer-autumn, frost-sensitive annual that thrives in a well-drained, rich, fertile, loamy soil in a sunny location. It grows well in most States.

With the advent of the newer, dwarf cultivars the plant is becoming more popular as a 'front of the border' bedding plant, or for window boxes or pot plants. The taller cultivars are also very attractive and worthy of a place in the border.

The most popular cultivar colour is purple, where the 19 mm (0.7 in) wide, or wider flowers are closely packed, like a raspberry fruit or clover head. These 'flowers' are in fact 'chaffy-bracts', which enclose the insignificant flowers. The flowers-bracts, if picked when just fully open, can be dried with their heads hanging down and used as long-lasting flowers.

White and pink flowered forms are available.

The Texan-Mexican *Gomphrena haageana aurea* has red bracts and orange florets, which fuse into rich orange.

Gomphrenas require ample watering, plus feeding when the buds appear with a well-balanced, liquid, soluble, flower fertiliser, suitable for gomphrenas and applied as the manufacturer instructs.
Propagation: Thinly sow the seeds of globe amaranthus in seed growing containers, 6 mm (0.2 in) deep, in a damp, recommended, seed raising compost, under glass if necessary, at 16–21°C (61–70°F); winter-spring-summer in subtropical areas; spring and early summer elsewhere.

The seeds will germinate within 5–21 days (mine germinated in 5 days). Prick out the seedlings into small pots, or containers of damp, recommended, potting compost. Harden off the seedlings and plant them directly where they are to grow and flower, but only when all danger from frost is past and the ground has warmed up.

The seeds can also be sown in the open, in nursery seedbeds in spring-summer, when all danger from frost is past and the soil has warmed up, with the strongest seedlings being planted out directly where they are to grow and flower, 150–300 mm (6–12 in) apart, depending on cultivar.

Seeds can also be 'station sown': that is a few seeds are sown in clumps where the plants are to grow and flower, but the seedlings are thinned out, keeping only the strongest at each station.

Gomphrenas can also be grown as pot plants.

In English gardens sow the seeds thinly in seed raising compost, late winter-early-mid spring (Feb-March-April), under glass at 16–21°C (61–70°F), and treat as half-hardy bedding annuals. Or they can be grown on as pot plants. Flowers midsummer on.
Pests and diseases: Reasonably free.
Cultivars/varieties: Globosa Mixed, height 250 mm (10 in), pink to red. Globosa Mixed Colours, height 450–600 mm (18–24 in), white, pink, flesh pink, red, purple. Dwarf Purple Buddy 200–300 mm (8–12 in), brilliant purple. *G. haageana aurea.*
Family: Amaranthaceae.

***Gypsophila* (baby's breath, chalk plant)** The strength of the hardy, spring-summer-autumn flowering gypsophilas lies in their ability to 'lift' other flowers.

There are two principle forms that can be grown from seeds: either annual as in the Caucasian *Gypsophila elegans*; height 450–600 mm (18–24 in); or perennial as in the southeast European-Asian *Gypsophila paniculata*; height 900 mm (36 in).

But we shall concern ourselves with *G. elegans*, which has 12 mm (0.5 in) wide flowers in white, pink or deep pink. The leaves are small and grey-green.

Gypsophilas thrive in full sun, but not too hot, in a well-dug, well-drained, neutral or alkaline soil. Excessive fertiliser applications can lead to rank growth, therefore bear in mind that these plants originated on reasonably starved, chalky soils.
Propagation: The 'shot-pellet' like, brown-black seeds of *G. elegans* can be sown at any time of the year, except in the hottest months of summer in hot areas; or the coldest months of autumn-winter in cooler areas.

You can sow small successions of seeds, say every 8–10 weeks; or every 4 weeks, if you do much floral decoration.

Dig over the soil where the gypsophila is to grow and flower, breaking and raking it down into a fine tilth. Remove any debris. Gently but thoroughly firm the soil to take the seeds. Make sure the soil is approximately neutral as gypsophilas deteriorate in an acid soil.

Sow the seeds in a sheltered, sunny spot (in row for cut flowers), 200–300 mm (8–12 in) apart. Rake the seeds carefully into the tilth, or cover them with seed raising compost or finely sieved soil, at a depth the seed merchant recommends on his packet. Gently water the seeds using a fine spray. The plants will germinate and develop quickly.

You can station-sow the seeds in clumps, dotted about to make an odd spot useful. Don't bother to thin out the seedlings as they can help support each other, unless you have really oversown, then thin them out carefully as gypsophilas resent root disturbance and react by producing less vigorous growth.

Or you can thin out the seedlings to say 450 mm (18 in) apart, but they will have to be supported with twiggy sticks, or similar.

You can grow gypsophilas in seed raising containers of damp, recommended, seed raising compost, and prick them out into pots of damp, recommended, potting compost, then grow them as fleeting pot plants, but they will need support.

In English gardens sow the seeds of *G. elegans* in early autumn (Sept) in mild winter areas, or spring elsewhere, directly where they are to grow and flower. Flowers early summer to autumn, but flowering time depend on when seeds are sown.
Pests and diseases: Reasonably free.
Cultivars/varieties: (annuals) *G. elegans* White or Pink or Carmine. Elegans Mixed, white, pink, carmine. 'Carminea Elegans', height 500 mm (20 in), carmine flowers. 'Covent Garden', height 500 mm (20 in), large white flowers.
Family: Caryophyllaceae.

***Helianthus* (sunflower)** The North American annual sunflower *Helianthus annuus*; height 1–3 m (39 in–10 ft); is one of the easiest plants to grow. The cultivar flower sizes can vary from 125–150–350 mm (5–6–14 in). The sunflower is also the State of Kansas flower-emblem.

The huge flowers of the traditional sunflower, up to 350 mm (14 in) wide, which appear summer, and on, are yellow-petalled with brown-purplish centre discs, borne on tall, 3 m (10 ft) stems. Be aware that the flowers usually face the sun. These annual sunflowers, because of their height and singular appearance, are usually restricted to the back of the border.

H. a. 'Flore-Pleno' is a double-flowered form. There are also less tall sunflower cultivars, in flower colours from orangey, to yellow, to whiteish.

Sunflower leaves are rough, hairy and heart-shaped.

The annual 'cucumber-leaf' sunflower *H. debilis cucumerifolius*, and its cultivars; height 1–2 m (39–79 in); have flowers 75–150 mm (3–6 in) wide, in shades and tints of yellow, red or purple, with the petal bases in darker zonal bands. There are double-flowered cultivars.

Sunflowers prefer a sunny, sheltered spot, in a well-drained, fertile soil, but the tall plants will still need staking. They need frequent dead-heading, i.e. removing of spent flowers, to prolong their flowering period and prevent self-seeding. They also need copious watering during dry spells.

Feed sunflowers in spring once the shoots have matured into young stems, and to increase flower production, with a well-balanced, liquid, soluble, flower fertiliser, suitable for sunflowers and applied as the manufacturer instructs.

Cut down and tidy up the foliage after flowering.

Propagation: Annual sunflower seeds can be sown late winter-spring (also at other times) in subtropical areas; spring-early summer elsewhere; but only if any danger from frost risk is past and the soil has warmed up.

Dig up and break down the soil into a fine tilth, raking out any debris. Annual sunflower seeds can be 'station sown'; that is sow a few seeds in the spots directly where they are to grow and flower, 450–600 mm (18–24 in) apart for the tall cultivars, 300 mm (12 in) apart for the dwarf, but eventually keeping only the strongest seedling in each group. The seeds are planted into the tilth surface 12–25 mm (0.5–1 in) deep.

Or the seeds can be sown broadcast over the area directly where they are to grow and flower (although this method uses up much seed), and covered with fine soil, 12–25 mm (0.5–1 in) deep.

Seedlings should appear from 3–10 days and on, depending on soil temperature. Thin them out 300–450–600 mm (12–18–24 in) apart, depending on cultivar size and spread.

Seeds can also be sown singly in 100 mm (4 in) pots of recommended seed raising compost, under glass at 16–18°C (61–64°F). Grow the seedlings on, harden them off, if necessary in a cold frame, and then plant them out directly where they are to grow and flower, but only when any danger from frost is past and the ground has warmed up.

This method of propagation, however, would be used only if you wanted early plants, as annual sunflower seeds germinate and grow so quickly.

In English gardens sow the seeds of annual sunflowers outside in mid-spring (April), but only when danger from frost is past, directly where they are to grow and flower, 12–25 mm (0.5–1 in) deep, in a sunny, sheltered spot. 'Station plant' the seeds, a few at each station, at the correct distance apart. Thin out the seedlings leaving only the strongest. Or the seeds can be sown, in early spring (March), under glass, at 14–16°C (57–61°F), singly in pots, and treated as half-hardy annuals. Flowers midsummer on.

Pests and diseases: Reasonably free.

Cultivars/varieties: 'Sun Giant', height 3 m (10 ft), huge flowers. 'Sungold', height 1 m (39 in), yellow double flowers 150–200 mm (6–8 in) wide. 'Bronze Shades', height 1.5 m (5 ft). 'Tall Russian', large flowered.

Family: Asteraceae.

***Helichrysum* (straw flower, everlasting daisy, paper daisy)** The Western Australian *Helichrysum bracteatum*; height: prostrate up to 1.2 m (48 in), but usually less, particularly the dwarf cultivars; is a short-lived, spring-summer flowering, variable perennial, or annual. Annuals can be grown from seed; perennial cultivars from vegetative propagation.

Helichrysum species, varieties and cultivars are now established as great garden favourites. They are available in white, yellow, goldish, orangey, pink, reddish, purplish or brownish, with some having flushed, zone-banded variations of these colours.

The 'lacquered', crisp-paper, or dry-straw, pointed-petalled, daisy-like, 50–75 mm (2–3 in) wide 'flowers', borne on erect stems, are in fact highly coloured bracts. The true flowers are less significant, and found as a raised, sometimes pointed tuft at the centre of the bracts.

The foliage, generally, is loose, sprawling, lance-like and grey-green.

Helichrysums look well in groups and drifts in a native plant garden, but they are equally at home as border, or bedding plants. They will self-seed in undisturbed gardens.

Other helichrysum annuals are *H. cassianum* (syn. *Schoenia cassiana*) and *H. davenportii*. The short-lived perennials *H. collinum* and *H. elatum* are treated as annuals.

Helichrysums prefer a neutral, moderately fertile, well-drained, sunny, sheltered site. They respond to sensible watering during dry weather and are reasonably hardy except in colder areas.

If using fertiliser choose one suitable for these Australian native plants (as many Australian plants have their own fertiliser likes and dislikes), and apply it as the manufacturer instructs for helichrysums.

Remove spent flowers as these can make the plants look scruffy. Helichrysum blooms can be used as dried flower floral decoration.

Propagation: Dig over the site where the helichrysums are to grow and flower, breaking down the soil into a fine tilth and removing any debris.

Seeds can be sown winter in subtropical areas; or early spring-summer temperate areas; spring in cool areas.

Broadcast the seeds thinly, and rake them lightly into the soil tilth, to a 3–5 mm (0.1–0.2 in) depth. Or cover the seeds with a thin layer of granulated peat, or similar, to create natural germinating conditions.

Water the seeds carefully using a fine spray. Thin out the seedlings 250–350 mm (10–14 in), usually 300 mm (12 in) apart. Flowers should appear midsummer on.

Or the seeds can be sown in a nursery seed bed and transplanted when large enough to handle, directly where they are to grow and flower.

Or you can sow the seeds at 16–18°C (61–64°F), under glass where necessary, in late autumn-early winter in seed compost containers, using a recommended seed raising compost. Keep the seeds pleasantly moist.

The seeds need light to germinate.

The seeds should germinate within 7–10 days, but some may appear in as little as 3 days, so check daily. Prick out the seedlings into 75–100 mm (3–4 in) pots, and grow them on. Harden them off, if necessary in a cold frame, and plant them out directly where they are to grow and flower, when any danger from frost is past and the ground has warmed up.

Should any significant flower variations be produced from these seedlings, then you can propagate them vegetatively.

In English gardens, *H. bracteatum* is treated as a pot grown half-hardy, summer-flowering annual. Sow in seed raising compost, late winter-early spring (Feb-March), at 16–18°C (61–64°F). Flowers midsummer, and on.

Pests and diseases: Mildew, verticillium wilt.

Cultivars/varieties: *H. bracteatum*, height 600 mm (2 ft). Bright Bikini Formula Mixed, height 300 mm (12 in), white, pink, crimson, yellow. Double Mixed, height 900 mm (3 ft). 'Hot Bikini', height 300 mm (12 in), scarlet. Monstrosum Double Mix, height 750 mm (30 in), pink, scarlet, gold. Tom Thumb, height 450 mm (18 in), mixed colours.

Family: Asteraceae.

***Heliotropium* (heliotrope, cherry pie)** The frost-sensitive Peruvian *Heliotropium* × *hybrida*; height 450 mm–1 m (18–39 in); is a sprawly perennial that can be grown from seeds.

The 75–150–225 mm (3–6–9 in) wide, terminal clusters of tiny, starry, heliotrope-scented (like vanilla icecream only sweeter) flowers appear above heavily-wrinkled, mint-like leaves, winter-spring-summer, depending on district climate. Hybrids are available with intense purple or white flowers.

Heliotropes like a free-draining, moisture retaining, rich, organic soil in a humid, sunny spot; not a hot dry site, and with shelter from fierce winds.

Heliotropes can also be trained as half-standard or standard plants, and in this mode they can be used as accent plants. For this purpose they are grown in pots and staked with stout canes.

Feed heliotropes with a well-balanced, liquid, soluble flower fertiliser, suitable for heliotropes and applied as the manufacturer instructs.

Cut down any spent flowers to prolong flowering, and any floppy foliage to keep the plant compact.

Propagation: Thinly sow the seeds in seed compost containers, on top of a damp, recommended seed raising compost; spring and autumn subtropical areas spring and autumn temperate areas; spring-summer cold areas; under glass if necessary at 16–21°C (60–70°F).

Press the seeds gently to anchor them to the compost. The seeds need light to help them germinate; but keep them out of direct sunlight when under glass.

Gently mist water the seeds using a fine spray, keeping the compost pleasantly moist. The seeds can take a few days or up to one month to germinate.

Prick out the seedlings, when they are large enough to handle easily, into containers of damp, recommended compost or preferably 100 mm (4 in) pots, and grow them on. Harden them off if necessary in a cold frame, and plant them out directly where they are to grow and flower, but only when any danger from frost is past and the soil has warmed up.

Nip back the growing tips when the plants have become established, and are approximately 75–100 mm (3–4 in) high, to encourage side shooting and compact growth. Heliotropes will grow outside provided the temperature does not go below 8–10°C (46–50°F).

In English gardens sow the seeds in seed raising mix, under glass, late winter or early spring (Feb-March), at 16–21°C (60–70°F). Do not cover the seeds, gently press them on to the compost to anchor them. Treat the plants as half-hardy annuals. Flowers summer.

Pests and diseases: Reasonably free.

Cultivars/varieties: Pacific Hybrids, height 300 mm (12 in), blue shades. 'Marine', height 450–600 mm (18–24 in), royal purple.

Family: Boraginaceae.

***Helipterum* (syn. *Rhodanthe*) (paper daisies, everlasting daisies)** The Australian annual *Helipterum manglesii* (syn. *Rhodanthe manglesii*); height 300 mm (12 in); blooms spring-summer. It bears 25 mm (1 in) wide, white or pink or deep-pink, papery flowers, the deep pink fading through lighter shades as the plant ages.

H. albicans, with 30 mm (1.2 in) wide, yellow or white flowers in summer, is a variable perennial that can be grown from seeds. *H. a.* ssp. *alpinum* has rougher-textured flowers, with purple reverse.

H. floribundum is an annual to 400 mm (16 in) tall, bearing, in spring, masses of 20 mm (0.8 in) wide, white, papery flowers.

Helipterums like hot sunshine and a well-drained, light, reasonably fertile soil.

They can also be fed, when the buds appear, with a well-balanced, liquid, soluble flower fertiliser, suitable for helipterums and applied as the manufacturer instructs.

Helipterums make excellent cut and dried flowers.

Helipterums will self-seed in the right conditions.

Seedlings must be protected from any damaging frosts.

Propagation: Dig over the soil, breaking it down into a fine tilth. Rake out any debris. Firm the soil gently, but firmly. Thinly sow the seeds broadcast-fashion, or in rows, autumn to spring in subtropical and frost-free temperate areas.

Elsewhere, the seedlings will have to be protected from frost. Or the seeds can be sown later, in spring, directly where they are to grow and flower. Rake them into the top 3 mm (0.1 in) of soil. Keep the soil pleasantly moist.

Thin out *H. albicans* seedlings to 300 mm (12 in) apart. Thin out *H. floribunda* seedlings to 200 mm (8 in) apart. Thin out *H. manglesii* seedlings to 250 mm (10 in) apart.

In English gardens broadcast, or sow the seeds in rows, in mid-spring (April), directly where they are to grow and flower. Germinating seedlings have to be protected in hard frost districts. Helipterum seedlings do not transplant well.

But for earlier flowers you can sow a few seeds in pots, late winter-early spring (Feb-March) under glass, at 16–18°C (61–64°F), keeping the strongest seedling in each pot. Treat these plants as half-hardy annuals.

Pests and diseases: Reasonably free, sometimes aphids.

Cultivars/varieties: Mixed Colours.

Family: Asteraceae.

***Hibiscus* (rose-mallow)** The Southern United States, summer-flowering *Hibiscus moscheutos* cultivars; height 600 mm–1.5–1.8 m (2–5–6 ft); are frost-tender perennials that can be grown as half-hardy annuals.

These cultivars produce eye-catching, 200–250 mm (8–10 in) wide, radar-dish, funnel-shaped flowers, in white, white with red eye, pink, or soft pink with red eye, rose, or deep red.

The tall cultivars can be used as background plants, or accent plants, and the smaller ones as bedding or pot plants.

Rose-mallows prefer a light, well-drained loam, rich in well-rotted, organic matter.

They need copious water when growing well, and applications, once the buds form, of a balanced, liquid, soluble flower fertiliser, suitable for these plants and applied as the manufacturer instructs.

Propagation: Seeds are sown under glass approximately 6 to 8 weeks before the last expected frost in your area, or approximately 2 months before the usual planting out time in your locality.

The hard-coated seeds can be soaked in water for say 12 hours before sowing, to help speed up germination.

Sow the seeds individually into 75 mm (3 in) peat pots, using a damp, recommended seed raising compost, under glass if necessary, at 18–21°C (64–70°F).

Hibiscus roots resent disturbance, and that is why you sow them in peat pots, so that you can plant out the seedlings pots and all.

The seeds can take up to 3 weeks to germinate, but keep an eye on them as they may come up much sooner. Harden off the seedlings, if necessary in a cold frame. Plant them out 900 mm–1.2 m (36–47 in) apart, in full sun, but only when all danger from frost is past and the ground has warmed up.

In English gardens sow the seeds in early-spring (March), in seed raising compost, individually in 75 mm (3 in) pots, at 18–21°C (64–70°F), and treat them as half-hardy plants. Flowers midsummer, and on.

Pests and diseases: Aphids, mealy bugs.

Cultivars/varieties: Dwarf Dixie Belle Mixed, height 600 mm (2 ft), pink, shell pink with red eye, rose, red. Southern Belle, height 1.5 m (5 ft), white, white with red eye, pink, rose, deep red.

Family: Malvaceae.

***Hunnemannia* (Mexican tulip poppy, golden cup)** At first glance the frost-sensitive, spring-summer flowering, Mexican perennial *H. fumariifolia* (syn. *H. fumariaefolia*); height 600–900–1.2 m (24–36–48 in); looks very much like a California poppy, but it is more shrubby in appearance, and generally taller. It has blue-green, finely-cut, carrot-like foliage.

The Mexican tulip poppy is usually treated as a tender annual in frost prone districts. It is, however, an easy plant to grow from seeds.

The yellow, creamy-smooth, cup-shaped flowers, 62–75 mm (2.5–3 in) wide, enclose a delicate cluster of yellow anthers. Mexican tulip poppies, which is unusual for poppies, can be used as cut flowers provided the cut is sealed.

The Mexican tulip poppy appreciates a neutral, sandy, free-draining loam. It bitterly resents root disturbance.

Propagation: Dig over the site where the plants are to grow and flower, when it is easy to work, breaking down the soil into a fine tilth. Gently but thoroughly firm it.

Plant the seeds of the Mexican tulip poppy directly where they are to flower and grow, as they do not transplant well.

Sow in autumn-winter, subtropical areas; or after any danger from last frost is past, in other areas. Barely rake the seeds into the surface tilth.

Gently water the seeds using a fine spray. Seedlings germinate in up to 20 days at 20°C (68°F) soil temperature. Carefully thin out the seedlings, without disturbing the roots of those left, 150–250–300 mm (6–10–12 in) apart. Keep the plants watered during dry, summer spells.

Or you can sow 3–5 seeds into 75 mm (3 in) peat pots, using damp, recommended sandy-loam potting compost, about 6 to 8 weeks before the usual planting time in your locality; or 6 to 8 weeks before the last frost is expected in your locality; under glass in frost prone areas, at 13–18°C (55–64°F).

Remove the weakest seedlings keeping only the strongest one in each pot. Harden off the seedlings, if necessary in a cold frame, and plant them out carefully, 200–300 mm (8–12 in) apart, directly where they are to grow and flower, but only when all danger from frost is past and the ground has warmed up.

Germinating the seeds in peat pots means that the roots need not be disturbed at planting time, as you plant the seedling pot and all.

In English gardens sow the seeds early-spring (March), in seed compost, under glass at 13–18°C (55–64°F), 3–5 seeds to each individual 75 mm (3 in) pot, or 75 mm (3 in) peat pot. Leave only the strongest seedling in each pot.

Treat the plants as half-hardy annuals. Or sow the seeds outside in mid-late spring, but only when all danger from frost is past. Mexican tulip poppies will be cut down by the first heavy frost. Summer flowering.

Pests and diseases: Reasonably free.

Cultivars/varieties: 'Sunlight', height 600 mm (2 ft), yellow.

Family: Papaveraceae.

***Iberis* (candytuft)** There are various Mediterranean-European, British and Western Asian, annual and perennial candytufts grown in our gardens, but the two we shall discuss are *Iberis amara* and *I. umbellata*.

The annual *Iberis amara*; height 300–400 mm (12–16 in); is the sweetly-scented, spring-summer flowering, white-flowered rocket or hyacinth-flowered candytuft. It produces a 50 mm (2 in) long, tight cluster of flowers around the stem, similar to the flowers of a hyacinth.

The leaves are toothed or lobed, lance to broad-ended.

The spring-summer flowering annual *I. umbellata*, globe or common candytuft; height 200–400 mm (8–16 in) depending on whether the plants are dwarf cultivars or otherwise; is most widely grown.

In late spring-summer-autumn, clusters of flowers, flattish, slightly domed in the centre, like an umbrella, and up to 50–75 mm (2–3 in) wide, are produced. They are available in white, pink, red and purple, and shades and tints of these colours.

The plant has narrow, lance-like leaves.

Both hyacinth flowered and globe candytufts are grown from seeds.

Candytufts are used for massed bedding, border edges, or rockeries and the like.

They prefer full sun, a neutral, well-drained, reasonably fertile soil, and applications, when the buds are forming, of a well-balanced, liquid, soluble, flower fertiliser, suitable for candytufts and applied as the manufacturer instructs.

Candytufts are also used as cut flowers.

Cutting off any spent flowers will help prolong the flowering period.

Propagation: Dig over the flowering site, breaking down the soil into a fine tilth. Rake out any debris, and gently but thoroughly firm the soil to take the seeds.

Sow the seeds; autumn-early winter in subtropical areas; spring or late summer-autumn temperate areas; spring or late summer-early autumn in cooler areas; 6 mm (0.2 in) deep, directly where the plants are to grow and flower, as they resent root disturbance. Germination should take place in 5–15 days at 16–20°C (61–68°F) soil temperature.

Or the seeds can be 'station planted', that is, sow a few seeds in clumps 150 mm 6 in) apart. Carefully thin out the seedlings, but leave two or three clumped together rather than upset the seedlings' roots.

Space *I. amara* 150 mm (6 in) apart; and *I. umbellata* 225 mm (9 in) apart, to provide a tight, carpet-mass of flowers.

Or a few seeds can be sown in individual, small pots of damp, recommended seed raising compost, in early spring under glass, at 16°C (61°F). Carefully thin out the seedlings in the pots, keeping only the strongest.

Harden off the seedlings, if necessary in a cold frame, and plant them out directly where they are to flower and grow, when all danger from frost is past and the ground has warmed up.

Or you can prick out small seedlings into punnets of damp recommended potting compost, grow them on, harden them off, and plant them out when danger from frost is past. But bear in mind that the seedlings may react adversely to root disturbance.

In English gardens sow the seeds in early autumn (Sept), and then again in spring (March and on), in successions if so desired, to prolong the flowering period, directly where the seeds are to grow and flower. Or sow seeds under glass at 16°C (61°F), in late winter-early spring (Feb-March) in small pots of damp, recommended seed raising compost. Keep only the strongest seedling in each pot. Treat these plants as half-hardy annuals. Flowers early summer, and on.

Pests and diseases: Reasonably free.

Cultivars/varieties: Ruffled White Hyacinth, height 400 mm (16 in), pure white ruffled. Dwarf Fairy Mixed, height 200 mm (8 in), shades and tints of white, lilac, silver pink, carmine, maroon. Umbellata Mixed.

Family: Brassicaceae.

***Impatiens* (balsam, busy-lizzie, sultan's balsam, touch-me-not)** The species of impatiens listed below, and their cultivars, are treated as tender, frost-sensitive plants, and are grown in filtered shade, although some hybrids are more tolerant of sun than others.

Impatiens are mostly summer-flowering, but if treated as heated-greenhouse plants, then many can be flowered in winter or spring.

The cultivars of the East African perennial *Impatiens wallerana* (syn. *I. walleriana*), busy-lizzie; height 150–750 mm (6–30 in); are among the most widely used summer-bedding plants in Australia.

I. sultanii, sultan's balsam, a perennial from the warmer parts of Asia-Zanzibar; height 600–900 mm (24–36 in); has now been placed under the species *I. wallerana* by one authority.

I. wallerana and *I. sultanii* have been crossed to produce colourful F hybrids; height 150–600 mm (6–24 in); which are popular as border plants, bedding plants, window-box, pot and hanging basket plants.

The 5-petalled flowers are 25–50 mm (1–2 in) wide, in white, orange, pink, lavender, red or striped bicolours, with a 'dorsal-fin' spur at the rear of the flower.

Their foliage consists of oval, light-green, shiny leaves, with nearly 'see-through' stems.

These cultivars have been cross-bred with New Guinea *Impatiens* species *I. schlecteri*, giving rise to attractively-leaved, frost-sensitive plants that are known as 'New Guinea Impatiens'.

New Guinea cultivars are grown as greenhouse or indoor pot plants. They can be grown outside in summer in warm, moist, frost-free areas, in a partially shaded, sheltered location.

Their germination rate may be lower than *I. wallerana*, therefore be prepared to sow more seeds.

The Indian-Southeast Asian annual *Impatiens balsamina* (syn. *I. balsaminafera*), balsam; height 200–900 mm (8–36 in); has cultivars that are mostly semi-double azalea flowered, or semi-double camellia flowered.

These blooms are 37–62 mm (1.5–2.5 in) wide, in shades and tints of white, yellow, pink or red, with a typical 'dorsal-fin' spur above the flower petals.

The foliage has watery-looking stems, like watercress, with pale green, lance-like leaves.

The cultivars of *I. capensis* are usually grown as greenhouse pot plants. They are erect plants bearing drooping but attractive, spotted blooms.

I. balsamina and *I. wallerana*, and their cultivars, are frost sensitive, and need warm, sheltered, filtered shade, a cool root run, and a well-drained, rich, organic soil.

The New Guinea cultivars are much grown as greenhouse plants in cooler areas.

Given the right growing conditions, that is moist and permanently warm, *I. wallerana* seed will explode from their capsules with impatient urgency (hence their name *Impatiens*), and self-seed. But hybrids will not breed true to type.

Propagation: I. wallerana seeds can be sown any time in warm, frost-free locations, where night temperatures do not drop below 15–18°C (59–64°F), directly where they are to grow and flower.

Dig over the soil breaking it down into a fine tilth, and remove any debris. Gently but thoroughly firm the soil to take the seeds.

Thinly sow the seeds, and barely press them on to the tilth surface to anchor them. Water gently with a fine misting spray. Don't let the seeds dry out, and keep the soil pleasantly moist.

Thin out the seedlings, leaving only the strongest, 225–450 mm (12–18 in) apart, depending on cultivar. Or the thinned out seedlings can be transferred to another bed, or into pots. Flowers should appear spring-summer from autumn-winter sowings, and summer from spring sowings.

Impatiens seedlings are susceptible to damping-off diseases, and perhaps, because of this, are better grown in seed compost containers, where more control over their growth can be exercised.

Seeds can be sown in a heated greenhouse or indoors in a well-lighted place, 6–8 weeks before the last frost is expected in your location, at 21–24°C (70–75°F), using a damp, recommended, seed raising compost.

Press the seeds gently on to the compost surface. Mist spray the seeds, or place the container in a shallow dish of water until the moisture just glistens on the compost surface, then remove the container. You can cover the container with a sheet of glass to help reduce evaporation. But constantly check the compost. Don't let the seeds dry out. Gradually lift the glass and finally remove it as the seedlings germinate.

Prick out the seedlings into pots of damp, recommended potting compost, and grow them on. Harden them off in a cold frame, and plant them out directly where they are to grow and flower, when all danger from frost is past and the ground has warmed up sufficiently.

Or sow the seeds in spring, or late summer-mid autumn in temperate areas; early-mid spring, or late summer-mid autumn in cooler areas; in frost-free conditions, and under glass where necessary.

Impatiens balsamina seeds can be sown all year round, or late winter-spring-summer in subtropical areas; spring-early summer in temperate areas; and spring-summer in cold areas, in frost-free conditions and under glass where necessary, at 21–24°C (70–75°F).

Impatiens can be grown on as pot plants.

In English gardens sow the seeds of *I. wallerana*, and its cultivars, early spring (March), under glass, in seed raising containers using a recommended seed raising compost, at 21–24°C (70–75°F). Treat them as half-hardy annuals. Eventually transfer the seedlings into 100 mm (4 in) pots, harden them off, and plant them out directly where they are to grow and flower, but only when all danger from frost is past and the ground has warmed up sufficiently. Summer flowering.

For *I. balsamina* follow the same method suggested for *I. wallerana*.

I. wallerana and its cultivars can be grown as indoor pot plants, lightly-shaded, and out of direct sunlight. They will cope at 13–15°C (55–59°F), and above, winter temperature. At lower temperatures the plants will deteriorate.

Pests and diseases: Aphids, red spider, slugs, damping-off, leaf spot, powdery mildew, rust.

Cultivars/varieties: Baby Mixed, height 150 mm (6 in), pink, salmon, carmine, red, orange. Balsam Super Double Mixed, height 450–600 mm (18–24 in), camellia flowered. Futura Mixed F_1 Hybrid, height 200 mm (8 in), clear colours. Super Elfin Mixed F_1 Hybrid, height 200 mm (8 in), many different colours. 'Sweet Sue', 300–600 mm (12–24 in), deep orange. 'Zig Zag', height 200–250 mm (8–10 in), bicoloured white on pink, rose, salmon, scarlet, orange.

Family: Balsaminaceae.

***Ipomoea* (morning glory)** The spring-summer-flowering morning glories are climbers with twining stems, and should be planted next to strong supports, such as tripods, trellises, fences and the like, for them to display their full beauty.

Or they can be grown as trailing hanging-basket or pot plants. Morning glory cultivars can provide a brilliant mix of light and dark colours.

The Mexican *I. violacea* (syn. *I. imperialis, I. rubro-caerulea, I. tricolor*); height 2.5 m (8 ft) or more; is a half-hardy perennial that is grown as an annual.

The species has blueish-reddish-purplish, yellow-throated, 100 mm (4 in) wide, trumpet-like flowers, that open in the morning, and fade and close in the afternoon, but are soon replaced by others.

It has delightful cultivars which are grown for their blue and white striped, or sky blue-white throated, or white-cream with gold-yellow throated trumpet-flowers, up to 125 mm (5 in) wide.

The Japanese *I. nil* grows to 3 m (10 ft) or more, with either violet-blue, or rose with white throat, or blueish, 50 mm (2 in) wide trumpets; some flower trumpets turn in at the edges. There is a larger, scarlet-flowered cultivar.

The Mexican *I. coccinea* is the red morning glory, a half-hardy annual which reaches a height of 1.5–2.5 m (5–8 ft), and has 37 mm (1.5 in) long, scarlet-yellow throated flowers. The leaves are pointed, slender to heart-shaped.

The tropical American *I. purpurea* is a half-hardy annual, the common morning glory, that quickly grows to a height of 3 m (10 ft), or more, with dull-green, heart-shaped leaves. It has cultivars of white, bluish, pink, red or purple, 75 mm (3 in) trumpet-flowers.

Morning glories prefer full sun and a well-drained, sandy loam, with moderate to good watering in hot weather. Do not feed these plants with fertilisers high in nitrogen, as this could lead to much foliage growth, but fewer flowers. Dead-head (remove) any spent flowers to lengthen flower production.

Certain morning glories, such as *I. learii*, can be unwelcomely vigorous, and therefore should be avoided.

You may find that ipomoeas are sometimes listed in seed catalogues as 'convolvulus', but there are beautiful convolvulus plants that are not ipomoeas. (See under *Convolvulus* in this book.)

Propagation: Dig over the soil where the plants are to grow, breaking it down into a fine tilth. Rake out any debris. Firm the soil to take the seeds.

Seeds of morning glories can be sown in winter and spring subtropical areas; early spring in frost-free temperate areas; late-spring in the cooler areas, after any danger from frost risk is past.

'Station plant' 2 or 3, or more seeds, 6 mm (0.2 in) deep, 200–300 mm (8–12 in) apart, where they are to grow and flower, close by a support they can climb. Very carefully thin out the seedlings keeping only the strongest at each station. Morning glories resent root disturbance.

The hard-coated seeds of *I. violacea* can be soaked in tepid water for 24 hours to speed up germination.

Or sow 2 or 3 morning glory seeds, spaced out, in individual, 75 mm (3 in) peat-pots, containing damp, recommended seed raising compost. Very carefully thin out the seedlings, keeping only the strongest in each pot. The seedlings are grown on, hardened off, and planted out pots and all, thereby minimising root disturbance.

Or in cool areas sow 2 or 3 seeds, early to mid spring under glass at 18–21°C (64–70°F), in individual 75 mm (3 in) peat-pots containing damp, recommended seed raising compost. Very carefully thin out the seedlings keeping only the strongest in each pot. Harden off the seedlings, and plant them outside when all danger from frost is past and the ground has warmed up.

In English gardens sow 2 or 3 seeds, early to mid spring (March-April), under glass at 18–21°C (64–70°F), in individual 75 mm (3 in) peat-pots containing damp, recommended seed raising compost. Very carefully thin out the seedlings keeping only the strongest in each pot. Treat them as half-hardy plants. But soak the seeds of *I. violacea* for 24 hours in tepid water before sowing them. Flowers midsummer.

Or sow the seeds directly where they are to grow and flower when all danger from frost is past, 12 mm (0.5 in) deep 200–300 mm (8–12 in) apart, a few seeds in each station. Provide a suitable support for the plants.

Pests and diseases: Aphids, red spider, white flies.

Cultivars/varieties: Early Call Mixed, white, pink, lavender, blue, violet. 'Cardinal Climber', red, white throat. 'Heavenly Blue', height 3 m (10 ft), intense, sky-blue. Flying Colours, trained to 2.5 m (8 ft), white, pink, blue.

Family: Convolvulaceae.

***Ipomopsis* (skyrocket, standing cypress)** The Californian *Ipomopsis rubra*; height 900 mm–1.8 m (3–6 ft) is a frost-sensitive plant that can often be found listed under *Gilia rubra* (syn. *G. coronopifolia*).

It is an attractive, half-hardy, spring-summer-flowering biennial, or annual, depending on when and how the seed is sown. It has tubular-trumpet, 5-petalled, star-ended 25–37 mm (1–1.5 in) rich-scarlet flowers, which spring out from the main column-spike on short side-branches.

The blooms are accompanied by needle-like foliage. The flower spike usually needs support when growing.

Ipomopsis prefers a sunny, free-draining soil, in a sheltered position. It is better mass-planted 225–250 mm (9–10 in) apart to achieve an impressive block of scarlet, and to allow the plants to give each other physical support.

Propagation: Dig over the site where the plants are to grow and flower, breaking down the soil into a fine tilth. Rake out any debris.

Sow the seeds 6 mm (0.2 in) deep; autumn in subtropical and temperate areas; spring in cooler areas. Thin out the seedlings 225 mm (9 in) apart.

Or sow the seeds in pots of damp, seed-raising compost, early autumn in subtropical and temperate areas; spring in cold, frost-prone areas.

You can, in cold, frost prone areas, sow the seeds, earliest spring, in pots of damp, recommended seed raising compost, under glass at 15–16°C (59–61°F), or in a cold frame. Carefully thin out the seedlings keeping only the strongest in each pot.

Or sow the seeds in seed compost containers of damp, seed raising compost. Prick out the seedlings, when large enough to handle, into 100 mm (4 in) pots of damp, recommended, potting compost.

Grow the plants in a cold frame in frost-prone areas, but don't let the seedlings 'stew' under the glass during summer. Ventilate and shade them if necessary.

Pot the plants up into larger pots before they become pot-bound. Overwinter them under glass in frost-prone areas, and plant them out when the danger from frost is past and the soil has warmed up.

Take care not to damage the foliage or roots when removing the plant from the pot.

In English gardens sow the seeds in earliest summer (June) in pots of seed raising compost, under glass at 15–18°C (59–65°F), or in a cold frame. Very carefully thin out the seedlings, keeping only the strongest seedling in each pot. Flowers midsummer.

Or sow the seeds in seed raising compost. Pot them up into larger pots of potting compost, and grow under glass in winter. Plant them out, properly hardened off, when the danger from frost is past and the ground has warmed up, or leave them in a cool greenhouse, in pots, for early flowering.

Pests and diseases: Reasonably free.

Cultivars/varieties: Species as above.

Family: Polemoniaceae.

***Isatis* (dyer's woad)** *Isatis tinctoria*; height 1 m (39 in); a short-lived perennial, usually grown in the garden as a biennial border plant.

It was used for the production of the famous blue dye known as dyer's woad, which was extracted from its 100 mm (4 in) oblong, pointed leaves. But today isatis is grown in gardens for its mass of 4-petalled, simple-cross, yellow flowers, typical of the cabbage family, of which it is a member.

From a rosette of leaves rises a spike, at the end of which are borne many branches, smothered with hosts of yellow flowers. En masse, in spring in temperate areas, and early summer in cold areas, they are very eye-catching.

The plants, when fully grown, may need staking as they do tend to flop. Isatis likes a neutral, fertile, free-draining soil.

Propagation: Sow the seeds of isatis as soon as they are ripe in summer, directly where they are to flower and grow. The seeds are large and arrow-shaped, and can be placed singly.

The primary root emerges from the middle of the seed and pushes into the soil, and at the same time pushes the seed case up above ground like an arrow-shaped shield. Thin out the seedlings to 300 mm (12 in) apart.

In English gardens sow the fully-ripened seeds in summer, directly where they are to grow and flower, and thin them out 300 mm (12 in) apart. They should flower the following early summer.

Pests and diseases: Reasonably free.

Cultivars/varieties: Species as above.

Family: Brassicaceae.

***Kochia* (summer cypress, mock cypress, burning bush)** The European-Asian *Kochia scoparia* var. *triphylla*; height: up to 1 m (39 in); spread: to 600 mm (24 in); is a 'summer' half-hardy annual that grows like a small, dense-foliaged, light-green cypress.

Before it dies its foliage turns reddish-maroon to vivid red, to brownish, looking, at its colour peak, as though it were on fire; hence its common name.

K. scoparia 'Childsii' is a more compact, neater plant.

The summer cypress has many uses in the garden, either as a border hedge, an accent plant, or a backdrop to annuals.

It is also grown in 125 mm or 175 mm (5 or 7 in) pots, using damp, recommended, potting compost. Special attention has to be paid to the pot plants' watering, making sure that they don't dry out.

Kochias produce small greenish flowers, which are insignificant. In warm areas kochias are prolifically self-seeding, and the seedlings should be removed when seen. The plants can be sparingly and lightly trimmed, like a hedge, to keep them tidy.

Propagation: Seeds are sown early spring, in warm, frost-free locations, 3 mm (0.2 in) deep, barely covered as they need light to germinate, directly where they are to grow and flower.

Or they can be sown in seed compost containers, using a damp, recommended seed raising compost, for early-mid summer mature plants.

Seeds are sown late winter-early spring, or 6 to 8 weeks before the last expected frost, under glass, in cold areas, in seed compost containers using a damp, recommended seed raising compost, at 16–21°C (61–70°F).

Prick out the seedlings into containers of damp, recommended potting compost, and grow them on. Harden off the seedlings in a cold frame, and plant them out directly where they are to grow and flower 450–600 mm (18–24 in) apart (450 mm if used as hedges, and 600 mm for 'cypress trees'), when any danger from frost is past and the ground has warmed up.

Or the seeds can be sown in late spring, when all the danger from frost is past, directly where they are to grow and flower, at 450–600 mm (18–24 in) stations (clumps), keeping only the strongest plant at each station. Kochias prefer a sunny, well-drained, reasonably fertile soil, and sheltered site.

In English gardens sow the seeds in early spring, under glass, in seed compost at 16–21°C (61–70°F), and treat them as half-hardy annuals. Or the plants can be grown on as pot plants in a cold greenhouse.

Pests and diseases: Reasonably free.
Cultivars/varieties: As above.
Family: Chenopodiaceae.

***Lagurus* (rabbits' tails, hare's tail grass)** The Mediterranean western European *Lagurus ovatus*, an ornamental annual grass, produces a silky-white, egg-shaped, woolly, 25–37 mm (1–1.5 in) long 'rabbit's tail' of seeds at the top of 300–600 mm (12–24 in), sometimes longer, rigid stems. The foliage is grey-green.

These seed heads, when dried, seem to have found a permanent place in florists' shops, either in their natural fawny colour or dyed in various colours.

But they can also be used as foliage plants, as low growing background plants, or grouped in the border or grown in pots. And massed, like wheat in fields, the seedheads wave and ripple in the breeze.

Lagurus is found growing naturally in sandy soil near the sea. It prefers a sunny, well-drained, reasonably fertile soil.

Propagation: Seeds can be sown in early spring in warm, mild, frost-free, temperate areas, or later in cool areas, when all danger from frost is past, and as soon as the soil can be worked easily, directly where the plants are to grow and flower. The seedlings are thinned out to 100–150 mm (4–6 in) apart.

Or in cool areas sow the seeds in peat pots, in a light frost free place, using a recommended seed raising compost, 6 to 8 weeks before the last expected frost. Harden the seedlings off and plant them out in spring, when all danger from frost is past.

In English gardens sow the seeds late summer-autumn (Aug-Sept), in seed compost containers using a damp, recommended seed raising compost. Pot the seedlings on, and over-winter them in a cool greenhouse or cold frame. Plant the seedlings out in mid-spring (April), directly where they are to grow and flower. Flowers in early summer, and on.

Pests and diseases: Reasonably free.
Cultivars/varieties: Species as above.
Family: Poaceae.

***Lathyrus* (sweet pea)** The Italian-southern European sweet pea *Lathyrus odoratus* was introduced into cultivation during the early 18th century.

But more particularly we are concerned with its cultivars, which are extremely popular as cut flowers, such as the Spencer and Cuthbertson strains.

Sweet peas are deliciously fragrant, tendrilled, climbing plants, with 25–50 mm (1–2 in) 'butterfly' looking flowers.

Sweet pea heights vary:

(a) 'Dwarf' sweet peas; height 600 mm (12 in) approximately, which are used as container, bedding, edging or rockery plants.
(b) 'Intermediate' dwarf sweet peas; height 450 mm (18 in).
(c) 'Semi Dwarf' sweet peas; height 300–900 mm (24–36 in).
(d) 'Tall' sweet peas; height 2–3 m (79 in–10 ft).

Tall sweet peas are usually grown in rows running north-south for maximum sun on both sides. If you intend having more than one row, then make sure that the rows don't overshadow one another.

Many years ago, when I was studying commercial glasshouse sweet pea culture, the rows ran north-south, double rows, only 225 mm (9 in) apart, but these double rows were separated by wide, 1.2 m (47 in) paths. And these paths were planted with a suitable, low growing, market 'catch crop' at the same time.

If you want tall climbing sweet peas as a garden feature, then bear in mind that the flowers will try to face north towards the sun. (South in the northern hemisphere, of course.)

Sweet peas can be trained up trellises, wire fences, free-standing tripods or columns; these particular devices being installed before the sweet peas are planted.

The stem bases of tall sweet peas can look untidy, and are best hidden from view by suitable low shrubs or other flowers.

The flowers, some with ruffled, wavy petals, are available in shades and tints of white, cream, pink, red, blueish, mauve and purple; some picotee-edged; some bicoloured. To the best of my knowledge there is no true yellow sweet pea.

But it is the perfume of the sweet pea, as well as the glorious colours of the blooms, which is sought.

Many years ago, gardeners grew mixtures of the old 'grandifloras'. They certainly had, and no doubt still have, the real sweet pea perfume! But they are smaller flowered, and I don't know if they are available in Australia.

Sweet peas will flower, depending on location, in winter, spring, summer or autumn, but they are always grown cool; not too hot or too cold.

The preparation for annual sweet peas is all-important to ensure a good crop of flowers, but today the addition of farmyard manure is considered by some to cause scorch.

Sweet peas like a sunny, sheltered, neutral (pH 5.5–7.0), well-drained, moist, organic soil. Good drainage is essential. Even if the dwarf cultivars are grown in containers, they still must have good drainage.

Heavy soils can be opened up with clean, coarse sharp sand, but such a soil is of little use if it forms a natural water-holding basin. Sandy soils would benefit from the inclusion of well-rotted compost or peat.

When digging the soil for sweet peas don't bring up heavy clay to the top surface, as sweet peas love a crumbly textured surface. If your ground is heavy, and if practical, you can raise the sweet pea bed to say 150 mm (6 in) above surrounding ground level, to help facilitate drainage.

Rotate your sweet pea bed locations each year to prevent the build up of fungus disease.

Sweet peas are members of the legume (pea) family: Fabaceae (syn. Papilionaceae, Leguminosae). The legume family manufactures nitrogen salts from the soil using nitrogen-fixing nodules on its roots; and that is why clover, also a legume, always looks so green. Therefore, use only a base-dressing fertiliser specifically compounded and recommended for sweet pea cultivation, and apply it as the manufacturer instructs for sweet peas.

Sweet peas can be grown as cool temperature plants starting life at 15.5–21°C (60–70°F), say 18°C (64°F), dropping to 13–14°C (55–58°F), and grown on, but no lower than 5°C (40°F).

Extremes of temperature, and extremes of watering practices, cause 'bud drop'. Too high a temperature produces short stems. Therefore a steady temperature and suitable watering are important. Flowers should appear in 14 weeks, possibly longer from sowing.

However, if you intend growing exhibition flowers, consult a book on growing exhibition plants, as their treatment can be different.

During dry weather water the plants copiously in the morning to encourage flower stem growth. Flowers should be picked when fully open as they don't open in water. Pick regularly, preferably early in the morning when the plants are turgid, to provide beautiful cut flowers, and help prolong the plant's flowering period.

Water sweet peas regularly, if need be, and feed them with a suitable sweet pea fertiliser applied as the manufacturer instructs for sweet peas. Wayward shoots will need to be redirected. Remove any spent flowers as soon as they fade, to prolong the flowering, unless you wish to keep the seeds.

As a rule always write out a label with the name of the plant, date, and so on, before you open any seed packet, and don't wait until you have finished and forgotten what is what.

Propagation: The seeds can be sown mid summer-late autumn (March-April) in sub-tropical and temperate areas. Mid summer-autumn in cool but mild winter areas; and early spring (Sept) in cold areas. But the best months to sow depends somewhat on the particular cultivar. Check the packet for sowing details.

Sow the seeds outdoors in early spring when the soil is still cool, but can be worked easily, and when no damaging frost will occur. Frost can damage sweet pea flowers.

Or in cool areas sow the seeds under glass, or in a warm suitable, light situation indoors, at 18°C (64°F), 6 to 8 weeks before normal spring planting out time. The seedlings are hardened off in a cold frame before planting out.

You can sow the seeds in long-barrelled,

sweet pea pots, or sweet pea peat pots, using damp, recommended seed raising compost. Keep the compost pleasantly moist.

If you sow the seeds in seed compost containers, then prick out the seedlings into 75 mm (3 in), preferably, sweet pea pots of damp, recommended, potting compost. Grow them on, and plant them out directly where they are to grow and flower.

It may be that in a packet of healthy, mixed seeds, some seeds are better looking than others. Don't be seduced into choosing only the 'good looking' ones, as you may be discarding darker coloured flowers. If you only want to sow a few seeds, then divide them equally into good-looking, fair-looking and not-so-good-looking samples.

Some seeds are hard-thick skinned. You can nick, and lift up a fraction of the hard testa (skin) of the seeds with a small knife, opposite the eye. This can be a little tricky and dangerous, particularly with a sharp knife. Or you can carefully file the hard testa, also opposite the eye, with a nail file, taking care not to damage the seed's flesh in both cases, as this could be counter-productive.

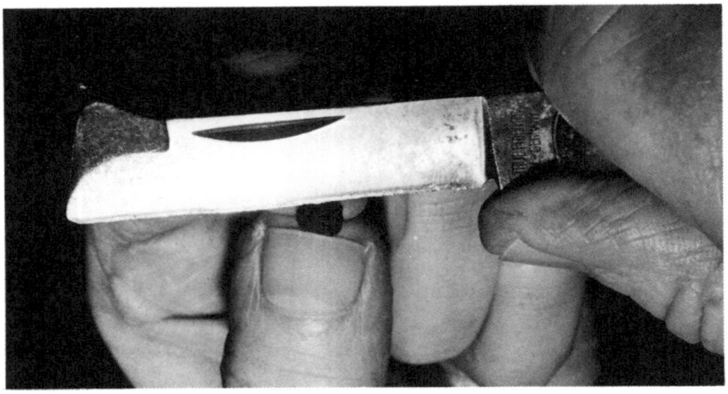

Nicking sweet pea seeds using a knife (n.b. the danger)

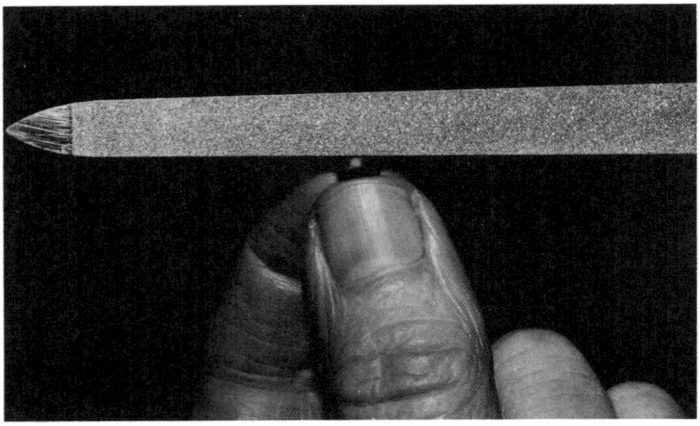

Nicking sweet pea seeds using a nail file

Some gardeners practise 'swelling' the seed. Place a small handful of damp, granulated peat, not wet, squeeze it to make sure, in a small plastic bag. Mix the seed with the peat, not forgetting to label the bag with seeds' name.

Seal the bag and place it in a cool spot, 13°C (55°F), for 2 days. Usually the seeds are swollen ready for planting out into pots. Any that haven't swelled can have their skins nicked, opposite the eye.

My latest batch of sweet pea seeds, using the damp-peat method, chitted in 4 days, and in 7 days I had shoots.

Or draw out shallow drills 25-31 mm (1-1.2 in) deep in the prepared soil, directly where the sweet peas are to grow and flower. Push the seeds individually into the drill-soil, 75 mm (3 in) apart; or 150 mm (6 in) apart for cut flowers. Cover the seeds with crumbly soil, well-rotted fine compost or vermiculite, and gently press the drill with the head of the rake, or a board, to firm the soil above the seeds.

Water is necessary to germinate the plants, but permanent waterlogging is taboo. Give the seeds a good drink, and then let them absorb it before giving them another. Too much water can cause the seeds to fail. But don't let them dry out either. Keep the soil just pleasantly moist. The seeds should germinate within approximately 10-14 days at 13-18-21°C (55-64-70°F).

The emerging shoots will flop about over the ground, and usually need twiggy support until they reach the climbing mesh, or what have you. But handle these young shoots carefully.

Pinch out the growing tip of the tall growing sweet peas, when the plant is approximately 200 mm (4 in) tall, or more specifically above the second or third leaves, to encourage side branches to emerge at the junction of these leaves. That is unless you are growing the plants for top quality blooms. Then you would let the plant's leader grow on. But consult a specialist book on sweet peas.

In English gardens, the flowering ground can be dug over during late autumn-winter incorporating a sweet pea fertiliser suitable for that time of the year, and applied as the manufacturer instructs for sweet peas.

The seeds can be sown early spring (March) at 16-21°C (61-70°F), say 18°C (64°F), into 75 mm (3 in) sweet pea pots containing potting compost. Gradually harden off the sweet pea seedlings in a cold frame for planting out, usually late spring. Or the seeds can be sown mid-autumn (Sept). Prick the seedlings out into pots. Overwinter the pots of autumn sown seedlings, plunged in clean sharp sand, in a cold frame. Harden them off, and plant out usually mid-spring. Flowers appear early summer, and on.

Or sow the seeds, early autumn in mild winter areas, or early spring, directly where they are to grow and flower, and follow the instructions on the seed packet.

Pests and diseases: Aphids, slugs, thrips, anthracnose, bud drop, damping off, downy mildew, foot and root rot, powdery mildew, spotted wilt.

Cultivars/varieties: 'Air Warden', height: climbing 2 m (7 ft) and more, scarlet-cerise, sweet scent. Dwarf Bijou Mixed, height 300 mm (12 in), ruffled flowers. Early Choice Mixed, height 2 m (7 ft), mixed colours. Early Multiflora Gigantea Colorama Mixed, good colour, many large flowers to a stem. 'Little Sweetheart', 200 mm (8 in), large flowering. Multiflora Mixed, climber, white, pinks, medium blue. 'Noel Sutton', height: climbing 2 m (7 ft) and more, a good 'blue', sweetly scented. Royal Mixed, height: climber, large blooms. 'Seventh Heaven', 2-3 m (7-10 ft), large flowers, many carried on one stem. Snoopea Mixed, height 600 mm (2 ft). 'Swan Lake', height: climbing to 2 m (7 ft) and more, pure white, heavenly scented. Tiffany, early flowering mixture, large, frilled flowers. Also various single colours in shades and tints of white, apricot, red, pink, blue.

Family: Fabaceae/Papilionaceae.

***Lavatera* (rose mallow, annual mallow, tree mallow)** The modern cultivars of the Mediterranean, bush-shrubby annual *Lavatera trimestris*; height: up to 600 mm-1.2 m (24-48 in); are widely grown.

They provide 75-100 mm (3-4 in) wide, trumpet, radar-dish, crinkly summer blooms in various glowing shades and tints of white, pink and mauve. The blooms are relatively fleeting, but are borne prolifically on the plant.

The 75 mm (3 in) wide juvenile foliage is up-facing and borne at the end of stems like a round artist's palette. Later the plant produces maple-leaf-shaped leaves.

Self-sown seedlings should be removed as soon as they are noticed. Lavateras can be used as summer 'hedges', or border plants. They succeed in a well-drained soil, in full sun.

Fertilise the young plants with a balanced, liquid, soluble flower fertiliser, suitable for lavateras and applied as the manufacturer instructs.

The plants will flop in windy sites, and should be staked. They rapidly wilt if short of water, but don't overwater, as lavateras don't like a waterlogged soil, and this could lead to 'rust' fungus disease. Remove any spent flowers to prolong the flowering period.

L. arborea, the tree mallow, is a half-hardy annual, and is also grown.

Propagation: Dig over the ground where the plants are to grow and flower, breaking it down into a fine tilth. Rake out any debris.

'Station sow' *L. trimestris* seeds, in spring, in rows, 2 or 3 seeds at each station. Or 'station sow' the seeds haphazardly. Rake them lightly into the tilth surface. They should germinate between 10–21 days at 21°C (70°F) soil temperature.

Thin out the seedlings 450–600 mm (18–24 in) apart, keeping only the strongest.

Or seeds can be sown indoors, in late winter, 6 to 8 weeks before the usual spring planting out time in your location. I sowed mine in reasonably warm conditions in pots, in late winter, and they germinated in 5 days, producing stocky plants. Plants grown in this fashion have to be hardened off before they are planted outside.

In English gardens sow the seeds, early-mid spring (March-April), directly where they are to grow and flower. Flowers midsummer, and on.

Pests and diseases: Red spider (on pot plants), rust.

Cultivars/varieties: 'Mont Blanc', height 525 mm (21 in), pure white. 'Silver Cup', height 600 mm (24 in), glowing carmine rose.

Family: Malvaceae.

Leptosiphon **(stardust flower)** The Californian *Leptosiphon hybridus* (syn. *Gilia lutea, Linanthus androsaceus luteus*) is a petite, pretty, hardy annual; height 100–200 mm (4–8 in); which is used for edges, window boxes, and out-of-the-way places like paving cracks.

It is called stardust flower because the flowers appear scattered over the plant like stars.

Leptosiphons flower early summer-autumn, providing a mass of tubed, 5-petalled, star-shaped flowers, 8–12 mm (0.3–0.5 in) wide, borne on unusually long stems, in shades and tints of cream, yellow, orange, pink and red.

The shiny, dark green 'leaves', 13–25 mm (0.5–1 in) long, are arranged like pointed, needle-like, wheel spokes, clustered in whorls around the stem.

Leptosiphons like a sunny location, and a well-drained soil.

Propagation: Dig over the ground where the plants are to grow and flower, when it is easy to work, breaking it down into a fine tilth. Rake out any debris, and gently but thoroughly firm the soil to take the seeds.

Sprinkle the seeds carefully over the prepared surface, in early spring, or after any danger from frost is past in frost-prone areas, and rake them into the fine tilth to a depth of 3 mm (0.1 in). Gently but firmly press the seeds to anchor them to the soil.

Water the seeds carefully using a fine spray. Don't allow the seeds or seedlings to dry out, but keep the soil pleasantly moist.

Thin out the seedlings 100 mm (4 in) apart. The seeds will germinate in approximately 10–15 days, but my leptosiphon seeds germinated in a quicker time, with excellent germination.

In English gardens sow the seeds early-mid spring (March-April), or later in hard, frost-prone areas, where they are to grow and flower. Thin out the seedlings to 100 mm (4 in) apart. Flowers appear in summer.

Pests and diseases: Reasonably free.

Cultivars/varieties: Species as above.

Family: Polemoniaceae.

Limnanthes **(meadow foam, fried eggs, poached-egg flower)** The prolific, star-like, 18–25 mm (0.7–1 in) wide, spring-summer, usually 5-petalled flowers of the North American *Limnanthes douglasii*; height 150 mm (6 in); appear above delicate greenish bracts. These blooms are a band of yolk-yellow, edged with white, and that's why they are called poached, or fried eggs.

Limnanthes is used to edge paths, and to decorate the front of the border. It is a reasonable ground-cover plant, although not weed-suppressive. Its flowering stems bend upwards to display its flowers to the sun. These are vaguely perfumed, although I cannot smell the perfume easily. They are visited regularly by bees. The delicate foliage looks like a cross between maidenhair fern and carrot leaves.

Limnanthes likes a cool moist, root run, a sunny site, but not hot and humid, and a summer mulch. Feed the plants regularly, as soon as the buds appear, with a well-balanced, liquid, soluble flower fertiliser, suitable for limnanthes, and applied as the manufacturer instructs.

Propagation: Dig over the soil where the plants are to grow and flower, breaking the soil down into a fine tilth and raking out any debris. Gently firm the soil to take the fine seeds, as they have to stay very close to the surface.

Thinly sow the seeds, late summer, autumn or early winter, depending on the severity of your local climate; or sow in spring in frost-prone areas; in clumps large enough to give an effective display, 150 mm (6 in) apart. Barely cover the seeds, 1.5 mm (0.1 in) deep, with finely-sieved soil, compost or vermiculite, and gently firm to anchor them to the soil.

Gently but thoroughly water the soil using a fine spray, keeping it moist until germination, and then water the seedlings when necessary. Carefully thin out the seedlings to 100 mm (4 in) apart. Germination should take place in up to 21 days.

Or the seeds can be sown early spring under glass at 18°C (64°F), in seed compost containers, using a damp, recommended seed raising compost. My limnanthes seeds germinated with a high success rate in 7 days.

Prick out the seedlings into pots of damp, recommended potting compost as soon as they are large enough to handle. Grow the seedlings on, harden them off, if necessary in a cold frame, and plant them out where they are to grow and flower, but only if the danger from frost is past and the ground has warmed up. Limnanthes will self-seed in mild conditions.

I grew some plants as pot plants for the house. The foliage trailed over the pot edges, and the flower stems turned up to the light. But possibly limnanthes would look better as pot plants if a few plants were clustered in low, 150 mm (6 in) flower pans.

In English gardens, thinly sow the seeds in early spring (March-April), or early autumn (Sept) in mild winter areas, directly where they are to grow and flower, in a sunny, but not hot and humid, well-drained, fertile soil. Flowers early summer, on.

Pests and diseases: Reasonably free.

Cultivars/varieties: Species as above.

Family: Limnanthaceae.

Limonium **(statice, sea lavender)** The new cultivars of the spring-summer flowering, Mediterranean perennial *Limonium sinuatum*; height 300–750 mm (12–30 in); are available in an exciting colour range: white, yellow, orange, red, purple, blue, and shades and tints of these colours.

Statice is treated as an annual, and is used to provide border displays or pot plants, or for cut flowers; or, as is more likely, dried cut flowers. Their 'crepe-papery' flowers are shaped like tiny, ragged-edged trumpets, and are arranged in 75–100 mm (3–4 in) long clusters at the top of the spike, like birds on a telephone line.

Even the mid to dark green, wavy, winged, flower stems, which rise from the centre of a rosette of lobed leaves, are curiously fascinating.

Statice grows well in full sun in a neutral, well-drained, fertile soil. It is fairly tolerant of heat and salt-spray. Water the plants only when conditions are dry, as they resent a waterlogged soil.

L. suworowii, the Russian (Turkestan) statice, is also popular as a cut flower or pot plant. It produces 450 mm (18 in) tall, thin, curling 'candle spikes' of tiny, pink flowers. These flower spikes are also known as 'rats' tails', but if this is so, then they must have been attached to some very pretty rats.

Propagation: Dig over the soil where the plants are to grow and flower, raking out any debris. Gently firm the soil to take the seeds.

Packet seeds can be fine and clean, but picked seeds can also include the dried flowers, and are difficult to separate, but try; or sow the seed as is.

'Station sprinkle' the fine seeds, 3 or 4 to a station, 300–375 mm (12–15 in) apart; all year through in warm, moist, subtropical areas; early spring-summer in temperate areas; late spring in cold areas, but only when all danger from frost is past.

Cover the seeds with a 5 mm (0.2 in) depth of finely sieved soil, and gently firm them with the head of the rake, or a board, to anchor them to the soil.

The seeds should germinate within 1 to 4 weeks at 20°C (68°F) soil temperature. Water the seeds keeping the surface moist until germination, and water the seedlings and plants as and when required. Thin out the seedlings 300–375 mm (12–15 in) apart.

Or the seeds can be sown in seed compost containers using a damp, recommended seed raising compost, at 16–20°C (61–68°F). In cold areas, sow in late winter, under glass, 6 to 8 weeks before normal late spring planting out time. Cover the seeds with 5 mm (0.2 in) of seed compost, and water them gently with a fine spray.

Prick out the seedlings into 75–100 mm (3–4 in) pots, using a damp, recommended potting compost. Move the plants up into bigger pots if they look like becoming pot bound. Harden off the seedlings, if necessary in a cold frame, and plant them out directly where they are to grow and flower, but only if any danger from frost is past and the ground has warmed up.

Or sow a few seeds in individual pots. Carefully thin out the seedlings, keeping only the strongest in each pot. Sowing the seeds in pots helps to minimise transplantation root disturbance, which statice does not like.

In English gardens, thinly sow the seeds, late winter-early-spring (Feb-March), or 6 to 8 weeks before the last expected frost in your locality, under glass, in seed compost containers, using damp, recommended seed raising compost, at 16–20°C (61–68°F), and treat the plants as half-hardy annuals. Flowers midsummer, and on.

Or sow the seeds, mid-spring (April-May), directly where they are to grow and flower. But it is possible, when sown this late, and if followed by a cold, wet summer, that there may not be enough good growing weather for the flowers to peak.

Pests and diseases: Reasonably free, occasionally mildew.

Cultivars/varieties: *L. s.* 'Heavenly Blue'. *L. s.* 'Rosea'. *L. s.* 'Yellow'. New Hybrids Mixed, height 360–370 mm (14–15 in), colourful variety of flowers. Sinuata Mixed, height 500 mm (20 in). *L. suworowii*, height 700 mm (28 in), bright rose.

Family: Plumbaginaceae.

***Linanthus* (mountain phlox)** The Californian *Linanthus grandiflorus* (syn. *Gilia grandiflora*); height 300–375 mm (12–15 in); is an annual plant that produces a profusion of lavender pink-white, 25 mm (1 in) wide, 5-petalled, delicately furrowed, soft-textured, trumpet flowers. These blooms appear spring-summer, and on, depending on the sowing date and location. My flowers are mostly white with a breath of pink.

The flowers arise from 25–31 mm (1–1.2 in) long, needle-fine foliage, that is whorled in clusters, like pointed wheel spokes, around the wiry stem.

Mountain phlox prefers a well-drained soil in a sunny location and, although it has a low water requirement, it seems to flower more prolifically if watered occasionally during dry spells. Commonsense is needed here.

Propagation: Dig over the soil when it is easy to work, directly where the plants are to grow and flower, breaking it down into a fine tilth. Rake out any debris, and firm the soil gently but thoroughly to take the seeds.

Sow the seeds thinly and evenly, late summer-autumn, subtropical areas; late winter-spring mild temperate areas; and spring in cold, frost-prone areas, after any danger from frost is past. Rake the seeds lightly into the top tilth, and firm them gently but firmly to anchor them to the soil.

Gently but thoroughly water the seeds using a fine spray, and don't allow them to dry out. Keep the ground pleasantly moist until the plants are well established, then water them when they need it. Even though the mountain phlox is reasonably tolerant of dry spells, the flowering period can be prolonged by watering during dry spells.

Seeds germinate in approxiamtely 14–21 days, although mine germinated in 10 days. Thin out the seedlings to 200–300 mm (8–12 in) apart.

Or sow a few seeds in individual 50 mm (2 in) pots of dampened, recommended seed raising compost, and grow them on. Thin out the seedlings keeping only the strongest in each pot, and grow them on, either as bedding plants or, as I have done with a few seedlings, as unusual pot plants.

I potted them on into 75 mm (3 in) pots, and then into 125 mm (5 in) pots of damp, recommended, potting compost. Indeed, I have one beside me as I write this, and I have only just noticed that the flowers have a very fine, delicate fragrance, but it is barely discernible.

In English gardens sow the seeds in late spring (April-May), or after the last expected frost in your area, and only then if the ground has warmed up, directly where the plants are to grow and flower; thinning them out to the required distance, 200–300 mm (8–12 in) apart.

Or sow the seeds earlier in a cold frame, early-spring, in 50 mm (2 in) pots of recommended seed raising compost, and grow them on as individual plants, making sure they are hardened off sufficiently before planting them out in the garden, but after any danger from frost is past and the ground has warmed up.

Or as stated above they can be potted up into 75 mm (3 in) pots, and from there on 2 sizes into 125 mm (5 in) pots of recommended potting compost.

Pests and diseases: Reasonably free.

Cultivars/varieties: Species as above.

Family: Polemoniaceae.

***Linaria* (toad flax, eggs and butter)** The Mediterranean linarias are winter-spring, or summer flowering, depending on location and sowing times. They are dainty, narrow-leaved plants resembling small snapdragons (antirrhinums), and are of the same family, except that linarias have a long flower spur.

The principal forms of 'annual' garden linaria are the colourful cultivars of *Linaria bipartita* and the Moroccan *Linaria maroccana*; height 230–450 mm (9–18 in); mostly 200–300 mm (8–12 in).

The 12 mm (0.5 in) long flowers are available in pastel shades and tints of yellow, orange, pink, and purple; some bicoloured. Some are splashed with separate colour blotches of white, pink or orange, on the lower part of the flower. Most flowers have a yellow nectary sighting spot.

Linarias should flower within approximately 3 months from sowing.

They can be used as bedding or edging plants, or in groups of 3 or 4 as pretty 125 mm (5 in) pot plants. But they look best clumped in small, but bold, groups where they can be seen easily. Recently I saw them massed effectively on a side-road traffic roundabout. They are also used as cut flowers.

Linarias prefer a well-drained, neutral, fertile, sandy soil, in a sunny spot, or light shade; but not full shade.

They require sufficient, but careful watering when germinating, and during the early seedling and plant stage. Don't waterlog them as they grow older, but don't let them dry out either; a good soaking once a week in dry weather will suffice. But keep checking, as in sandy soils they can dry out rapidly.

Feed the plants, when they are growing well, with a well-balanced, soluble, liquid, flower fertiliser, suitable for linarias and applied as the manufacturer instructs.

Trim off the first flush of dead and fading blooms to prolong the flowering period.

Propagation: Dig over the soil where the plants are to grow and flower, breaking it down into a fine tilth. Rake out and remove any debris. Gently but firmly press the soil to take the fine seeds.

Thinly sow the seeds, 6 mm (0.2 in) deep, late summer to early winter subtropical areas; mid summer to late autumn temperate areas; late summer to mid autumn, or early to mid spring in cooler areas. Linarias are not susceptible to ordinary light frosts, but in very cold climates spring sowings are best.

Sowing the seeds thinly helps save the bothersome chore of thinning out later on.

Or they can be sown indoors in a cool spot where they receive adequate light, 6 to 8 weeks before normal spring planting out time, in seed compost containers using a recommended seed raising compost.

Prick out the seedlings, when large enough to handle, into containers of damp, recommended, potting compost, and grow them on. Harden off the seedlings, if necessary in a cold frame, and plant them out directly where they are to grow and flower.

Water the seeds thoroughly, but carefully, using a fine spray. Don't allow the soil surface to dry out in dry weather until the seedlings are well established. Then water the seedlings, and mature plants, as and when needed.

Germination should take place within 2 weeks at 20°C (68°F). My *L. bipartita* seeds germinated under glass in 4 days, and very good germination it was.

The seedlings, if overcrowded, should be thinned out 50–100 mm (2–4 in) apart; some recommend 150 mm (6 in). Any weeds that could dominate are removed carefully, and as soon as possible. Any future cultivation should be kept very shallow, so as not to upset the delicate linaria roots.

In English gardens thinly sow the seeds of the hybrids in late winter, early-spring (Feb-April), in seed compost containers using seed raising compost, and place in a cold frame. Prick out the seedlings, when large enough to handle, into containers of damp, recommended potting compost, and grow them on. Harden off the seedlings, and plant them out mid-late spring (April-May) where they are to grow and flower, but only when any danger from frost is past. Flowers early summer, and on.

Or sow the seeds early-mid spring (March-April), directly where they are to grow and flower.

Pests and diseases: Reasonably free.

Cultivars/varieties: Crown Jewels, height 225–300 mm (9–12 in), shades and tints of carmine pink and purple, splashed with yellow or orange. Fairy Bouquet Mixed, height 200–250 mm (8–10 in), wide range of bright colours.

Family: Scrophulariaceae.

***Linum* (flax, scarlet flax)** The North African-Algerian, summer-flowering, hardy annual *Linum grandiflorum*; height 375–450 mm (15–18 in); is a beautiful, red-flowered species, known as scarlet flax.

The shallow-saucer, 5-petalled, star-shaped, 31–37 mm (1.2–1.5 in) wide flowers are borne on delicate, pale green stems.

But the cultivar *L. g.* 'Rubrum' has flowers of bright glowing crimson with an intense red centre eye-spot; height 300 mm (12 in).

The leaves are narrow, wish-wash green, pointed, and vaguely reminiscent of undernourished carnation leaves.

Linum blooms are fleeting, but the plants are fruitful. You can, however, sow the seeds at say 3 or 4 week intervals, to provide a succession of flowers. They are not considered as cut flowers.

Linums like a well-drained soil and good sunlight, otherwise they will not flower to perfection.

They are usually well-branched and tend to support each other, although they can get knocked about in rough weather.

Propagation: Annual flax, usually, is difficult to transplant. Dig over the area where the plants are to grow and flower, breaking the soil down into a fine tilth, and rake out any debris. Gently but firmly press the soil to take seeds.

Thinly sow the seeds of *L. grandiflorum*, and *L. g.* 'Rubrum', directly where they are to grow and flower; autumn in mild temperate areas; and early spring in cooler areas.

Carefully thin out the seedlings to 150–200 mm (6–8 in) apart, some prefer 250 mm (10 in) apart, and keep them moderately watered.

Or in cold areas sow a few seeds in individual 75 mm (3 in) peat pots, 6 weeks before the last expected frost in your locality, using a damp, recommended seed raising compost, under glass, at 13–16°C (55–61°F). Sowing in peat pots helps to reduce root disturbance.

Carefully thin out the seedlings leaving the strongest in each pot. Harden off the seedlings in a cold frame, and plant them out, peat pot and all, when any danger from frost is past and the ground has warmed up.

In English climate gardens sow the seeds of *L. grandiflorum*, early-mid spring (March-April), directly where they are to grow and flower. Thin out the seedlings 150–200 mm (6–8 in) apart. Flowers early summer, and on.

Pests and diseases: Reasonably free.

Cultivars/varieties: As above.

Family: Linaceae

***Lisianthus* (prairie gentian)** The Mexican-tropical South American summer flowering, annual F_1 hybrids of *Lisianthus russellianus* (syn. *Eustoma russellianum*) height 600 mm (24 in); have 75 mm (3 in) wide, cup-like blooms, similar to huge, loose tulip blooms, both single and double form. Flowers are available in white, cream, pink, violet-blue, purplish and bicoloured.

Prairie gentians are used as border plants, pot plants, or as cut flowers. They have fine, wiry, cane-like stems.

The leaves are borne in opposite pairs clasping the stem. They are waxy, blue-green, egg-shaped-pointed, approximately 75 mm (3 in) long, and 50 mm (2 in) wide, and appear as though dusted with flour.

Prairie gentians thrive best under good sunlight and dry conditions. They prefer a moderately fertile soil, with good drainage. Do not expose the young plants or seedlings to hot sun, drying winds, cold drafts or frosts.

Feed mature plants with a well-balanced, soluble, liquid fertiliser, suitable for prairie gentians and applied as the manufacturer instructs.

Propagation: Mix the seeds with several times their own volume of clean, fine, silver sand to ensure even distribution.

Thinly sow the seeds, the size of hundreds and thousands, in seed compost containers, autumn or spring, or 6 to 8 weeks before the normal spring planting out time in your location, indoors under glass at 20–25°C (68–77°F). Scatter the seeds on top of the damp, recommended seed raising compost, or cover them with only a breath of fine sand, just pressing them on to the top of the compost surface, with a flat, clean board, or similar.

Water the seeds thoroughly, and cover the container with a sheet of glass; or place it inside a clear plastic bag. Keep the compost just pleasantly moist during germination.

Remove the glass, or take the container out of the plastic bag, once the seeds have germinated, and progressively give the seedlings more light. But not direct sunlight through the greenhouse glass.

Germination should take place in approximately 15 days, but keep a weather-eye open just in case. It is mid-spring as I write this, and we have had 3 successive days of 37.7°C (100°F) and over. The point being that the seeds could germinate quicker, or seedlings could become stressed in such heat.

Prick out the seedlings when 3 pairs of true leaves have appeared, 38 mm (1.5 in) apart both ways, into containers of damp, recommended potting compost; or singly into 75 mm (3 in) pots. Keep the seedlings at 20–25°C (68–77°F).

To ensure proper growth, lightly shade the seedlings until they have rooted into the compost, then remove the shade allowing maximum light, but not scorching sunlight, to reach the plants. Prairie gentians are slow growing in their early stages, and therefore it is essential that the utmost care be taken to nurture them at this stage.

When the plants have produced 4 to 5 true leaves, harden them off, if necessary in a cold frame, and transfer them directly into the beds where they are to grow and flower, 150 mm (6 in) apart, but only if all danger from frost is past and the ground has warmed up.

Or pot them singly into 125 mm (5 in) pots, using a damp, recommended potting compost, and grow them as pot plants.

You can remove the growing tips to induce a larger number of stems and flowers. Pinch out the shoots when the stems have grown to the third node; that is pinching out above the second node. But to obtain an even larger number of stems and cut flowers, pinch out above the third or sixth node. But I prefer them as single stemmed pot plants, and they still produce a reasonable number of flowers.

Thin cane support may be needed for the plants when they have grown to a height of about 200 mm (8 in), to hold up the heavy flowers and stems.

In English gardens, grow prairie gentians as outlined above, but treat them as half-hardy tender annuals and grow them as greenhouse pot plants.

Pests and diseases: Reasonably free.

Cultivars/varieties: Single Colours: Pink Pearl, White, Blue. Single Mixture, white, pink, blue. New Alpine Series, height 850 mm (34 in), double flowered: white, pink or blue. New Cocktails, bicoloured flowers. Cocktail Lilac, clear lavender, pure white. Prairie Gentian F_1, height 600 mm (2 ft), white, creamy pink, violet blue.

Family: Gentianaceae.

Lobelia Lobelia is one of the world's most popular summer bedding plants and is grown in great quantities.

The frost-prone, tufted or trailing, perennial cultivars of the winter-spring-summer flowering, South African *Lobelia erinus (L. e. compacta pumila, L. e. pendula)*; height 100–250 mm (4–10 in); are treated as annuals.

The flowers, borne singly on delicate 31 mm (1.2 in) stalks, are 6–12 mm (0.2–0.5 in) wide, with 3 larger lower petal-lobes, and 2 minute, upper petal-lobes, like little rabbit ears. They are available in white, carmine-pink, dark-blue, light-blue, rose with white centres, purple, and shades and tints of these colours.

Lobelia cultivars are used for border edges, windowboxes, pot plants, and other like purposes. The trailing cultivars can hang down for 600 mm (24 in), or more, and are ideal for hanging baskets. Lobelia is used extensively in combination with white alyssum, petunias, geraniums, and a host of other summer bedding plants.

The flowers grow in profusion in winter, spring or summer, depending on locality, and when sown, or until cut down by frost.

The 31–50 mm (1.2–2 in) long, tooth-edged, egg-shaped pointed, or lance-like foliage is also densely attractive, being either a fresh-green, bronzey-green, or stained with purple.

Lobelia prefers a cool, temperate climate, partially shaded, with sun for part of the day, and a fertile, well-drained, but 'moisture-holding' soil, sheltered from hot, drying winds. But it will grow in most ordinary garden soils.

Water the plants sensibly, at regular intervals during dry weather. Indiscriminate watering will splash mud over the plants.

Trim off the first flush of dead flowers to prolong the flowering.

Feed lobelia, when flowering begins, with a well-balanced, soluble, liquid, flower fertiliser, suitable for lobelia and applied as the manufacturer instructs.

Propagation: Thinly sow the extremely fine seeds, mixed with several times their own volume of clean, fine, silver sand to aid uniform sowing, in seed compost containers, on top of damp, recommended, seed raising compost; late summer-winter in subtropical areas; late summer-autumn in temperate areas; late summer-early autumn, or early-mid spring, or summer in cool, frost-prone areas; in a greenhouse where necessary at 16–21°C (61–70°F), or possibly slightly lower depending on the seedman's recommendations, as some cultivars prefer lower temperatures.

Or sow seeds indoors 8 to 10 weeks before normal spring planting out time, in a greenhouse, as above, where necessary.

Gently press the seeds on to the compost surface using a clean, flat board.

Stand the container in a dish of tepid water and let the moisture soak through the compost until it just glistens on the surface; then remove the container. But be careful as water pooling will 'float' away the fine seed. Germination can take up to 21 days.

It may be difficult to prick out the seedlings individually, so they are 'patch planted'; that is a few plants are transplanted together, 19 mm (0.7 in) apart, into containers of damp, recommended potting compost. Grow them on.

Harden off the seedlings, if necessary in a cold frame, and plant them out directly where they are to grow and flower, when all danger from frost risk is past, and the ground has warmed up. Space plants about 100–150 mm (4–6 in) apart.

Flowers appear in profusion approximately 3–4 months after sowing.

Or seeds can be sown in a prepared seedbed, and pricked out to directly where they are to grow and flower; spring-summer in cool areas.

In English gardens treat the plants as half-hardy annuals. Sow the seeds in late-mid spring (Feb-April) in seed compost containers, under glass, at 16–21°C (61–70°F), and treat the seedlings as half-hardy plants. Flowers summer, and on.

Pests and diseases: Damping off, leaf spot, stem rot.

Cultivars/varieties: 'Cambridge Blue', height 100 mm (4 in), azure blue. 'Colour Cascade', trailing, shades and tints of white, carmine, lilac, mauve, purple and blue. 'Crystal Blue', height 100 mm (4 in), deep blue. 'Crystal Palace Compacta', height 150 mm (6 in), dark blue. 'Mrs Clibran', height 100 mm (4 in), deep-purplish with white eye. 'Rosamund', height 100 mm (4 in), carmine rose with white eye. 'Pendula Sapphire', height 150 mm (6 in), deep blue, white eye, for hanging baskets and so on. 'Snowball', height 150 mm (6 in), snow white. 'String of Pearls', height 100 mm (4 in), mixed colours.

Family: Campanulaceae.

***Lobularia* (sweet alyssum, sweet alice)** The Mediterranean-West Asian-near Eastern perennial sweet alyssum, *Lobularia maritima*; height 75–150–250 mm (3–6–10 in); is one of the most widely grown of all late winter-spring-summer and autumn bedding plants. It seems to flower and flower, self-seeding like mad. But, usually, it is grown as an annual.

Each flower cluster is borne on 25–50 mm (1–2 in) stems, above flattish grey-green foliage. The 5 mm (0.2 in) wide, strongly-scented, 4 flat-petalled, cross-shaped flowers are available in white, cherry-cerise, lilac-pink, rose-pink, violet-red, violet or purple.

Seeds are available as mixtures or as separate colours. You can mix plants to your own satisfaction, particularly when growing them in containers.

Sweet alyssum forms a dense carpet of flowers and is used for border edges, ground-cover, pot and rockery work, and so on.

It likes a sunny, well-drained, neutral soil, and tolerates drought remarkably well. But when watering sweet alyssum give the roots a good, deep drink, say once a week during dry, hot spells, and not a succession of small waterings.

Regular applications, when the plants are growing well, of a well-balanced, soluble, liquid, flower fertiliser, suitable for sweet alyssum and applied as the manufacturer instructs, will produce a profusion of flowers.

Carefully trim off the dead and spent flowers when the first flush of blooms is past, and reap a second crop.

Carefully remove any weeds when they are young, to prevent disturbing the sweet alyssum's fine roots.

Propagation: Thinly sow the seeds, 2 mm (0.1 in) deep, in seed compost containers, using a damp, recommended seed raising compost; late summer-autumn-early winter (or for much of the year) subtropical areas; summer-mid autumn or spring in temperate areas; spring-summer-early autumn in cool areas; under glass where necessary at 11–18°C (52–64°F).

Or sow the seeds indoors in a frost-free, light place, late winter, say 6 to 8 weeks before the usual spring planting out time in your location.

Prick out the seedlings, when they are large enough to handle, into containers of damp, recommended potting compost. Harden off the seedlings, and plant them out directly where they are to grow and flower, but only when all danger from frost is past and the ground has warmed up.

Or the seeds can be sown early-spring directly where the plants are to grow and flower.

Dig over the ground, when it is easy to work, breaking it down into a fine tilth, and rake out any debris. Gently but firmly press the soil to take the seeds.

Thinly sow the seeds, and rake them lightly into the top tilth, 2 mm (0.1 in) deep. Press them lightly with the head of the rake, or a board, to anchor them to the soil.

Water the seeds carefully, using a fine spray. Germination occurs in 5 to 14 days at 11–18°C (52–64°F) soil temperature.

Thin out the seedlings 75–150–200–300 mm (3–6–8–12 in) apart, depending on the growth and spread of the cultivar; but generally 150 mm (6 in). Keep the seeds and seedlings moist until they are established, then water them as need be. Plants should flower within 2 months.

In English gardens sow the seeds under glass in late winter-early spring (Feb-March), in seed compost at 11–18°C (52–64°F), and treat the plants as half-hardy annuals. Or sow the seeds, mid-late spring (April-May), directly where they are to grow and flower. Flowers appear early summer and on.

Pests and diseases: Caterpillars, stem rot.

Cultivars/varieties: 'Oriental Night', height 100 mm (4 in), violet purple. 'Pastel Carpet', height 100 mm (4 in), white, pink, rose, violet. 'Rosie O'Day', height 100 mm (4 in), shades of rose pink. 'Snow Cloth', height 150 mm (6 in), pure white. 'Wonderland', height 100 mm (4 in), deep, cherry cerise. 'Wonderland Purple', height 100 mm (4 in), deep purple. 'Wonderland White', height 100 mm (4 in), pure white.

Family: Brassicaceae.

***Lonas* (golden ageratum, African daisy)** The northern and southern Mediterranean annual *Lonas inodora* (syn. *L. annua*); height 300 mm (12 in); looks like a dwarf, fern-leaved, golden-flowered yarrow, although many liken it to a golden form of the blue ageratum.

The golden-yellow, flat flowerheads, which appear as clusters of 'look-alike', tiny, shaving brushes, are from 50–75 mm (2–3 in) wide, but have no perfume. The flowers are also used in dried flower arrangements. Lonas will flower spring-summer-autumn, depending on climate and location.

Lonas is effective if planted in bold clumps, in borders or beds, otherwise it can look a bit insipid. It thrives in a well-drained soil, in a warm, sunny, sheltered site.

Propagation: Thinly sow the seeds in seed compost containers, using a damp, recommended, seed raising compost, indoors in a light place, 6 to 8 weeks before the normal planting out time in your locality.

The seeds will germinate in 5–7 days at 18–21°C (64–70°F) soil temperature. Mine, sown late winter, germinated in 5 days at 16–18°C (61–64°F).

Cover the seeds with fine compost and place them in a dark, warm place to germinate. Move the container, as soon as the seedlings appear, into good light, but not hot sunlight. I covered my seeds with black plastic, removing it as soon as the seedlings appeared, to prevent them from being drawn-up and spindly.

Prick out the seedlings, when large enough to handle, into small pots of damp, recommended potting compost, and grow them on. Harden them off, if necessary in a cold frame, before planting them out directly where they are to grow and flower, 150 mm (6 in) apart. But only when any risk from frost is past and the ground has warmed up.

If the plants look like becoming pot-bound, then pot them up into 75 mm (3 in) pots of damp, recommended, potting compost.

Or the seeds can be sown late winter in mild winter areas, or late spring in cooler areas, directly where the plants are to grow and flower.

Dig over the soil when it is easy to work, breaking it down into a fine tilth, and remove any debris. Firm the soil to take the seeds, which are small and chaff-like.

Sow the seeds thinly to minimise thinning out later. Thin out the plants 150 mm (6 in) apart. Water the plants during dry spells.

In English gardens treat lonas as a half-hardy annual, sowing the seeds under glass late winter-early spring, at 16–18°C (61–64°F). Or sow them outdoors, early-mid spring (March-April), directly where they are to grow and flower.

Pests and diseases: Reasonably free.

Cultivars/varieties: Species as above.

Family: Asteraceae.

***Luffa* (loofah, bathroom sponge)** The Old World, now tropical, frost-tender smooth-luffa, *Luffa cylindrica* (syn. *L. aegyptiaca*) is used as an ornamental climbing plant.

The fruits of *L. cylindrica* look like fat versions of small, continental cucumbers, up to 300 mm (12 in) long, and 75–100 mm (3–4 in) diameter. Luffa is a member of the cucumber family.

The 75–125 mm (3–5 in) wide, 'starfish' yellow flowers are fleeting, but attractive. Luffa is possibly native to tropical India, and other tropical areas, and is grown world-wide, but the Japanese have given it special attention.

As a tropical plant it prefers a long, hot, summer growing season, fruiting in late summer-autumn. If planted out it will reach the fruiting stage in temperate areas usually by mid-autumn; however, the time it fruits depends on the previous spring and summer weather.

In cooler climates the luffa may never reach the fruiting stage, unless, perhaps, grown under glass as a greenhouse plant in warm, humid conditions.

Luffa likes full sunlight, a light, organic, moisture-retaining, fertile soil, and frequent watering at all stages of growth, or the large, 'maple leaf' leaves will soon flag.

Fertilise the plants with a fertiliser suitable for cucumbers. Too much nitrogen leads to lush foliage but few fruits. Train the vines up the supports as soon as practical.

Propagation: In warm, moist areas, where the temperature is 20°C (68°F) and above, sow the seeds directly where they are to grow and flower, on small mound-hills, 1.8 m (6 ft) apart, say 2 or 3 seeds (which look like water melon seeds) to each spot, 12–25 mm (0.5–1 in) deep. Here they clamber over the ground like marrows.

The plants can also be grown as a garden feature, for example as single plants up a tripod, or trained over a trellis, with the seeds planted 300–600 mm (12–24 in) apart and 12–25 mm (0.5–1 in) deep.

Or the seeds can be started indoors, under glass, at 20–21°C (68–70°F), say 2 seeds to a 75 mm (3 in) peat pot, pushed upright into the compost, 12–25 mm (0.5–1 in) deep. Eventually, but carefully, remove one of the seedlings, when approximately 50 mm (2 in) tall, leaving only the strongest.

Keep the luffa seedlings out of direct sunlight at these early stages, but gradually introduce them to more light after germination. But not direct sunlight, not until after they are well established, and never under glass, unless the glass is shaded. Glass can concentrate sun rays like a magnifying glass; think of how heat comes through a car window!

The seeds can be soaked in tepid water overnight, some say 24 hours, to speed up germination, which can take up to 21 days.

Harden off the seedlings, and plant them outside directly where they are to grow and flower, when they have made their 3rd or 4th leaf, or say 75–100 mm (3–4 in) high. But only if all danger from frost is past, the ground has warmed up sufficiently, and the weather is cloudy to allow the plants to adapt more easily. Or you could shade them for a short time, but be aware that too much darkness will turn the seedlings yellow and drawn.

In English gardens treat the luffa as a tender annual, sowing the seeds in 75 mm (3 in) peat pots of seed raising compost, late winter-mid spring (Feb-April), at 20–21°C (68–70°F), eventually potting the seedlings on into larger pots of potting compost and growing them as greenhouse plants.

Or grow the plants under glass, then harden them off, and plant them out directly where they are to grow and flower, when all danger from frost is past and the ground has warmed up sufficiently. But in cold, wet summers the luffa may never achieve fruition.

Pests and diseases: Red spider, cucumber diseases.
Cultivars/varieties: Species as above.
Family: Cucurbitaceae.

***Lunaria* (honesty)** The southern European-Mediterranean *Lunaria annua* (syn. *L. biennis*); height 500 mm–1 m (20–39 in); is an erect, many-branched quick-growing biennial, which is sometimes grown as an annual.

The fragrant, 12 mm (0.5 in) wide blooms, like petite, stock-flower blooms, are usually magenta-pink and 4-petalled. The tuft-rosette of leaves grows 150 mm (6 in) or more in the first year. Then the mostly solitary stems, which carry the cluster of flowers, appear in the second season mid spring-summer.

But honesty is grown principally for its flat-disc, oval to circular, pointed, pale-brown, bladder-like, 31–38 mm (1.2–1.5 in) long seed cases.

The outers of these seed cases are carefully peeled away to expose the white-translucent, papery membrane. This opaque silver lining looks 'moon-like', hence the name *Lunaria*. And it is these membranes that are used in flower arrangements.

It is called honesty because the seed case, as it matures, exposes the seeds for all to see.

The magenta-pink, sometimes white or purplish flowers are also attractive, and these, plus the sharply-toothed, lush, heart-shaped, pointed leaves, make honesty a useful border plant. There is also a variegated-leaf cultivar.

Occasionally, honesty can display flowers and seed cases at the same time, but at this stage in its life the plant can look scruffy.

Honesty is a hardy plant, and thrives in cool areas such as Melbourne. Recently, however, in temperate Australia, I saw a bed of well-developed young plants flattened after 3 days of 38°C (100°F) temperatures. But a second planting made a few weeks later seems to be surviving.

Honesty tolerates some sun, but being of woodland origin prefers partial-dappled shade, and a well-drained, reasonably fertile soil.

Give the plants sufficient water during dry spells. Feed honesty, when the plants are budding up, with a well-balanced, soluble, liquid flower fertiliser, suitable for honesty and applied as the manufacturer instructs.

Flower stalks carrying the seed cases needed for dried flower arrangements should be cut summer-autumn once they have matured. Hang them up to dry in a cool, dry spot that has buoyant, circulating air. Carefully peel off the outer cases once they are dry, which is relatively easy to do, to expose the translucent membranes.

Honesty plants, if left where they are growing and flowering, will self-seed, providing for future flowers. They may become a weed nuisance by providing too many seedlings, and these surplus seedlings will have to be removed.

Propagation: Dig over the soil when it is easy to work, breaking it down into a fine tilth, and gently firming it to take the seeds.

Sow the seeds 3 mm (0.1 in) deep; autumn-winter subtropical areas; autumn and spring temperate areas; autumn and spring cold areas; either directly where they are to grow and flower or in rows in a nursery seedbed. The seeds germinate in approximately 12 to 30 days in a reasonably warm soil temperature.

Thin out those seedlings sown in their permanent flowering quarters or in a seedbed, 300–400 mm (12–16 in) apart. When large enough to handle easily, transplant those seedlings in the nursery holding-bed to their permanent flowering quarters 300–400 mm (12–16 in) apart. Or the seeds can be sown in seed compost containers. Prick out the seedlings when they are large enough to handle into small pots of recommended potting compost, grow them on, and then harden them off, and then plant outside.

Or in cold areas you can sow the seeds indoors, in good light, 3 mm (0.1 in) deep, in early spring, in seed compost containers, using a damp, recommended potting compost, and grow them on. Harden off the seedlings in a cold frame, and plant them out when the danger of frost is past and the ground has warmed up.

In English gardens sow the seeds, late spring or early summer (May-June), in rows in a nursery seedbed, or directly where they are to grow and flower.

During early autumn to earliest spring, either transplant the seedlings to their permanent quarters, or thin them out, 300–400 mm (12–16 in) apart. They should flower, in due season, late spring-early summer.

Pests and diseases: Occasionally cabbage pests and diseases.
Cultivars/varieties: Mixtures, or White.
Family: Brassicaceae.

***Lupinus* (lupin, lupine)** The cultivars of the popular Mexican annual *Lupinus hartwegii*; height 600–900 mm (30–36 in); are available in shades and tints of white, yellow, pink, blue and mauve. But those old favourite annual lupins 'Blue Pearl', 'Pink Pearl' and 'White Pearl' may still be obtainable.

Annual lupin 'pea' flowers are arranged loosely on 300 mm (12 in) tall spikes. Annual lupins are suited to most areas, particularly from Brisbane southwards. They flower, winter-spring-summer, depending on location and planting time.

The soft leaflet-foliage is like 7 or more hairy fingers.

Annual lupins are not to be confused with the more dramatic perennial lupins; for example the Russell lupins, which are not discussed here.

Annual Lupins prefer a slightly acid to neutral, well-drained, light soil, in a warm-sunny, or partially shaded, sheltered position. They need ample watering when growing.

They are members of the pea family, and if you look closely at the flowers you will see their 'pea flower' characteristics, and this is important when considering their fertiliser requirements.

They do not like an excessive amount of nitrogen fertiliser, as they manufacture their own nitrates (a pea family characteristic); neither do they like fresh animal manure around their roots. Feed sparingly with a fertiliser suitable for lupins, and applied as the manufacturer instructs for lupins. Remove spent flowers regularly.

Propagation: Annual lupin seeds should be sown directly where they are to grow and flower, as the seedlings do not transplant readily.

Dig over the ground, when it is easy to work, directly where the plants are to grow and flower, preferably in sun in cooler areas, or partial shade in warmer areas, breaking the soil down into a fine tilth, and removing any debris. The seeds can be soaked for 24 hours in tepid water prior to planting.

Sow seeds of annual lupins autumn-winter subtropical and temperate areas; autumn or spring in cooler areas; but in hard frost areas you can leave sowing until spring.

Draw out (trench) the drills (rows), to a depth of 19–25 mm (0.7–1 in). The seeds are large enough, with care, to be placed individually in the drills.

'Station sow' a few seeds in clumps, 300 mm (12 in) apart, pressing the seeds on to the bottom of the trench. Cover the seeds with sieved soil, fine compost or similar. Germination can be erratic, taking up to 21 days, possibly more, at 13–18°C (55–64°F) soil temperature.

As an experiment, I sowed annual lupin seeds in containers of damp, recommended, seed raising compost, and they germinated in 5 days with good results. I pricked them out when they were very small into 50 mm (2 in) long pots, and from there into 100 mm (4 in) pots; they were subsequently hardened off and placed outside. But I wasn't entirely satisfied with this method of propagation.

Seeds should not be allowed to dry out;

neither should they be waterlogged.

In English gardens sow the seeds of the annual lupins, early-spring (March-April), directly where they are to grow and flower. Thin out the seedlings 300 mm (12 in) apart. Flowers summer.

Pests and diseases: Slugs, snails.
Cultivars/varieties: Hartwegii Mixed, height 750 mm (30 in), white yellow, rosy mauve, blue. 'Pink Pearl', shell pink. 'Blue Pearl', deep blue. 'White Pearl'. Height 600–750 mm (24–30 in).
Family: Fabaceae/Papilionaceae.

***Lychnis* (rose-campion, Maltese cross)** The scarlet petals of the perennial east Russian-Siberian-Turkish Bosporus *Lychnis chalcedonica* (Maltese cross); height 450–900 mm (18–36 in); seem to blaze on hot sunny days.

The shape of these late spring-mid summer flowers resembles the St John's Ambulance Brigade insignia.

L. chalcedonica has flower cultivars in white, pink or bright red, each approximately 25–31 mm (1–1.5 in) wide, borne in flat topped clusters, 75–100 mm (3–4 in) across, sometimes more.

Its leaves are plain green and lance-like, occasionally evergreen.

L. chalcedonica makes a useful bedding or border plant in warmer areas. It is also used as a container plant. It is one of the more important species of campion grown in Australian gardens.

The south European-central Asian *Lychnis coronaria* (syn. *Agrostemma coronaria*), rose-campion, is an old garden favourite; height 500–900 mm (20–39 in). It has single, 'glowing-fluorescent', rich magenta-pink, 25–37 mm (1–1.5 in) wide flowers. But is also has white, pink and crimson cultivars.

It is a short-lived perennial that can be treated as an annual. It flowers late spring-summer.

Its 'awkwardly' branched flowering stems arise from a clump of very distinctive, white-woolly, egg-shaped to lance-like, evergreen leaves.

Trim off all the spent flowers to keep lychnis plants tidy, and to prevent self-seeding, particularly from *L. coronaria*. The many-branched lychnis species can get knocked around in windy locations, and may need supporting.

Lychnis are not fussy about soil, provided it is well-drained, sheltered, and receives a good amount of sun. They also like adequate watering during dry spells.

The flowers grown from lychnis seeds can be variable.

Propagation: Thinly sow the seeds in late winter or spring, for *L. chalcedonica*, or say 8 to 10 weeks before the usual spring planting-out time at your location, in seed compost containers, using a damp, recommended, seed raising compost.

Place the container indoors in good light, or in a greenhouse or cold frame if necessary. Keep the compost pleasantly moist.

Seedlings can be hardened off and pricked out into nursery holding-beds, or planted out directly where they are to grow and flower; *L. chalcedonica*, 300–600 mm (12–24 in) apart.

Those transplanted into the nursery holding-beds can be lifted with a garden trowel and planted out, with the roots still contained in a ball of soil, into their permanent quarters mid-late autumn, when weather conditions permit; for example: not too hot.

L. coronaria can be grown as an annual, with seeds sown late winter at 14–18°C (57–64°F), in a greenhouse where necessary, keeping the compost pleasantly moist.

Prick out the seedlings into small pots of a damp, recommended potting compost. Grow the seedlings on, harden them off, if necessary in a cold frame, and plant them out, in late spring, directly where they are to grow and flower; 300–450 mm (12–18 in) apart.

Or ripe seeds can be sown in spring, directly where they are to grow and flower, and thinned out to the correct distance apart.

In English gardens sow the seed *L. chalcedonica* in late spring-earliest summer (May-June), in seed raising compost, and place in a cold frame or similar to germinate. Be aware of the need to ventilate and shade the young seedlings from hot direct sunlight being concentrated through the glass. Transplant hardened off seedlings into a nursery holding-bed. Finally plant them out, mid-autumn, directly where they are to grow and flower.

L. coronaria can be treated as a half-hardy annual by growing the seeds under glass, mid-late winter at 14–18°C (57–64°F). Lychnis can flower from mid-summer on.

Pests and diseases: Reasonably free.
Cultivars/varieties: As above.
Family: Caryophyllaceae.

***Lythrum* (purple loosestrife)** The European-temperate Asian perennial *Lythrum salicaria*; height 600–1.8 m (2–6 ft); has small, pink-purple, star-shaped flowers clustered tightly in a 225–300 mm (9–12 in) 'corncob' group, all along the tall, candle-pointed spike.

The leaves are dullish, darkish green and slightly oval to lance-shaped, and not particularly attractive.

Lythrum prefers a moist soil, in a partially shaded site, or sun. It will grow well in organic garden soils, but it must have ample water during dry spells. Tidy up the stems after flowering. Feed yearly with a well-balanced, proprietary brand of fertiliser suitable for lythrums and applied as the manufacturer instructs.

Named cultivars do not come true from seeds.

Propagation: Thinly sow the seeds, autumn in frost-free areas, directly where they are to grow and flower; or sow in early spring. Or seeds can be sown outside late spring-early summer in cold areas. Plant out, or thin out the seedlings 450 mm (18 in) apart.

Or sow the seeds in seed compost containers, using a damp, recommended, seed raising compost, winter, under glass at 16–18°C (61–64°F). Prick out the seedlings into small pots of damp, recommended potting compost, grow them on, harden them off, and plant them out directly where they are to grow and flower.

In English gardens sow the seeds mid-spring (April) in seed compost containers, using a recommended seed raising compost, under glass at 16–18°C (61–64°F). Prick out the seedlings into 75 mm (3 in) pots, and grow them on. Harden off the seedlings, and plant them out, late spring-early summer, into a nursery holding-bed. Finally transplant them in autumn to directly where they are to grow and flower. Or put the pots outdoors after hardening off and transplant in autumn.

Or plant the 'hardened-off' seedlings out directly where they are to grow and flower.

Or the seeds can be sown directly outside, late spring-early summer (May-June).

Flowers from the early sowings appear during summer.

Pests and diseases: Reasonably free.
Cultivars/varieties: Mixed.
Family: Lythraceae.

***Machaeranthera* (Tahoka daisy)** The western United States *Machaeranthera tanacetifolia* (syn. *Aster tanacetifolius*); height up to 600 mm (24 in); is an annual or biennial, daisy-like flower.

The 39–50 mm (1.5–2 in) wide blooms have sensitive, lavender-blue petals, with bright-yellow centres, similar to, but much finer than, a michaelmas daisy's.

The pale-green foliage is delicately shredded like fine, fern-carrot foliage.

Tahoka daisy flowers late spring-summer, depending on location and sowing times. It can be used as part of a border scheme or for cut-flowers, although the flowers tend to close up somewhat at night.

Tahoka daisy needs regular watering during dry spells to prevent the ferny foliage from scorching. It likes an open, free-draining, loamy-sandy soil, in a sunny spot.

Propagation: Dig over the site where the plants are to grow and flower, and when it is easy to work, in late winter-late spring. Break the soil down into a fine tilth, and rake out any debris. Gently firm the soil to take the seeds.

Thinly scatter the fluffy seeds over the area, when all danger from frost is past, and rake them into the tilth surface. Press the soil lightly but firmly to anchor the seeds to the soil.

Water the seeds well using a fine spray. Don't allow the seedbed to dry out until the seedlings are well established, then water the plants when they need it.

The seeds should germinate in approximately 10 days. Thin out the seedlings 150–225 mm (6–9 in) apart. Flowers should appear in approximately 3 months. Mine took exactly 3 months to begin flowering, but in good growing conditions.

Or sow the seeds late winter-early spring under glass in seed compost containers using a damp, recommended seeding compost at 16°C (61°F), or a little below. Correct temperature control is imperative as temperatures above 18°C (64°F) can cause the seeds to react adversely.

I found, with my particular Tahoka daisy sowing time, that trying to maintain such a low temperature was difficult, and this resulted in spasmodic germination. However, those seeds that did germinate and flower were extremely lovely, and worth waiting for.

Prick out the seedlings into small pots of damp, recommended, potting compost, and grow them on. Harden them off, if necessary in a cold frame, before planting them out directly where they are to grow and flower, when any danger from frost is past and the ground has warmed up.

Space the seedlings 150–225 mm (6–9 in) apart.

In English gardens sow the seeds late winter-early spring (Feb-March) under glass, in seed compost containers, using a damp, recommended seed compost at 16°C (61°F), or a little below, and treat them as half-hardy pot-grown annuals.

Pests and diseases: Reasonably free.
Cultivars/varieties: Species as above.
Family: Asteraceae.

***Malcolmia* (Virginia, Virginian stock)** The Mediterranean *Malcolmia maritima*; height 150–200–300 mm (6–8–12 in); is neither a true stock, as stocks are members of the *Matthiola* genus, nor does it come from Virginia.

But it is a spring-flowering, hardy annual of the same family as the stocks, and has a deliciously sharp-sweet scent. Virginia stock is used as an edging plant, and for window boxes and the like.

It flowers approximately 4 weeks from seed-sowing, producing a mass of variable white, pink, lilac, rose or reddish, 12–19 mm (0.5–0.7 in) wide, 4-petalled, 'cross' flowers. And these flowers are freely borne for 5 to 8 weeks, depending on whether it is very hot, or not. Virginia stock seems to flower and flag quickly in hot, humid conditions.

Virginia stocks will grow in most soils, provided they are positioned in a sunny and sheltered spot. Self-sown seedlings occur prolifically in undisturbed soil.

Prepare the soil with a well-balanced, proprietary flower fertiliser, prior to sowing the seeds, and applied as the manufacturer instructs for Virginia stocks. You can feed the plants, when the buds are forming with a well-balanced, liquid, soluble, flower fertiliser, suitable for Virginia stocks, applied as the manufacturer instructs.

Be careful if you bother to thin out Virginia stocks, or weed around them, as their delicate roots are easily pulled up.

Propagation: Dig over the soil, when it is easy to work, where the plants are to grow and flower, breaking it down into a fine tilth and raking out any debris. Gently but firmly press the soil to take the fine seeds.

Sow the seeds in succession, if so desired, very thinly to obviate the need to thin them out later on, which is a fiddly job; autumn subtropical areas; summer-autumn and spring in temperate areas; and summer-autumn and spring in the cooler areas.

Scatter the seeds over the prepared soil and lightly rake them into the tilth, barely covering them. Gently water the seeds using a fine, misty spray.

The seeds germinate in approximately 5 days, usually as thick as mustard and cress, although they can take longer. Thin out the seedlings, if necessary, 75–100 mm (3–4 in) apart.

Or the seeds can be sown in seed compost containers using a recommended seed raising compost. My seedlings germinated in 5 days. I pricked them out into containers of damp, recommended, potting compost, when they were large enough to handle, and grew them on for flowering.

But quite frankly, this latter method is a bit 'Rolls-Royce' for the humble little Virginia stock. But you know, I have a soft spot for Virginia stocks, having cut my gardening teeth on such plants in my salad days, years ago.

In English gardens sow the seeds very thinly to avoid thinning out later, directly where they are to grow and flower. Begin sowing in spring (March-April) and make a succession of sowings, every 4 to 6 weeks to mid-summer, provided you don't get fed up with them. And sow again in early autumn (Sept).

Pests and diseases: Reasonably free.
Cultivars/varieties: Dwarf Mixed.
Family: Brassicaceae.

***Malope* (mallow-wort)** The Spanish-North African *Malope trifida*; height 750 mm–1 m (30–39 in); is related to the hollyhock and hibiscus. It is a hardy annual, erect and bushy, and usually doesn't need staking.

But the species is not often grown in Australia, although its white, or rose-red-mauve cultivars-natural varieties, with their deeper-pink veins radiating up from the centre of the flower, are well worth a place in the flower border.

The flowers are 50–75 mm (2–3 in) wide at the mouth, 5-petalled trumpets, that seem to glow fluorescent-pink with darker coral veins segmenting each petal. The top of each petal is folded back creating a ring of light at the top of the flower.

Some people use them as cut flowers. The 'maple leaf' leaves are dullish green.

Malopes are uncomplaining plants, and will grow in an ordinary, light, well-drained, neutral garden soil.

Propagation: Dig over the soil where the seeds are to grow and flower, when it is easy to work. Rake it into a fine tilth, removing any debris. Gently firm the soil to take the seeds.

Sow the seeds autumn in frost-free areas; early spring in mild climates; raking them just into the surface tilth, and gently firm them to anchor them to the soil. Water gently using a fine spray.

Or in cold areas, sow a few seeds in 75 mm (3 in) pots, using a damp, recommended seed raising compost, late winter, indoors in a frost-free place in good light, but not hot direct sunlight. Thin out the seedlings keeping the strongest in each pot.

Harden off the seedlings in a cold frame, and plant them out directly where they are to grow and flower, but when all danger from frost is past and the ground has warmed up.

Space the plants 225–300 mm (9–12 in) apart. Flowers will appear November-January in temperate areas.

In English gardens sow the seeds, early-mid spring (March-April), directly where they are to grow and flower, and barely cover them with fine soil. Thin out the seedlings to 225–300 mm (9–12 in) apart, and grow them on. Flowers summer.

Pests and diseases: Reasonably free.
Cultivars/varieties: As above.
Family: Malvaceae.

***Matricaria* (feverfew)** The summer-flowering, Great Britain-Caucasus *Matricaria eximia* (syn. *Chrysanthemum parthenium*); height 225–500 mm (9–20 in), although a short-lived perennial, is often treated as an annual, to obtain neat, compact, floriferous plants.

It is a hardy plant for cool-temperate areas. It flowers autumn, winter, spring, or early summer, depending on location and when the seeds were sown.

Feverfew grows as a clump, producing myriads of 19–25 mm (0.7–1 in) wide, fried-egg, open-daisy flowers, above bright green, chrysanthemum-like, pineapple-eucalyptus fragrant foliage.

There are cultivars available in single or double daisy-form, or anemone-pompon form, with white, or golden-yellow flowers; some cultivars have golden foliage. Feverfew will flower in the first year from seed if treated as a half-hardy annual.

Feverfew is used for borders, windowboxes, garden edges, and pot work. It will grow on most soils, but prefers a light, well-drained, moderately fertile soil, in a sunny, sheltered spot.

M. eximia florepleno (syn. *C. p. florepleno*) is a taller flowered form.

Propagation: Seeds can be sown later winter and spring subtropical areas; spring in temperate areas; autumn and spring in cooler areas; in seed compost containers using a damp, recommended seed raising compost.

In cold areas, sow the seeds late winter-spring, indoors in a warm, light place, at 16–21°C (61–70°F), say 8 to 10 weeks before the usual spring planting-out time in your location.

Firm the compost to present a firm base on which the seeds will settle, but not sink. The seeds must have light to germinate.

Sow the seeds on top of the compost, and water them with a misting spray. Or better still stand the container in a shallow dish of water, allowing the moisture to soak up through the compost and just glisten on the compost surface; then remove the container. Don't allow the water to pool and float the seeds away. Keep the seeds moist at all times.

Prick out the seedlings into containers of damp, recommended potting compost and grow them on. When they are large enough to handle and transplant easily, move them out directly where they are to grow and flower.

If the seedlings have been grown soft, under heat, then make sure that they are hardened off, if necessary in a cold frame, before planting them out of doors.

Or you can dig over the site, when it is easy to work, where the plants are to grow and flower. Break the soil down into a fine tilth and remove any debris. Gently but thoroughly firm the soil so that the seeds will stay on the surface.

The seeds can be broadcast, or sown in small, straight rows; early spring or autumn in cooler areas. Or the seeds can be sown in nursery beds, and later transplanted. Gently press the seeds to anchor them to the soil surface, and mist water them using a fine spray.

Germination should take place within 15 days, at 21°C (70°F) soil temperature. Thin out the seedlings to 225–300 mm (9–12 in) apart (some gardeners like to plant the more dwarf cultivars as close as 150 mm (6 in) apart). Water the plants when need be during dry spells, but don't overwater them.

In English gardens sow the seeds, early-mid spring (March-April), directly where they are to grow and flower. Thin them out to 150–225–300 mm (6–9–12 in) apart, according to cultivar. Or you can sow the seeds late winter-early spring (Feb-March), under glass, at 16–21°C (61–70°F), in seed raising compost, and treat them as half-hardy annuals. Flowers early summer, and on.

Pests and diseases: Aphids, caterpillars, slugs, snails, leaf spot, powdery mildew, scorch.
Cultivars/varieties: Species as above. Double White Stars, height 600 mm (24 in). Tom Thumb White Stars, height 225 mm (9 in), yellow centred, white button flowers, broad outer petals.
Family: Asteraceae.

***Matthiola* (stocks)** The Greek, winter-spring-summer flowering *Matthiola bicornis*; height 300–400 mm (12–16 in); is a sprawly, straggly-looking plant, with dull-green leaves.

The 19 mm (0.7 in) wide, 4-petalled, cross-shaped, greenish-backed, pinky-white flowers, are carried on 150–225 mm (6–9 in) stems. The blooms seem to turn in on themselves during the day, and perhaps, because of this, you would plant night-scented stock where you didn't particularly want to see it.

But at evening and night the flowers open up and exude their sweet, but powerful perfume. Coming across this fragrance unexpectedly is one of the joys of gardening. Planting distance 150–200 mm (6–8 in) apart.

Matthiola incana **cultivars**
The cultivars of the grey felted leaved, southern European, winter-spring-summer flowering *Matthiola incana*; height 120–750 mm (5–30 in); planting distance: 200–400 mm (8–16 in) apart (height and distance apart being according to cultivar); are the popular 'stocks' found in great abundance.

They are hardy biennials or short-lived perennials; some being treated as annuals. They carry 25 mm (1 in) wide, single or double flowers, massed in white, cream, pink, purple or yellow; most colours except orange and blue.

M. incana can be classified as follows:

(1) Brompton Stocks (biennials); height up to 450 mm (18 in).
(2) East Lothian Stocks, or Intermediate Stocks (biennials, or can be treated as half-hardy annuals in cold climates); height up to 375 mm (15 in).
(3) Ten Week Stocks (annuals); height 300–750 mm (12–30 in) depending on the stock strain.
(4) Trysomic Stocks (annuals); height up to 400 mm (16 in).

Popular stocks in Australia are:

(a) Austral Stocks Mixed, or separate colours in white, cream, apricot, copper, raspberry and white bicolour, salmon-pink, carmine-pink, lilac, lavender and dark lavender.
(b) Dwarf Ten Week Mixed Bedding; annual.
(c) Giant Column Non-Branching Mixed, or in separate colours of white, cream, buff, pale pink, rose-pink, lavender, purple, or shades and tints of these colours.
(d) Excelsior Column Mixed; annual. Wide colour range.
(e) Giant Perfection Mixed, shades and tints of white, cream, pink, lavender, purple.
(f) Trysomic Stocks Blends; many double blooms. There is one Trysomic Stock known as Trysomic 7 Week Mix, which, in the correct growing conditions, can produce flowers in just 7 weeks from sowing. Colours: white, pink, rose, crimson, dark blue, purple.
(g) Stock Pigmy Mixed; height 120–150 mm (5–6 in); double flowers in white, cherry, bright scarlet, royal purple.

Try to avoid growing stocks in soil that has been used recently for any of the cabbage family such as: candytuft, isatis, kale, sweet alyssum, virginia stock, wallflowers and many other plants, as stocks, being of the same family, are prone to many of the same diseases.

Stocks like a well-drained, organic, neutral soil, or even a little limy (alkaline), and a sunny location. They do not usually need staking, although some of the taller cultivars will fall over in windy areas; stake where necessary.

Water stocks thoroughly during dry spells, but don't waterlog them as this leads to root rot.

Treat the soil with a flower fertiliser suitable for stocks, and apply it as the manufacturer instructs for stocks. Stocks are sensitive to potash deficiency.

Stock seedlings can suffer from heat-stroke in hot, drying winds, and shade protection may have to be given. But the shade must be removed as quickly as is feasible to prevent drawing up of the seedlings. It is an accepted practice to plant seedlings in the cool of the day to give them time to adjust overnight, but keep an eye on them.

Water the plants copiously during dry weather, but don't waterlog them.

Propagation: M. bicornis is easy to grow from seeds in a well-drained soil, in light shade in hot areas, or full sun in cooler areas.

Prepare the ground when it is easy to work, breaking it down into a fine tilth, and removing any debris. Gently but firmly press the soil to take the fine seeds. Sow the seeds all year through in subtropical areas; spring and summer elsewhere.

Seeds can also be sown in seed compost containers, using a damp, recommended, seed raising compost. Prick out the seedlings into pots or containers, grow them on, and plant out directly where they are to grow and flower.

They should flower within 12 weeks. Bear in mind that they are not particularly attractive as flowers; although it is a matter of opinion.

Sowing times: The time taken between the sowing and flowering of *M. incana* stocks can vary considerably according to the cultivar grown, and you would refer to the specialist instructions given on the seed packet. After all, some stock cultivars can take 20 to 25 weeks to flower from sowing; other cultivars can flower within 12 weeks; and one cultivar, given the correct growing conditions, can flower in 7 weeks!

M. incana seeds, however, can be sown: late summer-early-mid autumn subtropical areas; mid-late summer-mid autumn in temperate areas; summer in cooler areas. But I repeat, check the packet for specialist instructions given on the packet concerning seed sowing times.

In cold areas you can sow annual summer-flowering stock seeds late winter-early mid spring (or later, depending on the instructions given on the packet concerning the time it takes for the plants to flower from sowing the seeds), in seed compost containers, under glass at 14–16°C (57–61°F), and treat them as half-hardy plants.

Prick out the seedlings into containers, or pots of damp, recommended, potting compost, and grow them on. Harden them off, and plant them out directly where they are to flower and grow, but when all danger from frost is past. Don't plant out any seedlings that are suspect or straggly.

Or sow the seeds in late spring-early summer, directly where they are to grow and flower, but once the soil warms up, thinning out the seedlings to the required distance apart.

Sow stock seeds as thinly as possible, to provide room for the seedlings to 'show' themselves without becoming overcrowded; this also helps reduce the incidence of damping-off disease.

Dig over the soil when it is easy to work, where the plants are to grow and flower, raking it into a fine tilth, and remove any debris. Gently but firmly press the soil to take the seeds.

It is imperative that you sow the seeds thinly directly where they are to flower and grow, in shallow drills, the drills being 350 mm (14 in) apart, barely covering the seeds, say a maximum of 3 mm (0.1 in) deep. Sowing the seeds thinly means that you don't have to separate seedlings unnecessarily. Thin out the seedlings to 150–200–250 mm (6–8–10 in) apart, depending on cultivar, transplanting any surplus seedlings somewhere else.

There are various methods of selecting double-flowered seedlings when pricking out Trysomic Stocks. But be circumspect when sorting out seedlings; don't become too fussy and end up with hardly any plants. Gardening is meant to be fun! Read the instructions on the packet.

In English gardens sow the seeds of *M. incana* summer blooming annuals, late-winter early-mid spring (Feb-April), in seed compost containers, under glass at 14–16°C (57–61°F), and treat them as half-hardy plants. But check the details on the packet for specialist instructions for a particular cultivar, concerning sowing times; particularly with regard to the quick-flowering annuals.

Or sow the seeds in mid-late spring, directly where they are to grow and flower, but once the soil warms up, thinning out the seedlings to the required distance apart. But again check the instructions given on the packet.

Pests and diseases: Aphids, caterpillars, alternaria leaf spot, bacterial blight, botrytis, damping off, foot rot, fusarium wilt, potash deficiency, white blight and collar rot.

Cultivars/varieties: Many and varied, but see above.

Family: Brassicaceae.

Maurandya **(syn.** ***Asarina*****) (climbing penstemon)** The summer-flowering Mexican *Maurandya barclaiana* (syn. *Asarina barclaiana, Maurandia barclaiana*) can climb 2.1–3 m (7–10 ft), or even up to 4.5 m (15 ft) in warm, moist conditions.

The 50–75 mm (2–3 in) long, white, pink or violet-purple flowers, depending on species and variation within the species, borne on solitary stems, are pendulous, tubular-bell, star-ended, with white throats.

Maurandyas are extremely frost sensitive and, as pot plants, demand a minimum winter temperature of 10°C (50°F).

But they can be treated as annuals. They are planted outside in the garden in temperate areas, but only after any danger from frost is past and the ground has warmed up. However, in mild winter, temperate areas they can become perennials.

Maurandyas cling by using tendrils, but are usually tied on to the support. They look impressive on garden tripods or trellis-work, or similar. If grown as greenhouse plants they are kept in check by judicious pruning in late winter.

Some gardeners use maurandyas as hanging-basket plants. They are grown on in 125 mm (5 in) pots of damp, recommended potting compost, and the pot is placed into the hanging basket. Special attention has to be paid to the plant's watering to ensure that it does not dry out.

Maurandyas make excellent screens, as

their dark or light or dull-green, ivy-like, triangular leaves completely clothe their supports. They prefer a well-drained, rich, organic, fertile, neutral soil in a sunny, sheltered site, or light shade in hot areas.

Water maurandyas well during dry weather. Feed them with a well-balanced, soluble, liquid, flower fertiliser, suitable for maurandyas and applied as the manufacturer instructs.

Propagation: Sow the seeds, mid winter-spring, in seed compost containers, using a recommended seed raising compost, in a greenhouse if necessary, at 16–21°C (61–70°F).

Or sow the seeds indoors in a warm, light place, late winter, say 6 to 8 weeks before the usual spring planting-out time in your location.

Prick out the seedlings when large enough to handle into 75–100 mm (3–4 in) peat pots, and grow them on. Harden them off, if necessary in a cold frame, before planting them outside, when all danger from frost is past and the ground has warmed up.

If using maurandyas as greenhouse plants, then pot the seedlings singly into 100 mm (4 in) pots of damp, recommended, potting compost; from there pot them on 2 sizes into 150 mm (6 in) pots; and then into 200 mm (8 in) pots, as and when required.

Keep maurandyas in a light area, although not exposed to direct sun through the glass, and in a warm, buoyant, greenhouse atmosphere.

In cold areas keep the roots of greenhouse maurandya plants just moist over winter.

In English gardens treat maurandyas as frost-tender greenhouse plants, the seeds being sown late winter-early spring (Feb-March), at 16–21°C (61–70°F). Or sow the seeds indoors in a warm, light place, late winter, say 6 to 8 weeks before the usual spring planting-out time in your location. They can also be planted outside, in mild areas, in late spring-summer, once hardened off, and when all danger from frost is past and the soil has warmed up sufficiently. Flowers late spring, and on, under glass; and mid summer, and on, outside.

Pests and diseases: Aphids.
Cultivars/varieties: Species as above.
Family: Scrophulariaceae.

***Mentzelia* (blazing star)** The Californian hardy annual *Mentzelia lindleyi* (syn. *Bartonia aurea*); height 300–600 mm (12–24 in); is well named as blazing star. (But be aware that *M. laevicaulis* is also known by this name.)

The 'fleeting' 31–62 mm (1.2–2.5 in) wide, 5 pointed-petalled, 'sheriff's badge' flowers of *M. lindleyi*, with their concentrated clutch of central stamens and deeper-yellow eye, do seem to blaze like polished gold in our hot sunlight.

The flowers have a delicate perfume, which is not obtrusive.

The stems are wiry, but seemingly fragile in the early stages. The leaves are dull green, narrow, very pointed, with occasional notches opposite each other up the leaf, like little shark fins.

Mentzelia flowers are produced freely spring-summer, depending on location and how the seeds were sown.

Mentzelias make useful border plants. They must have a sunny, open, site, and free-draining soil.

Propagation: Dig over the soil, when it is easy to work, where the plants are to grow and flower. Rake it down into a fine tilth, and remove any debris. Firm the soil to take the seeds.

Broadcast the seeds, or plant them in small rows, early-spring or autumn in mild winter areas; or spring in cold areas; barely raking them into the top tilth. Cover the seeds with a 6 mm (0.2 in) depth of fine compost or vermiculite, and gently firm them to anchor them to the soil. Seeds can take up to 14 days to germinate; my mentzelia seeds, sown under glass, took 5 days.

Thin out the seedlings to 200–400 mm (8–16 in) apart. Gently spray with water using a fine spray. Keep down weeds and watch out for snails.

As a conceit, and because mentzelias are difficult to transplant outside in the garden, I grew some under glass, in damp, recommended seed raising compost, with the seeds being sown in late winter.

I pricked out the seedlings into small pots of damp, recommended, potting compost, and grew them on as interesting, but 'fleeting' pot-plant flowers. The flowers appeared in mid-spring, and one of the plants in flower is looking at me now as I write this.

In English gardens dig over the soil, when it is easy to work, where the plants are to grow and flower. Rake it down into a fine tilth and remove any debris. Firm the soil to take the seeds.

Broadcast the seeds, or plant them in small rows, earliest mid-spring (March-April), barely raking them into the top tilth. Thin out the seedlings to 200–400 mm (8–10 in) apart. Mentzelias are summer-flowering.

Pests and diseases: Reasonably free.
Cultivars/varieties: Species as above.
Family: Loasaceae.

***Mimosa* (sensitive plant)** The Brazilian *Mimosa pudica* makes an attractive pot plant. The fame of *M. pudica* lies in the fact that the leaves, especially in the temperature range of 24–29°C (75–85°F), when touched, immediately withdraw, which is not only fascinating but gives rise to the question 'why?'

This withdrawing habit is referred to in the name: *mimosa* (mimic); *pudica* (bashful).

Mimosa pudica is becoming a principal weed in many countries, rapidly colonising vast areas because of its ability to adapt to harsh conditions, the lack of natural competition, and the absence of natural predators.

M. pudica can grow from semi-prostrate to 200 mm–1 m (8–39 in) tall. In some areas it is grown as a frost-tender, greenhouse annual. But it behaves like a perennial in permanently warm locations.

The flowers are 8 mm (0.3 in) wide, pinkish, fluffy and egg-shaped, followed by 'pineapple' seeds which are hard and bristled, with powerfully-sharp prickles, and are easily transported by animals and humans.

The leaves form opposite each other on a central vein, like a fishbone, or miniature palm leaves. It is a thorny plant, and this is one reason why children should not be allowed to touch it, but they can be shown by adults.

Experiments have shown that fresh seeds will germinate in 14 days. Older seed will still germinate well, taking up in 28 days, at 25°C (77°F) soil temperature.

There may be regulations regarding the growing of *Mimosa* species in your State, therefore check to make sure.

In English gardens *M. pudica* can be grown as a frost-tender, greenhouse plant. Seeds are sown late winter-early spring, in seed raising compost, at 19–25°C (65–77°F).

Seeds should germinate in approximately 8–14 days (variable). Prick out the seedlings when large enough to handle into 75 mm (3 in) pots of damp, recommended, potting compost. From there pot them on 2 sizes into 125 mm (5 in) pots.

Grow them on as well-lighted (not direct sunlight) greenhouse plants, but give them light shade during hot, sunny weather, and ventilate the house once the temperature moves above 21°C (70°F). Keep them at 8 to 10°C (46–50°F) minimum winter temperature. Apply normal, greenhouse-floor, damping-down techniques when necessary. Feed the plants, when needed, with a well-balanced, soluble, liquid flower fertiliser, suitable for mimosas, applied as the manufacturer instructs. Flowers midsummer, and on.

Pests and diseases: Reasonably free.
Cultivars/varieties: Species as above.
Family: Fabaceae/Papilionaceae.

***Mimulus* (musk mimulus, monkey flower)** There are many western North American and western South American *Mimulus* species. But it is the attractive cultivars: height 100 mm (4 in) and slightly taller; particularly some of the newer F_1 hybrids, that are sought.

The 'grinning-mouth', funnel-bell shaped flowers can be up to 50 mm (2 in) wide, and are available in red, yellow, creamy, some white, or mixed variations of these colours, plus red mottling, spotting or freckling.

Generally, mimulus cultivars are frost-sensitive short-lived perennials, that can be grown as annuals.

Garden mimuluses like a moist soil, or a soil that can be kept damp, in a shady location. They rapidly deteriorate in hot sunlight. Mimuluses are used as border plants, rockery plants, bog, or waterside garden-pond plants, or pot plants.

One of the great horticultural mysteries is: 'Why did the sweet perfume of the western North American musk flower, *M. moschatus*, disappear?'

At one time, prior to the beginning of this century, the musk flower was much in demand for its musk perfume, as well as for its fascinating, yellow flowers. Then early in the 20th century the perfume disappeared from the face of the earth. And no scented musk flower has appeared since.

The name 'mimulus' comes from the latin *mimus* meaning mimic-actor; referring to the gaping, mask-like, monkey-face flowers. And, no doubt, if you stared long enough at the flower, you could see a grinning monkey staring back.

Propagation: Seeds of many F_1 hybrids can be sown most times of the year, except during the very hot, or very cold months.

Usually they are sown in late winter-early spring and autumn; under glass where necessary. But they need a 15–18°C (59–64°F) temperature in which to germinate. They can be sown late spring-early summer in temperate areas, directly where they are to grow and flower, but only in suitably shady locations; or earlier in frost-free northern areas; also in shady locations.

Sow the seed in 75 mm (3 in) deep, seed compost containers, using a damp, recommended, sterile, soilless, seed raising mix, that wets quickly and easily. Dry compost will result in the demise of the seedlings.

The compost should also firm well, but not become compacted, to prevent the minute seeds from being washed below soil surface. You can make a compost using 2 parts by volume, acid, granulated sphagnum peat-moss, to 1 part, by volume, of vermiculite.

Place the compost into the container, and firm it thoroughly with your fingers and a clean, sterile block of wood, or similar.

You must work cleanly when growing mimuluses, as the F_1 hybrid seedlings are so delicate. Leave the compost 19 mm (0.7 in) from the top of the container. You can spray the compost with a suitable damping-off disease preventative.

Make sure that the compost is firm, thoroughly damp, but not waterlogged.

Very, very carefully mix the minute seeds with a small quantity of clean, sharp, fine silver sand, and pour the lot carefully on to a sheet of clean, white paper, folded to contain the seeds.

Or mix the seeds, still in their seed packet, with several times their volume of sand.

Sprinkle, surface sowing, the sand-seed mix evenly over the damp compost surface, the silver sand indicating where the seeds are falling, to avoid sowing too thickly in one spot.

Cover the seed container with a sheet of glass, as I did, or place the whole inside a clear, plastic bag.

The seeds in the plastic bag should not need watering, but don't just accept this, and keep a wary eye on them.

Any watering that needs to be done can be achieved by placing the container in a dish of water and letting the water soak up through the compost, so that the compost surface just glistens with moisture; then remove the container.

But be alert as too much water rising through the compost can cause the seeds to float to the container edges. Any heavy watering from the top will wash out the seeds, and the seedlings.

Pay particular attention to the germination. I always inspected my compost with a magnifying glass, as those microscopic green specks may not be easily seen, and any excess condensation from the glass or plastic bag can cause damping-off disease.

Remove the glass, or take the container out of the plastic bag, once germination has taken place, to prevent the seedlings being drawn or subjected to excessive condensation.

Germination should take place within 10 days at 15–18°C (59–64°F); although temperature fluctuations can alter this time. My seedlings took 16 days; some much longer.

Transplant the seedlings as soon as they can be handled into containers of damp, recommended, potting compost 50 mm (2 in) apart, or singly into 50 mm (2 in) pots, and grow them on. I used a 'V' notched plastic label to transfer my mimulus seedlings.

Grow the seedlings on; then transfer them into 75 mm (3 in) pots of damp, recommended, potting compost, and grow them on as half-hardy plants. Gradually harden them off, if necessary in a cold frame, and plant them outside, but only if any risk from frost danger is past and the ground has warmed up.

The distance apart depends on the species or cultivar, but is usually 150 mm–225 mm (6–9 in) between plants, and 225–300 mm (9–12 in) between rows.

Or you can grow the seedlings on as pot plants, potting on into bigger pots when necessary.

Frequent, but careful, waterings are necessary, and feeding the plant with a well-balanced, soluble, liquid, flower fertiliser, suitable for mimuluses, and applied as the manufacturer instructs, is also useful.

The minute F_1 seedlings are easily destroyed in their infancy, but once they are established you will wonder how such large plants came from such minute seeds and seedlings.

In English gardens treat the summer-flowering cultivars as half-hardy annuals.

Sow the more desirable cultivars in late winter (Feb), under glass, at 15–18°C (59–64°F), in seed compost containers. Take the precautions mentioned above.

Prick out the seedlings into 50 mm (2 in) pots of damp, recommended potting compost, and grow them as summer-shaded, greenhouse pot plants, potting them on two sizes at a time when required.

Pests and diseases: Reasonably free.
Cultivars/varieties: Calypso Mixed F_1 Hybrid, height 125–200 mm (5–8 in), orange, yellow, solid and bicolor. Queen's Prize Mixed, height 400 mm (16 in), finely spotted and blotched.
Family: Scrophulariaceae.

***Mirabilis* (marvel of Peru, four o'clocks)** The frost-tender, summer-flowering, tropical American *Mirabilis jalapa*; height 450–900 mm (18–36 in); is a tuberous perennial that has the ability to produce variable white, pink, red, yellow, 25–50 mm (1–2 in) long, 25–50 mm (1–2 in) wide, fragrant, fused-petalled trumpet-flowers.

For example, it can have pink and yellow harlequin-colours on the same flower, either in blocks, stripes, or splashes, and all on the same plant. It can also have tricoloured flowers.

The flowers are fleeting, theoretically, opening at 4 o'clock in the afternoon and fading the following day, but this is determined by location, temperature and cloud cover, which can extend the flowering period.

Mirabilises can be grown as annuals in cold areas. They appear as occasional weeds in temperate South Australia. The 100 mm (4 in) long foliage is bright green, narrow-heart-shaped, pointed, or lance-shaped.

Mirabilises are used as border plants, and can spread rapidly under the right temperature conditions.

They like a light, organic, moist, but well-drained soil, and a sunny, sheltered location. Water them well during dry spells. In cold areas the tubers of *M. jalapa* can be lifted and stored. Or in temperate-warm areas the foliage can be cleaned up after flowering and the roots left in the ground to grow on the next season.

Propagation: Dig over the site, when it is easy to work, directly where the plants are to grow and flower. Break the soil down into a fine tilth, rake out any debris, and gently firm the soil.

Sow the seeds, usually in spring, or at any time during clement weather once the seeds are ripe, directly where they are to grow and flower.

The seed should germinate in 14 days at 21°C (70°F) soil temperature. Keep them moist during germination, and thin out the seedlings to 300–600 mm (12–24 in) apart. Feed the plants regularly with a well-balanced, soluble, liquid, flower fertiliser, suitable for mirabilises and applied as the manufacturer instructs.

Or sow the seeds in late winter-early spring, or 6 to 8 weeks before the normal, frost-free, spring planting-out time in your location, in seed compost containers, using a recommended seed raising compost, at 18–21°C (64–70°F). Prick out the seedlings, when large enough to handle, into containers of damp, recommended, potting compost, and grow them on.

Harden off the seedlings in a cold frame before planting them outside directly where they are to grow and flower. But only if any danger from frost is past and the ground has warmed up.

In English gardens treat *Mirabilis* species as half-hardy plants. Sow the seeds in late winter-early spring (Feb-March), in damp, recommended seed raising compost, at 18–21°C (64–70°F). Mirabilises are summer flowering.

Pests and diseases: Aphids.
Cultivars/varieties: Marvel of Peru Mixed, height 1 m (39 in), white, rose, red, yellow. Species as above.
Family: Nyctaginaceae.

***Moluccella* (bells of Ireland, molucca balm, Irish bells, Irish green bellflower)** Why the spring or summer-flowering, west Asian-Asia Minor (Syrian) *Moluccella laevis*; height 375–900 mm (15–36 in); is called 'bells of Ireland' I do not know, except that the flowers are bell-shaped, and a pleasant green.

Moluccella is treated as a half-hardy annual in cold areas, but as a hardy annual elsewhere.

From out of a tuft of pale-bright green, coarsely-toothed, nettle-like leaves arise single or branched, 225–600 mm (9–24 in) flower-stem spikes, around which are clustered and whorled pale-green, 'cow-bell', 25 mm (1 in) wide, or wider, flowers, which are heavily criss-crossed with a network of white veins.

But these flowers are the calyces, and not the true flowers.

The true flowers, situated inside the bell, are vaguely fragrant and white, with two large petals like bell clappers, dominating a pinkish 'cotton-wool' ovary. There are also small spines on the flower stem.

Moluccellas like an open, sheltered, sunny site in cooler areas; and partial shade, with sun for part of the day, in warmer areas. They grow in most garden soils, although they prefer a well-drained, light, moderately-rich soil. They need staking. They need watering during dry spells. Moluccella flowers will self-seed if left on the plant, and if soil and temperature conditions are right.

Moluccellas are used extensively as fresh or dried cut flowers, with the leaves removed from the stem.

Propagation: First check the seed packet for any instructions concerning the pre-cooling period for the seeds to break their dormancy.

Dig over the soil in autumn-winter-early spring in subtropical areas; autumn or early spring temperate areas; or spring in cooler areas, once the soil is easy to work, directly where the plants are to grow and flower. Break the soil down into a fine tilth, and remove any debris. Gently firm the soil to take the seeds.

The seeds need light to germinate. 'Station sow' a few seeds in clumps 200–225 mm (8–9 in) apart, or sow them in drills, or scatter them, barely raking them into the top tilth.

Seeds can take up to 3 weeks to germinate,

and up to 3 months to flower. Keep them watered, and thin out the seedlings very carefully to 200–250–300 mm (8–10–12 in) apart. Moluccellas resent root disturbance and do not transplant easily.

Or the seeds can be sown in autumn, in seed compost containers, using a damp, recommended seed raising compost. The seedlings are pricked out into 75 mm (3 in) pots of damp, recommended potting compost, and grown on over winter, under glass if necessary. They may need potting up into larger pots.

Or the seeds can be sown indoors at 16–18°C (60–64°F), in a light place, 8 to 10 weeks before the usual frost-free, spring planting-out time in your location.

Harden off the seedlings, if necessary in a cold frame, before planting them out in spring, directly where they are to grow and flower.

In English gardens, check the packet for any seed pre-cooling instructions. Sow the seeds under glass in late winter-early spring (Feb-March) at 16–18°C (60–64°F), in seed raising compost, barely covering the seeds with compost, and treat them as half-hardy plants. Or sow seeds early-mid spring (March-April) outdoors, directly where they are to grow and flower. Flowers late summer.

Pests and diseases: Reasonably free.
Cultivars/varieties: Species as above.
Family: Lamiaceae.

Momordica The balsam apple, *Momordica balsamina*; height: clambering-climbing, approximately 2.1 m (8 ft); a tendrilled plant, is found from tropical-western Asia to Africa.

It is frost sensitive, and will only bear fruit in locations that have long, hot summers. It is not much grown as an ornamental plant.

Momordica balsamina has been found growing wild, as has *M. charantia*, in the far north of Australia, New South Wales and Queensland, but I have never seen seeds of these plants for sale in Australia, although I have seen the plants.

M. balsamina has 18–25 mm (0.7 in) wide, yellow, bell-shaped flowers. The 31–63 mm (1.5–2.5 in) long fruit is egg-shaped, warted, pale-yellow, changing to orangey when ripe.

The 38–75 mm (1.5–3 in) wide leaves are bright green, rounded to heart-shaped in outline, but deeply divided into 5 round-diamond-shaped, finger-like lobes.

M. charantia (balsam pear); height: clambering-climbing, approximately 2.1 m (8 ft); is similar to the balsam apple, except that its fruits can be larger and the leaves coarser-looking.

If sown under glass in temperate areas, late winter, the fruits begin to appear earliest-mid summer.

Momordicas require a sunny location, a rich, moist soil, and ample watering during dry spells. They look interesting when trained up a 1.8–2.1 m (6–7 ft) tall garden cone or tripod, or similar, as accent plants.

Propagation: The 12 mm (0.5 in) long seeds are sown, under glass if necessary, in individual 75 mm (3 in) peat pots of damp, recommended seed raising compost, 4 weeks before your usual planting-out time, or a month before the last frost is expected in your area, at 18–21°C (64–70°F), and grown on as single plants.

The plants are hardened off, if necessary in a cold frame, and planted out, 300 mm (12 in) apart, when all danger from frost is well past and the ground has warmed up.

In cool areas you could try growing them on in large pots, or boxes of damp, recommended potting compost, as cool greenhouse plants, shading and ventilating the house during hot weather.

The plants are sprawly when first planted out, and will be invaded by weeds as they sprawl. So carefully keep them weed free, but remember that their roots, shoots and tendrils are very delicate, and the flowers will drop off if handled carelessly. The plants must be kept watered during dry spells.

In English gardens treat momordicas as half-hardy plants, sowing the seeds in early spring (March), under glass at 18–21°C (57–70°F), and growing them on as single plants.

Pests and diseases: Various.
Cultivars/varieties: Species as above.
Family: Cucurbitaceae.

***Myosotis* (forget-me-not)** The cultivars of the European *Myosotis sylvatica*; height 300–400 mm (12–16 in); are the most widely grown forget-me-nots.

They are cool climate, shady area, winter-spring-early summer (depending on location) flowering plants, used extensively as under-plants for spring-flowering bulbs, and in other spring bedding schemes.

Forget-me-nots are also planted in semi-shady positions where they create a carpet of colour, or in rockeries, or as clumps of colour in a border scheme.

Forget-me-nots are frost-resistant, hardy perennials, usually treated as biennials, or as annuals, with new seedlings leading to bushy, compact plants each year. If left undisturbed they will self-seed.

The 6–8 mm (0.2–0.3 in) wide, 5-petalled flowers are fragrant and sky-blue. The centre-eye is bright yellow, shading to white. There are cultivars with flowers of rich-deep blues, pinks, carmines or white; plus other shades and tints.

The 100–150 mm (4–6 in) long leaves are soft, oblongish to lance-like, with minute, silky hairs.

Forget-me-nots prefer a rich, organic, sandy loam, moist, fertile soil. They will tolerate a sunny, but not hot, position, but will do well in a shady spot that receives a few hours morning sun.

Feed the plants, when they are growing well, with a well-balanced, soluble, liquid, flower fertiliser, applied as the manufacturer instructs.

Propagation: Dig over the seed bed, late summer-autumn, when it is easy to work, directly where the seeds are to grow and flower. Rake the soil down into a fine tilth and remove any debris. Gently but thoroughly firm the soil.

Sow the tiny, 'apple-pip' seeds directly into the well-prepared seed bed, and rake them into the soil, 6 mm (0.2 in) deep. A succession of sowings, say once every 14 days, can be made if an extended flowering period is desired.

Keep the seed bed pleasantly moist; not wet. The seeds must not be allowed to dry out. They should germinate within 28 days, and flower within 3 to 4 months from sowing.

Thin out the seedlings, 100–150 mm (4–6 in) apart. Then transplant, when they are large enough to handle easily, directly where they are to grow and flower, 225 mm (9 in) apart.

Be aware that the seedlings may flag rapidly in hot weather, and may need protection from the sun.

Or sow the seeds in seed compost containers using a damp, recommended, seed raising compost, 6 mm (0.2 in) deep. Prick out the seedlings into pots of damp, recommended, potting compost, or into nursery holding-beds 100–150 mm (4–6 in) apart. Grow them on, and transplant them directly to where they are to grow and flower.

Seedlings may need over-winter protection in hard-frost areas, under glass cloches, or grown on in a cold frame, and planted out when the bad weather is past.

Or sow the seeds under glass, late winter-early spring, in seed compost containers, using a recommended seed raising compost, 6 mm (0.2 in) deep, at 18–21°C (64–70°F).

Prick out the seedlings into pots of damp, recommended compost, and grow them on. Harden them off, and move them out into a nursery holding-bed, until you are ready to plant them out into their permanent flowering quarters.

In English gardens sow the seeds, mid-late spring-early summer (April-May-June), in seed raising compost. Place the container in a cold greenhouse or cold frame. Or sow the seeds in a nursery seedbed, outside in the garden. Transplant the seedlings into nursery holding-beds, and grow them on until they are planted out, in early-autumn, directly where they are to grow, for flowering in mid-spring.

Pests and diseases: Grey mould, powdery mildew.
Cultivars/varieties: Cottage Garden Mixture, height 200 mm (8 in), white, blues, carmine rose. 'Blue Ball', height 150 mm (6 in), ultramarine blue. 'Little Blue Bird', height 300 mm (12 in). 'Royal Blue Improved', height 300 mm (12 in), rich, deep blue.
Family: Boraginaceae.

Nemesia The cultivars of the South African *Nemesia strumosa*; height 150–400 mm (6–16 in); are upright, densely-branched plants, that produce eye-catching displays of funnel-scoop flowers. They are usually grouped as cultivars of *N. s. suttonii.*

The scented flowers, which appear in winter-spring, depending on location, can be 19–50 mm (0.7–2 in), or more wide, in shades and tints of white, pink, yellow, red, purple and blue; some having spotted throats.

There are 4 small, rounded petals, similar to two pairs of rabbits' ears, above the ovary, with a much larger (usually much more than half the flower), pot-bellied, bottom petal.

The foliage is light green, with 81 mm (3.2 in) long, large-lobed, lance-like leaves, which grow opposite each other on the stem.

In my opinion nemesias are best mass-planted in beds of their own, although they do make excellent border and container plants.

Nemesias will grow in most soils, but prefer a neutral, or slightly acid, well-drained, organic soil, preferably in a sheltered, sunny, but not hot, spot.

Nemesias don't like hot, humid conditions, such as those encountered in the warm, moist north. But they will put up a near-perfect show if the winter-spring conditions in these areas are cool and reasonably dry. However, any hot sun during spring will cause the plants to deteriorate.

Feed the plants, when they are growing well,

with a well-balanced, liquid, soluble, flower fertiliser, suitable for nemesias, and applied as the manufacturer instructs.

Water nemesias carefully, using a fine spray, to avoid spoiling the velvety flowers. Prune off spent blooms to encourage further flowering.

Propagation: Dig over the site, when it is easy to work, directly where the plants are to grow and flower. Break down the soil into a fine tilth and remove any debris. Gently firm the soil to take the seeds.

Thinly sow the seeds in shallow drills, 6 mm (0.2 in) deep, or sow them broadcast fashion; late summer-autumn subtropical areas; late summer-autumn temperate areas. Rake the seeds into the top tilth barely covering them. Water them carefully using a fine spray, and ensure that the seeds and seedlings do not dry out during dry spells. Seedlings appear in 5 to 14 days.

Thin out the seedlings 100–125 mm (4–5 in) apart for the dwarf cultivars, and 200–225 mm (8–9 in) apart for the larger cultivars.

Or sow the seeds in seed compost containers using a damp, recommended seed raising compost. Prick out the seedlings into containers of damp, recommended, potting compost, and grow them on. Harden off seedlings, if necessary, and plant them out directly where they are to grow and flower. Flowers should appear within 4 months.

In cold areas you can treat nemesias as half-hardy annuals. Sow the seeds under glass in late winter-early spring, in seed compost containers, using a damp, recommended, seed raising compost. Seeds should germinate within 2 weeks at 16–21°C (61–70°F).

Prick out the seedlings into containers of damp, recommended, potting compost, and grow them on. Harden them off in a cold frame, and plant them out when all danger from frost is past and the ground has warmed up.

Keep a constant check for any signs of damping-off disease.

Seedlings can be decimated by hard frosts.

In English gardens sow the seeds latest winter-early spring (Feb-March), under glass, at 16–21°C (61–70°F), in seed raising compost, and treat them as half-hardy annuals. Flowers early summer, and on.

Pests and diseases: Foot and root rot, damping off.

Cultivars/varieties: Carnival, height 300 mm (12 in), white, rose pink, cerise, scarlet, crimson, orange, plus many in-between shades and tints. Dwarf Compact Carnival, height 200 mm (8 in), blood red, orange yellow, orange red. Dwarf Carnival Mixed (hulled).

Family: Scrophulariaceae.

***Nemophila* (baby blue eyes)** The Californian spring-summer flowering *Nemophila menziesii*, height 150–225 mm (6–9 in); is an overlooked, but easy to grow, hardy, frost-resistant, spreading-tufted, groundcover annual.

It thrives in a cool winter-spring sun, or in a semi-shady position, in warmer areas.

Above the foliage rise masses of 19–37 mm (0.7–1.5 in) wide, 5 fused-petalled, bowl-saucer-shaped, clear-sky blue flowers, with contrasting white centre-eyes, and 5 black-tipped stamens. The flowers are borne singly on 50 mm (2 in) stems, which lift them above the foliage.

The pale green, leather-feathery leaves are deeply lobed, almost to the mid-rib.

These uncomplaining plants will grow in most garden soils, but they prefer a sandy, organic, moisture-holding soil in a cool, partially shaded spot.

Feed the plants regularly with a well-balanced, liquid, soluble flower fertiliser, suitable for nemophilas, and applied as the manufacturer instructs.

Nemophilas are used as groundcover plants, border plants, rockery plants and pot plants.

Occasionally, nemophilas are sown to flower in tandem with spring-flowering bulbs, forming a striking blue and white under-carpet. The bulbs are planted before the nemophila seeds are sown.

Also grown is *N. maculata*, the 'five-spot' nemophila, which has white flowers with a purple spot at the tip of each petal.

Propagation: Dig over the soil, when it is easy to work; in late summer-mid autumn subtropical areas; late summer-autumn temperate areas; late summer-mid autumn and early spring in cool areas; early spring in cold areas; directly where the plants are to grow and flower.

Break the soil down into a fine tilth and rake out any debris. Gently firm the soil to take the seeds.

Thinly sow the fine, gritty seeds in shallow drills (rows), or carefully broadcast them in clumps 300 mm (6 in) apart. You can mix sand with the seed to ensure even distribution. Barely cover the seeds, 1.5 mm (0.1 in) deep, with fine sand, sieved soil, or similar. Gently firm the seeds to anchor them to the soil. Water carefully using a fine spray, and do not let them dry out.

Germination should occur within 14 days; too hot a soil temperature causes nemophila seeds to fail.

Thin out the seedlings very carefully, as nemophilas resent root disturbance, to 150 mm (6 in) apart.

Flowering should occur within 14 weeks; mine began flowering exactly 13 weeks after sowing.

To grow nemophilas as pot plants, sow a few seeds directly into 50 mm (2 in) pots of damp, recommended, seed raising compost, and grow them in a cold frame, but only if necessary. Thin out the seedlings, leaving one strong seedling in each pot. Grow them on, and transfer say 2 or 3 plants into a 125 mm (5 in) pot of damp, recommended potting compost, for flowering.

Or sow a few seeds in a 125 mm (5 in) pot of seed raising compost, and keep the best 3 seedlings.

As an experiment I have sown nemophila seeds into punnets of seed raising compost, the seeds germinating in 5 days at 17°C (63°F) soil temperature. I pricked the seedlings out, very early on, into pots of damp, recommended, potting compost, and got good results. But, as I said, nemophilas don't like root disturbance.

In English gardens sow the seeds early-mid spring (March-April), directly where the plants are to grow and flower. Thin out the seedlings. Flowers appear early-mid-late summer.

Pests and diseases: Aphids.

Cultivars/varieties: 'Baby Blue Eyes', height 200–300 mm (8–12 in), sky blue, with white eyes.

Family: Hydrophyllaceae.

***Nicandra* (shoo-fly plant, apple of Peru)** The Chilean shoo-fly plant, *Nicandra physalodes violacea*; height 300 mm–1.2 m (12–47 in); is a summer-autumn flowering, strong-growing annual.

The 25–37 mm (1–1.5 in) wide, violet-blue, white-centred, bell-shaped blooms have 5 fascinating, tiny, purple blotches at the base of each petal.

Each flower is enclosed by a Chinese-lantern-like calyx before it opens up, which enlarges after flowering, to enclose the rounded seeds. The flowers are open only for a few hours from midday on, seemingly to catch the sun.

The flowers are supposed to keep flies and insects at bay, hence its common name.

The 39–150 mm (1.5–6 in) long leaves are mid-green, spear-shaped-pointed, with large, irregular lobes.

Nicandras prefer a deep, rich, organic, well-drained, but moisture-holding soil, in a sunny location.

They need frequent watering during dry spells, and feeding occasionally with a well-balanced, liquid, soluble, flower fertiliser, suitable for nicandras and applied as the manufacturer instructs.

N. physalodes has the reputation of causing bloat in sheep grazing on cereal crops, in areas where it has established as a weed. Because of this there may be regulations concerning the growing of this plant. Check with your local State agricultural department.

Propagation: Sow the seeds, late winter-early spring, in compost containers using a damp, recommended, seed raising compost, at 16–21°C (61–70°F). Prick out the seedlings into 75 mm (3 in) pots of damp, recommended, potting compost.

Grow the seedlings on; harden them off, if necessary in a cold frame, and plant them outside, 300–600–900 mm (12–24–36 in) apart, when all danger from frost is past and the ground has warmed up.

Or in mild, temperate areas, 'station sow' a few seeds in spring 300–600–900 mm (12–24–36 in) apart, directly where the plants are to grow and flower, but only when the soil is easy to work, and any danger from frost is past and the ground has warmed up. Keep the strongest seedling in each clump.

In English gardens sow the seeds under glass, in late winter-early spring (Feb-March), in seed raising compost, at 16–21°C (61–70°F), and treat them as half-hardy annuals. Flowers midsummer, and on. Or sow seeds, late spring, directly where they will grow and flower.

Pests and diseases: Reasonably free.

Cultivars/varieties: Species as above.

Family: Solanaceae.

***Nicotiana* (flowering tobacco)** The fragrant, South American *Nicotiana alata grandiflora*; height 300 mm–1 m (12–39 in) depending on species or cultivar; has satiny flowers in shades and tints of white, cream, yellow, yellow-green, pink, red and chocolate, borne on upright sprays.

The 50 mm (2 in) wide, tubular-trumpet, flaring, star-ended, 'sheriff's badge' flowered cultivars and F_1 hybrids are frost-tender perennials that are usually grown as annuals.

Also grown are cultivars of *N.* × *sanderae*; height 450–750 mm (18–30 in); sweetly-scented, and also available in various colours. The flowers of certain *N. alata* × *N. forgetiana* cultivars stay open all day.

It is possible that there may be restrictions in your State concerning the growing of flowering tobacco plants. Check with your local State agricultural department.

Nicotianas are used as bedding plants, and prefer a rich, organic, moisture-holding, but well-drained soil, in a sunny location, or light shade in hotter areas.

Keep any weeds down, and water the plants when necessary during dry spells. Dead-heading spent flowers will prolong the flowering period.

Propagation: For summer-flowering plants, sow the seeds late winter-early spring, under glass where necessary, in seed compost containers, using a damp, recommended, seed raising compost, at 14–21°C (57–70°F).

Or sow the seeds indoors, in a warm, 14–21°C (57–70°F), light place, say 8 weeks before the usual frost-free, spring planting-out time in your location.

Carefully, and thinly, sprinkle the seeds over the surface of the compost, and press them onto the compost surface to anchor them. Water using a fine, misting spray. Germination should take place within 12–20 days.

Prick out the seedlings into containers or pots of damp, recommended potting compost, and grow them on.

Harden off the seedlings in a cold frame, and plant them outside, 300 mm (12 in) apart, directly where they are to grow and flower, but only when any danger from frost is past and the ground has warmed up. Or grow the seedlings on as 125 mm (5 in) pot plants.

In English gardens sow the seeds, late winter-very early spring (Feb-March), under glass, in seed raising compost, at 14–21°C (57–70°F), and treat them as half-hardy annuals. Flowers early summer, and on.

Pests and diseases: Aphids.

Cultivars/varieties: White, height 400 mm (16 in). Lime Green, height 400 mm (16 in). Lilac, height 800 mm (32 in).

Family: Solanaceae.

***Nierembergia* (blue cap flower)** The Argentinian *Nierembergia caerulea violacea* (syn. *N. caerulea*); height 150–375 mm (6–15 in), depending on species and cultivar; is a moderately hardy, but still frost-sensitive perennial, that is usually grown as an annual to provide tight, fresh plants.

The 7–25 mm (0.3–1 in) wide flowers (depending on species and cultivar), are cup-shaped, in shades of pale-lavender to violet-blue to purple, with spidery, pale yellow centres. And if you study the flower closely you will see a 'purple-snowflake' star.

Nierembergia is a mounded-hummock, sub-shrubby plant that spreads up to 250 mm (10 in), or more. The wiry-stemmed, bland-smelling foliage consists of 12 mm (0.5 in) long, bright-green, delicate, needle-like leaves.

Nierembergias can be used as edging plants, border plants, window box or rockery plants, or as unusual pot plants.

It is mid-late spring, and I have in front of me a *N. caerulea* plant, growing in a 75 mm (3 in) pot. It has 40 violet-blue blooms!

Nierembergias will grow in most moderately fertile, free-draining soils, in a sunny, but not hard-hot, sheltered position. They wilt rapidly in dry weather.

Trim off the faded and spent blooms after the first flower-flush to encourage further flowering.

Propagation: Sow the seeds in autumn-winter subtropical areas; autumn and early winter, or spring, warm temperate areas; autumn and spring in cool areas. But under glass where necessary, in frost-prone areas.

In frost-free areas, dig over the ground breaking it down into a fine tilth, and rake out any debris.

Thinly sow the seeds in drills (rows), covering them with 3 mm (0.1 in) layer of sand, or finely sieved soil. Water the seeds and seedlings carefully using a fine spray. Seedlings can take 7, or 15, or up to 30 days, or more to emerge, depending on the soil temperature.

Thin out, or transplant the seedlings to directly where they are to grow and flower, 150 mm (6 in) apart.

To exercise more control, sow the seeds in seed compost containers, indoors in good light, 8 to 10 weeks before the usual planting out time in your location, using a damp, recommended seed raising compost.

Prick out the seedlings into containers, or pots, of damp, recommended, potting compost, and grow them on. Harden off the seedlings, if necessary in a cold frame, and plant them out directly where they are to grow and flower, when all danger from frost is past and the ground has warmed up.

Or grow them as pot plants, starting and flowering them in 75 mm (3 in) pots, or potting them on 2 sizes to 125 mm (5 in) pots, using a damp, recommended potting compost.

Pay particular attention to their watering, as nierembergias flag quickly.

Plants may take 4–5 months, or longer, to flower from seed sowing.

In cold, hard-frost areas sow the seeds autumn and spring, under glass at 14–21°C (57–70°F).

Sow seeds in seed compost containers, using a damp, recommended seed raising compost. Prick out the seedlings into containers or pots of damp, recommended, potting compost, and grow them on.

Harden them off in a cold frame, and plant them out directly where they are to grow and flower, 150 mm (6 in) apart, but only when all danger from frost is past and the ground has warmed up.

In English gardens sow the seeds, late winter-early spring (Feb-March), in seed raising compost, at 14–21°C (57–70°F), and treat them as half-hardy plants; or grow them on as pot plants. Flowers early summer, and on.

Pests and diseases: Reasonably free.

Cultivars/varieties: 'Purple Robe', height 150 mm (6 in), deep lavender. 'Violet Supreme', height 150 mm (6 in), blue flowers, yellow eye.

Family: Solanaceae.

***Nigella* (love-in-the-mist)** The bushy, southern European, western Asian *Nigella damascena*; height 375–600 mm (15–24 in); is a mostly spring-early summer, flowering plant, more suited to border-planting in cooler and temperate areas.

The 37–50 mm (1.5–2 in) wide, semi-double flowers have spoon-shaped, pointed petals. They are veiled by delicately-spidery, lacy, thread-fine, foliage-bracts, like a mist; hence the name.

The traditional flower colour is blue, but now flowers come in shades and tints of white, blue, and pink.

Above the flower is a whorl of flat projections that are spaced around the flower like six running legs. The flowers are followed by crowned, ornamental, inflated, bladder-like, approximately 25 mm (1 in) wide seed pods, which some gardeners keep as dried flowers.

Nigellas can be used as cut flowers.

The foliage is fern-like. Nigellas will self-seed in an undisturbed soil.

Nigellas thrive in most well-drained soils, but prefer a not-too-rich soil, in a sheltered, reasonably sunny, not hard-sun, site. They do well in a cool, partially-shaded site.

Remove spent flowers, if not keeping them as dried flowers, to prolong the flowering period. A succession of sowings can be made to extend the flowering season.

Propagation: Dig over the site where the plants are to grow and flower, breaking it down into a fine tilth. Rake out any debris. Gently firm the soil to take the seeds.

Thinly sow the seeds in late summer-autumn in most areas; also spring in cold areas, covering the seeds with 3 mm (0.1 in) of sieved soil. Press the seeds gently to anchor them to the soil. Water gently using a fine spray.

Seeds should germinate within 3–4 weeks. Keep the seedlings watered during dry spells. Very carefully thin them out to 225–300 mm (9–12 in) apart, as nigellas object to root disturbance.

Flowers should appear within 12 weeks, possibly longer.

I experimented by sowing the seeds in seed compost containers, using a damp, recommended, seed raising compost. I got excellent germination in 5 days. The seedlings were pricked out into small pots of damp, recommended, potting compost, and grown on. However, the transplantation death-toll was horrific, though some survived.

In English gardens sow the seeds, in early-mid spring (March-April), where they are to grow and flower, barely covering the seeds with soil. Thin out the seedlings to 225–300 mm (9–12 in) apart. Nigellas are summer flowering.

Pests and diseases: Reasonably free.

Cultivars/varieties: Persian Jewels, height 350 mm (14 in), white, light rose, dark rose, carmine, light blue.

Family: Ranunculaceae.

***Nolana* (Chilean bell-flower)** The spring-summer flowering Chilean *Nolana paradoxa*; height 150 mm (6 in); has 25 mm (1 in) wide, pale-purple, primrose-like flowers, with egg-yolk yellow centres. It is a perennial that is grown as an annual.

The dull-green, 38 mm (1.5 in) long leaves, borne on trailing stems, are pointed-egg shaped and slightly hairy.

Nolana physioides; height 250 mm (10 in); has 18 mm (0.7 in) wide, pale-mauve, white-centred, trumpet flowers. The 25 mm (1 in) long, pointed-egg shaped, dull green leaves, are spattered with tiny, black dots.

Nolanas are not much grown in Australia, although I have seen splendid specimens of *N. paradoxa* and *N. physioides*. But I also notice that they can suffer badly from stress in hot sunlight.

Nolanas like a sandy-organic, free-draining soil.

N. humifusum and *N. prostrata* are also grown.

Propagation: Sow the seeds late winter-spring, in seed compost containers, using a damp, recommended, seed raising compost, under glass if necessary, at 15–21°C (59–70°F).

Prick out the seedlings, when large enough to handle, into 75 mm (3 in) pots of damp, recommended potting compost, and grow them on.

Harden off the seedlings, if necessary in a cold frame, and plant them out directly where they are to grow and flower, but only when all danger from frost is past and the ground has warmed up.

Or dig over the soil when it is easy to work, early spring in warm and temperate areas, later in cold areas, directly where the plants are to grow and flower. Break down the soil into a fine tilth and remove any debris. Gently firm the soil to take the seeds.

Thinly sow the seeds, and barely rake them into the top tilth. Water gently using a fine spray. Germination can take a few weeks. Thin out the seedlings to 100–150 mm (4–6 in) apart, in rows 150–225 mm (6–9 in) apart.

In English gardens sow the seeds late winter-early spring, under glass, in seed raising compost, at 15–21°C (59–70°F), and treat seedlings as half-hardy plants.

Pests and diseases: Reasonably free.
Cultivars/varieties: Species as above.
Family: Nolanaceae.

Ocimum **(ornamental basil)** The tropical Asian (also Mediterranean since recorded history) ornamental basil, *Ocimum basilicum*; height 300–600 mm (12–24 in); is a half-hardy annual that has attractive, shiny coppery to bronze-green, to purple leaves.

These leaves are 63 mm (2.5 in) long, serrated, bubbled, pointed-egg shape, and are borne opposite each other, in pairs, up the square-sided leaf stems. Basil leaves exude a powerfully aromatic, spicy-minty fragrance.

The small, pink-purple, whitish, tubular flowers are insignificant, and not really wanted, indeed, they are often removed to increase foliage growth. But these flowers, if closely examined, are seen to be beautiful and delicate.

Ornamental basil is clumped in groups, not over-dominating, as contrast plants in beds and borders, or in fragrant gardens.

Ornamental basil likes a free-draining, organic soil, in a warm sheltered, sunny or semi-shaded position. Water the plants well during dry weather.

Propagation: Thinly sow the seeds, 6 mm (0.2 in) deep, in seed compost containers, using a damp, recommended seed raising compost; late autumn-winter-spring subtropical areas; spring-earliest summer in temperate areas; but after any danger from frost.

Or you could sow the seeds indoors, say 6 to 8 weeks before the normal planting-out time in your location.

Germination can take up to 14 days, although my ornamental basil germinated in 5 days, from seeds sown in early spring.

Prick out the seedlings into pots of damp, recommended, potting compost, and grow them on. From there plant the seedlings out directly where they are to grow, 200–300 mm (8–12 in) apart.

Or dig over the site, when it is easy to work, where the plants are to grow, breaking it down into a fine tilth and raking out any debris. Gently firm the soil to take the seeds.

'Station sow' a few seeds in clumps 200 mm (8 in) apart, directly where they are to grow, and thin out the seedlings, keeping only the best looking.

In cold areas sow the seeds in early spring in seed compost containers using a damp, recommended seed raising compost, under glass at 13–21°C (55–70°F).

Prick out the seedlings when large enough to handle into containers, and grow them on. Harden off the seedlings in a cold frame, and plant them outside, latest-spring, 200–300–450 mm (8–12–18 in) apart, directly where they are to grow and flower, but only when all danger from frost is past and the ground has warmed up.

Or seeds can be sown directly where they are to grow, but only if any danger from frost is past and the ground has warmed up.

In English gardens sow the seeds in early spring (March) in seed raising compost, under glass at 13–21°C (55–70°F), and treat them as half-hardy plants. Or the seeds can be sown late spring (May), directly where they are to grow, but only if any danger from frost is past and the ground has warmed up.

Pests and diseases: Reasonably free.
Cultivars/varieties: 'Dark Opal', height 450–600 mm (18–24 in), shiny, purple bronze foliage.
Family: Lamiaceae.

Oenothera **(evening primrose)** The Chilean perennial *Oenothera acaulis*; height from prostrate to 100–300 (4–12 in); is known as the Mississippi primrose, and has fragile, 39–75 mm (1.5–3 in) wide, white, spring-summer blooms. These flowers move through shades of cream to shell-pink.

It has narrow, 150 mm (6 in) long, lance-shaped, grey-green leaves. It is used for edging work, borders, and the like.

The North American *Oenothera biennis* is a flower that has naturalised in the coastal areas of Adelaide and the eastern States. It is an erect biennial; height 500 mm–1.2 m (20–47 in). The slightly-scented, pale-lemon flowers are 38–50 mm (1.5–2 in) wide. It can become invasive; indeed magnificent specimens can be found in the smallest of pavement joints.

The leaves are dull green and lance-like.

The perennial, southern-central United States, spring-summer flowering *Oenothera missouriensis*; height up to 150 mm (6 in) and higher; with lance-like, dullish-green leaves, is a most popular evening primrose, with sparkling-yellow flowers up to 75 mm (3 in) wide.

The spring-summer flowering, Texan-western South American *Oenothera rosea*; height more or less prostrate; is a delightful perennial that has soft-pink, up-facing, daylight-flowering, 18 mm (0.7 in) wide, blooms. It is a vigorous little plant, which could dominate rockeries, and the like.

Some evening primrose species carry a breath of beautiful fragrance.

Oenotheras will grow in most well-drained garden soils, but it has to be in a sunny spot. Water the plants well during dry spells.

Propagation Dig over the site where the plants are to grow and flower, when it is easy to work, in midsummer-autumn, or early spring, depending on your climate. Break down the soil into a fine tilth and rake out any debris. Gently firm the soil to take the seeds.

Thinly sow the seeds over the prepared area, and rake them lightly into the surface tilth. Gently firm the seeds to anchor them to the soil. Carefully water the seedbed using a fine spray, and don't allow the seeds, or young seedlings, to dry out.

Seeds should germinate in up to 30 days, at 15–21°C (59–70°F). Mine germinated in 7 days; germination time always depending on growing conditions.

Thin out the seedlings to 150–225–450 mm (6–9–18 in) apart according to species.

In cold areas seed can be sown mid spring, in seed compost containers, using a damp, recommended seed raising compost. Place the container in a cold frame or greenhouse to germinate the seeds, making sure that they don't dry out. Be aware that unexpected hot weather could stew seedlings under glass, so protect them if necessary.

Prick out the seedlings when large enough to handle singly into 50–75 mm (2–3 in) pots of potting compost, and grow them on.

Harden off the seedlings and plant them out in late spring-early summer, when any danger from frost is past, into nursery holding-beds, and grow them on. Move them out in mid-autumn, to directly where they are to grow and flower.

Or for those evening primroses that can be treated as annuals for flowering the same year, sow the seeds late-winter in seed compost containers, using a recommended seed raising compost, at 15–21°C (60–70°F). Prick out the seedlings into 50–75 mm (2–3 in) pots of recommended potting compost.

Harden off the seedlings, and plant them out late spring-early summer, when any danger from frost is past and the ground has warmed up.

In English gardens sow the seeds mid spring (April) in seed raising compost. Place the container in a cold frame to germinate the seeds. Prick out the seedlings and grow them on. Harden them off, and move them into nursery holding-beds, and grow them on. Plant out, in mid-autumn (October), directly where they are to grow and flower. Evening primroses are mostly latest-spring-summer flowering. Or the seeds of annuals can be sown late winter-early spring (Feb-March) in a greenhouse, in seed raising compost.

Pests and diseases: Reasonably free.
Cultivars/varieties: Species as above.
Family: Onagraceae.

Onopordum **(Scotch thistle)** I am of the opinion that the true heraldic Scotch thistle is based on the stoutly-erect, summer-flowering, hardy biennial *Onopordum acanthium*; height 1–2 m (39–80 in) or higher. They are few in Scotland, but more numerous in Europe and western Asia, and are found in Australia. They are not often grown in gardens.

The 'shaving-brush' flowers, approximately 50 mm (2 in) wide, are of the classic mauve-purple that one associates with Scotland's national emblem.

The plant starts off as a very spiny rosette of 500 mm (20 in) long, by 75 mm (3 in) wide, lobed, silver, grey-green felty, matted-hair leaves. The rest of the foliage is silver grey-white, very spiny along the leaf margins, with spiny wings up the stem. The leaves are oblong, lance-like and toothed, ending with a long, orange spine.

These spiny leaves can be hazardous to young children.

The mauve-purple flowered *Onopordum bracteatum* is very similar to the above.

Onopordums succeed in most well-drained soils, but grow tallest in a rich, organic soil, in sun or filtered shade.

If you feel you have to grow these very spiny plants, then remove the spent flowers as soon as possible to prevent self seeding, which may become a problem, as thistles are among our worst agricultural pest plants, a really bad one being *Onopordum acaulon*, the stemless onopordum.

Propagation 'Station sow' the seeds 375 mm (15 in) apart, directly where they are to grow and flower, in a prepared seedbed, and grow them on. Thin out the seedlings keeping the strongest in each clump.

Or sow a few seeds in 75 mm (3 in) peat pots keeping the strongest seedling in each pot, and planting them out, peat pot and all, directly where they are to grow and flower.

In English gardens sow the seeds, late spring (May), directly where the plants are to grow and flower, in a prepared seed bed, and thin out the seedlings to 300-375-900 mm (12-15-36 in) apart. Onopordums do not transplant well. Remove any spent flowers to prevent self-seeding. Flowers midsummer, but bear in mind that they are biennials.

Pests and diseases: Slugs, snails.

Cultivars/varieties: Species as above.

Family: Asteraceae.

Osteospermum **(African daisy, veldt daisy)** You will often see the South African osteospermums, a group of sub-shrub perennials, catalogued under *Dimorphotheca* species, but they do have differences; and *Dimorphotheca ecklonis, D. barberae* and *D. fruticosum* should be considered here as *Osteospermum ecklonis, O. barberae* and *O. fruticosum*.

Osteospermum barberae is the evergreen, perennial, pink veldt daisy; height 600-900 mm (24-36 in). The pink-purple flowers, borne on single stems, are 62-75 mm (2.5-3 in) wide, with a prominent, dark blue-purplish centre-disc.

The narrow, lance-like to oval, sappy, 50-63 mm (2-2.5 in) long, occasionally-toothed, dark-green leaves form mound-like clumps. *O. barberae* flowers late winter-early summer, giving a sparkling display, but only in sunny weather.

Osteospermum ecklonis is the perennial, evergreen, white veldt daisy; height 600-900 mm (24-36 in). The 62-75 mm (2.5-3 in) wide flowers have dazzling, pure-white petals radiating around a glowing, navy-violet-purple, yellow-stamened centre-disc. It flowers beautifully late winter-spring, in sunny weather.

The 75-150 mm (3-6 in) long leaves are occasionally toothed, narrow and lance-like, or oblong and lance-like.

Osteospermum fruticosum has leaves and flowers similar to *O. ecklonis*, but it is low-growing and spreads effectively, proving to be one of the best mild climate groundcover plants.

In dull weather the petals of osteospermums close, showing a dull, paler under-surface.

O. barberae and *O. ecklonis* can be planted in large pots in a sunny location.

Osteospermums are grown in all States, but must have a sunny site. In cold areas they must have a sunny, warm, sheltered location, as osteospermums are frost-sensitive. Indeed, in hard-frost areas they would be grown as annuals, or protected over-winter against hard frost and excessive wetness.

Osteospermums prefer a well-drained, open soil, in a sunny location. Removing spent blooms will prolong the flowering period.

Propagation Sow the 6 mm (0.2 in) long seeds in seed compost containers, using a damp, recommended, seed raising compost, 6 mm (0.2 in) deep at 16-21°C (59-70°F).

Prick out the seedlings when large enough to handle into small pots of damp, recommended potting compost. Grow them on, harden them off, and plant them out when all danger from frost is past and the ground has warmed up.

Or dig over the soil of a nursery-seedbed, when it is easy to work; all year round in the frost-free, warm, moist north; early winter-to summer in temperate areas, but only if the soil is warm enough for seed sowing, that is 16-21°C (60-70°F). Break down the soil into a fine tilth and rake out any debris.

Sow the seeds and rake them into the top tilth. The seeds should germinate in up to 15 days at 16-21°C (60-70°F) soil temperature. Thin out the seedlings, and grow them on.

Transplant them out, 300 mm (12 in) apart, when they are large enough to handle easily, directly where they are to grow and flower.

In cold areas sow the seeds in early spring, under glass, in damp, recommended seed raising compost, at 18-21°C (64-70°F) and grow them on as half-hardy annual pot-bedding plants.

In English gardens osteospermums are usually grown as annuals. Sow the seeds, late spring (May), directly where they are to grow and flower. Or sow the seeds in early spring (March), in seed raising compost, at 18-21°C (64-70°F), and grow them on as half-hardy annual pot or bedding plants. Osteospermums should flower midsummer on.

Pests and diseases: Reasonably free.

Cultivars/varieties: Osteospermum × 'Starshine', height 300-900 mm (1-3 ft), pink, rose, carmine, all with yellow centre 'eye'. Species as above.

Family: Asteraceae.

Papaver **(poppy)** Poppies are one of the mainstays of spring-summer bedding, and are available in all colours except blue. (I am not including *Meconopsis betonicifolia*, the Himalayan blue poppy, in this section.)

Some poppy flowers produce distinctive, slender, brandy-glass-shaped, capped and pointed seedpods, which look attractive to some gardeners and untidy to others.

Poppy foliage, mostly, is blue-green and finely divided.

The Asian-Arctic-Sub-Arctic *P. nudicaule*, the winter-spring flowering Iceland poppy; height 375-600 mm (15-24 in); is a short-lived perennial that is grown extensively as an annual, or biennial or half-hardy annual in certain cold climates.

The 450-600 mm (18-24 in) wiry flower shoots arise from a pleasant-green clump of leaves, and produce magnificent, single, 63-100 mm (2.5-4 in) wide, fragrant, crinkly, satiny, tissue-paper-petalled, cup-shaped flowers, in shades and tints of white, yellow, orange and scarlet.

Remove spent flowers to prolong flowering period. Iceland poppies need a well-watered, well-drained, fertile, rich-organic soil, and a 'bud-breaking', sunny sheltered site, particularly a morning-mid day, sunny, sheltered site.

The Reverend W. Wilks, in the late 19th century, decided to 'select' the annual, black centred, Great Britain-European, (Flanders) field poppy, *P. rhoeas*. And he bred the now famous strain known as Shirley poppies.

Although not as spectacular as Iceland poppies, they are well worth growing; particularly the 75 mm (3 in) wide, glistening, fragile cultivars, which come in white, pink, yellow, red, some bicolours, white-based, single or double, but without the classic black centre.

The annual poppy *P. rhoeas* is also grown in gardens, and on hot, spring-summer days these magnificently glowing-red, black-throated flowers open up and drink in the sun. Their powerful, strong-sweet fragrance, once smelt, is never forgotten.

The Armenian-eastern Turkey perennial *P. orientale*, oriental poppy; height 600 mm-1.2 m (24-47 in); is a hardy perennial that grows large clumps of coarse, hairy foliage.

This in turn is followed by magnificent scarlet flowers, 75-100 mm (3-4 in) wide, or wider, most having dark blotches at their throats. Flowers are available in shades and tints of white, pink and red. Oriental poppies usually need staking.

P. alpinum; height 250 mm (10 in); is a short-lived perennial that is grown as an annual, having 25-50 mm (1-2 in) wide, white, pink, yellow or orange, single flowers and fine foliage.

Feed poppies when they are growing well, with a well-balanced, soluble, liquid, flower fertiliser, suitable for the above poppies and applied as the manufacturer instructs.

The Iceland poppy is used as a cut flower.

The opium poppy is the Middle-Eastern *P. somniferum*.

Propagation Most poppies resent transplantation, and are best sown where they are to grow and flower. Iceland poppies, however, may survive transplantation.

Sow the Iceland poppy seeds early autumn-winter in subtropical areas; mid-late summer-autumn temperate areas; late summer-earliest autumn in cooler areas.

Be prepared to nurse summer-sown seedlings through the hot, midsummer period by growing, or keeping them, in a cool, shaded position before hardening them off, and planting them out directly where they are to grow and flower. Flowers should appear in 4-6 months.

Mix Iceland poppy seeds with several times their own volume of dry, fine, silver sand, to ensure thinner distribution.

Sow the seeds in compost containers, on top of damp, recommended seed raising compost, in rows to aid pricking out.

Cover the fine seeds with a breath-sprinkling of compost, gently pressing them to anchor them in. Gently mist water the seeds, and place them in a dark place to germinate. But constantly check, and don't allow the seedlings to become drawn and spindly in the dark, or dry out.

Germination can take place in 5-14 days at 16-21°C (61-70°F). Carefully prick out the seedlings, when they are just large enough to handle, into containers of damp, recommended, potting compost, 31-50 mm (1.2-2 in) apart. Some gardeners transplant the seedlings directly into 75 mm (3 in) peat pots of damp, recommended, potting compost to prevent transplantation root disturbance. Grow the seedlings on, harden them off, and transplant them outside during cool weather, 300–450 mm (12–18 in) apart.

Make sure that the seedling crown is above ground level, otherwise the plant will rot. Carefully and gently water the plants until they are well established. Weed carefully around them, as any root damage causes the poppies to react by producing twisted, or unsightly, stems.

Or dig over the site directly where the poppies are to grow and flower, breaking it down into a fine tilth, and raking out any debris. Gently firm the soil to take the minute seeds, otherwise they will disappear.

Thinly sow the seeds, barely raking them into the soil, and press them to anchor them in. Water carefully using a fine spray. Thin out the seedlings to the correct distance apart.

Dig over the site directly where the *P. rhoeas* Shirley poppies are to grow and flower. Break down the soil into a fine tilth and rake out any debris. Gently firm the soil to take the seeds.

Thinly sow the seeds in autumn-winter in subtropical areas; autumn and early winter temperate areas; and spring cool areas; barely raking the seeds into the soil. Water carefully using a fine spray.

Thin out the seedlings to 300 mm (12 in) apart. Give them the same treatment as Iceland poppies, but Shirley poppies can flower earlier.

In English gardens, sow the seeds of annual poppies, including Shirley poppies, in early-mid spring (March-April); or Iceland poppies, early summer (May-June); directly where they are to grow and flower, barely covering them with soil. Thin out the seedlings: *P. nudicaule* 300–450 mm (12–18 in) apart; *P. rhoeas* 300 mm (12 in) apart; *P. alpinum* 200–225 mm (8–9 in) apart. Flowers of *P. nudicaule, P. alpinum* and *P. rhoeas* appear late spring-summer.

Pests and diseases: Anthracnose, bacterial blight, downy mildew.

Cultivars/varieties: Iceland Poppy: Artist's Glory, 450–600 mm (18–24 in), white, rose pink, salmon, lemon, gold, apricot. Kelmscott Giant, giant flowers, white, red, yellow, orange, and intermediate shades and tints. Oregan Rainbow Mixed, height 450–600 mm (18–24 in), pinks, magentas, lilacs, greens, semi-doubles, bicolours, picotee. Sunglow, red, gold, orange, many pastel shades. Alpinum Mixed, height 150 mm (6 in), scarlet, yellow, orange, apricot. Soldiers' Poppy, 450 mm (18 in), blood red, four black blotches. Shirley Poppy Fairy Wings, 375–450 mm (15–18 in), pure white, dusty pinks, reds, bright greys, to blues, mottled purples, picotees. Shirley Poppy Mixed, height 800 mm (32 in), double blooms, pink, carmine, crimson, scarlet, plus picotee and bicolours. Oriental Poppy Mixed, 750 mm (30 in), pink, rose, red.

Family: Papaveraceae.

***Pelargonium* (geranium)** The name 'geranium' is still used when referring to the frost-sensitive, South African *Pelargonium* species, although *Geranium* is a separate genus.

The floriferous, compact, evergreen, perennial, sub-shrubby *Pelargonium × hortorum* F_1 hybrids; height 250–450 mm (10–18 in); can be grown from seeds. They have 12–25 mm (0.5–1 in) wide flowers, with 5 to 8, or more, petals, in shades and hues of white, pink and red, and bicolors, borne on many stemmed, rounded clusters.

F_1 hybrids can flower in approximately 14–20 weeks from germination. The main flush of blooms occurs early to mid-spring to summer, but less proliferous from there on, although indoor pot grown plants can flower at any time of the year.

The 75–125 mm (3–5 in) wide leaves are either circular, heart-shaped or kidney-shaped, usually toothed around the edges, and can be light green, dark green or zoned in bands of different colours. Pelargonium flower stems are soft and fleshy, and are easily snapped.

F_1 hybrid pelargoniums are used for border edges, massed planting in beds, pot, tub or container plants, window box plants and indoor plants.

Pelargoniums require a well-drained, light, free-draining loam, with a slightly acid-neutral soil pH and, most important, a sunny site. Pelargoniums prefer temperate to cool summer climates, and may suffer badly in the northern hot, humid, summer months.

Water the plants very gently at ground level, during dry weather only, and avoid spraying the foliage. Waterlogging leads to stem disease, and we who have grown pelargoniums as bedding plants know that heavy rain, or a wet season, can reduce their effectiveness dramatically.

Feed the plants when they are growing well, with a well-balanced, soluble, liquid, fertiliser, suitable for pelargoniums, and applied as the manufacturer instructs. Dead-heading the spent blooms will prolong the flowering period.

Propagation Seed can be sown all year round in frost-free and temperate areas. In cold areas sow seeds from winter to late spring, but refer to the seedsman's instructions. It is important to use clean containers throughout, as damping off and other seedling diseases can decimate pelargonium seedlings.

Sow the seeds 1 mm (0.1 in) deep; 6 mm (0.2 in) apart, in rows 50 mm (2 in) apart, in seed compost containers, using a damp, recommended, soilless, seed raising compost, under glass where necessary, at 16–25°C (61–77°F). But the seeds will germinate erratically in erratic soil temperatures. For more even germination results try to maintain a steady soil temperature of 24°C (75°F).

It is imperative to use a properly sterilised (pasteurised) seed raising compost.

Water the seeds by standing the container in a shallow dish of water, allowing moisture to soak up through the compost until it just glistens on the compost surface. Then remove the container.

Cover the container with a sheet of glass, and keep the compost pleasantly, and uniformly, moist at all times.

Seeds germinate erratically, in 7–28 days, but more uniformly at a steady soil temperature.

Remove the glass immediately the seeds emerge to help prevent damping off disease.

Prick out the seedlings, 50 mm (2 in) apart, when large enough to handle, into containers of damp, recommended, potting compost, or singly into 50 mm (2 in) pots of damp, recommended, potting compost, and grow them on.

Constantly be aware of the possibility of damping off and other seedling diseases.

Harden off the seedlings, and plant them out directly where they are to grow and flower, 300 mm (12 in) apart, when all danger from frost is past, and the ground has warmed up.

You can grow the plants on as pot or container plants, as opposed to bedding plants. But bear in mind that pelargoniums are frost-sensitive, and as mature pot or garden plants need a minimum 8–10°C (46–50°F) winter temperature.

In English gardens sow the seeds under glass, early or mid or late winter (Dec-Jan-Feb), in seed raising compost, at 16–25°C (61–77°F), or try to maintain a constant 24°C (75°F), and treat the plants as half-hardy, pot-grown, bedding plants.

They must be taken inside before any winter frosts occur, otherwise they will be killed. Or take cuttings from F_1 hybrids you admire, well before the frosts strike, and grow the cuttings on under glass. Pelargoniums are late spring-summer flowering.

Pests and diseases: Whiteflies, alternaria leaf spot, blackleg, grey mould, rust, spotted wilt.

Cultivars/varieties: Choice Mix F_1 Hybrid, 450 mm (18 in), white, rose pink, deep red, scarlet. Orbit Mixture F_1, height 350 mm (14 in), white, soft pink, salmon pink, cherry red, fiery red, scarlet, 'geranium red', coral orange. Speckles F_1, height 300–375 mm (12–15 in), scarlet, cherry or rose, flecked, splashed, stippled petals; backgrounds white, pink, or salmon. There are many more such as: Sprinter F_1; Startel F_1.

Family: Geraniaceae.

***Penstemon* (bearded tongue)** The Mexican, tender perennial *P. hartwegii*; height 600 mm (24 in); is the principal parent in a range of luxurious, hybrid penstemons known as *P. × gloxinioides*; height 600–900 mm (24–36 in); the mid to southern United States (Nebraska to Texas) *P. cobea* being the other parent.

The felty, foxglove-gloxinia flowers, borne on 300–900 mm (24–36 in) tall spikes, are 38–50 mm (1.5–2 in) long, drooping and bell-shaped, with 5-lobed petalled mouths.

They are available in shades and tints of white, cream, pink, scarlet, and crimson, usually with white throats; some having spotted throats.

A 'bearded-tongue' stamen is conspicuous inside some penstemon flower bells, hence its common name.

Penstemons flower spring-summer, depending on climate. Named cultivars are propagated by vegetative means, but you can grow superb penstemons in mixed colours from seeds.

The glossy, bright green leaves are pointed-egg-shaped or lance-like.

Although penstemons are perennials they are grown as annuals (being half-hardy in cold areas). But they will grow as perennials in frost-free areas.

Penstemons grow well in most cool, temperate garden soils, provided they are well-drained, friable, in partial shade, but with sun for part of the day. Water penstemons during dry spells.

Penstemons can be used as cut flowers. Cut back spent blooms to prolong flowering.

Propagation: Sow the seeds indoors in a cool place, in good light as the seeds need light to germinate, 8 to 10 weeks before the usual planting-out time in your location, in seed compost containers, using a damp, recommended seed raising compost.

Or in cold areas sow the seeds under glass, late winter-spring, and grow them on at 13-15°C (55-59°F).

Cover the seeds with a breath of compost, 3 mm (0.1 in) deep, not forgetting that the seeds require light to germinate. Carefully mist spray, and don't allow the compost to dry out. Seeds should germinate in 2-3 weeks.

Prick out the seedlings into small pots, or containers, of damp, recommended, potting compost, and grow them on, at say 13°C (55°F). Harden off the seedlings, if necessary in a cold frame, and plant them out directly where they are to grow and flower, 300–375 mm (12–15 in) apart, when all danger from frost is past and the ground has warmed up.

In English gardens sow the seeds, in seed raising compost, late winter-early spring (Feb-March), under glass, at 13-15°C (55-59°F), and treat them as half-hardy pot-grown, or container, bedding plants. Flowers early summer, and on.

Pests and diseases: Reasonably free.
Cultivars/varieties: Sensation Mixed Colours. Sentinel Hybrids Mixed, 750 mm (30 in), rose, scarlet, purple, orange, shades with contrasting throats.
Family: Scrophulariaceae.

***Perilla* (beefsteak plant)** The purple-leaved, Japanese-Chinese-Indian *Perilla frutescens* (syn. *P. oxymoides*); height 600–900 mm (24–36 in); is grown principally as a foliage plant, providing an effective contrast with white, yellow, orange or other dazzling summer bedding flowers.

It is a hardy annual in warm climates, but half-hardy in cold climates It is quick and strong growing.

P. frutescens crispa laciniata has bronzey-purple, oval-pointed, 50–75 mm (2–3 in) long, 'waxy-sheen', crispy, crumpled, bubbled, rip-saw toothed edged, nettle-like leaves.

Perilla leaves are borne opposite each other on the square stems, and when gently bruised these leaves give off a savoury-spicy-cinnamon perfume.

Perillas grow in most well-drained, fertile garden soils, in a sunny spot, but not hard sun. The young, white, or blush of pink, tubular-flower spikes can be removed to maintain foliage compactness.

Propagation: Thinly sow the seeds, under glass where necessary; late winter-mid spring or early spring in cold areas; in seed compost containers, using a damp, recommended seed raising compost, at 18-21°C (64-70°F). Gently press the seeds on to the compost surface; do not bury them.

Mist spray the seeds with water, and don't let the compost dry out. The seedlings should germinate within 20 days; mine took only 8 days.

Carefully prick out the seedlings, when large enough to handle, into containers of damp, recommended, potting compost, and grow them on, but be aware that the young roots grow rapidly.

I pricked my seedlings out into 50 mm (2 in) pots, and from there into 100 mm (4 in) pots. But you can prick out the seedlings straight into 75 mm (3 in) pots, to avoid disturbing the roots unnecessarily

Harden off the seedlings before planting them out directly where they are to grow, but only when all danger from frost is past and the ground has warmed up. Perillas can also be grown as pot plants.

Or the seeds can be sown outside, in late spring, directly where they are to grow and flower, but only when all danger from frost is past, and the soil has warmed up and can be worked easily. Carefully thin out the seedlings to 300 mm (12 in) apart.

In English gardens sow the seeds under glass late winter-early spring (Feb-March), at 18-21°C (64-70°F), and treat them as half-hardy plants.

Pests and diseases: Reasonably free.
Cultivars/varieties: Species and cultivars, as above.
Family: Lamiaceae.

Petunia The cultivars of the South American *Petunia* × *hybrida*; height 225–375 mm (9–15 in); seem to get more magnificent each year. Petunias are usually treated as half-hardy annuals, being easily destroyed by frosts.

They are used as bedding plants, rockery plants, container plants, balcony plants, window box specimens, pot plants, rockery plants, and so on.

They are spring or summer bedding plants. But this depends on climate, or when the seeds are sown and grown on. For example, in certain temperate areas in public display sites, in late spring, pot grown petunias, grown under glass and hardened off, provide reasonable bedding displays.

Petunia flowers are trumpet-shaped, with many cultivars being ruffled and double-petalled, to my knowledge in all colours except full yellow and orange.

The foliage feels tacky when touched, and the leaves are light-mid-dark green and egg-shaped.

Petunias prefer a light, fertile, well-drained, neutral to slightly acid soil, in a sheltered, sunny location. Too rich a soil promotes leaves at the expense of flowers.

Petunias need sufficient water during dry spells, but not heavy watering that will spoil the flowers.

Removing spent and dead flowers will prolong and increase the flowering period.

Hybrid petunias are classed into 4 convenient groups:

(a) Grandiflora (large-flowered); height 300–350 mm (12–14 in).
(b) Multiflora (many flowered); height 300–350 mm (12–14 in).
(c) Nana Compacta (dwarf compact); height up to 150 mm (6 in).
(d) Pendula (trailing); spreading to 900 mm (36 in).

And of these Grandiflora and Multiflora reign supreme, and are divided into single or double-flowered.

(1) Grandiflora: These are bushy compact plants, and F_1 hybrids are available with plain or frilled-edged, single or double flowers, 75–100 mm or possibly 125 mm (3–4–5 in) wide, in shades and tints of white, rose, cream, yellow, pink, red, lavender, mauve, purple and blue; also bicolours and stripes.

Many are marked with white centre-stars, or coloured markings or veinings. Some are 'picotee', for example, red trumpet with a white, frilly edge.

Grandifloras, because of their larger flower size, are more weather vulnerable than the smaller-flowered cultivars, but in good weather they are beautiful, although not as floriferous as Multifloras.

(2) Multiflora: These are compact, bushy plants; height 150-300 mm (6–12 in); which bear masses of flowers; hence the name. There are many F_1 hybrids offered, with 50–75 mm (2–3 in) wide blooms in shades and tints of white, cream, yellow, pink, red, mauve and blue; also bicolours, and mixtures of these colours. Many are marked with white centre-stars, or coloured markings, or veinings.

Being smaller flowered they are more weather resistant, and are used extensively in public garden displays.

(3) Nana compacta: These are the dwarf varieties; height 150 mm (6 in); with 50 mm (2 in) wide flowers. They are available in pink, red, violet and blue, and mixtures of these colours.

(4) Pendula: These, as the name suggests, are trailing petunias, used extensively as hanging-basket, window box and ground cover specimens; height 150 mm (6 in); spread 600–900 mm (24–36 in); available in many colours.

Propagation: Seeds are sold either as fine seed or pelleted.

The fine seeds can be mixed with several times their own volume of fine, clean, silver sand, to ensure more even seed distribution. The seeds need light to germinate.

Petunia sowing times are: late autumn-winter-spring in subtropical areas; early to mid-spring in temperate areas, under glass if necessary, and on to early summer if a succession of plants is wanted; mid spring-early summer in cooler areas, under glass, or indoors, in good light, 6 to 8 weeks before the usual spring planting-out time in your location, at 15-21°C (59–70°F).

Sow the seeds in compost containers using a dampened, recommended seed raising compost. Gently press the seeds just onto the compost surface. Mist spray the compost with water, and don't allow it to dry out, but just keep it pleasantly moist.

Or place the container in a shallow dish of water until moisture soaks up through the compost, and just glistens on the compost surface; then remove the container. Don't let the water pool on the compost surface.

Seeds should germinate in 5 to 15 days depending on compost temperature.

Pelleted petunia seeds can be spaced 12 mm (0.5 in) apart, in 'V' shaped, furrowed rows, 3 mm (0.1 in) deep.

Prick out petunia seedlings, when large enough to handle, into containers, or into 50 or 75 mm (2–3 in) pots of recommended potting compost, and grow them on.

Harden off the seedlings, if necessary in a cold frame, before planting them outside; 150-250 mm (6–10 in) apart for small-flowered singles; 250-400 mm (10–16 in), usually 300 mm (12 in), apart for large flowered and doubles, but not until all danger from frost is past and the ground has warmed up.

Those seedlings in 50–75 mm (2–3 in) pots can also be potted up into 125 mm (5 in) pots, and from there into 175 mm (7 in) pots; to 225 mm (9 in) pots.

In English gardens sow the seeds in seed compost, late winter-early-mid spring (Feb-

March-April), under glass at 15-21°C (59-70°F), and treat the seedlings as half-hardy annuals. Petunias should flower early summer on.

Pests and diseases: Aphids, alternaria blight, crown rot, foot and root rot, fusarium wilt, virus.

Cultivars/varieties: Bonanza Mix F_1 Hybrid, height 200 mm (8 in), double flowers, bright colours. Carnival, height 300 mm (12 in), mixed colours, large blooms. Cascade Mixture F_1 Hybrid, height 300 mm (12 in), bright clear colours, large single flowers. Double Victorious Mixed F_1 Hybrid, height 300 mm (12 in), rose pink, carmine rose, deep salmon rose, salmon, violet blue, white purple, plus bicolours. Fluffy Ruffles Mixed, height 250 mm (10 in), shades and tints of white, pink, lavender, wine. Nana Compacta Choicest Mixed, dwarf, brilliant colours. Petunia Picotee Mixed, height 300 mm (12 in), grandifloras in rose and white, red and white, velvet and white, blue and white. 'Red Petticoat', height 250-350 mm (10-14 in), red base, pure white wavy margins. 'Starfire' F_1 Hybrid, height 250 mm (10 in), scarlet, contrasting white stripes. 'Sundance', light salmon. There are many, many, more cultivars.

Family: Solanaceae.

***Phacelia* (California bluebells, wild heliotrope)** Californian phacelias are spring-early summer flowering in hot summer areas, and summer flowering in colder areas.

Phacelia companularia; height 200-250 mm (8-10 in); is a hardy annual that produces bushy plants covered in up-facing bell-shaped, intense gentian-blue flowers 18-25 mm (0.7-1 in) wide.

The foliage is dark green, ovalish, with leaf edges that are occasionally well toothed.

It is used as an edging or rockery plant.

Phacelia tanacetifolia (wild heliotrope); height 600-900 mm (24-36 in) has 12 mm (0.5 in) wide, fragrant, spidery-whiskered, pale lavender, bell-shaped blooms, clustered in groups at the end of the small flower spikes.

It is a hardy annual which starts off as a rosette of 'fern leaves', followed by erect, wiry stems. These stems bear 63-75 mm (2.5-3 in) long, dull-dark green, touch-hairy, fine-shredded, fragrant, fern-like foliage. This phacelia can be used as a border plant, but it may need staking.

Bees are very much attracted to phacelias.

Phacelias must be grown in a sunny location, but not hard-hot sun. They suffer badly in hot, humid conditions, preferring reasonably warm, dry, day-growing conditions, with a temperature drop during the night.

They grow well in most soils, although *P. campanularia* prefers a well-drained, sandy loam.

Phacelias have a low water requirement, but they do like some water during extreme dry spells.

Propagation: Dig over the soil where the plants are to grow and flower, breaking it down into a fine tilth. Rake out any debris, and gently, but thoroughly firm the soil to take the seeds.

Thinly sow the seeds, late summer, autumn and early winter, over the prepared area, and barely rake them into the surface tilth, as they need light to germinate.

In cold, frosty areas, sow the seeds in spring once the ground has warmed up.

Gently press the seeds to anchor them to the soil. Gently water the soil, and seedlings, using a fine spray. Don't allow the seeds or seedlings to dry out until they are well established, and then water the plants when they need it.

Thin out the seedlings: *P. campanularia* 150 mm (6 in) apart; *P. tanacetifolia* 300-375 mm (12-15 in) apart.

As an experiment I sowed seeds of *P. tanacetifolia* under glass, mid winter, temperate area, in a warm, not hot, temperature, in a seed punnet, using a recommended seed raising compost. The germination, which occurred in 5 days, was very good. I pricked out the seedlings into pots of recommended potting compost, and grew them on as pot plants.

In English gardens sow the seeds, early to mid spring (March-April), directly where the plants are to grow and flower. Barely cover the seeds. Thin out to the required distance. Phacelias are summer-flowering.

Pests and diseases: Slugs, snails.

Cultivars/varieties: Species as above.

Family: Hydrophyllaceae.

Phlox The Texan-New Mexican *Phlox drummondii*; up to 375 mm (15 in); is treated as a half-hardy annual in cold climates. It is spring, summer, or autumn flowering, depending on location, and time of sowing.

The sparkling, 5-petalled, fringed-edged, or smooth-edged, 25-37 mm (1-1.5 in) wide flowers, are borne in tightly packed, flattened clusters, on erect stems, 75-100 mm (3-4 in) across, in shades and tints of white, pink, lavender and purple; some are bicoloured, and some have white centre-stars.

The rounded bush of foliage consists of small, dull green, 50-75 mm (2-3 in) long, oblong to lance-like leaves.

P. drummondii grows well in a hot, sunny spot. It prefers a rich, fertile, well-drained, but moisture-retaining soil.

Feed the plants, when they are budding up, with a well-balanced, liquid, soluble, flower fertiliser, suitable for phloxes, and applied as the manufacturer instructs. Don't over-feed phlox, as this leads to foliage at the expense of flowers.

Carefully water the plants well during dry spells, but don't deluge them with a heavy overhead spray, as this flattens the flower clusters.

Dead-head (remove) any spent flowers to prolong the flowering period.

Plant *P. drummondii* cultivars in beds on their own, or as edging plants, pot plants, rockery, window box or container plants.

P. drummondii is split into 3 sections:
(1) 'Large Flowered'; height 300-400 mm (12-16 in); is the large-flowered annual phlox, available in mixed or separate colours.
(2) 'Dwarf Compact'; height to 200-225 mm (8-9 in); is the dwarf-compact, large-flowered, annual phlox, in mixed or separate colours.
(3) 'Star Fringed'; 150-200 mm (6-8 in); is the pointed, star-shaped annual phlox, in mixed or separate colours.

Phlox drummondii make a useful cut flower.

Propagation: Thinly sow the seeds, and cover them with a 3 mm (0.1 in) thickness of compost, in seed compost containers, using a damp, recommended seed raising compost, under glass where necessary; late autumn-winter in sub-tropical areas; early spring-summer temperate areas; spring-summer in cold areas, at 15-18°C (59-64°F).

Gently press the compost to anchor the seeds. Keep the seed container in a dark place until the first signs of germination, then move the container into good light, but not hot, direct sunlight. Mist spray the compost with water, keeping it just pleasantly moist. The seeds should germinate within 15 days at 15-18°C (59-64°F), but check regularly.

Prick out the seedlings into pots of damp, recommended potting compost, and grow them on. Harden off the seedlings, if necessary in a cold frame, and plant them out directly where they are to grow and flower, 150-225 mm (6-9 in) apart, when all danger from frost is past and the ground has warmed up. They should flower within 10 weeks.

Or the seeds can be sown directly where they are to grow and flower, when all danger from frost is past and the ground has warmed up. Dig over the soil when it is easy to work, breaking it down into a fine tilth. Rake out any debris, and gently but thoroughly firm the soil to take the seeds.

Sow the seeds, covering them with a 3 mm (0.1 in) depth of fine soil or vermiculite, and firm them with the head of the rake, or a board, to anchor them to the soil. Carefully water the seeds and seedlings using a fine spray. Very carefully thin out the seedlings to the required distance apart.

In English gardens sow the seeds in seed compost, late winter-mid spring (Feb-April), at 15-18°C (59-64°F), and treat them as half-hardy annuals. *P. drummondii* is summer flowering.

Pests and diseases: Slugs, snails, aster yellows, leaf blight, leaf spot, powdery mildew, root and crown rot.

Cultivars/varieties: Dwarf Compact Beauty, height 200 mm (8 in), white, pink, salmon, crimson, yellow, mauve, violet, blue. Cecily Mixed, height 200 mm (8 in), wide colour range. Drummondii Mixed, height 350 mm (14 in), bright colours, contrasting 'eyes'. Dwarf Twinkle Star, height 200 mm (8 in), brilliant colours, starred, fringed pointed petals. Grandiflora Mixed, height 350-450 mm (14-18 in), the best colours.

Family: Polemoniaceae.

***Physalis* (Chinese lantern)** The summer-flowering, hardy perennial, southeast European-Japanese-Chinese *Physalis alkekengi*, and its variety the Japanese *Physalis a. franchettii*, are grown in the garden for their 'Chinese lanterns'. These lanterns are flame to bright-orange, inflated, 50-62 mm (2-2.5 in) long, heart-shaped, membrane-papery pods.

P. alkekengi; height to 375 mm (15 in); has 50 mm (2 in) long by 37 mm (1.5 in) wide, dull green, crinkly-veined, slightly hairy, rounded-triangular, or oval-pointed, occasionally-toothed leaves.

The unbranched stems produce 12 mm (0.5 in) wide, white flowers in the axils of their leaves, which in turn are followed by orange, red-brown berries, with the flower calyces (outside green petals) enclosing the berries to form the 'Chinese lantern'.

P. a. franchettii is taller; height to 600 mm (24 in); but with the same green, rounded-triangular, or pointed, egg-shaped leaves. The flowers are 12-19 mm (0.5-0.7 in) wide and produce orange berries, which in turn are enclosed by the calyces to form 62 mm (2.5 in) long lanterns.

The underground roots of Chinese lanterns can be very invasive, and this should be considered carefully before growing them. Some gardeners, however, grow Chinese lanterns as annuals, to help overcome the invasive root problem. But broken bits of crown left in the soil will shoot, so be sure to remove the whole plant, roots and all.

P. alkekengi, and its varieties, prefer a sunny, well-drained soil. But not too hot a spot in temperate and warmer areas.

Propagation: Thinly sow the seeds in seed compost containers, late winter-earliest spring, under glass where necessary, at 18–21°C (64–70°F). Use a damp, recommended, seed raising compost, covering the seeds with only the merest breath of compost, as light aids germination.

Seeds should germinate in 12 to 28 days. Prick out the seedlings into 75 mm (3 in) pots of damp, recommended, potting compost, and grow them on. Harden them off, if necessary in a cold frame, and plant them outside directly where they are to grow and flower, when all danger from frost is past and the ground has warmed up.

Or sow the seeds in seed compost early to mid spring under glass in a cold frame, unheated glasshouse, or similar. Plant out the seedlings directly where they are to grow and flower; or into a nursery holding-bed, and from there transplant them, in autumn, directly to where they are to grow and flower.

Or for perennial plants you can sow the seeds directly into a prepared seed bed in spring. Thin out the seedlings, and later transplant them to their permanent flowering quarters: *P. alkekengi* 450 mm (18 in) apart; *P. a. franchettii* 600 mm (24 in) apart.

Or you can 'station sow' a few seeds in clumps, 450 mm (18 in) apart, directly where the plants are to grow and flower.

In English gardens sow the seeds in seed compost early to mid-spring (March-April), under glass in a cold frame, unheated greenhouse, or similar. Plant out the seedlings directly where they are to grow and flower; or into a nursery holding-bed, and from there transplant them, in autumn, directly to where they are to grow and flower.

Or sow the seeds in seed compost containers, late winter-earliest spring (Feb-March), under glass, at 18–21°C (64–70°F), and treat as half-hardy plants. Plants flower mid-summer on, with the 'Chinese lanterns' appearing in autumn.

Pests and diseases: Reasonably free.

Cultivars/varieties: Species as above.

Family: Solanaceae.

***Platycodon* (balloon flower, Chinese bellflower)** The Chinese-Japanese, northeast Asian, hardy herbaceous perennial, *Platycodon grandiflorum*; height 225–600 mm (9–24 in), depending on variety-cultivar; has beautiful blue flowers, but there are also white, pinkish, dwarf, and double-flowered varieties and cultivars.

Balloon flowers are mostly temperate to cool climate plants.

The common name 'balloon flower' refers to the 'hot-air' balloon shape of the flower buds. The buds burst open to produce front- or up-facing, 38–75 mm (1.5–3 in) wide, brilliant-blue, distinctively violet-blue veined, flattish-bell-shaped, star-ended flowers. These flowers appear late spring-summer in short-stemmed clusters.

The silver, blue-green, spear-shaped, toothed foliage is very attractive.

Balloon flowers grow well in a well-drained, organic soil, in a sheltered, sunny location, but they resent hard sunlight. And although quick growing, they seem to take a few seasons to become established.

But once established the whitish, fleshy roots do not tolerate disturbance kindly, therefore be careful when weeding around them. Also be careful if ever lifting old plants to separate the crowns.

Balloon flowers need watering well during dry spells.

Feed them with a well-balanced, liquid, soluble, flower fertiliser, when the plants are young, vigorous, and growing strongly, and apply it as the manufacturer instructs.

The taller forms of balloon flower tend to flop, and support may be needed.

Cut down the dead foliage, after flowering has finished and, if necessary in cold areas, cover the crowns with peat, but be aware that slugs and the like can take up residence in the peat. Also mark the spot so that you know that the plant is there.

Propagation: Thinly sow a few seeds in small pots to reduce transplantation shock, early to late spring, under glass if necessary, using a damp, recommended, seed raising compost. Cover them with only a breath of compost, as light is needed for germination.

Thin out the seedlings, very carefully, as at this stage they are fragile and brittle, leaving only the strongest in each pot. Grow them on, and plant them out directly where they are to grow and flower.

Or sow the seeds, early spring to late summer, in a prepared seed-bed, or directly where they are to grow and flower. Sow them thinly, and cover them with only a breath of fine soil or vermiculite, for as stated balloon flower seeds need light to germinate. Gently firm the seeds to make contact with the soil, using the head of the rake, or a board.

Water carefully, but thoroughly with a fine spray. The seeds should germinate in 10–15 days at 21°C (70°F). Thin out the seedlings to 300–450 mm (12–18 in) apart.

Or transplant them directly where they are to flower and grow, 300–450 mm (12–18 in) apart, as early as possible, before fleshy roots have formed as these roots are extremely fragile.

Or, if too late, you can delay transplantation until the plant goes into its dormant period, but again take great care.

In English gardens sow the seeds in seed compost, earliest spring, under glass. Prick out the seedlings into small pots of damp, recommended, potting compost, as soon as possible, as these young seedlings are fragile and brittle, and resent transplantation.

Or sow a few seeds directly into small pots, keeping only the strongest seedling in each pot. Harden off the seedlings, and plant them outside directly where they are to grow and flower, 300–450 mm (12–18 in) apart. Flowers early summer, and on.

Or the seeds can be sown in late spring-early summer (May-June), directly where they are to grow and flower. Carefully thin out the seedlings to the required distance apart. Each seedling develops a tap-root, which if broken causes the plant to fail.

Pests and diseases: Reasonably free.

Cultivars/varieties: Fuji Mixed, height 600–800 mm (24–32 in). Grandiflorus Mixed, 225–450 mm (9–18 in), blue shades, some white, some shell pink.

Family: Campanulaceae.

***Portulaca* (sun plant, pig face)** The popular, Brazilian annual *Portulaca grandiflora*; height 100–150 mm (4–6 in); is a prostrate, trailing, clambering plant, that has succulent, fleshy, reddish stems.

Its cultivars are the most widely garden grown of all the portulacas. Depending on climate, they are late spring, summer or autumn flowering.

The 25 mm (1 in) wide, sometimes wider, wavy- and 5-petalled single, or semi-double, or double, saucer-shaped, dazzling flowers, have a bold centre-group of yellow stamens.

Flowers are available in shades and tints of white, yellow, red and purple. Some flowers close up during the day, and during dull weather, although new cultivars have been bred to extend the day flowering time.

The narrow, bright green leaves are round and pointed, like short, thick needles, and clump together like moss plants.

Portulacas must have a well-drained garden soil, in full sun, and only need watering during dry spells, as they are moderately drought resistant.

Portulacas are used for rockeries, garden edging, window boxes, pot plants, and so on.

Propagation: Dig over the soil when it is easy to work, in late autumn-winter-mid spring in subtropical areas; spring-early summer temperate areas; and spring-early summer in cold areas, provided there is no danger from frost.

Break down the soil into a fine tilth, and rake out any debris. Gently but firmly press the soil to take the seeds.

Thinly sow the seeds, and gently rake them into the tilth barely covering them with 5 mm (0.2 in) of fine soil or vermiculite, as they need light to germinate. Gently press them with the head of the rake, or a board, to anchor them to the soil.

Carefully water the seeds and seedlings using a fine spray, keeping the soil just pleasantly moist until the seeds germinate and become established. Water carefully and sparingly after that. Seeds should germinate within 15 days at 20–25°C (68–77°F).

Thin out the seedlings to 100–125–150 mm (4–5–6 in) apart, and gently water-in around the seedling roots using a fine spray. Weeding at these spacings can be a problem, but do be careful. Flowers can appear in approximately 6 weeks.

Or sow the seeds in seed compost containers, using a damp, recommended, seed raising compost, 6 to 8 weeks before the usual planting out time in your location, under glass where necessary, at 16–21°C (61–70°F). Press the seeds gently on to the compost surface. Mist spray the seeds and seedlings keeping the compost just pleasantly moist.

Prick out the seedlings into containers of damp, recommended potting compost. Grow them on, and harden them off, if necessary in a cold frame, before planting them out directly where they are to grow and flower, when all danger from frost is past and the ground has warmed up.

Portulacas will self seed in undisturbed,

suitable growing conditions.

In English gardens sow the seeds in seed compost containers, late winter-early spring (Feb-March), under glass, at 16–21°C (61–70°F), and treat the plants as half-hardy annuals.

Or sow the seeds on to a prepared seed bed, in late spring (April-May), provided damaging frosts are past, directly where they are to grow and flower. Flowers early summer, and on.
Pests and diseases: Aphids, damping off.
Cultivars/varieties: Large Flowered Double Mixed, mostly double, semi-double blooms. All Double Mixed, height 80–100 mm (3–4 in), double and semi double brilliant blooms. 'Sundance', high percentage of large double, semi-double flowers, whites, creams, pinks, reds, oranges. *P. oleracea* 'Wildfire', 50 mm (2 in), rose, yellow, apricot.
Family: Portulacaceae.

Primula The most widely grown primulas in Australia are *Primula × kewensis, Primula malacoides, Primula obconica* and *Primula × polyantha*; and of these the cultivars of *Primula malacoides* and *Primula × polyantha* are most popular.

The perennial *Primula × polyantha*; height 150–250 mm (6–10 in); is a hybrid of *P. vulgaris*, the common primrose; *P. elatior*, the oxlip; *P. veris*, the cowslip; and possibly *P. juliae*, the 'colourful' Caucasus primula; and possibly others.

Polyanthuses are variously listed as 'Polyantha', 'Polyanthus', *P. × polyantha, P. variabilis* or *P. × variabilis*; but double check to make sure that you get the polyanthuses you want.

The 31–38–50 mm (1.2–1.5–2 in) wide, 5 or more petalled primrose-flowers, borne in large clusters, are carried on stout, leafless stems, well above the crinkly, foliage rosette.

Flowers are available in shades and tints of white, cream, pink, red and blue, usually with a contrasting yellow centre-eye.

Polyanthuses are used mainly as bedding plants, but they are also used widely as pot plants, particularly the more dwarf cultivars. Several excellent strains and F_1 hybrids are available. Flowers appear winter-spring-summer.

Polyanthuses prefer a neutral or slightly acid, moist, rich, organic, free-draining, but moisture retaining soil. They dislike hard-sunlight areas, but thrive in a sheltered, partially shaded, location. They are grown in shade-houses as perennial plants, but in my opinion polyanthus are better grown as 'annuals'.

Keep the plants well watered during dry spells, as they suffer rapid dehydration in hot, dry weather.

Feeding the plants, when they are growing well, with a well-balanced, liquid, soluble, flower fertiliser, suitable for polyanthuses and applied as the manufacturer instructs, will produce good leaf and flower formation.

Primula malacoides, the Chinese fairy primrose; height 250–450 mm (10–18 in); is a perennial that is usually grown as an annual, but in certain temperate areas, usually shaded, it does naturalise.

The delicately-slender stems carry the candelabra whorls of 12 mm (0.5 in) wide, 5-petalled, notch-ended, somewhat daisy-like, 'fairy' flowers well above the mid-green, faintly-hairy, rosette of leaves. The vaguely fragrant flowers can be had in shades and tints of white, pink, red, lilac-blue and purplish, many with a contrasting, yellow centre-eye. Flowers appear winter-early spring, 3 to 4 months after sowing; but sometimes longer.

P. malacoides prefers an open, sunny location in cool areas, but partially shaded sites in warmer areas, and a neutral or slightly acid, well-drained, rich-organic soil.

Feeding the plants with a well-balanced, liquid, soluble, flower fertiliser, suitable for primulas, and applied as the manufacturer instructs, will improve leaf and flower formation.

P. malacoides resents root disturbance when growing well, therefore be extra careful when weeding around them.

The perennial *Primula obconica*; height 225–375 mm (9–15 in); is used mostly for pot work. The bountiful clusters of 25–50 mm (1–2 in) wide flowers, in shades and tints of white, cream, pink, red, purple and blue, are borne majestically above the egg-shaped, slightly hairy leaves.

Some people are very allergic to certain types of primula, such as *P. obconica*, so be aware of this.

The perennial hybrid *P. × kewensis*; height 375 mm (15 in); was first bred at Kew Gardens, England. It has 19 mm (0.7 in) wide, intense, bright yellow, fragrant blooms, borne in up-facing, candelabra-whorls around the stem. The stem and base of the flowers seem to be coated with a waxy, 'flour-like' substance. The light-green, spoon-shaped leaves are well-toothed around the edges.

Remove dead and spent primula blooms to prolong the flowering season.
Propagation: Thinly sow ripe-fresh polyanthus seeds in seed compost containers, usually mid to late summer to early autumn in subtropical areas; mid to late summer, and on through autumn in temperate areas; late summer to mid autumn in cold areas, under glass if necessary, to provide late spring-early summer flowers.

Or the seeds can be sown, provided they are fully ripe and viable, latest spring-earliest summer-early autumn.

Use a damp, recommended, sand-granulated peat, seed compost that has been flooded and allowed to drain, but is still damp. Press the seeds on to the compost surface.

Mist spray the seeds, and cover them with a sheet of glass. Never allow polyanthus seeds to dry out, or germination will be curtailed; possibly terminated. Seeds should germinate in 21–28 days at 15–20°C (59–68°F). Temperatures above 21°C (70°F) tend to induce seed dormancy.

Constantly check the compost to make sure that it is moist.

Remove the glass immediately the seedlings appear, and grow them on in good light, but not direct sunlight, at a cool, if possible, 10°C (50°F); or grow them on in a shadehouse.

Prick out the seedlings, when large enough to handle, into containers or pots of damp, recommended potting compost, and grow them on.

Gradually harden off the seedlings, and transplant them into a nursery holding-bed, until you are ready to plant them directly where they are to grow and flower, 150 mm (6 in) apart for a 'solid display', but wider for a standard winter-spring display. Or keep growing them on in pots, potting on as necessary, and then plant them out.

Water the roots well before moving them from a holding bed, taking as large a root-ball of soil as is feasible, to lessen transplantation shock.

Sow the seeds of *P. malacoides* in seed compost containers, mid to late summer-autumn, at 16–21°C (61–70°F). Use a damp, recommended, seed raising compost, cover the seeds with a sheet of glass or similar, and place the container in a shady place for the seeds to germinate.

Remove the container, and sheet of glass, etc., as soon as the seedlings appear, or they will become drawn and leggy. But do not expose them to hot sunlight.

Seeds germinate in 14–21 days at 21°C (70°F), but check regularly to avoid drawn or 'stewed' seedlings.

Prick out the seedlings into containers, or small pots of damp, recommended, potting compost, and grow them on, but not in hard, direct sunlight; a shadehouse would be suitable. Grow them on, harden them off, and then transplant them directly where they are to grow and flower, at 250 mm (10 in) apart.

Sow seeds summer-autumn in temperate areas; and sow seeds summer-mid autumn in cold areas at 16–21°C (61–70°F).

Or as pot plants, grow them on in 75 mm (3 in) pots of damp, recommended, potting compost, and pot them finally into 125 mm (5 in) pots.

In English gardens sow only ripe polyanthus seeds in seed compost, just pressing them onto the top of the damp compost, mid-late spring to early autumn (April-May-Sept), or as soon as you get the seeds, as they quickly lose their viability. Place the container in a cold frame or cold greenhouse, and cover it with a sheet of glass, or similar, to maintain humidity around the seeds.

Or sow the seeds in a greenhouse, mid-winter to early-spring, at say 15–20°C (59–68°F). If polyanthus seeds are allowed to dry out, then germination can be poor. Also be aware that hot sun through the glass can 'stew' young seedlings. Therefore lightly shade the germinating seedlings to prevent sun scorch.

Prick out the seedlings, when they are large enough to handle, into containers of damp, recommended, potting compost, and grow them on. Then transplant the seedlings, once hardened off sufficiently, out into a nursery holding-bed until you are ready to plant them out, usually early autumn (Sept), or spring, directly where they are to grow and flower.

Pot grown seedlings can be 'plunged' outdoors for eventual planting out, or potted on into larger pots, and grown on as pot plants. 'Plunge' means to sink the pots into sand, or similar, up to their rims, to keep the roots cool, and prevent unnecessary drying out of the pots.

Sow the seeds of *P. malacoides* in seed compost, late winter-earliest-mid spring (Feb-March-April), under glass at 16–21°C (61–70°F). Cover them with a sheet of glass or similar. Remove the glass, etc., once the seeds germinate.

Prick out the seedlings into 75 mm (3 in) pots of damp, recommended, potting compost, and grow them on 'plunged' in clean sharp sand, in a shaded cold frame over summer, giving any ventilation necessary.

In autumn, pot up the plants into 125 mm (5 in) pots of damp, recommended potting compost, and grow them on as indoor pot plants at 13°C (55°F).

Feed the plants when the flowering stems are forming, with a well-balanced, soluble, liquid flower fertiliser, suitable for primulas and applied as the manufacturer instructs for primulas.

P. × *polyantha* flowers March-May; *P. malacoides* flowers December-April; *P. obconica* flowers December-March.

Pests and diseases: Aphids, caterpillars, crown, foot and root rot, grey mould, leaf spot.

Cultivars/varieties: Polyanthus: Pacific Giant Jewel Mixed, height 150 mm (5 in), bright pink, rose, scarlet, and white, pink, velvet red, yellow. Pacific Giants Mixed, height 250 mm (10 in), wide colour range. Reselected Pacific Mixed, height 250 mm (10 in), mostly rose, bright red orange, also white, lavender, golden yellow, clear deep blue. Super Pacific Giants Mixed, 250 mm (10 in), white, pink, rose, carmine, crimson, scarlet, yellow, blue. Giant Bouquet Mixed, height 200 mm (8 in), large blooms, many colours. *P. malacoides:* Lavender Lady. Lollipops Mixed, all shades. Malacoides Mixed. *P. obconica* Giant Mixed height 250 mm (10 in), white, pink, rose, salmon, red, deep red, copper red, mid blue.

Family: Primulaceae.

Pyrethrum The cultivars of the hardy, spring to summer flowering, Caucasus *Pyrethrum roseum* (syn. *Chrysanthemum coccineum*); height 500–750 mm (20–30 in); are also known as the florists' pyrethrums.

Pyrethrums have 50–75 mm (2–3 in) wide, single, semi-double, and double, daisy-like flowers, with delicate petals, almost dahlia-like in texture. The flower colours are white, pink, red, or mauve, usually with prominent yellow centres.

Seeds are usually available in mixed colours. Pyrethrum seeds are short lived, so sow them as soon as possible. The seeds from named cultivars do not necessarily breed true to type.

Pyrethrum foliage is much finely-divided, almost fern-like.

Pyrethrums are used extensively in the mixed or herbaceous border, in temperate and cooler locations.

Pyrethrum aureum is the 'Golden Carpet Moss'; height 100 mm (4 in); which is used for bedding, but is famous for its use in floral clocks and the like.

Pyrethrum ptarmicaeflorum; height 150–200 mm (6–8 in); a half-hardy perennial, usually treated as a half-hardy annual, is grown principally for its finely divided, lacy, silver-grey, fern-like foliage, that looks as though it has been flattened between two boards. It is used as a spring bedding plant in temperate areas, but only when all danger from frost is past and the ground has warmed up. It can be used in combination, for example, with dwarf cinerarias, or other dwarf plants.

P. roseum likes a well-drained, light soil, in a sheltered, sunny location, but it can be buffeted by winds, and usually needs supporting.

Water the plants well during dry weather, and cut back the flowering stems after flowering.

Feeding the plants, when they are growing well in spring, with a well-balanced, liquid, soluble, flower fertiliser, suitable for pyrethrums, and applied as the manufacturer instructs, will help extend the flowering season. A second crop of flowers may be produced.

The white-flowered pyrethrum of commerce is *Chrysanthemum cinerariaefolium*; height 450 mm (18 in). It is a strong-smelling plant with 19–25 mm (0.7–1 in) wide, white flowers.

Propagation: Dig over the soil, when it is easy to work, where the *Pyrethrum roseum* plants are to grow and flower, breaking it down into a fine tilth. Rake out any debris. Gently, but thoroughly, firm the soil to take *Pyrethrum roseum* seeds.

'Station sow' a few seeds, 375 mm (15 in) apart, in summer-early autumn, or spring in cool areas, but surface sow them only. Don't bury them. Water the seed bed keeping the soil pleasantly moist.

Thin out the seedlings keeping only the strongest in each clump. The seeds should germinate in approximately 21 days at 18°C (64°F) soil temperature. Don't let the seedlings or plants dry out.

In English gardens sow *P. roseum* seeds in seed raising compost, earliest spring (March), under glass at 14–16°C (57–61°F), and press them on to the damp surface of the compost. Don't bury them.

Prick out the seedlings into small pots of damp, recommended, potting compost, grow them on, harden them off, and plant them out when all danger from frost is past. *P. roseum* flowers late spring-summer.

Pests and diseases: Reasonably free.

Cultivars/varieties: Robinson's Giants, height 750 mm (30 in), pink, red, mauve. Superb Mixture, height 750–900 mm (30–36 in) semi-double, single flowers, in white, pink, rose, red.

P. aureum 'Golden Carpet Moss'; *Pyrethrum ptarmicaeflorum; Pyrethrum cinerariaefolium.*

Family: Asteraceae.

***Ranunculus* (turban buttercup)** The late winter or spring-flowering, southeast European-Oriental *Ranunculus asiaticus*; height 200–450 mm (8–18 in); is a tuberous plant, being hardy only in mild, temperate locations. In cold areas it should be treated as a half-hardy perennial. Plants can be grown easily from seeds.

The hybrid, globular ranunculus flowers, 75 mm (3 in) or more wide, are mostly semi or double-flowered, in shades and tints of white, pink, red and yellow, and are borne on erect, stiff stems.

The densely massed plain-green leaves, ovalish in outline, are divided into deeply-cut segments.

Ranunculuses are used as bedding plants, border clumps and container plants.

R. asiaticus grows well in a rich, well-drained, light, organic soil, in a sunny, sheltered location. If necessary, dress the soil with a well-balanced flower fertiliser, applied as the manufacturer instructs for ranunculuses.

Or feed the plants, when the flowers begin budding up, with a well-balanced, liquid soluble, flower fertiliser, suitable for ranunculuses and applied as the manufacturer instructs.

The tubers are lifted when the leaves turn yellow, and stored in a frost-free place.

Propagation: Some of the newer hybrid strains flower in approximately 5 months from seeds. In mild winter areas the seeds are sown in autumn. In cold areas with cool summers the seeds are sown indoors during winter. Check the seed packet.

Or thinly sow ranunculus seeds, 6 mm (0.2 in) deep, in small rows, in seed compost containers, using a damp, recommended, seed raising compost, late summer-autumn subtropical areas; late summer-early autumn elsewhere, for spring flowers. Cover the seeds with a 6 mm (0.2 in) layer of sand of compost.

Some gardeners sow the seeds in late autumn, to miss the summer or early autumn heat, but the flowers do not usually appear until late spring.

Place the container in a cool, partially shaded spot, protected from hard sunlight and hot drying winds. Keep the compost pleasantly moist. The seeds germinate in approximately 18 days at 18–20°C (64–68°F).

Prick out the seedlings, when large enough to handle, into containers or pots of damp, recommended potting compost. Grow the seedlings on. Harden them off and plant them out, when established, 50–75 mm (2–3 in) tall, directly where they are to grow and flower, 150–200 mm (6–8 in) apart.

Don't let the seedlings' roots stifle each other before planting them out.

Or sow the seeds into seedbeds, and transplant them from there.

Observation of the plants when they are growing determines which tubers should be kept. Once flowering is finished, and the foliage has died down, usually late spring-early summer, carefully ease up the tubers with a fork, or spade.

Let the stems dry off, and clean off the dead foliage from the tubers. Separate these tubers into size and colour, and store them in a cool, dry, frost-free place, in dry granulated peat, or even paper bags, until the next planting season. But check the tubers frequently during the dormant season to make sure that none are rotting.

Plant these tubers, 25–50 mm (1–2 in) deep, with the 'claws' pointing downwards, late summer-early to late autumn; but only at the correct planting time at your location.

Ranunculus tubers have a comparatively short life, and are usually discarded after 2 or 3 seasons; you will observe the plants when flowering, and note if they are worth keeping for another season.

But in my public garden bedding displays, I would use fresh seedlings each year, as the show I got from the modern seed mixtures was excellent.

In English gardens you could sow the seeds in seed compost, as for cold climate above. However, named cultivar ranunculus tubers are much planted in English gardens for late spring or summer flowers.

Pests and diseases: Damping off, powdery mildew, root rot, wilt.

Cultivars/varieties: Bloomingdale F_1 Hybrid Dwarf Mixed Colours, height 200 mm (8 in), double flowers. Double Florentine Mixed, height 450 mm (18 in), bright colours.

Family: Ranunculaceae.

***Ratabida* (red Mexican hat)** The North American *Ratabida columnaris* (syn. *R. columnifera*); height 300–900 mm (12–36 in); is not a well-known flower in Australia, although its flowers would rate among the most unusual grown in gardens.

The 6 mm (0.2 in) thick, domed, high-centred stamen collection protrudes 12–18 mm (0.5–0.7 in) out from the petals, like a finger. The 18–25 mm (0.7–1 in) long, red and golden-yellow petals are swept back. Indeed the whole flower looks like a colourful, small dart without the point.

Golden anthers appear all up the high centre as the flower matures, creating a fascinating splash of bright-red, yellow and gold.

The cylindrical-domed high centre, and down-sweeping petals give rise to the common name, Mexican hat (sombrero).

Ratabidas are free-flowering plants with a long flowering period.

The foliage is a light, pleasant green, 5 mm (0.2 in) wide, with 31 mm (1.2 in) long lobes.

Ratabidas grow in most soils provided it is not in full shade, indeed, they thrive in full sun. They require little, but adequate, water once fully established.

Propagation: Dig over the site where the plants are to grow and flower, breaking it down into a fine tilth. Rake out any debris. Gently but thoroughly firm the soil to take the seeds.

Sow the seeds summer, autumn, late winter, or spring in frost-free areas, or early spring in cold areas, but only when the worst of the winter weather has passed and the soil has warmed up.

Rake the seed lightly into the top tilth. Lightly but firmly press the soil to anchor the seeds. Water gently but thoroughly, using a fine spray, keeping the soil pleasantly moist until the seedlings are well established, and then water them as, and when, required.

Germination takes place in approximately 5-15 days at 15-20°C (59-68°F) soil temperature. Thin out the seedlings to 300-375 mm (12-15 in) apart. The flowers should appear in approximately 8 to 12 weeks, when grown as annuals.

I sowed ratabida seeds, latest winter at 16-21°C (61-70°F), using a damp, recommended seed raising compost. The seeds germinated in 6 days, and I pricked them out, as soon as they were large enough to handle, into 50 mm (2 in) pots of damp, recommended potting compost. The plants were hardened off, and grown outside when all danger from frost was past.

But I have before me as I write this, a ratabida in a 50 mm (2 in) pot that, as a seedling, was pricked out into the pot on 22 August. It is now December, and the plant is 600 mm (24 in) tall, and still putting on a brave show of flowers. However, this plant is being grown in this manner for experimental reasons only.

In English gardens treat ratabidas as half-hardy plants. Sow ratabida seeds in seed compost, mid spring at 16-21°C (61-70°F).

Pests and diseases: Reasonably free.
Cultivars/varieties: Species as above.
Family: Asteraceae.

***Reseda* (mignonette)** The North African *Reseda odorata*; height 200-450 mm (8-18 in); is grown for its exquisite, spicy fragrance.

However, if you examine a mignonette flower closely you will see that it is a lovely little bloom, with bunches of orange-red, minute, 'bell-clapper' stamens protruding like grapes from insignificant white-yellow, 6 mm (0.2 in), wide flowers.

These flowers are produced at any time of the year, depending on climate and sowing times.

Mignonette is a branching, hardy annual, with erect growth, and spoon-shaped, smooth, plain-green leaves.

Sow mignonette where you want to smell its perfume. It is used in hardy annual borders, massed in drifts, or as pot plants.

Mignonette likes a neutral, or slightly acid, or slightly limy (alkaline), rich, well-drained soil, in a sunny location. Or for hot sun areas, partial shade, but sun for part of the day.

Remove spent blooms to prolong the flowering period.

Propagation: Dig over the site where the plants are to grow and flower, breaking it down into fine tilth. Rake out any debris. Gently, but thoroughly, firm the soil to take the seeds.

Sow the seeds in small rows, autumn-winter in subtropical areas; early spring-summer or autumn-winter in temperate areas; usually spring-summer (sometimes autumn) in cool areas; but only when the worst of winter weather has passed.

Lightly, but firmly, press the soil to anchor the seeds. Don't bury them, as they need light for germination; or at the most 6 mm (0.2 in) deep. Gently but thoroughly water the seeds using a fine spray, keeping the soil pleasantly moist.

Mignonette should germinate in 15 to 20 days at 15-20°C (59-68°F) soil temperature. Thin out the seedlings to 100-200 mm (4-8 in) apart.

The flowers should appear in approximately 12 weeks.

Mignonette seedlings do not transplant readily, and this is the reason why the seeds are sown directly where the plants are to grow and flower.

But if you carefully take surplus, thinned-out seedlings, at the 2 leaf stage, you could try transplanting them, or potting them on, but don't bank on their survival. I transplanted mignonette seedlings, but only achieved fair-to-middling results.

In English gardens sow the seeds, early-mid spring (March-April), directly where the plants are to grow and flower. Or sow under glass at 13-18°C (55-64°F) in very early spring, and treat as half-hardy annuals. Flowers early summer, and on.

Pests and diseases: Reasonably free.
Cultivars/varieties: Crimson New York Market. Large Flowered Mixed, height 300 mm (12 in). 'Machet Ruben', height 450 mm (18 in), reddish, scented flower spikes.
Family: Resedaceae.

***Ricinus* (castor-oil plant)** *The tropical African Ricinus communis*; height usually to 3 m (10 ft), although I have seen them taller; is a soft-woody, perennial shrub or tree.

The cultivars are grown in some countries for their bronze or purple foliage; the foliage being highly decorative, like an outstretched-hand of 'maple' leaves, with 7-9 deeply-cut, serrated, pointed, finger-lobes. The leaves are 150-300 mm (6-12 in) long and 100-400 mm (4-16 in) wide.

The creamy, insignificant 6-12-25 mm (0.2-0.5-1 in) wide, male and female, 'ageratum-like' flowers, are borne separately on the same plant. These are followed by clusters of roundish, prickly-spiny, mottled-brown seedpods.

There are a few cultivars of ricinus, mostly with green-white, bronzey, reddish-purple or blackish purple foliage. Kept reasonably small, up to 1.5 m (5 ft) they make attractive accent plants, although they may have to be staked.

The problem with the castor-oil plant is that it is considered a pest plant in some States, as its shiny 'tick' seeds, and to a lesser extent the leaves, contain a 'Ricin' phytotoxin substance, which is very poisonous to animals and people.

The common *R. communis* can be seen growing wild in temperate and warm areas. It grows well, only too well, in a rich, organic soil, in a sunny, sheltered location. Check with your local department of agriculture for more information concerning this plant in your State.

In English gardens the seeds are sown singly in 75 mm (3 in) pots, 18-25 mm (0.7-1 in) deep, late winter-early spring (Jan-March), under glass at 21-25°C (70-77°F) using a proven seed raising compost. Seeds can be nicked to speed up germination. The seedlings are pricked out into 125 mm (5 in) pots of potting compost, allowed to establish their roots, and grown on, gradually reducing the temperature. The young plants are hardened off in a cold frame, and planted out directly where they are to grow, but only when all danger from frost is well past and the ground has warmed up. Or they are grown on as 200-225 mm (8-9 in) pot plants under glass, at 8-10°C (46-50°F) minimum winter temperature.

Pests and diseases: Reasonably free.
Cultivars/varieties: As above.
Family: Euphorbiaceae.

***Rudbeckia* (black-eyed susan, cone-flower, gloriosa daisy, marmalade daisy)** The summer flowering, United States *Rudbeckia bicolor* (syn. *R. hirta pulcherrima*); height 600 mm (24 in); is an erect, many-branched biennial that is treated as an annual. It produces 50 mm (2 in) wide, bright yellow flowers, with a blackish centre cone-disc.

It has bristly-to-the-touch foliage, and plain-green, oblong leaves. It is not as much grown, or as popular, as those that follow.

The summer-autumn flowering *R. hirta*; height 750-900 mm (30-36 in); although a perennial, is usually grown as an annual or biennial. The 75 mm (3 in) wide daisy flowers are brightest yellow with a dominating, blackish, brown-purple, centre cone-disc.

But it is the prolific Giant Tetraploids; height 250-900 mm (10-36 in), with their 75-125-175 mm (3-5-7 in) wide flowers, that catch the eye. These blooms can be chestnut mahogany-red, orange-gold or yellow; some bicolours, with purple-brown, mahogany, or even green, centre cone-discs.

In the 'tetraploid', double-flowered hybrids, much of the dark-brown centre cone-disc is covered with extra petals.

The 75-125 mm (3-5 in) long, dark-green foliage is narrow egg-shaped, to oblong, to lance-like, and covered with bristly-to-the-touch hairs.

These perennial rudbeckias are used as 'dramatic clump' bedding plants.

Rudbeckias succeed in a well-drained, fertile, well-maintained garden soil, preferably in an open, sunny location, sheltered from high winds, otherwise they may need staking.

Cut down the spent flowers of the perennials after flowering to prolong flowering.

Feed the plants, when they are growing well, with a well-balanced, soluble, liquid, flower fertiliser, suitable for rudbeckias and applied as the manufacturer instructs.

Propagation: Thinly sow the seeds of *R. hirta*

and the Giant Tetraploids 6 mm (0.2 in) deep, in seed compost containers, using a damp, recommended seed raising compost, late autumn to early spring in subtropical areas; late winter-spring temperate areas; spring in cooler areas. Place the container, if necessary, in a cold frame for the seeds to germinate.

Or the seeds can be sown, once the soil is easy to work, mid-late spring in cooler areas, directly where the plants are to grow and flower.

Or for earlier plants in cold areas, you can sow the seeds late winter, or 6 to 8 weeks before the usual frost-free, spring planting out time in your location, at 16–21°C (60–70°F); the seeds will take approximately 10–20 days to germinate.

Prick out the seedlings into containers of damp, recommended potting compost, and grow them on. Harden them off, if necessary in a cold frame, and plant them out directly where they are to grow and flower, but when all danger from frost is past, in cold areas, and the ground has warmed up. Flowers should appear in approximately 3 to 4 months from sowing.

Or 'station sow' a few seeds in clumps, directly where they are to grow and flower 250–300 mm (10–12 in) apart, and thin out the seedlings, keeping only the strongest in each group. Flowers should appear summer and/or autumn depending on climate and location.

In English gardens sow the seeds in mid-spring (mid April), directly where they are to grow and flower. Or sow seeds in seed compost containers, late winter-early spring (Feb-March), and place them in a cold frame to germinate.

Or for earlier plants sow the seeds early-mid spring, under glass, at 16–21°C (60–70°F), in seed raising compost, and treat the plants as half-hardy plants. Flowers midsummer, and on.

Pests and diseases: Slugs, snails.

Cultivars/varieties: Caravelle Mixed Tetra, height 900 mm (3 ft), large flowers, bright yellow, gold, orange, mahogany. 'Goldilocks', height 250–375 mm (10–15 in), double, semi-double gold, 75–100 mm (3–4 in) wide flowers. 'Marmalade', height 675 mm (27 in), free flowering, up to 125 mm (5 in) wide, brilliant orange, chocolate centres.

Family: Asteraceae.

***Salpiglossis* (velvet-flower, painted tongue)** The Chilean, summer-flowering *Salpiglossis simuata*; height 450-600-900 mm (18–24–36 in) depending on cultivar; is related to the petunia and looks reasonably similar, but is slightly more exotic, and has 5 prominent, notched petal lobes.

These 50 mm (2 in) wide, or wider, funnel-shaped flowers are available in shades and tints of white, fawn, yellow, orange, lavender-pink, red, scarlet, crimson and blue. They are velvet-textured, raised-patterned flowers, heavily veined with a deeper colour, and having a contrasting golden-yellow, patterned throat.

There are large-flowered hybrids, and many new F_1 hybrids; tall and dwarf. Salpiglossis is a half-hardy annual in frost-prone areas, but it seems to perform better in cool-warm, not hot, weather.

The leaves are a dull, light green, 50 mm (2 in), or more, long, smooth-edged when young, wavy-edged later, and slightly hairy to the touch.

Salpiglossis is used as a bedding plant, and some cultivars, because of their height, can be used towards the back of the flower border.

Salpiglossis prefers a reasonably rich, organic, fertile soil, in a sheltered, sunny location.

Flowers appear late spring on, depending on location, but generally 3 to 4 months after seed sowing.

Early tip pruning of the plants, when young, increases the production of side branches. Tall plants may need supporting with sticks or canes. Remove spent or dead flowers to extend the flowering season.

Feed the plants, unless the soil is already rich in nutrients, and when they are growing well, with a well-balanced, liquid, soluble, flower fertiliser, suitable for salpiglossis, applied as the manufacturer instructs. But be circumspect with the feeding of salpiglossis, as too much fertiliser causes the plants to deteriorate rapidly.

Propagation: Dig over the soil when it is easy to work, and sow the seeds, late winter-spring in subtropical areas; early spring-summer temperate areas; spring in cooler areas, when all danger from frost is past, directly where the plants are to grow and flower. Break down the soil into fine tilth, and remove any debris.

Gently, but thoroughly, firm the soil to take the seeds. Mix the seeds with a few times their own volume of clean, dry, fine, silver sand. Thinly sow the seeds in small rows, over the prepared soil, and cover them with a 3 mm (0.1 in) depth of finely sieved soil or vermiculite. Firm the rows gently with the head of the rake, or a board, to anchor the seeds.

Gently, but thoroughly, water the seedlings using a fine spray, keeping the soil pleasantly moist, and then water the plants when they require it.

Germination should take place within 14–21 days (mine took 7 days) at 20°C (68°F). Thin out the seedlings to 150–300 mm (6–12 in); say 225 mm (9 in) apart.

Or sow a few seeds in small pots of damp, recommended seed raising compost, under glass if necessary, at 13–21°C (55–70°F), and thus minimise root disturbance. Carefully thin out the seedlings keeping only the strongest in each pot and grow them on.

Harden off the seedlings, if necessary in a cold frame, before planting them out, 225 mm (9 in) apart, directly where they are to grow and flower, when all danger from frost is past and the ground has warmed up.

Or you can sow the seeds in seed compost containers, under glass if necessary, also at 13–21°C (55–70°F).

Bear in mind that salpiglossis seedlings do not transplant readily, although there are differing opinions regarding this.

I recently experimented with transplanting my salpiglossis seedlings singly into 5 mm (2 in) pots of damp, recommended, potting compost. The transplantation casualty-rate was horrendous; only 2 successes! However, in my second sowing the transplantation success rate was somewhat higher, but still far from satisfactory.

You could try transplanting the seedlings as early as possible in an attempt to improve the success rate, but success cannot be guaranteed. Prick out the seedlings into pots of damp, recommended, potting compost.

In English gardens sow a few seeds in small pots of seed raising compost, to minimise root disturbance; mid winter-early spring (Jan-March), under glass at 13–21°C (55–70°F). Carefully thin out the seedlings keeping only the strongest in each pot and grow it on. Or you can experiment by sowing the seeds in seed compost containers. Treat the seedlings as half-hardy annuals.

In mild winter areas you can sow the seeds, late spring (May), directly where they are to grow and flower, thinning out the seedlings to 225 mm (9 in) apart. Salpiglossis are summer flowering.

Pests and diseases: Aphids, aster yellows, foot and root rot.

Cultivars/varieties: Bolero Mixed, height 600–700 mm (24–28 in), blue, rose, crimson, gold, blue. Emperor Royal Mixed, height 900 mm (36 in), shades and tints of rose, crimson, purple, blue.

Family: Solanaceae.

Salvia The most famous bedding salvia is the Brazilian *Salvia splendens* (scarlet sage); height 300–600 mm (12–24 in); and its cultivars. It is a half-hardy perennial which is grown as an annual.

The 'flower' consists of a true tubular flower of a glowing scarlet, which is enclosed by an equally scarlet bract (false flower).

The true flower is a narrow, 31-62 mm (1.2-2.4 in) long, scarlet, 'spaghetti-tube', ending with two protruding, pouting lips. This is enclosed by a 25 mm (1 in) long, ridged, bell-shaped bract, of the same scarlet colour, and it also looks like a pouting fish.

There are approximately 20-30 pendulous flowers, tightly packed in 'candelabra' whorls around 150-200 mm (6-8 in) tall spire-like spikes. It is the scarlet bracts that people consider as the flowers. *S. splendens* now has white, pink and purplish hybrids.

The 75-100 mm (3–4 in) long, strong-green leaves, borne on square stems, are narrow heart-shaped, pointed, and toothed. These leaves contribute considerably to the plant's attractiveness.

An old favourite annual, the southern European *S. horminum* (syn. *S. viridis*), has been much improved, and is available in bract colours of white, pink and blue, which if massed in bold clumps form an attractive garden feature.

Another old garden favourite, the Mexican *S. patens* (gentian sage); height 600 mm (24 in); has clean, light-blue flowers. The Texan *S. farinacea* (mealycup sage); height 700 mm (28 in); is also a perennial that is grown as an annual, and because of its height can be planted to the back of the flower bed or border. It has spikes of mid to deep blue, or white and blue flowers, and light green leaves. The new cultivars are particularly attractive.

S. splendens, and its cultivars, are mostly used as bedding plants, although some gardeners grow them as pot and container plants. Salvias demand a rich, well-drained soil, in the sunniest location, and occasional feedings, when they are growing well, with a well-balanced, liquid, soluble, flower fertiliser, suitable for salvias and applied as the manufacturer instructs.

Flowers appear late spring-early summer on, according to method of growing and location.

Some gardeners in warm, mild winter climates, cut down the spent flowers, and keep *S. splendens* for more than one year. But to be honest, I prefer fresh plants each year.

Keep *S. splendens* watered during dry spells, but avoid excess watering during the flowering period.

Propagation: S. splendens, the scarlet sage, is frost tender. For controlled results, thinly sow the seeds in seed compost containers, using a damp, recommended, seed raising compost; late summer-spring (and at other times) in subtropical areas; late winter-early spring-summer temperate areas; and spring in cold areas, or 6 to 8 weeks before the usual frost-free, spring planting out time in your location, under glass at 16–24°C (60–75°F).

Gently press the seeds on to the top of the compost to anchor them. Don't bury them as they need light to germinate.

Gently, but thoroughly, mist water the compost using a fine spray, keeping it pleasantly moist. Remember that salvia seedlings are prone to damping-off disease when subjected to excess water and humidity. Commonsense in watering and heat control is called for.

Seeds should germinate in 5–12–21 days depending on soil temperature. Transplant the seedlings when they are large enough to handle into containers or 75 mm (3 in) pots of damp, recommended, potting compost.

Those grown in pots develop into superior, larger plants, particularly if the growing tips are pinched out to induce branching, but only when the plants have produced enough stem joints to provide sufficient sideshoots. I would use pot-grown salvias to provide spectacular, important, public garden displays.

Grow the seedlings on, and harden them off, if necessary in a cold frame. Plant them out directly where they are to grow and flower, 400 mm (16 in) apart large cultivars; 200 mm (8 in) apart dwarf cultivars, but only when all danger from frost is past, and the ground has warmed up.

Or the seeds can be sown directly where they are to grow and flower in frost-free areas, or in any area provided the soil is warm enough. Sow the seeds in temperate and cooler areas, mid or late spring, directly where they are to grow and flower, but only when all danger from frost is past and the soil is warm enough.

But be aware that it will be approximately 3 months before you see flowers, and the plants are usually cut down by the first frost. However, there are new cultivars being bred that will flower sooner. Thin out the seedlings to 200–400 mm (8–16 in) apart, according to the size and spread of the cultivar.

Sow seeds of *Salvia horminum*, spring or summer, directly where they are to grow and flower, 3 mm (0.1 in) deep. Thin out seedlings to 300 mm (12 in) apart. Flowers appear in 3 months.

In English gardens sow seeds of scarlet sage in seed compost, late winter-early spring (Feb-March), under glass at 16–24°C (61–75°F). Prick out the seedlings, when they are large enough to handle, into containers or small pots and treat the plants as half-hardy annuals. Other salvias grown as annuals can be sown in the heated greenhouse in early spring, and treated as above. *S. splendens* flowers appear mid summer on.

Pests and diseases: Glasshouse pests, leaf eating insects, damping off.

Cultivars/varieties: 'Bonfire', height 600 mm (2 ft), scarlet. 'Carabiniere', height 250–300 mm (10–12 in), brilliant red. Dress Parade Mixed, height 350 mm (14 in), white, pink, rose, scarlet, purple. Dwarf Pigmy, height 300 mm (12 in), scarlet. 'Early Bonfire', height 600 mm (2 ft), scarlet. Spangles, 300 mm (12 in), white, pale pink, pale lilac, scarlet, salmon and red and white bicolour. Salvia Clary Sage Mixed, 450 mm (18 in), white, pink and blue. *Salvia horminum* 'Tricolor', white, pink, blue. *Salvia farinacea*, 600 mm (24 in), wedgewood blue. The attractive cultivars of *S. farinacea*: 'Argent', 500 mm (20 in), compact, white; and 'Victoria', height 500 mm (20 in), compact, violet blue; can be used as a 'matched pair' in the flower bed. I have seen 'Victoria' in effective combination with red salvias and grey foliage.

Family: Lamiaceae.

***Sanvitalia* (creeping zinnia)** The Mexican frost-tender annual *Sanvitalia procumbens*; height 150–200 mm (6–8 in), has 18–25 mm (0.7–1 in) wide, notched-pointed petalled, double yellow, or orange cultivars.

These pert, bright-yellow or orange, 25 mm (1 in) wide daisy flowers, are dominated by a large blackish-brown-purplish centre-disc eye. Sanvitalia is late spring or summer flowering.

Sanvitalia's 30 mm (1.2 in) long, mid-green leaves are egg-shaped-pointed in outline. It is a fairly prostrate plant, spreading by trailing stems.

Sanvitalia succeeds in most gardens, but prefers a light, well-drained soil, in an open, sunny location. It is tolerant of dry weather, but water sanvitalias sensibly during dry spells.

It is used for groundcover, mass bedding, edging plants, hanging baskets and rockery cascades. I have before me, as I write this, a 'Mandarin Orange' sanvitalia, being grown as a 75 mm (3 in) pot plant.

Be aware that sanvitalia seedlings, and mature plants, resent root disturbance.

Propagation: Dig over the soil, directly where the plants are to grow and flower, but only when it is easy to work. Break it down into a fine tilth, and rake out any debris. Firm the soil gently, but thoroughly, to take the seeds.

Thinly sow the seeds outdoors directly where the plants are to grow and flower, when all danger from frost is past. Do not bury them, as they need light to germinate. Press them with the head of the rake or a board to anchor them to the soil. Water gently but thoroughly, using a fine spray.

Seeds will germinate in 7 to 10 days at 20–25°C (68–77°F) soil temperature. Carefully thin out the seedlings to 150 mm (6 in) apart. Some gardeners thin out as close as 75 mm (3 in) apart, the theory being that sanvitalias like crowding. But they will spread to 225 mm (9 in).

Or for earlier flowers in cool areas, sow a few seeds in 75 mm (3 in) peat pots of damp, recommended seed raising compost, indoors in a warm, light place in late winter, or 6 to 8 weeks before the usual, frost-free, spring planting out time, in cold locations. Very carefully thin out the seedlings leaving the strongest in each pot, and grow them on.

Harden off the seedlings, if necessary in a cold frame, and plant them out where they are to grow and flower, peat pots and all, in late spring, or when all danger from frost is past.

Or potted seedlings can be moved on into 125 mm (5 in) pots of damp, recommended, potting compost, to form interesting, low-growing 'cushion' pot plants.

In English gardens dig over the soil directly where the plants are to grow and flower, breaking it down into a fine tilth. Rake out any debris, and firm the soil gently but thoroughly to take the seeds.

Sow the seeds thinly, early to mid spring (March-April), but don't bury them in the soil, as they need light to germinate. Press the seeds to anchor them to the soil. Carefully thin out the seedlings to 75–150 mm (3–6 in) apart.

Or sow the seeds, early spring (March) under glass in pots, and treat them as half-hardy annuals. Flowers midsummer, and on.

Pests and diseases: Reasonably free.

Cultivars/varieties: Species as above. 'Mandarin Orange', orange, double flowers.

Family: Asteraceae.

***Scabiosa* (pincushion flower, sweet scabious)** The southern European *Scabiosa atropurpurea*, the sweet scabious; height 450–900 mm (18–36 in); is the best known scabious.

It is a hardy annual that grows prolifically in spring or summer, and has spicy-fragrant, 37–50 mm (1.5–2 in) wide, spongy, 'posy' flowers in subdued shades or tints of white, pink, red or purple.

The domed, pincushion flowers are a mass of smaller flowers each with protruding pinhead, reproductive organs, which give rise to the plant's common name of 'pincushion'.

The flowers grow from a rosette of oblong, coarsely toothed leaves, but the upper leaves are fine and deeply lobed.

Scabiosa stellata, the drumstick scabious, produces a mass of lilac, powdery-blueish flowers, on 150–300 mm (6–12 in) stiff stems. However, the 37 mm (1.5 in) wide, drumstick seedheads, used for dried flower arrangements, are also sought.

Scabiouses prefer a fertile, well-drained, neutral or slightly alkaline (limy) soil, in an open, sunny location.

They are used as border plants, and also as cutflowers, the 'drumstick' dried flowerheads of some being in demand by florists.

Water scabiouses during dry spells. The taller plants may need staking, but usually they seem to manage on their own.

Feed the plants, when they are budding up, with a well-balanced, liquid, soluble, flower fertiliser, suitable for scabious and applied as the manufacturer instructs.

Propagation: Dig over the soil when it is easy to work, directly where the plants are to grow and flower, breaking it down into a fine tilth. Rake out any debris, and firm the soil gently but thoroughly to take the seeds.

Thinly sow the seeds late summer and autumn in subtropical and temperate areas; late summer or mid to late spring in cool areas.

Rake the seeds gently into the top tilth, and press them with the head of the rake or a board to anchor them. Water gently but thoroughly using a fine spray, and don't allow the seedbed to dry out. Keep it just pleasantly moist until the seedlings are well established, and then water the plants when they need it.

Seeds should germinate within 20 days at 21°C (70°F). Thin out the seedlings to 225–300 mm (9–12 in) apart. Flowers should appear in approximately 12–16 weeks.

Or seeds can be sown indoors, in a warm, 13–16°C (55–60°F), light place, 6 mm (0.2 in) deep, in seed compost containers, using a damp, recommended, seed raising compost, 2 or 3 weeks, or even 8 weeks for earlier flowers, before the usual, frost-free spring planting out time, in your location. Cover the seeds with sieved compost or vermiculite.

Prick out the seedlings into containers of damp, recommended potting compost, harden them off, and plant them out directly where they are to grow and flower.

In English gardens thinly sow the seeds of the annual scabious, early to mid spring, directly where the plants are to grow and flower. Thin out the seedlings to 225–300 mm (9–12 in) apart. They should flower summer to autumn.
Pests and diseases: Slugs snails, powdery mildew.
Cultivars/varieties: Choice Mixed, height 600 mm (2 ft), mixed colours. Imperial Giant Hybrids, height 600–900 mm (2–3 ft), white, pink, crimson, lavender, blue. *S. stellata*, drumstick, height 450–600 mm (18–24 in), powder blue.
Family: Dipsacaceae.

Schizanthus **(poor man's orchid, butterfly flower)** Although the frost-sensitive cultivars of the Chilean *Schizanthus pinnatus*; height 450 mm–1.2 m (18–47 in); and *Schizanthus* × *wisetonensis*; height 450 mm (18 in) or up to 1.2 m (47 in); can be grown outside early spring in warm climates, or summer in cool climates, as garden bedding annuals, they are grown mostly as pot plants or hanging basket plants, under cover in a shadehouse or shaded greenhouse.

And here the butterfly-clusters of cascading flowers can be shown to perfection. Under glass they usually provide a winter-spring floral display.

The 37 mm (1.5 in) wide, butterfly-like, saucer-depression flowers, are available in shades, tints, and bicolours of white, pink, red, crimson and violet, each having a yellow, spotted throat.

The pale green, sticky, lacy, deeply-cut foliage is almost fern-like. Schizanthuses can quickly burn up in any hot sun.

They prefer a rich, organic, well-drained light soil, in a sheltered, dappled-light location; or sunnier in cold areas. Keep the plants well watered during dry spells. Feed them when they are growing well, with a well-balanced, liquid, soluble flower fertiliser, suitable for schizanthus and applied as the manufacturer instructs.

Schizanthuses have to be staked with suitable canes or similar, particularly before the tall cultivars become massed with flowers. But some firms are now breeding much smaller cultivars, 150–350 mm (6–14 in) tall.
Propagation: Sow the seeds 3 mm (0.1 in) deep, in seed compost containers, using a damp, recommended seed raising compost, under glass if necessary, at 13–18°C (55–64°F); autumn-early winter for winter-spring flowering in subtropical areas; late summer-autumn temperate areas; late summer-autumn in cooler areas.

Or early spring in cold areas, under glass, at 13–18°C (55–64°F), for flowering out of doors. Higher growing temperatures may cause the seeds to react adversely.

Press the seeds lightly with a wooden block, or similar, to anchor them to the compost. Mist water the compost using a fine spray, and keep it pleasantly moist. Do not let the seedlings dry out.

Place the container in a dark place for the seeds to germinate, but remove it immediately the seedlings emerge, and place into good light, otherwise the seedlings will become drawn and spindly; but do not place them in hot sunlight.

The seedlings should germinate in approximately 8–14–21 days, but inspect the seed containers daily, just in case the seedlings appear *before* the 8th day.

Prick out the seedlings into 75 mm (3 in) pots of damp, recommended potting compost, and grow them on.

Once the plants are growing well, and when the plant and side-shoots are approximately 75 mm (3 in) tall or long, carefully tip prune the growing shoots and side branch shoots of the young plants. Tip pruning and side-shoot pruning early on form dense, bushy, then cascading plants, which become smothered in blooms. But take great care as the plants are brittle.

Grow the plants on over winter in a shadehouse in warm areas, or in a greenhouse in cooler areas, at a minimum temperature of 8–10°C (46–50°F). Schizanthus will not tolerate hot temperatures.

To prevent the plants from becoming root-bound, pot them on, when and if necessary, progressively from 75 mm (3 in) pots to 125 mm (5 in); to 175 mm (7 in); to 225 mm (9 in) pots of damp, recommended potting compost; or into hanging baskets of potting compost.

Flowers should appear in approximately 14 weeks from sowing. Turning each pot alternatively 180 degrees towards the direction of the sun's light, to prevent the plant from growing on one side, may help to produce a bushier 'all-round-flowered' plant.

Those seedlings that are to be planted outside, directly where they are to grow and flower, should be hardened off at the 75 mm (3 in) pot stage, if necessary in a cold frame, and planted out, 300 mm (12 in) apart, when all danger from frost is past and the ground has warmed up.

Or the seeds can be sown in rows; late summer to early winter in warm, moist, frost-free areas; and after the last frost in other areas, directly where they are to grow and flower.

In English gardens sow the seeds under glass, in seed compost containers, at 13–18°C (55–64°F), early-mid spring (March-April) for flowering out of doors. Treat those plants to be planted outside as tender annuals, ensuring that they are properly hardened off before planting them outside, when all danger from frost is past and the ground has warmed up. Sow seeds late summer-early autumn (Aug-Sept) at the same temperature as for indoor greenhouse pot plants. Gradually reduce the temperature of the greenhouse pot plants, and provide a winter minimum of 8–10°C (46–50°F). Shade and ventilate the greenhouse when necessary. Pay particular attention to the plants' watering needs, as they can dry out rapidly. Summer flowering outside.

Or sow seeds, mid-late spring (April-May), outside directly where they are to grow and flower.
Pests and diseases: Aphids, damping off, various rots, virus.
Cultivars/varieties: Angel Wings Mixed, height 350 mm (14 in), bright colours, gold centres. Dr Badger's Hybrids, large flowers, brilliant colours. Hit Parade, height 300 mm (12 in), large colour range. Star Parade, height 200 mm (8 in), orchid-like blooms.
Family: Solanaceae.

Senecio **(florists' cineraria)** The Canary Island, frost sensitive, *Senecio* × *hybridus* (syn. *Senecio cruentus, Cineraria cruentus*); height 150–600 mm (6–24 in); is better known as the florists' cineraria.

Possibly it is listed in certain seed catalogues under 'Cineraria', but do be aware that there are other plants known as cinerarias.

Although a perennial, *S.* × *hybridus* is treated as a cool-season, half-hardy annual.

Florists' cinerarias are commonly grown in warm, moist, and temperate Australia as either winter or spring, massed bedding plants; but they are also grown as cool-greenhouse pot plants. In cold areas cinerarias are grown as warm-greenhouse pot plants.

There is a wide range of cultivars, with 18–63 mm (0.7–2.5 in) wide, velvety, daisy-like flowers, in shades and tints of white, pink, red, lavender, mauve or blue, in single or bicolours; some having distinct, white-eyed, zonal-bands of colour; all with a large, dark, centre-eye disc.

Cinerarias can be classified into 4 groups:
(1) *S. hybridus grandiflorus* (large flowered hybrids)
(2) *S. h. intermedius*
(3) *S. h. stellatus* (star-shaped flowers)
(4) Double flowered.

But every year more and more hybrid crosses are being produced, so that now from the seed catalogue you can, for example, choose:
(a) Large-Flowered; height 600 mm (24 in)
(b) Semi-Dwarf Large-Flowered; height 350 mm (14 in)
(c) Double Large-Flowered; height 300 mm (12 in)
(d) Dwarf-Multiflora Large-Flowered; height 225 mm (9 in)
(e) Extra-Dwarf Large-Flowered; height 150 mm (6 in).

So to choose the cinerarias you want: (1) study the catalogue; (2) choose the plant height you want; (3) choose the colour(s) you want; (4) choose the flower formation you want, for example, single, double, large- or small-flowered; (5) choose those suitable for either bedding or pot plants, or both.

The 18–63 mm (0.7–2.5 in) wide flowers are produced above the foliage in 250–300 mm (10–12 in) wide, dome-mound clusters. They appear late winter-early spring, or later, according to location and the method used to grow them.

The foliage is much branched, with heart-shaped-pointed leaves, up to 200 mm (8 in) long, with irregular, toothed, leaf margins.

Florists' cinerarias prefer a well-drained, fertile soil, partial shade with sun for part of the day, but protected from hot sunlight, in a frost-free, sheltered location.

This year's bedding displays in certain temperate parts of Australia have suffered badly from unusually high spring temperatures.

They also appreciate regular feeds of a well-balanced, liquid, soluble, flower fertiliser, suitable for cinerarias and applied as the manufacturer instructs.

Watering is a key factor in growing cinerarias. Water that is too cold may cause shock, and possible collapse; which can also happen if the plants are waterlogged. Therefore sensible, regular, tepid-warm watering is needed.

Cinerarias, when grown in pots, demand a top quality potting-compost; one that holds water like a sponge, but does not become waterlogged. Attention must be paid to the watering needs of pot grown cinerarias, by never letting them dry out.

Pot cinerarias need feeding regularly with a well-balanced, soluble, liquid, flower fertiliser, suitable for cinerarias, and applied as the manufacturer instructs.

Propagation: Thinly sow the seeds in seed compost containers, using a damp, recommended seed raising compost; autumn-early winter subtropical areas; late summer-autumn temperate locations; mid-summer-mid autumn, but under glass, in cooler areas, at 13–16°C (55–61°F), as florists' cinerarias will not survive frost damage.

But seedlings growing under glass will have to be protected from strong sunlight by suitable greenhouse shading, and must receive adequate ventilation if and when necessary.

Carefully and thinly sow the seeds pressing them gently on to the compost surface, as they need light to germinate. Mist water the compost with a fine spray.

Or place the container in a shallow container of tepid-warm water, letting the moisture soak up through the compost, until it just glistens on the surface, but doesn't pool. Remove the container.

Don't let the compost, or seedlings dry out, but keep the compost just pleasantly moist. Water the plants, once they are established, when they need it, also with tepid-warm water.

The seeds should germinate in approximately 15 days, but they may germinate sooner, or later, than this, so be prepared.

Prick out the seedlings, when they are large enough to handle, into 75 mm (3 in) pots, or 75 mm (3 in) peat pots, of damp, recommended, potting compost. Using peat pots reduces root disturbance when transplanting or potting on the seedlings later on.

When suitably hardened off, plant out the large cultivars, 300 mm (12 in) apart; dwarf cultivars 200 mm (8 in) apart; directly where they are to grow and flower, but only when all danger from frost is past and the ground has warmed up.

Carefully pot on those seedlings needed as pot plants from 75 mm (3 in) pots to 125 mm (5 in) pots; and then up two sizes, if required, into 175 mm (7 in) pots of damp, recommended potting compost; and on into 225 mm (9 in) pots if necessary. Take great care not to disturb the roots when repotting the plants.

Pot plants should be grown in cool conditions, 13–16°C (55–61°F), with a winter minimum of 8–10°C (46–50°F). In hot climates, they need to be grown as shadehouse or bushhouse pot plants. Flowers should appear approximately 20 weeks after sowing. Deadheading spent flowers will help prolong the flowering period.

In English gardens sow the seeds in seed compost containers, mid spring to late summer (April-Aug), under glass at 13–16°C (55–61°F). Use a damp, recommended, seed raising compost. Prick out the seedlings into 75 mm (3 in) pots, or 75 mm (3 in) peat pots, of potting compost, and grow them on until the roots are established.

Check pertinent literature, and packet instructions as cinerarias require specialist treatment.

Pests and diseases: Aphids, leaf miner, thrips, grey mould, powdery mildew, mosaic-streak viruses.

Cultivars/varieties: Cindy Multiflora Formula Mix, height 250 mm (10 in), pink, carmine, dark red, blue, copper shades. Double Mixed, height 300 mm (12 in), large colour range, many doubles. Dwarf Multiflora Mixed, height 225 mm (9 in), large flowered. Erfurt Palette Mixed, height 250 mm (10 in); rich colour range. Large Flowered Exhibition, height 600 mm (24 in). Pretty Girl Mixed, height 400 mm (16 in), good colour range. Large Flowered Hybrids, height 150–200 mm (6–8 in), various colours.

Family: Asteraceae.

***Senecio* (dusty miller)** The Mediterranean, half-hardy perennial *Senecio bicolor* (syn. *S. cineraria, S. maritima, Cineraria bicolor, C. maritima*); height 600–750 mm (24–30 in); although not as glamorous as the florists' cineraria, is widely used, particularly its cultivars, principally for their perfect, 'go-with-any-colour', silver-grey, deeply-lobed, or fern-like foliage.

The 'lift' dusty miller gives to bedding plants is eye-stopping. It is a good idea, however, to plant fresh, young seedlings at each planting, pinching out the growing tips to form bushy plants. Older plants can look leggy and scruffy, and the yellow flowers produced by this plant are not particularly attractive.

But if dusty millers are grown in the sub-shrubby mode, in groups of their own, then these older plants, and their 25 mm (1 in) 'shaving-brush' flowers, have a separate attraction.

S. bicolor prefers an average to dry soil, in full sun.

Propagation: Sow the seeds, under glass if necessary, in seed compost containers, using a damp, recommended, seed raising compost, late-summer, autumn in subtropical areas; late winter-early spring in temperate locations; early-spring in cold areas, at 16–21°C (61–70°F).

Carefully and thinly sow the seeds pressing them gently on to the compost surface, as they need light to germinate. Mist water the compost with a fine spray, using tepid-warm water, and never let the compost or seedlings dry out, keeping the compost pleasantly moist.

Seedlings should appear in approximately 10 days. Prick them out once they are large enough to handle, into containers, or 75 mm (3 in) pots, of damp, recommended potting compost, and grow them on.

Harden off the seedlings, if necessary in a cold frame, and plant them out directly where they are to grow and flower, 150–250–300 mm (6–10–12 in) apart, but only if any danger from frost is past and the ground has warmed up.

In English gardens sow the seeds under glass, late winter-early spring (Feb-March), at 16–21°C (61–70°F). Prick out the seedlings into containers, or straight into 75 mm (3 in) pots of a damp, recommended potting compost, and treat the plants as half-hardy annuals.

Pests and diseases: Reasonably free; wet season rot.

Cultivars/varieties: 'Silver Lace', 200 mm (8 in), silver white foliage.

Family: Asteraceae.

***Silene* (catch-fly, campion, rose of heaven)** The north-western Mediterranean *Silene coeli-rosa* (syn. *Lychnis coeli-rosa, Viscaria elegans, Viscaria oculata*); height 250–300 mm (10–12 in); is a hardy, frost-resistant annual.

When massed, the upfacing, spring-summer, rose-pink purple, 'propeller' flowers seem to sparkle like a constellation.

There are many *S. coeli-rosa* cultivars, ranging in height from 150–450 mm (6–18 in), in shades and tints of white, pink, red or lavender-blue blooms.

The 5-petalled flowers, borne singly on 50 mm (2 in) long, wiry stalks, are approximately 25–37 mm (1–1.5 in) wide, and some have a dark pink stained centre-throat, with the classic catch-fly bulbous throat, albeit reduced in size, behind the flowers.

The rough-to-the-touch, dull-grey, branched foliage, bears 37–87 mm (1.5–3.4 in) long, 6–12 mm (0.2–0.5 in) wide, oblong-pointed, or narrow-pointed leaves.

S. coeli-rosa grows in most neutral garden soils in a sunny location in cool areas, but seems to thrive better in a partially-shaded spot in warmer areas.

As an experiment I grew silenes as pot plants in a shade-frame, and they bloomed and bloomed, from mid spring, and on.

S. coeli-rosa is used as a cut flower.

Silene starki (ragged robin); height 150–250 mm (6–10 in); a hardy annual, is also grown. Other *Silene* species and cultivars are grown as well.

Water the plants adequately during dry spells.

Propagation: Dig over the soil, when it is easy to work, directly where the plants are to grow and flower, breaking it down into a fine tilth. Rake out any debris, and firm the soil gently but thoroughly, to take the seeds.

Thinly 'station sow' the seeds in clumps 150–200 mm (6–8 in) apart; late autumn-winter or even spring in subtropical areas; late winter-early summer temperate areas; spring in cooler areas.

Rake over the soil to ensure even seed distribution, burying the seeds no deeper than 3–6 mm (0.1–0.2 in). Or cover the seeds with finely sieved soil or vermiculite. Press the seeds and soil lightly, but firmly, with the head of the rake or a board to anchor them to the soil.

Water the seeds gently but thoroughly using a fine spray, and don't allow the seeds or seedlings to dry out until they are well established. Water the seedlings when they need it.

Seeds should germinate in approximately 14 to 21 days, but germination time depends on the weather conditions. Thin out the seedlings to 150 mm (6 in) apart, although if sown thinly enough the plants don't usually need thinning.

Care must be taken when weeding and thinning, as silene roots are shallow growing and sensitive to disturbance.

Flowers should appear in approximately 12 weeks from sowing.

Or thinly sow the seeds in seed compost containers, using a damp, recommended, seed raising compost. Cover them with 3–6 mm (0.1–0.2 in) of sieved compost or vermiculite. Gently firm them with a small wooden block, or similar. Mist spray the compost with water, and keep it pleasantly moist. Then water the seedlings when they need it.

Seeds can germinate in 5 days in warm conditions. Prick out the seedlings, when large enough to handle, into 50 mm (2 in) pots of damp, recommended potting compost, and grow them on. Harden off the seedlings and plant them out directly where they are to grow and flower 150–200 mm (6–8 in) apart.

In English gardens, dig over the soil, when it is easy to work, in early to mid spring (March-April), and thinly 'station sow' the seeds in clumps 150–200 mm (6–8 in) apart, directly where they are to grow and flower. Flowers summer.

Pests and diseases: Reasonably free.

Cultivars/varieties: Species as above; *S. coeli-rosa* 'Blue Angel', and *S. c.* 'Rose Angel'. Love Hearts, height 300–400 mm (12–16 in), white, pink, red, blue.

Family: Caryophyllaceae.

***Stylomecon* (wind poppy)** The western North American, frost resistant annual *Stylomecon heterophylla*; height 450–600 mm (18–24 in); is a relatively new addition to the annual garden display.

The glowing, orange blooms can reach up to 100 mm (4 in) wide, but mine did not grow as wide as that; only 50 mm (2 in) wide. The flowers have blunt, tooth-edged petals, and are arranged like 4-petalled propellors. The foliage is pale green and deeply lobed.

Wind poppies prefer semi, or deeper shade; but not heavy shade. They flower for 2 to 3 months during the late spring and/or summer.

They grow well in most garden soils, although they must have good drainage, and ample watering during dry spells. Wind poppies are used on their own in small drifts, or in the mixed border.

Propagation: Dig over the soil when it is easy to work, and sow the seeds late summer, autumn, early winter in subtropical areas; early spring in temperate areas; spring in cold areas. Break down the soil into a fine tilth, and rake out any debris. Gently but thoroughly firm the soil to take the seeds.

Thinly sprinkle the seeds over the area directly where they are to grow and flower. Lightly rake them into the top tilth, barely covering them, and then gently firm with the head of the rake, or a board, to anchor them to the soil.

Gently water the seeds using a fine spray, and don't allow the seedbed surface to dry out until the seedlings are well established, then water the plants when they need it.

Seeds should germinate in up to 21 days. Carefully thin out the seedlings to 300–375 mm (12–15 in) apart.

As an experiment I sowed some wind poppy seeds in punnets, indoors late winter, and they germinated in 4 days. I pricked them out into 50 mm (2 in) pots and grew them on, and they flowered indoors 42 days from germination. But the plants seemed a little unhappy in such an environment. The seedling transplantation success rate was bad, which leads me to suppose that wind poppies resent root disturbance.

In English gardens, sow the seed mid spring (April), outdoors directly where they are to grow and flower.

Pests and diseases: Reasonably free.

Cultivars/varieties: Species as above.

Family: Papaveraceae.

***Tagetes* (marigolds)** The tagetes listed below originated in Mexico or the United States, and not in Africa or France, as perhaps one would suppose.

Most tagetes have a powerful scent, but there are some African (American) marigold cultivars that are odourless.

Tagetes are frost sensitive, being treated as half-hardy annuals in colder climates.

They are mostly summer-autumn flowering, although French marigolds appear earlier in spring in warm, moist, frost-free, northern locations.

Tagetes are shallow rooting and soon dry out, and are easily damaged by careless weeding.

Tagetes marigolds are not the traditional 'pot marigolds', which are discussed under *Calendula* species.

Tagetes marigolds can be split up into 4 convenient groups:

(1) *Tagetes erecta*, the African (or American) marigold
(2) *Tagetes patula*, the French marigold
(3) *Tagetes tenuifolia (T. signata)*, the fine-leaved (signet) marigold
(4) *Tagetes* Triploid (Afro-French), the 'man-made' marigold.

T. erecta, the summer-autumn flowering African (American) marigold; height 600–900 mm (24–36 in), is an upright, dominating, many branched marigold, and is used in various annual border situations.

The bright yellow flowers are approximately 50 mm (2 in) wide; although many of the new hybrids can be 100–125–150 mm (4–5–6 in) wide. There are hosts of garden hybrids and F_1 hybrids, ranging in height from 300–900 mm (12–36 in), each with a tightly-packed flower petal-mass (carnation or chrysanthemum form), or looser petalled in some semi-double cultivars.

Flowers are available in shades and tints from whitish to deep orange. Some cultivars have high-domed flowers up to 100–125 mm (4–5 in), or more, wide.

The dark green leaves are deeply cut, segmented, toothed, and almost bracken-like in appearance.

The long stems of the taller African marigolds can be hidden by fronting them with smaller plants. Try to avoid overhead watering, if possible, as the taller cultivars can be knocked about by heavy sprays. Space African Marigolds 300–450 mm (12–18 in) apart.

T. patula, the sometimes autumn, or spring-summer flowering French marigold; height 350–500 mm (14–20 in), is a bushy, floriferous plant bearing 37–50 mm (1.5–2 in) wide, brownish-red yellow, single flowers.

This plant has been hybridised to produce many splendid, 150–250 mm (6–10 in) tall cultivars, with single, semi-double, or double (crested) flowers, up to 65 mm (2.5 in) wide, in shades and tints of mid-yellow, to gold, to flame, to mahogany-red; plus bicolours.

The French marigold prefers a cooler climate than the African marigold. New cultivars, however, have recently been introduced, and these are more resistant to summer heat. In cold climates French marigolds can be sown, in spring, under glass, and will grow to perfection during the summer. Space French marigolds 150–300 mm (6–12 in) apart, depending on the cultivar spread.

T. tenuifolia (syn. *T. signata*), the fine-leaved, or signet marigold; height 600 mm (24 in); has threadish-like, sweet smelling leaves, and 25 mm (1 in) wide flowers. It has a varietal form *T. t. pumila*, the dwarf fine-leaved marigold, which has been used to breed cultivars; height 150–200 mm (6–8 in) tall; in flower colours ranging from mid-yellow to mid-orange.

The beauty of these cultivars lies in their ability to smother the plant with small, bright, yellow or orange flowers, usually early summer. Space signet/fine-leaved marigolds 300 mm (12 in) apart.

T. Triploid; height 250–350 mm (10–14 in), is a man-made race of marigolds, produced from crossing African (American) marigolds with French marigolds, resulting in sterile-seeded mules: that is they set no seeds, and are the result of complicated species crossing. These hybridised seeds are expensive and not generally available in Australia.

Triploids produce lovely, floriferous plants. They have inherited much of the flower size of the African marigolds, and the dwarf, compact habit of the French marigolds, resulting in flowers 50–75 mm (2–3 in) wide, in yellow, gold, orange or reddish shades and tints. But bear in mind that each year variations of these plants are being produced. Space triploid tagetes 300 mm (12 in) apart. If seed is available.

Tagetes will grow in most well-cultivated, well-drained, moderately fertile, not too rich soils, in a sunny location. But hot, hard sunlight causes the flowers to decline. French marigolds, usually, flower earlier than African (American) marigolds. In warm, temperate areas the fine-leaved signet tagetes can be a mass of bloom by early summer.

Removing spent marigold flowers will improve the appearance of the plant, particularly of the taller, or large-flowered cultivars. Dead-heading, however, can be a little daunting when dealing with the smaller-flowered tagetes.

Fertilise the plants when they are growing well with a well-balanced, liquid, soluble, flower fertiliser, suitable for tagetes, and applied as the manufacturer instructs.

Tagetes, to me, always look best regimented in rows and sweeps in formal garden beds, and I would always arrange my public garden displays in this fashion. But it is a matter of opinion.

Plant out the seedlings, preferably late in the day or on a cloudy day to help prevent flagging, and water the root area carefully with a fine-rosed watering can, or similar.

Propagation: Generally African marigold seeds are sown in spring in subtropical, temperate, and cool areas; and French marigolds are sown in autumn in the same areas. But as you may find out by observation and discussion, seeds are sometimes sown at times other than those mentioned above, or below.

Sow the seeds in seed compost containers, under glass where necessary, at 16–21°C (60–70°F), using a damp, recommended, seed raising compost.

African marigolds: In subtropical areas sow seeds winter-spring; in temperate areas late winter-early spring; in cold areas mid to late spring.

French marigolds: In subtropical areas sow seeds late summer-early autumn; temperate areas late summer-autumn; cool areas early-late summer, but these sowings are cut down by heavy frost, or spring, for summer flowering.

Thinly sow the seeds over the seed raising mix, cover them with a 5 mm (0.2 in) layer of sieved compost or vermiculite, and gently firm them, using a wooden block or similar.

Mist spray the compost with water using a

fine spray. Keep it pleasantly moist, and don't let the seeds or emerging seedlings dry out until they are well established. Then water the plants when they need it. Correct watering must be kept up at all times with tagetes, or else they wilt rapidly and are soon attacked by white-spot insects.

Germination should occur in approximately 5-14 days, at 21-25°C. Prick out the seedlings into containers of damp, recommended potting compost, and grow them on.

Harden off the seedlings, if necessary in a cold frame, and plant them out directly where they are to grow and flower 150-450 mm (6-18 in) apart, depending on cultivar height and spread, when all danger from frost is past and the ground has warmed up.

Flowers should appear in approximately 12-16 weeks from sowing time. Water the plants well during dry spells, avoiding overhead watering, if possible, with the taller African cultivars.

Or in subtropical-tropical areas, French marigold seeds can be sown in rows, late summer-early autumn; and African marigold seeds can be sown late winter-spring; both directly where the plants are to grow and flower, thinning them out to the required distance.

Seeds can be sown in cooler areas in rows, directly where they are to grow and flower, when all danger from frost is past and the ground has warmed up; but bear in mind that they can take 3 to 4 months to flower and are cut down by frost. So find out from a competent authority when your first frost is due, and work back from there.

In English gardens sow the seeds in seed compost, late winter-mid spring (Feb-April), under glass at 16-21°C (60-70°F), and treat the plants as half-hardy annuals. The flowering period is early summer-mid autumn.

Pests and diseases: Slugs, foot rot, grey mould, leaf spot, wilt and stem rot.

Cultivars/varieties:

African: Crackerjack Mixed, height 600 mm (2 ft), yellow, gold, orange, carnation flowered. 'Hawaii Golden' (odourless), to 750 mm (30 in), large flowered. 'Hawaii Orange' (odourless) to 750 mm (30 in), large flowered. 'Inca Orange', height 300 mm (12 in), flowers fully double orange, up to 100-125 mm (4-5 in) wide. 'Inca Yellow', height 300 mm (12 in), bright yellow, flowers 100-125 mm (4-5 in) wide. 'Jubilee Golden Hybrid', 450-600 mm (18-24 in), gold flowers, 100-125 mm (4-5 in) wide. 'Perfection Yellow', height 450 mm (18 in), dense, double, rounded flowers.

French: Brocade Mixed, height 200 mm (8 in), yellow, gold, red, mahogany, and bicolours. 'Janie Gold', crested flowers, golden orange. 'Orange Sophia', height 350 mm (14 in), bright orange. 'Red Cherry', height 300 mm (12 in), bright cherry. 'Queen Sophia', 350 mm (14 in), bronze, russet, with yellow edge. 'Yellow Sophia', height 350 mm (14 in), bright yellow.

Signet: 'Lemon Gem', height 150 mm (6 in), bright, clear lemon. 'Tangerine Gem', height 150 mm (6 in), deep orange.

There are many, many more African and French marigold cultivars.

Family: Asteraceae.

Thunbergia The thunbergias discussed below are treated as frost-sensitive, warm-season annuals in cold climates, or as greenhouse pot plants.

But in temperate frost-free Australia, and warmer areas, they are used as perennial twining climbers in the garden, on fences and trellis; or from window boxes; or in large hanging baskets; or climbing in large containers with suitable support.

The popular South African *Thunbergia alata*, black-eyed Susan; height 1.8-3 m (6-10 ft); is a perennial that can be used as an annual.

Its flowers start as dark-purple tubes, which expand into 38-50 mm (1.5-2 in) wide, flared, 5 rounded-petalled, flat-trumpet, orange flowers, with a prominent brownish-black centre eye.

Black-eyed Susans are also available in pale-yellow, buff and white flower variations. The 'Chinese lantern' flower pods are also attractive.

The bright green, ivy-like leaves have winged leaf stalks.

T. alata can cover or hide a fence in a season, and in temperate areas can provide a succession of blooms from early spring on, depending on climate.

The tropical east African *Thunbergia gregorii* (syn. *T. gibsonii*), clock vine, golden glory vine, orange clock vine; height 1.8-3 m (6-10 ft); is a rapid-growing, evergreen perennial, with 5-lobed, pure-orange, trumpet flowers, 38 mm (1.5 in) wide, borne on long 75 mm (3 in) long stalks. Flowers appear mid spring to mid autumn.

The leaves are dull green, hairy, and rounded-triangle in shape.

Thunbergias grow well in a reasonably fertile soil in a warm, sunny location, but they need copious water during dry spells.

Tidy up the foliage after flowering, during the dormant period, removing any dead leaves and stems. Sparingly feed thunbergias, once the plants are growing well, with a well-balanced, liquid, soluble, flower fertiliser, suitable for thunbergias and applied as the manufacturer instructs.

Propagation: 'Station sow' a few seeds of *T. alata* in clumps; winter-spring in subtropical areas; spring-summer elsewhere, directly where they are to grow and flower, 6 mm (0.2 in) deep, 450-600 mm (18-24 in) apart.

But only sow the seeds when all danger from frost is past and the ground has warmed up, as even the slightest frost will kill seedling thunbergias.

Seedlings should appear in approximately 10-15 days at 21-24°C (70-75°F). Thin them out to approximately 600 mm (24 in) apart.

Or the seeds can be sown in 75 mm (3 in) pots, or 75 mm (3 in) peat pots, of damp, recommended, seed raising compost, earliest spring, under glass if necessary, at 21-24°C (70-75°F) temperature. Thin out the seedlings leaving the strongest in each pot.

Harden off the seedlings, if necessary in a cold frame, and plant them out directly where they are to grow and flower, when all danger from frost is past and the ground has warmed up.

In English gardens sow the seeds, in seed raising compost, late winter-mid spring (Feb-April) at 21-24°C (70-75°F), and treat them as tender, half-hardy plants. Flowers early summer, and on.

Or pot the plants on as required, and grow them as pot plants, going up eventually to 225 mm (9 in) pots. Keep them in a greenhouse, lightly shaded during the hot summer months.

Ventilate the greenhouse during the hottest months, but bear in mind that thunbergias grow outside in such places as temperate and warm Australia. Therefore don't grow them in too dark an environment, or too cold a temperature.

Overwinter the plants at say 15°C (60°F), keeping them just moist. But water them copiously when they are growing well, particularly during dry spells.

Tidy up the foliage after flowering, during the dormant period, removing any dead leaves and stems. Flowers appear mid summer-mid autumn.

Pests and diseases: Reasonably free.

Cultivars/varieties: Thunbergia alata Mixed.

Family: Acanthaceae.

***Thymophylla* (Dahlberg daisy)** The summer-flowering, Texan-Mexican frost-tender annual *Thymophylla tenuiloba* (syn. *Dyssodia tenuiloba*); height 100-150 mm (4-8 in); is little known in Australia. But it bears a mass of 12 mm (0.5 in) wide, yellow daisy flowers, above thread-like, aromatic foliage.

Dahlberg daisies prefer a sunny spot, and are used as edging plants, or massed in small beds of their own. They thrive in a well-drained, or light, sandy-loam soil. Do not overwater Dahlberg daisies, as waterlogging causes them to deteriorate.

Propagation: In frost-free areas the seeds can be sown late winter-early spring, directly where they are to grow and flower. Dig over the soil, when it is easy to work, breaking it down into a fine tilth. Remove any debris and gently, but thoroughly, firm the soil to take the seeds.

Mix the seeds with several times their own volume of dry, silver sand, to ensure even distribution. Thinly sow the seeds, but do not rake them into the surface tilth, and gently press them with a board, or similar, to anchor them to the soil. Gently water in the seeds using a fine spray.

Thin out the seedlings once they germinate, to 150-225 mm (6-9 in) apart.

In frost-prone areas, sow the seeds when all danger from frost is past, and the ground has warmed up, but bear in mind that the plants will take 4 months, maybe more, to reach the flowering stage.

Or sow the seeds in seed compost containers, earliest spring, under glass at 16-21°C (61-70°F). Prick out the seedlings into small pots of damp, recommended, potting compost, and grow them on. Harden them off in a cold frame, and plant them out directly where they are to grow and flower, when all danger from frost is past and the ground has warmed up.

In English gardens sow the seeds in seed compost, under glass at 16-21°C (61-70°F), in early-spring (March), and treat them as half-hardy annuals.

Pests and diseases: Reasonably free.

Cultivars/varieties: Species as above.

Family: Asteraceae.

***Tithonia* (Mexican sunflower)** The new summer-autumn flowering cultivars of the Mexican-Central American, warm-season annual *Tithonia rotundifolia* (syn. *T. speciosa*); height 750 mm-1.2 m (2.5-4 ft), with their 75-88 mm (3-3.5 in) wide, glowing orange-scarlet, 'sunflower-dahlia' flowers, are spectacular.

The leaves are heart-shaped-pointed, and somewhat coarse.

Mexican sunflowers prefer a sunny,

sheltered location, and a well-drained soil, moderately rich in organic matter. Do not over-water them as they are reasonably drought resistant, and only need watering during dry weather.

Keep them weed free in their early stages of growth, as slugs, who hide in the weeds, love the young seedlings.

The taller cultivars may need corral-staking. Mexican sunflowers are used as background, or 'easy-to-spot' border plants. They are also used as cut flowers.

Remove spent flowers to prolong the flowering period. Tithonias seed freely, so remove unwanted seedlings before they become a pest.

Propagation: 'Station sow' the large seeds directly where they are to grow and flower, 6 mm (0.2 in) deep, winter-spring in subtropical areas; spring and summer elsewhere, when all danger from frost is past, and the ground has warmed up. The seeds should germinate in approximately 10–11 days at 16–24°C (61–75°F).

Thin out the seedlings to 600–900 mm (24–36 in) apart, depending on the spread of the cultivar. Flowers should appear within 4 months from sowing.

Or in cooler areas, sow a few seeds in 75 mm (3 in) pots of seed raising compost, earliest spring, under glass, at 16–21°C (61–70°F). Seed should germinate in approximately 5–10 days. Thin out the seedlings, leaving only the strongest in each pot, and grow them on.

Harden off the seedlings in a cold frame, and plant them outside directly where they are to grow and flower, when all danger from frost is past and the ground has warmed up.

In English gardens sow the seeds in 75 mm (3 in) pots of seed raising compost, earliest spring (March), under glass at 16–21°C (61–70°F). Thin out the seedlings, keeping only the strongest in each pot, and grow them on. Treat the plants as half-hardy annuals. Flowers midsummer, and on.

Pests and diseases: Reasonably free.

Family: Asteraceae.

Torenia (wishbone plant) The tropical Asian-Indo-Chinese *Torenia fournieri*; height 200–300 mm (8–12 in); is a summer-flowering, warm-season, annual plant that thrives in a filtered light location.

It has stiff, square stems, and 31 mm (1.2 in) long, by 13 mm (0.5 in) wide flowers, that vaguely resemble open-mouthed antirrhinums; indeed they are of the same family. The petals are pale lilac-blue, with a velvety, dark-purple blotched, bottom lip. There are also two dark-purple 'cheek' blotches, and a yellow sighting-spot in the throat.

The plant derives its common name from the chicken wishbone-shaped stamens found inside the flower's throat. The flower-pods are like tiny Chinese lanterns, and so are the seed pods. A white form is known.

The foliage is shiny-green, with occasional bronzeing, 50 mm (2 in) long, by 31 mm (1.2 in) wide, rippled, tooth-edged and heart-shaped pointed.

Torenias prefer an organic, moisture-holding, friable soil, in a partially shaded spot. Or more sun in cool summer areas.

Water the plants freely during dry spells.

Feed the plants, when the flower buds are forming, with a well-balanced, liquid, soluble, flower fertiliser, suitable for torenias. This should help extend the flowering period, and increase flower size.

Torenias are useful for low-border edges, edging plants, pot plants, and window boxes.

Propagation: Sow the seeds in seed compost containers, on top of damp, recommended seed raising compost; late winter-spring in subtropical areas; late winter to early summer in temperate areas; and spring-early summer in cold areas, under glass if necessary, at 16–21°C (61–70°F).

Press the seeds with a wooden block, or similar, to anchor them to the compost. They should germinate in approximately 15 days.

Prick out the seedlings into 75 mm (3 in) pots of damp, recommended potting compost, and grow them on.

Harden off the seedlings, if necessary in a cold frame, and plant them out directly where they are to grow and flower, 150–200 mm (6–8 in) apart, when all danger from frost is past and the ground has warmed up.

Flowers should appear in approximately 12–16 weeks from seed sowing; mine flowered in 12 weeks from a late winter sowing.

Or 'station sow' a few seeds in clumps 150 mm (6 in) apart, directly where the plants are to grow and flower, and when there is no danger from frost to the emerging seedlings. Thin out the seedlings leaving only the strongest in each clump.

In English gardens, sow the seeds in seed compost, late winter-mid spring (Feb-April) under glass, at 16–21°C (60–70°F). Prick out the seedlings into 75 mm (3 in) pots of damp, recommended potting compost, and grow them on. Treat them as half-hardy annuals. Finally plant them out into a sheltered, moist, partially shaded soil location. Torenias can be grown as pot plants, using 125 mm (5 in) pots. They flower mid-summer.

Pests and diseases: Reasonably free.

Cultivars/varieties: Species as above. 'Fournieri Blue'. 'Little Gem', height 200–300 mm (8–12 in), velvety blue.

Family: Scrophulariaceae.

***Trachelium* (throatwort)** The Mediterranean *Trachelium coeruleum*; height 300–900 mm (12–36 in); is a half-hardy perennial that is not much grown, although it is a classic border plant.

The minute mauve-blue flowers appear in 150–300 mm (3–6 in) flat-topped, or explosive clusters, held well above the foliage on strong, wiry stems.

The dark green leaves are narrow-ovalish, pointed and heavily toothed.

In warm climates tracheliums are grown as perennials, but in frost-prone, colder climates they are treated as half-hardy annuals.

Sown in the right conditions, tracheliums should bloom in the first summer from a winter-early spring sowing.

They grow well in partial shade, with sun for part of the day; or more sun in locations with cooler summers.

There is also a white form *T. c. album*.

Propagation: Sow the seeds directly into 50 mm or 75 mm (2–3 in) pots of a damp, recommended seed raising compost, mid winter, or 8 to 10 weeks before the last expected frost in cold areas, under glass, at 13–18°C (55–64°F).

The reason why the seeds are sown in pots is to keep the seedlings moving without a check, as the plants can take up to 5 months to flower from sowing. It is important, therefore, that the seeds are sown early enough for plants to bloom before they are cut down by frost.

Seeds take approximately 20 days to germinate. Carefully thin out the seedlings keeping the strongest in each pot, and grow them on. Pot on the seedlings, if they are about to outgrow their present pots, into larger pots of damp, recommended potting compost.

Harden them off in a cold frame, and plant them out directly where they are to grow and flower, 300–450 mm (12–18 in) apart, when all danger from frost is past and the ground has warmed up.

In English gardens sow the seeds, late winter-earliest spring (Feb-March-even April) under glass, in 50 mm or 75 mm (2–3 in) pots of seed raising compost, at 13–18°C (55–64°F). Thin out the seedlings, keeping only the strongest one in each pot.

Grow them as cool greenhouse pot plants; or harden them off in a cold frame, and plant them out in a sheltered spot, directly where they are to grow and flower, 300–450 mm (12–18 in) apart, when all danger from frost is past and the ground has warmed up. They should flower summer-autumn.

Pests and diseases: Reasonably free.

Cultivars/varieties: Species as above. Umbrella Series-Purple Shades height 600–900 mm (2–3 ft).

Family: Campanulaceae.

***Trachymene* (blue-lace flower, Rottnest Island daisy)** The Western Australian *Trachymene coerulea* (syn. *Didiscus caeruleus*); height 300–600 mm (12–24 in); is a summer-flowering annual, although it is treated as a half-hardy annual in cold climates.

It is an upright, erect plant with slightly hairy stems, bearing mounded, cushion-scabious flower clusters, like sunshade-umbrellas, 25–50 mm (1–2 in) wide, in a delicate, lacy lavender-sky blue. Each cluster of flowers consists of approximately 25 or more, 5 mm (0.2 in) wide, 5-petalled, star-like blooms. These flower clusters have a particular charm, in that each small flower stalk closes up, like fingers, to form attractive, 'shredded wheat' seed heads.

The leaves are pale-mid green, 50 mm (2 in) long, finely divided, or deeply lobed.

Trachymenes like a slightly acid-neutral, well-prepared, well-drained soil, in full sun or partial shade, in a sheltered location.

They are useful for planting in drifts. They may need supporting with twigs, or similar, in windy sites.

Carefully pinch out the growing tips to form bushier plants, but only when the plants have produced enough stem joints to provide sufficient sideshoots. Trachymenes make useful cut flowers. They can also be grown as pot plants, if necessary in a shaded greenhouse.

Feed the plants when they are growing well with a well-balanced, liquid, soluble, flower fertiliser, suitable for blue-lace flowers and applied as the manufacturer instructs.

Propagation: Dig over the soil when it is easy to work, directly where the plants are to grow and flower, breaking it down into a fine tilth. Rake out any debris, and firm the soil gently, but thoroughly, to take the seeds.

Thinly, and evenly sow the seeds 5 mm

(0.2 in) deep; early autumn-winter and spring in subtropical areas; autumn and spring in temperate areas; late spring in cold areas, in small rows, directly where they are to grow and flower.

Water the soil gently using a fine spray, keeping it pleasantly moist until the seeds germinate and are well established, and then water the plants when they need it.

Seedlings appear in approximately 11–21 days at 21°C (70°F); my last trachymene sowings germinated in 11 and 16 days. Thin out the seedlings to 200–225 mm (8–9 in) apart.

Or in cold areas the seeds can be sown in seed compost containers, using a damp, recommended seed raising compost, late winter-early spring under glass at 15–18°C (59–64°F), covering them with a 5 mm (0.2 in) layer of finely-sieved compost or vermiculite.

Prick out the seedlings very carefully, as they resent transplantation, when they are large enough to handle, into 75 mm (3 in) peat pots of damp, recommended, potting compost, and grow them on.

Harden off the seedlings in a cold frame, and plant them out, 200–225 mm (8–9 in) apart, when all danger from frost is past and the ground has warmed up.

In English gardens sow the seeds in seed compost, earliest spring (March) under glass at 15–18°C (59–64°F), covering them with a 5 mm (0.2 in) layer of finely-sieved compost or vermiculite, and treat them as half-hardy plants. Or they can be potted on into 125 mm (5 in) pots of damp, recommended, potting compost, and grown on as pot plants in a lightly shaded greenhouse; the greenhouse being ventilated when necessary during hot weather. Flowers should appear from mid-summer (July-Aug), on.

Pests and diseases: Reasonably free.
Cultivars/varieties: Species as above.
Family: Apiaceae.

***Tropaeolum* (nasturtium)** The South American Andean, cool-season annual *Tropaeolum majus*; height or spread: 1.8–2.4 m (6–8 ft); can be grown as a climber or trailer. It has flowers 50–75 mm (2–3 in) wide, in creamy-white, pink, yellow, orange, bicolours or multicolours, with 5 broad, funnel-cup-shaped petals, with a prominent flower-sepal, nectar spur. The flower perfume is weak and strange.

The variable cultivars are widely grown. These range in height from 250–375 mm (10–15 in), and are divided into 4 convenient groups:

(1) Climbing or clambering, with a spread of 1.8–2.4 m (6–8 ft); these are used for trailing over walls, covering large, bare areas, and the like. They can be either single or double flowered, in shades and tints of cream, yellow, orange, red and dark-red.

(2) Dwarf Semi-Trailing or Clambering, with a spread of 900 mm-1 m (36–39 in); also used for bare spots, or hanging over small walls and so on, with semi-double or double flowers in shades and tints of cream, yellow, orange, scarlet and dark red; some having the nasturtium perfume.

(3) Dwarf Non-Trailing Compact; height 300 mm (12 in), with a spread of up to 600 mm (24 in); these are used as bedding plants, edging plants, and so on. They have semi or double flowers, some upfacing, having no spurs, in shades and tints of yellow and red; but some have distinctive, purple foliage surmounted by vivid scarlet flowers.

(4) Dwarf Non-Trailing Compact, similar to those above, but single flowered in shades and tints of yellow and red; some are multicoloured, and others bear their mass of flowers above green and white variegated foliage.

Thus you can see that there are many beautiful strains to choose from. They are used as climbing plants, or ground clambering and trailing plants, or hanging basket plants.

Nasturtiums are seen flowering prolifically spring-summer-autumn in the most starved of places, and that is one secret of growing nasturtiums successfully. But in hot, hard sunlight the flower production is reduced.

Gardeners sometimes scatter and sow a few nasturtium seeds to hide a bare spot that offends the gaze. Poor, meagre soils produce numerous flowers, whereas fertile soils produce masses of beautiful leaves, but fewer flowers.

The 125 mm (5 in) wide leaves, bright green on top, and dull green below, are flat, roundish, and wavy-edged, with the leaf stalk in the centre of the leaf, so that the whole looks like a flat sunshade. When crushed, these leaves and the stems have a powerful scent.

T. majus prefers a weakly fertile soil, or even a poor soil, well-drained, in a sunny location, although it will tolerate light, filtered shade. It also tolerates drought reasonably well, but water the plants during dry spells. It is frost sensitive.

T. majus makes a useful cut flower, particularly when arranged with the leaves.

The Peruvian-Ecuadorian *Tropaeolum peregrinum* (syn. *T. canariense*), the canary creeper; height 3–4 m (10–13 ft), is a short-lived perennial that is treated as an annual. The yellow, 18–25 mm (0.7–1 in) wide, fringed-feathery flowers, with green, curved spur, are irregular in outline.

The leaves are blue-green, 5-lobed, stubby fingered-hand like, with the leaf stem in the middle of the leaf, the whole looking like a flat, tatty sunshade.

The canary creeper prefers a reasonably fertile soil, and a warm, sunny, sheltered location, up against a wall, or fence, or trellis, or similar, but it will grow in filtered shade.

The plant starts off growing upright then tends to branch out.

Propagation: Dig over the soil when it is easy to work, directly where the plants are to grow and flower. Break it down into a fine tilth and remove any debris.

'Station sow' *T. majus* seeds, in clumps of 2 to 4 seeds, 600 mm (24 in) apart for the strong climbing-clambering forms; 450 mm (18 in) apart for the semi-climbing-clambering forms; 250 mm (10 in) apart for the dwarf forms; late summer-autumn-winter-early spring in subtropical areas; early spring to summer in temperate areas; spring-summer in cold areas, after frosts, directly where they are to grow and flower. Cover with 18–25 mm (0.7–1 in) of sieved soil or vermiculite.

Germination should occur within 7–14 days at 18°C (64°F). Thin out the seedlings keeping only the strongest in each clump. Nasturtiums do not transplant readily and can suffer transplant-shock and root disturbance shock, so be careful when weeding around them.

Flowers should appear in approximately 10 weeks from sowing.

T. majus will self-seed, and many new plants will appear through the old foliage.

'Station sow' 2 or 3 seeds of *T. peregrinum* in one clump 1 m (39 in) apart, and keep only the strongest seedling.

To produce earlier flowers in cooler areas, sow 2 seeds to a 75 mm (3 in) pot, or 75 mm (3 in) peat pot of damp, recommended, seed raising compost, under glass at 13–18°C (55–64°F), late winter-early spring.

Thin out the seedlings keeping only the strongest in each pot and, if required, grow them on as pot plants, moving them up into larger pots of damp, recommended potting compost, if necessary. Those plants to be used in the garden can be hardened in a cold frame, and planted outside, late spring-early summer when all danger from frost is past.

In English gardens 'station sow' 2 or 3 seeds of *T. majus*, in clumps, in mid-spring (April), directly where they are to grow and flower, 18–25 mm (0.7–1 in) deep, at the required distance apart, when all danger from frost is past.

'Station sow' 2 or 3 seeds of *T. peregrinum* (April-May) outdoors in clumps 1 m (39 in) apart, and keep only the strongest seedling.

Or to produce earlier flowers, sow 2 seeds to a 75 mm (3 in) pot, or 75 mm (3 in) peat pot of seed raising compost, under glass at 13–18°C (55–64°F), in late winter-early spring (Feb-March). Thin out the seedlings keeping only the strongest in each pot, and grow them on as pot plants; moving them up into larger pots if necessary.

Those plants to be used in the garden can be hardened off in a cold frame, and planted outside, latest spring-early summer (April-May). *T. majus* should flower early summer-early autumn (June-Sept); *T. peregrinum* should flower mid summer-mid autumn (July-Oct).

Pests and diseases: Aphids, thrips, red spider, bacterial wilt.
Cultivars/varieties: Alaska Dwarf Variegated, white and green marbled foliage. Golden or Scarlet Gleam Hybrids Mixed, height: trailing 2 m (7 ft). Jewel Dwarf Mixed, low growing, many blossoms. Whirlybird Mixed, 250 mm (10 in), bushy plant, open-faced flowers in cream, gold, tangerine, orange, cherry rose. *Tropaeolum peregrinum*.
Family: Tropaeolaceae.

***Ursinia* (jewel of the veldt)** The South African *Ursinia anethoides*; height 225–450 mm (9–18 in); is a perennial which is grown as an annual, or half-hardy annual in cold climates.

The 50–63 mm (2–2.5 in) wide, daisy-like flowers, borne on wiry stems, have beautiful zone-bands of fiery-orange, shading to bright yellow. Each flower has a purple centre disc, which is studded with bright yellow stamens. But, unfortunately, the buds hang their heads; as do the flowers in cloudy, dull weather, or in darkness. They are, therefore, not much good as cut flowers.

The leaves are pale green, finely divided and lacy.

Ursinias prefer a well-drained, light soil in a sunny, sheltered location. They are spring-summer flowering in temperate areas.

Propagation: Sow the seeds 3 mm (0.1 in) deep, in seed compost containers, using a damp, recommended seed raising compost, winter and spring in subtropical areas; spring and early summer temperate areas; spring and early summer in cold areas; under glass if need be, at 13–18°C (55–64°F).

Water the seeds gently with a fine spray, and keep the compost and seedlings pleasantly moist. Seedlings appear in approximately 15 days.

Prick out the seedlings when they are large enough to handle into containers, or small pots of damp, recommended, potting compost, and grow them on.

Harden off the seedlings, if necessary in a cold frame, and plant them out directly where they are to grow and flower, 150–200 mm (6–8 in) apart, but when all danger from frost is past and the ground has warmed up. Flowers should appear in approximately 16 weeks.

Or the seeds can be sown, late spring (earliest November) in cold areas, directly where they are to grow and flower.

In English gardens, sow the seeds in seed compost, late winter-earliest-mid spring (Feb-March-April), under glass at 13–18°C (55–64°F), and treat the plants as half-hardy annuals.

Or the plants can be grown as pot plants, either singly in a 100 mm (4 in) pot, or 3 plants to a 175 mm (7 in) pot. Flowers should appear early-mid summer to early autumn (June-July-Sept).

Or the seeds can be sown, late spring (earliest May), directly where they are to grow and flower.

Pests and diseases: Reasonably free.
Cultivars/varieties: Species as above.
Family: Asteraceae.

Venidio × arctotis (see below)

***Venidium* (monarch of the veldt, Cape daisy, Namaqualand daisy)** The South African *Venidium fastuosum*; height 450–600 mm (18–24 in) is a frost-sensitive annual, which is grown as a half-hardy annual in cold climates.

It has 75–100 mm (3–4 in) or wider, glowing, bright-orange daisy-like flowers, each petal having a distinctive, black, sighting-splash at its base. The large, blackish-purple centre-disc becomes studded with yellow stamens. But there are cream to deep-orange variations, and more dwarf forms.

The light green leaves, which are covered with silver-white hairs like ghosty cobwebs, are deeply lobed, starting off narrow at the base and widening and rounding at the top.

Venidiums prefer a well-drained, light, organic soil, in a sheltered, sunny location. Usually the plants, because of their heavy-headed flowers, need supporting with neatly arranged, small stakes. Venidiums are used as border plants, pot plants, and cut flowers.

Propagation: Dig over the soil when it is easy to work, directly where the plants are to grow and flower. Break it down into a fine tilth and remove any debris. Firm the soil gently, but thoroughly, to take the seeds. Thinly sow the seeds in late summer-autumn-winter-spring, subtropical areas; spring and early summer in temperate areas; late spring and early summer in cool areas.

Try not to bury the seeds, as they need light to germinate. Mixing the seeds with several times their own volume of clean, fine, sharp sand will ensure a more even distribution.

Gently but thoroughly water the seeds using a fine spray, and don't let the seed-bed dry out until the seedlings are well established, then water them when they need it.

Seedlings should emerge in approximately 10–15 days at 21°C (70°F). Thin them out to 300 mm (12 in) apart. Flowers should appear in approximately 16 weeks from sowing.

Or the seeds can be sown in seed compost containers, using a damp, recommended, seed raising compost, under glass, early spring in frost-prone areas at 16–21°C (61–70°F). Just press the seeds on to the top of dampened compost. Mist water them using a fine spray and don't let the compost dry out; keep it pleasantly moist. Water well-established seedlings when they need it.

Germination is variable, usually 10 days or more, but my venidiums germinated in 5 days, and flowered in 10 weeks, so be prepared.

Prick out the seedlings into containers or pots of damp, recommended potting compost, and grow them on. Harden them off, if necessary in a cold frame, before planting them out, 300 mm (12 in) apart, directly where they are to grow and flower, but only when all danger from frost is past and the ground has warmed up.

In English gardens sow the seeds in seed compost, late winter-early-mid spring (Feb-March-April) under glass, at 16–21°C (61–70°F), and treat the plants as half-hardy annuals.

Or in mild winter areas, the seeds can be sown, late-spring (May), directly where they are to grow and flower, and thinned out to the required distance apart. Flowers should appear in summer-autumn.

Pests and diseases: Reasonably free.
Cultivars/varieties: Species as above.
Family: Asteraceae.

Venidio × arctotis In 1952 a sterile, intergeneric hybrid between the closely related *Venidium fastuosum* and *Arctotis* species (discussed previously) was produced commercially. This gave rise to many different cultivars, propagated by cuttings, with flowers in shades and tints of white, yellow and red; self-coloured and bicoloured. I have not seen them growing in Australia.

***Verbascum* (mullein)** We are concerned here only with the white or yellow *Verbascum* species that flourish in temperate to cool climates, and can be grown from seed.

The Asia Minor *Verbascum bombyciferum*; height 1.2–2 m (47–79 in); is a biennial that begins as a rosette of oval-pointed leaves. Tall spikes of bright-yellow flowers spring up from the rosette.

The southern European *Verbascum longifolium* var. *pannosum* is a perennial; height 900 mm–1.2 m (36–47 in); and has very long, oblong to lancelike, lobed, pointed leaves. The flowers are deep yellow, with small, red-blotched centres.

The European *Verbascum nigrum* is a perennial; height 600–900 mm (24–36 in); and has heart-shaped, ovalish leaves. The flowers are yellow, splashed red-brown.

The Balkan-European *Verbascum phoeniceum*, a short-lived perennial, has ovalish leaves. The flowers are whitish or pink-purplish.

Verbascums thrive in most well-drained, moderately fertile, garden soils, in a sunny location. Staking is usually necessary when the plants grow tall or lank, or are growing in an exposed site.

Cut off any spent flower spikes, immediately below the last spent flower, to encourage the production of new flower spikes, and also to prevent the proliferation of self-sown seedlings; unless you are keeping the flower spike for a fresh supply of seeds, then you would select a fine specimen.

In too rich a soil they tend to produce foliage, but few flowers, and are apt to deteriorate.

Propagation: Verbascums flower late spring-early summer in mild, temperate locations, and already, early summer, seedlings are appearing around the parent plant of those allowed to self-seed. It is possible to sow the seeds as soon as they are ripe, but the seedlings would have to be nursed through the summer.

In temperate climates you can sow the ripe seeds in seed compost containers, late summer-early autumn, using a damp, recommended seed raising compost. Gently water in the seeds, using a mist spray, and don't let them dry out, but keep the compost just pleasantly moist.

Seeds take approximately 20 days to germinate. Prick out the seedlings into 125 mm (5 in) pots of damp, recommended, potting compost, and grow them on, plunged into sand to reduce the evaporation rate.

Or they can be pricked out from the seed container directly into a prepared seedling nursery-holding bed 150–200 mm (6–8 in) apart, and grown on.

During the dormant season, using a garden-trowel, lift the seedlings, and plant them out directly where they are to grow and flower, scooping up as large a soil root-ball around the plant as is feasible, to lessen root disturbance. Remember that verbascums can develop strong tap roots, and care must be taken not to damage these.

Space the verbascums 375 mm (15 in) apart for small verbascums; and 450 mm (18 in) for the taller.

Or sow the ripe seeds, in drills, outdoors in a prepared seedbed. Thin out the seedlings to 150–200 mm (6–8 in) apart.

Or 'station sow' a few seeds in clumps directly where the plants are to grow and flower, 375–450 mm (15–18 in) apart, keeping only the strongest to grow on.

In cold climates sow the seeds in seed compost containers, in mid-spring, using a damp, recommended seed raising compost. Gently water the seeds, using a mist spray, and don't let the compost dry out, but keep it just pleasantly moist.

Place the container in a cold frame to germinate the seeds, bearing in mind the possible need to shade-protect, or to ventilate the seeds and young seedlings if there is hot sunshine.

The seedlings can be hardened off and pricked out from the seed container, directly into a prepared seedling nursery-holding bed 150–200 mm (6–8 in) apart, and grown on; and from there, during the dormant season, planted out directly where they are to grow and flower.

Or prick out the seedlings into 125 mm (5 in) pots of damp, recommended potting compost, and grow them on. Harden off the young plants, and plunge them outside, up to their necks in sand, until you are ready to plant them out, directly where they are to grow and flower.

In English gardens sow the seeds in seed compost, mid-spring (April), and place them in a cold frame. Be aware that the seedlings may need protecting from hot, concentrated sunlight, through the glass, and may also need ventilation. Harden off the seedlings, and prick them out into a prepared, nursery holding-bed, 150–200 mm (6–8 in) apart, and grow them on. Plant them out in early-autumn (Sept), directly where they are to grow and flower.

Or prick out the seedlings into 125 mm (5 in) pots of damp, recommended potting compost, grow them on, and plunge them out of doors for planting out early autumn.

Or sow the seeds outdoors late spring-early summer (May-June) in a prepared seed bed. Thin the seedlings out if necessary, and from there plant them out directly where they are to grow and flower.

Flowers appear late spring or summer, depending on species and seed sowing date.
Pests and diseases: Reasonably free.
Cultivars/varieties: Species as above.
Family: Scrophulariaceae.

***Verbena* (garden verbena, vervain)** The spring-summer-autumn flowering *Verbena × hybrida* (syn. *V. × hortensis*) is a group of hybrids derived from various South American perennial species.

These hybrids make uncomplaining, summer bedding plants. They are, in my opinion, excellent for this use.

Verbena × hybrida; height 150–300–450 mm (6–12–18 in); is of prostrate habit, with shoots trailing to 500–600 mm (20–24 in). The small star-shaped flowers are borne in circles, as dense, 75 mm (3 in) wide, flat-topped clusters, like miniature cinerarias.

The flowers are available in many beautiful shades and tints, from white, to pink, red, purple and blue, with many being bicolours, having a distinct, white, centre-eye.

Although perennial they seem to be 'better set up' as annual bedding plants, grown to flower from seed in the first year. But they can be kept for a few years.

Verbena × hybrida can be divided into 2 convenient groups
(1) Tall, large flowered; height 300–450 mm (12–18 in) or more.
(2) Dwarf; height 150–300 mm (6–12 in).

The leaves of *V. × hybrida* are fernish, leathery-looking, dark green to dark green-greyish, with the leaf outlines narrow and notched, like rounded teeth.

Verbenas prefer a well-drained, rich, organic soil in a sunny location, although they are reasonably tough. Pinching out the growing tips encourages branching, but only when the plants have produced enough stem joints to provide sufficient sideshoots.

Water verbenas during dry spells, not excessively, and feed them with a well-balanced, liquid, soluble flower fertiliser, suitable for verbenas and applied as instructed.

Verbena × hybrida is used for summer bedding, edging, rockeries, pot plants, cut flowers, and hanging basket work. Dead heading, that is removing spent flowers, increases the flowering display.
Propagation: Sow a few seeds individually in 75 mm (3 in) pots of damp, recommended, seed raising compost, to minimise root disturbance; late summer to early spring in subtropical areas; late winter-spring-early summer in temperate areas; spring-early summer in cold areas, under glass where necessary, at 18–21°C (64–70°F).

Germination occurs spasmodically at approximately 20 days, but can take up to 4 weeks, or more. However, some of the new cultivars have a higher germination rate.

Water the seeds carefully as they soon rot in too-damp a compost. Thin out the seedlings, keeping only the best in each pot, and grow them on.

Harden off the potted seedlings, if necessary in a cold frame, and plant them out directly where they are to grow and flower, 225–300 mm (9–12 in) apart (depending on hybrid spread), but only when all danger from frost is past and the ground has warmed up.

Or in mild winter areas, the seeds can be sown directly where they are to grow and flower. Dig over the soil, when it is easy to work, breaking it down into a fine tilth. Rake out any debris and firm the soil gently, but thoroughly, to take the seeds.

'Station sow' the seeds in clumps 225–300 mm (9–12 in) apart, depending on hybrid spread, covering them with 6 mm (0.2 in) of sieved soil, compost or vermiculite, and gently firm them to anchor them to the soil.

Gently but thoroughly water the seeds using a fine spray, and don't let the seeds, seedbed, or seedlings dry out until the seedlings are well established, then water them when they need it. Thin out the seedlings as soon as it is easy to do, 100–300 mm (4–12 in) apart (depending on hybrid spread).

In English gardens sow the seeds in 75 mm (3 in) pots of seed raising compost, mid winter-early spring (January-March) at 18–21°C (64–70°F), and treat as half-hardy plants. Flowers should appear in early summer (June), and continue until cut down by the first frosts.
Pests and diseases: Reasonably free.
Cultivars/varieties: Gaiety Mixture, height 225 mm (9 in), bright colours. Ideal Florists' Strain, height 225 mm (9 in), compact, good colour range. Petite Mix, non trailing, bright colours. Springtime Mixed, height 300 mm (12 in), wide range, bright colours.
Family: Verbenaceae.

***Viola* (garden pansy, viola, horned viola, johnny jump-up, tufted pansy)** What is the difference between a modern pansy and a modern viola? Quite frankly, with all the cross-breeding, and back-crossbreeding between the species, it is not all that clear, although possibly in the seed catalogues you will see them listed specifically as 'Pansy' or 'Viola'.

Violas usually are smaller, and self (single coloured), borne on more compact plants, but you cannot necessarily rely on this. Pansies and violas, although perennials, are usually grown as annuals or biennials.

Originally, the British-European *Viola tricolor* (heart's-ease, or johnny jump-up) was crossed with the fragrant Peruvian *Viola cornuta* to create the first garden pansy hybrids, known as *V. × hybrida*. Then *V. tricolor* was crossed with *V. lutea*, (the mountain pansy), *V. altaica* and *V. cornuta*, producing the hybrids *Viola × wittrockiana* (syn. *Viola tricolor hortensis*), which are now grown in our gardens as pansies.

Viola × wittrockiana intergenetic hybrids; height 150–250 mm (6–10 in); are divided into winter-flowering (hiemalis), or summer-flowering pansies.

The velvet flowers, 25–100 mm (1–4 in) wide, are available in shades and tints of white, cream, yellow, orange, red, crimson, purple, blue, bicolours and tricolours, some hybrids even look jet-black.

The blooms have 5 rounded, overlapping petals, like ships' propellors, mostly with 'grumpy, moustached men' or 'doggy' faces, with a yellow centre-eye; but some are all one colour, known variously as single, solid, plain or self-coloured.

The edges of the mid-green, narrow-oval, or oblong, lance-like leaves are notched like rounded teeth.

One American seed firm, in a recent catalogue, under the winter-blooming section, offers climbing pansies, that grow several feet in height, ideal for forcing, and available in a wide flower colour range. But I have not seen them in Australia.

Viola tricolor, with its small, neat, three-coloured, viola-flowers is also grown in our gardens.

The 'tufted' pansy, or viola, is a cross between *V. tricolor, V. cornuta* and *V. williamsii*, and you may see these hybrids classified under *V. × wittrockiana*, but perhaps they should be listed as *Viola × williamsii*. Also check under 'Viola' in your seed catalogue.

There are many favourite 'tufted' pansy cultivars, with 37 mm (1.5 in) wide flowers and beautifully clear colours, in shades and tints of white, yellow, ruby-red and blue. Many tufted pansies can only be grown true from vegetative (non-flowering) basal cuttings. *Viola cornuta* is usually sold in mixed, pure colours.

Violettas, produced from *Viola 'Blue King'* × *V. cornuta*, are tufted, petite, oval or circular-shaped flowers, having a pleasant vanilla ice-cream fragrance. They produce masses of 25 mm (1 in) wide, or less, blooms, with no rays or markings, but with a bright gold, or orange centre eye.

Viola odorata, is the common sweet-violet.

Garden pansies can spread to 300 mm (12 in), but after a while tend to look scruffy, and that is one reason why, although perennials, they are grown as annuals and biennials, or are reproduced from cuttings.

Garden pansies and violas will grow in most garden soils that are well drained, moisture-holding, fertile and in a sunny location, with afternoon filtered shade, as they can suffer badly if exposed to hot, hard sunlight.

Recently, in spring, after two days of 38°C (100°F), our local pansies looked badly mauled.

Dead-heading, removing spent blooms, is important, as it increases the flowering display. Garden pansies are used for bedding displays, edging plants, pot plants, window box plants, and so on. Pinching out the growing tips of the plants, when young, encourages side branching, but only when the plants have produced enough stem joints to provide sufficient sideshoots.

Garden pansies like regular feeds of a well-balanced, liquid, soluble, flower fertiliser, suitable for pansies and applied as the manufacturer instructs. They dislike fresh manure around their roots.

Pansies and violas need watering well during dry spells, and do try, if possible or feasible, to 'gently' spray the soil and not the flowers, to avoid spoiling the delicate blooms. But I know from practical experience that this is not always feasible.

Flowers should appear in 4–5 months from seed sowing.

Check the seedman's instructions on the packet, and ascertain the flowering requirements.

Pansies and violas have various flowering times, depending on (a) whether they are winter or summer pansies or violas; or (b) the location; whether it is hot or temperate or cold; or (c) the variable sowing times So check before you buy.

Viola and pansy seeds, being so fine, are perhaps best sown in seed containers or pots. But they can be sown in sheltered seed beds.

Propagation: Thinly sow the seeds of *V.* × *wittrockiana* pansy hybrids in seed compost containers of damp, recommended, seed raising compost, at the most 5-6 mm (0.2 in) deep, in small rows; mid-late summer-autumn (Jan-May) subtropical areas; late summer-autumn (Feb-May) temperate areas.

Mist water the compost gently, but thoroughly, using a fine spray. Be especially vigilant, and never let the seeds or seedlings dry out, but keep the compost pleasantly moist.

Germination occurs in approximately 7-28 days, depending on soil temperature; but approximately 14 days at 18-21°C (64-70°F), so be prepared.

Prick out the seedlings when large enough to handle, 50 mm (2 in) apart, into seed compost containers, or singly into 75 mm (3 in) pots of damp, recommended potting compost, and grow them on in filtered shade for a few weeks.

Then plant the seedlings out directly where they are to grow and flower, 150-200 mm (6-8 in) apart, according to the spread of the hybrid. But remember that pansies must be protected from hot-harsh, or even strong sunlight, and hot or cold drying winds.

In cold areas sow the seeds in seed compost containers using a damp, recommended seed raising compost, late summer-autumn (Feb-March-April) and early spring (Sept). Prick out the seedlings singly into 75 mm (3 in) pots of recommended potting compost and grow them on.

Place the pots to overwinter in a cold frame, to protect the young seedlings from harsh weather. Harden off these seedlings in spring, and plant them out, directly where they are to grow and flower.

Or sow the seeds early spring in seed compost containers. Prick out the seedlings into 75 mm (3 in) pots of damp, recommended, potting compost, and grow them on.

Harden off the plants for a few weeks in filtered shade, and plant them out directly where they are to grow and flower. They should bloom late summer-autumn.

Seeds and seedlings can dry out rapidly, so pay special attention to their watering needs.

In English gardens thinly sow *V.* × *wittrockiana* pansy hybrid seeds, midsummer (July-earliest August), outside directly into a prepared seedbed. It may be advisable in southern areas, where mild autumns can push growth along, to delay the sowing until mid August. Seek local professional advice on pansies.

Prick out the seedlings from the seedbed into a nursery holding-bed, spacing them 100 mm (4 in) apart. Transplant these seedlings, in autumn (Sept-Oct), directly to where they are to grow and flower.

Or sow the seeds in seed compost containers using a damp, recommended seed raising compost. Place the seed compost container in a cold frame. Remember that hot sunlight through the glass could destroy the seedlings, so they must be protected from strong sunlight by suitable greenhouse shading for pansies, and ventilation; and also sheltered from hot drying winds.

Those seedlings growing in the cold frame can be pricked out into 75 mm (3 in) pots of damp, recommended, potting compost. The potted seedlings are overwintered in the cold frame, and planted out, early mid spring (March-April), directly where they are to grow and flower, 150-200 mm (6-8 in) apart. Make sure the plants are thoroughly hardened off before planting them out.

Pests and diseases: Slugs, black root rot, collar and stem rot, damping off, fusarium wilt, leaf spot, root rot, rust, and others.

Cultivars/varieties: 'Black Dream', height 150 mm (6 in), 'black' petals. 'Chantreyland', height 150 mm (6 in), apricot yellow, suffused orange. Clear Crystals, white, red, yellow, azure blue. Dream Series, height 150 mm (6 in): 'China Dream', soft yellow; 'Elderberry Dream', claret-purplish-rose; 'Oriental Dream', midnight blue; 'Snow Dream', pure white. Majestic Giants F_1 Hybrid Mixed, height 200 mm (8 in), large flowers, blotched, in white, deep rose, red, purple, blue, yellow. Roggli Giants, height 100 mm (4 in), large flowers. Roguish Ruffles Mixture, height 220 mm (9 in), heavily waved, larger flowers, blue, purple, bronze shades. Space Crystals, height 100 mm (4 in), bright colours. 'The Black Pansy', height 150 mm (6 in), midnight purple, bright yellow eye. *Viola tricolor.* There are many more.

Family: Violaceae.

***Xeranthemum* (immortelle, everlasting immortelle)** You could be forgiven for thinking that the southern European-Mediterranean *Xeranthemum annuum*; height 500-600-900 mm (20-24-36 in); was an Australian relative of the helichrysum and helipterum, as they are much alike.

Immortelle is a hardy annual only in Mediterranean climates. It is an uncomplaining plant that produces spring-summer, everlasting single, or semi-double, or double flowers in shades and tints of white, pink and pale-purple.

The crispy-papery, 37 mm (1.5 in) wide daisy-flowers are, however, flower-bracts, the 'true' flowers appearing as the centre-disc.

The downy, grey-green, 31 mm (1.2 in) long, by 8 mm (0.2 in) wide, oblong-pointed leaves, similar to lavender leaves but with a faint lemon smell, are borne on wiry stems.

Immortelle grows well in most soils provided they are well-drained and in full sunlight. Sow the seeds to create clumps, or drifts, in the flower border.

Immortelle may need twiggy support when young, to force the flowering shoots upwards. Be careful of the roots when working around them, as they are very susceptible to damage.

Immortelles can be used as cut flowers or dried-flowers. For dried-flowers take those blooms with long stems. Tie the flowers up in small bunches, and hang them upside down in a cool, shady place to dry off.

Propagation: Immortelles are frost sensitive. The seeds are sown directly where they are to grow and flower, as they do not transplant readily.

Dig over the soil when it is easy to work, directly where the plants are to grow and flower, breaking it down into a fine tilth, and rake out any debris. Firm the soil gently but thoroughly to take the seeds.

Sow the seeds thinly; autumn to spring in warm, frost-free areas; or spring in frost prone areas, when all danger from frost is past, in rows 300-375 mm (12-15 in) apart.

Rake the seeds barely into the top tilth, as they need light to germinate. Firm the soil with the head of the rake, or a board, to anchor the seeds to the soil.

Gently but thoroughly water the seedlings using a fine spray, and keep the soil and seedlings pleasantly moist until the seedlings are well established. Then water them when they need it.

Seeds can germinate in approximately 10-15 days, at 18-21°C (64-70°F). Thin out the seedlings to 150 mm (6 in) apart.

As an experiment I sowed immortelle seeds, under glass, in seed compost containers, using a damp, recommended, seed raising compost. The seeds germinated in 7 days, with plenty of seedlings. I pricked out the seedlings into 50 mm (2 in) pots, and achieved a reasonable transplantation success.

The plants were potted on into 125 mm (5 in) pots, hardened off, and grown outside in full sun, where they flowered profusely.

But I feel that it would be preferable, and possibly more productive, to sow the seeds directly where they are to grow and flower.

In English gardens dig over the soil directly where the plants are to grow and flower. Rake out any debris, and gently but thoroughly firm the soil to take the seeds.

Sow the seeds in spring (March-April), but after any danger from frost is past, in rows 300-375 mm (12-15 in) apart, and barely rake them into the top tilth.

Thin out the seedlings to 150 mm (6 in) apart. Flowers should appear mid summer-early autumn (July-Sept).

Pests and diseases: Reasonably free.

Cultivars/varieties: Mixed Colours.

Family: Asteraceae.

***Zea* (Indian corn, sweet corn, variegated corn)** The North-South American *Zea mays* (sweet corn); height 2.4 m (8 ft); a warm season, half-hardy annual, is known to most of us. And there are gardeners who use sweet corn as background plants in the flower border.

But there are *Zea mays* varieties and cultivars; height 900 mm-1.5 m (36-60 in); that are grown principally for their various coloured, coarse, grassy, rush-like stems, that are used in the flower border as accent plants. Some hybrids have coloured seeds.

The foliage can be green, white-striped; or white, pale-yellow and pink. There are green-leaved hybrids that have coloured cobs, with yellow, red, orange, and purplish seeds. These cobs are collected and used as dried seed decorations.

Some corn cob cultivars or varieties are not to be eaten, and you should check this before buying the seeds.

Zea mays is frost sensitive. It is grown in clumps to create an effect.

It is a gross feeder, and needs ample space to develop, plenty of close company of its own kind to ensure pollination, a fertile, rich organic soil, and an open, sunny location.

It also needs ample watering when growing, and regular weeding to keep down the competition.

Propagation: The seeds are sown after any danger from frost is past, directly where they are to grow and flower, into a prepared bed, as they resent root disturbance.

Place the seeds 25 mm (1 in) deep; late winter-summer in subtropical areas; late spring-early summer in temperate areas; late spring-early summer in cool areas, provided there is no danger from frost.

Dib in 3 or 4 seeds to a station, each station being 300–350 mm (12–14 in) apart, and keep the strongest seedlings at each. Don't let the seeds or soil dry out, but keep the soil pleasantly moist at all times. The seedlings should appear in approximately 5–10 days, depending on soil temperature.

In cold locations, start individual seeds under glass in mid-spring; or indoors in a warm, light place, say 2 to 3 weeks before the usual frost-free spring planting out time in your location.

Insert the seeds 25 mm (1 in) deep, in 75 mm (3 in) pots, or 75 mm (3 in) peat pots of damp, recommended, seed raising compost, at 16–21°C (61–70°F). Using peat pots means less root disturbance, as you plant the seedling still in its pot.

Don't let the seeds or compost dry out at any time.

The seedlings germinate quickly, approximately 5 days, and grow rapidly; so harden them off in a cold frame when they are approximately 100–150 mm (4–6 in) tall, and plant them out directly where they are to grow, 300–350 mm (12–14 in) apart, when the frost is over and the ground has warmed up.

In English gardens, *Zea mays* is treated as a half-hardy annual. Place individual seeds, under glass in mid-spring (April), 25 mm (1 in) deep, in 75 mm (3 in) pots, or 75 mm (3 in) peat pots of damp, recommended, seed raising compost, at 16–21°C (61–70°F). Treat seedlings as half-hardy annuals.

Or in mild winter areas, the seeds can be sown into a prepared bed, late spring-earliest summer (late May-earliest June), directly where they are to grow. Dib in 3 or 4 seeds to a station, each station being 300–350 mm (12–14 in) apart, and keep the strongest seedling in each.

Pests and diseases: Reasonably free.

Cultivars/varieties: Multicoloured, coloured seeds. 'Squaw', multicoloured seed cobs.

Family: Poaceae.

Zinnia The summer-autumn flowering, easy to grow, zinnia hybrids, grown so profusely in our gardens, are warm season annuals.

They have been bred from the daisy-flowered Mexican *Zinnia angustifolia* (the narrow-leaved zinnia); height 600–750 mm (24–30 in); and *Zinnia elegans* (the common, graceful zinnia); height 600–750 mm (24–30 in).

And it is the vast range of colourful hybrids that we admire so. Their heights range from 150–900 mm (6–36 in), in a host of shades and tints from white, to cream, yellow, greenish, pink, red and purple, indeed in every colour except blue.

Zinnias can be conveniently divided into 3 groups: (1) Giant-Cactus flowered; (2) Giant-Dahlia flowered; and (3) Dwarf hybrids; with the flower sizes varying from 31–187 mm (1.2–7.4 in) wide.

Gardeners have given zinnias recognisable flower-shape names; the two most famous being: cactus-quilled flowered; and dahlia flowered. There are also such beautifully descriptive names as: ball-flowered-ruffled; beehive flowered; button flowered; chrysanthemum flowered; formal flowered; gaillardia flowered; pompon flowered; scabious flowered—single, semi or double.

Z. angustifolia (syn. *Z. haageana, Z. mexicana*) is a half-hardy annual in cold climates, with golden-orange single flowers.

The form known as *Z. angustifolia* × *haageana*; height 300–450 mm (12–18 in); bears 37 mm (1.5 in) wide, bicoloured or zone-banded flowers. Some plants have flowers with strikingly different petal tips and edges. These blooms look like dahlias; either single, semi-double or double flowered, in shades and tints of white, yellow, orange, red, mahogany-red and chocolate-brown.

The dull green, oblong-pointed, stem-clasping leaves are borne in opposite pairs up the stem.

The species *Z. elegans* is a half hardy annual, with 62 mm (2.5 in) wide, purple flowers. The prominently-veined, dull green leaves, borne in opposite pairs, are wide, oval-pointed, stem-clasping, and spring from coarse, brittle, upright stems.

Zinnia linearis; height 250–300 mm (10–12 in); the 50 mm (2 in) wide, orange-flowered, linear-leaved, classical zinnia, is also popular as an edging plant for borders.

Zinnias thrive exceedingly well in the Australian climate, more so perhaps than they do in the United Kingdom; they are also very popular in the U.S.A.

They demand to be planted massed in beds of their own, the taller ones to the back of the border and the smaller ones to the front, but they can be used as edging and container plants. They are also useful as cut flowers, particularly the taller cultivars.

Zinnias thrive in a hot, dry climate, in full sun, sheltered from fierce winds, in a well-drained, slightly acid to neutral, fertile soil. But not excessively fertile, as too much nutrient causes an excess of foliage at the expense of flowers.

However if it is obvious that the plants need feeding, then use a well-balanced, liquid, soluble, flower fertiliser, suitable for zinnias and applied as the manufacturer instructs.

Zinnias need watering sensibly, as any prolonged period without water will cause the plant to wilt and possibly die. But don't waterlog them, as they are susceptible to disease in wet soil conditions. And try to keep the water off the foliage as this could lead to one of the zinnia's biggest problems: mildew.

Commonsense is the keyword when dealing with zinnias.

Remove spent flowers to increase the flowering display.

Zinnias are frost sensitive, and are planted out when all danger from frost is past and the ground has warmed up. They are then cut down by the first frost.

Be extra careful when weeding around zinnias, as I have seen zinnia beds decimated by heavy-handed hoeing.

Propagation: Final planting distance: Tall zinnias 400 mm (16 in) apart; Intermediate zinnias 300 mm (12 in) apart; Dwarf zinnias 200 mm (8 in) apart.

Sow the seeds late winter-spring in subtropical areas, directly where they are to grow and flower.

Dig over the soil when it is easy to work, breaking it down into a fine tilth. Rake out any debris, and firm the soil gently but thoroughly to take the seeds.

'Station sow' a few seeds in clumps the required distance apart, and rake them into the top tilth 5 mm (0.2 in) deep, or cover them with sieved soil, compost or vermiculite. Press the soil down lightly, but firmly, with the head of the rake, or a board, to anchor the seeds. Gently but thoroughly water using a fine spray and don't allow the seed or seedlings to dry out, keeping the soil pleasantly moist at all times.

Seedlings germinate in approximately 5–12 days at 21–25°C (70–77°F) soil temperature. Very carefully, as young zinnia roots are very sensitive to disturbance, thin out the seedlings to 200–400 mm (8–16 in) apart, depending on the ultimate height and spread of the plant.

The seeds can also be sown, early spring-summer in temperate areas; and spring in cold areas; under glass where necessary, at 16–21°C (61–70°F), directly into individual 75 mm (3 in) pots, or 75 mm (3 in) peat pots, of damp, recommended, seed raising compost to lessen subsequent root disturbance. Or indoors in a warm, light place, say 2 to 3 weeks before the usual frost-free spring planting-out time in your location. Cover the seeds with 5 mm (0.2 in) of compost or vermiculite.

Gently press the compost to anchor the seeds, and spray them with water using a mist spray. Don't let the seeds or seedlings dry out, but keep the compost surface just pleasantly moist. Seedlings germinate in approximately 5–12 days at 21–25°C (70–77°F) soil temperature.

Carefully thin out the seedlings keeping the strongest in each pot. Harden them off in a cold frame, and plant them out, directly where they are to grow and flower, 200–400 mm (8–16 in) apart, when all danger from frost is past and the ground has warmed up.

Or you could try growing the seedlings in seed compost containers using a damp, recommended seed raising compost. Prick out seedlings immediately they are large enough to handle, into 75 mm (3 in) pots, or 75 mm (3 in) peat pots, of damp, recommended, potting compost, to lessen future root disturbance, and grow them on.

As an experiment, I sowed seeds directly into pots, and directly into seed compost containers. Both lots of seeds germinated in 3 days. Those grown directly in pots were thinned out only, and those in containers were pricked out into pots.

Those grown directly in pots, at the time of writing, are a little ahead of those that have been pricked out into pots.

Or sow the seeds directly where they are to grow and flower, but only after the last frost and when the ground has warmed up. Zinnia seeds will stay dormant and then rot in a cold, wet soil.

In English gardens sow the seeds, early-mid spring (March-April), directly into 75 mm (3 in) peat pots of damp, recommended seed raising compost to lessen subsequent root disturbance, under glass, at 16–21°C (61–70°F). Keep the strongest seedling in each pot. Treat the plants as half-hardy annuals.

Or you can sow the seeds in seed compost containers, earliest-mid spring (March-April), under glass, at 16–21°C (61–70°F), in seed raising compost. Zinnias resent root disturbance very much, so very carefully prick out the seedlings, as soon as they are large enough to handle, into 75 mm (3 in) peat pots of damp, recommended, potting compost, and grow them on. Treat the plants as half-hardy annuals. Flowers should appear mid-summer on.

Or the seeds can be sown directly where they are to grow and flower, when any danger from frost is past.

Pests and diseases: Slugs, snails, damping off, alternaria blight, bacterial leaf spot, grey mould, powdery mildew.

Cultivars/varieties: Burpee Mixed Hybrids, height 900 mm (36 in), cactus flower type, good colour range. Cupid Mixed, height 225 mm (9 in), miniature double blooms. 'Envy', height 750 mm (30 in), dahlia flowered, chartreuse green. Peter Pan Mixed F_1 Hybrid, height 350 mm (14 in), white, cream, light pink, pink, red, plum, yellow, orange. 'Rose Pinwheel', height 300 mm (12 in), rose pink, yellow centre. Thumbelina Mixed, 150 mm (6 in), wide colour range. 'Persian Carpet' (haageana), height 300 mm (12 in). *Z. linearis* (Classic), height 300 mm (12 in) single orange. There are more.

Family: Asteraceae.

Index

Botanical and common names are listed here, cross referenced to aid plant identification. But it must be pointed out that common names can be misleading as, for example, in the case of 'African daisy'.